Science and Public Rea[s]

MW00846548

This collection of essays by Sheila Jasanoff explores how democratic govern-ments construct public reason, that is, the forms of evidence and argument used in making state decisions accountable to citizens. The term public reason as used here is not simply a matter of deploying principled arguments that respect the norms of democratic deliberation. Jasanoff investigates what states do in practice when they claim to be reasoning in the public interest. Reason, from this perspec-tive, comprises the institutional practices, discourses, techniques and instruments through which governments claim legitimacy in an era of potentially unbounded risks—physical, political, and moral. Those legitimating efforts, in turn, depend on citizens' acceptance of the forms of reasoning that governments offer. Included here therefore is an inquiry into the conditions that lead citizens of democratic societies to accept policy justification as being reasonable. These modes of public knowing, or "civic epistemologies," are integral to the constitution of contempo-rary political cultures.

Methodologically, the book is grounded in the field of Science and Technology Studies (STS). It uses in-depth qualitative studies of legal and political practices to shed light on divergent cross-cultural constructions of public reason and the reasoning political subject. The collection as a whole contributes to democratic theory, legal studies, comparative politics, geography, and ethnographies of modernity, as well as STS.

Sheila Jasanoff is Pforzheimer Professor of Science and Technology Studies at Harvard University's John F. Kennedy School of Government. A pioneer in legal and political studies of science and technology, she has written many widely cited articles and chapters and is author or editor of a dozen books, including The Fifth Branch (Harvard University Press), Science at the Bar (Harvard University Press), and Designs on Nature (Princeton University Press).

Science in Society Series

Series Editor: Steve Rayner
Institute for Science, Innovation and Society, University of Oxford

The Earthscan Science in Society Series aims to publish new high quality research, teaching, practical and policy-related books on topics that address the complex and vitally important interface between science and society.

Animals as Biotechnology
Ethics, sustainability and critical animal studies
Richard Twine

Business Planning for Turbulent Times
New methods for applying scenarios
Edited by Rafael Ramírez, John W. Selsky and Kees van der Heijden

Debating Climate Change
Understanding debate and agreement
Elizabeth L. Malone

Democratizing Technology
Risk, responsibility and the regulation of chemicals
Anne Chapman

Dynamics of Disaster
Lessons on risk response and recovery
Rachel A. Dowty Beech, Barbara Allen

Genomics and Society
Legal, ethical and social dimensions
Edited by George Gaskell and Martin W. Bauer

Influenza and Public Health
Learning from past pandemics
Tamara Giles-Vernick, Susan Craddock and Jennifer Gunn

Integrating Science and Policy
Vulnerability and resilience in global environmental change
Edited by Roger E. Kasperson and Mimi Berberian

Marginalized Reproduction
Ethnicity, infertility and reproductive technologies
Edited by Lorraine Culley, Nicky Hudson and Floor van Rooij

Nanotechnology
Risk, ethics and law
Edited by Geoffrey Hunt and Michael Mehta

Rationality and Ritual
Participation and exclusion in nuclear decision making, 2nd ed.
Brian Wynne

Resolving Messy Policy Problems
Handling conflict in environmental, transport, health and ageing policy
Steven Ney

The Limits to Scarcity
Contesting the politics of allocation
Lyla Mehta

Uncertainty in Policy Making
Values and evidence in complex decisions
Michael Heazle

Unnatural Selection
The challenges of engineering tomorrow's people
Edited by Peter Healey and Steve Rayner

Vaccine Anxieties
Global science, child health and society
Melissa Leach and James Fairhead

A Web of Prevention
Biological weapons, life sciences and the governance of research
Edited by Brian Rappert and Caitrìona McLeish

This collection brings together a quarter century of writing by Sheila Jasanoff on the sources and impacts of science and technology. In showing how they permeate public life, she demonstrates also that the field of Science and Technology Studies is no arcane specialty, but a research field of sweeping significance for law, history, administration, and the social sciences. At stake in the interactions of science with democratic institutions is public reason itself.'

Theodore M. Porter, UCLA, USA

'This book fascinatingly asks: What begins where all that seems solid, all that modernity has created, melts into air, leaving no shared ground to stand on? Sheila Jasanoff's exciting answer: a new age and style of public reason that can shed surprisingly clear light on a world in turmoil.'

Ulrich Beck, University of Munich, Germany & L.S.E, UK

'No one has contributed as much as Sheila Jasanoff to furthering our understanding of the importance of law in the complex relationships that develop between politics and technoscience. *Science and Public Reason* is more than a collection of her most significant articles on the subject; this seminal book opens entirely original perspectives on what, in a globalized world, a new alliance between science, techniques and democracy could and should be.'

Michel Callon, Ecole des mines de Paris, France

'Sheila Jasanoff's latest book demonstrates, once again, why she is at the very forefront of her field.'

Bruce Ackerman, Yale University, USA

Science and Public Reason

Sheila Jasanoff

Routledge
Taylor & Francis Group

LONDON AND NEW YORK

First edition published 2012
by Routledge
2 Park Square, Milton Park, Abingdon, Oxon, OX14 4RN

Simultaneously published in the USA and Canada
by Routledge
711 Third Avenue, New York, NY 10017

*Routledge is an imprint of the Taylor & Francis Group, an informa
business*

© 2012 Sheila Jasanoff

Firt issued in paperback 2013

British Library Cataloguing in Publication Data
A catalogue record for this book is available from the British Library

Library of Congress Cataloging-in-Publication Data
A catalog record has been requested for this book

ISBN: 978-0-415-52486-5 (hbk)
ISBN: 978-0-415-62468-8 (pbk)

Typeset in Times New Roman
by RefineCatch Limited, Bungay, Suffolk

Contents

Preface

David Winickoff

This is not the place to recite the academic honors Sheila Jasanoff has received, the institutions she has built, or the generations of scholars she has trained. Suffice it to say that she is globally recognized as a deeply influential and highly original public intellectual on the cultural forms of knowledge societies. Many members of the academy and beyond are familiar with her major books, including the *Fifth Branch, Science at the Bar*, and *Designs on Nature*. Also of importance are the great number of articles and book chapters that have appeared in edited volumes and periodicals of various kinds. It is a relief that she has finally done what many around her have been nagging her to do: issue a selection of these articles and essays that include some of her most cited articles as well as newer or harder-to-find pieces. This collection, however, is far from a pastiche of shorter works: with new essays, and overarching thematic development, it sets out novel theoretical contributions at the frontiers of science and technology studies (STS), political theory, and jurisprudence, and provides a new synthesis of her thought. *Science and Public Reason* will be an important resource for scholars in diverse fields, civil servants, and citizens alike grappling for new idioms in which to think about political life in an age so permeated by technology.

The internet and the Arab Spring, biofuels and global food systems, new nuclear states, climate change and "geoengineering". One does not have to look far to see how science and technology carry unique power in our unsettled world. They fuel its greatest aspirations and greatest fears, and sit at the center of its most difficult problems. How do modern democratic societies, as complicated and pluralist collectives, use and consider these powerful forces in contemporary life, and what are the implications for democracy of a world constituted by technology and permeated by technical rationality? This volume helps answer these questions, again revealing Jasanoff to be one of our foremost interpreters and guides.

Much work in science and technology studies (STS) has helped demonstrate the ways in which science is political. In these essays, Jasanoff reveals how power—especially in the form of political institutions such as the law and administrative agencies—is *epistemological*. She does this in part by drawing out and elaborating the theory of *coproduction*—a notion that she and other scholars in STS have been developing for some time, and for which she has been the central impresario. Coproduction is an analytical framework that sees science, technology, politics and culture as co-constitutional, operating together in an unfolding process. In this set of essays, we have theoretical specification as well as examples, both explicit and implicit, of a coproductionist approach that is rooted as much in Foucault and social theory as it is in administrative and constitutional legal theory. *Science and Public Reason* will help illuminate new epistemic dimensions of political cultures, raising new questions, and providing a powerful way of seeing for STS scholars, critical theorists, and jurists alike.

Science and Public Reason expounds three major themes in Sheila Jasanoff's work as a whole: first, that there are national cultures of rationality, what she has elsewhere called *civic epistemologies*; second, that institutionalized expertise produces new political forms as much as new knowledge; and third, that the law is a productive site in the politics of knowledge societies. All three constitute major innovations in the social studies of science, and have opened up frontiers for scholars in diverse fields. In this volume, these themes crystallize as packages of theory, methods and empirical illustration, and are brought together in an overarching whole. In her synthetic chapters, Jasanoff herself provides an extended discussion of these themes that I will not rehearse here. Nevertheless, I wish to say a few words about each one.

The notion that Western democracies differ in fundamental ways in how they deliberate upon, use, and govern technoscience remains one of Jasanoff's most original findings. These essays mark and illustrate different dimensions of this thesis. Surveying institutional differences and deciphering the dreamwork located in events, narratives, and collective symbols, she actually speaks more about political culture than science *per se*. In an era of globalization, one hears endlessly of the retreat of the nation state, the flatness of the world, and the irrelevance of the rule of law in the face of grand neoliberal forces. However, as a glance at any major newspaper would indicate, national political and legal structures persist and remain organizing forces even in a globalizing world. In fact, in an age of globalization, it is more important than ever to attend to the State as it rubs up uncomfortably against larger formations like the European Union, the WTO, the IPCC and the like.

Technical discourse and the credibility of experts, especially as they function in regulatory contexts, constitute the second theme, and is another area where Jasanoff has helped break new ground. Of interest to political theorists and STS scholars alike, Jasanoff's work registers, but moves beyond, the routinized dichotomies that populate existing thought in this arena: democracy versus technocracy, experts versus lay people, *inter alia*. The volume is interesting as well in that it reveals an evolution in her work and new directions in the arena of expert studies. In particular, we see the move from earlier work that explored the politics of expert advisory committees and "boundary work" in regulatory domains to more recent ideas about how modes and languages of technical rationality reshape public controversies themselves and produce hegemonic conceptions of due process.

One can easily see a connection between the prior two themes to the third, the turn to law. The omnipresence of this theme in the volume should come as no surprise: Sheila Jasanoff came to the field of STS on the heels of a Harvard Law School degree and a short stint as a practicing environmental lawyer. As recent

U.S. Supreme Court cases in environmental law indicate—e.g., the case of *Massachusetts v. EPA* where the state sued EPA for failing to regulate carbon as a "pollutant"—the work of environmental law, whether in litigation or compliance, often deals with challenges to the technical basis and process of regulatory rulemaking. In the U.S., rulemaking pursuant to environmental or health statutes must conform with an overarching law, the Administrative Procedures Act of 1946, which sets out a conception of due process in the regulatory state. This law, then, sits as a kind of constitution of regulatory power as among agency officials, experts, citizens, and the Federal courts, all of which are given certain powers to scrutinize the legitimacy of agency decisions. As Jasanoff explains in her introduction, the system affords legal standing to citizens to challenge regulations, and thus—in the U.S. system—courts have become an important place for the public legitimization of science. Laws of evidence and epistemic procedure, as well as the operation of judicial review and scrutiny, construct both public knowledge and the power to know. This theatre of actors and normative concerns is reflected in Jasanoff's core interests in regulation, public evidence and the law.

Science and Public Reason moves beyond judging, courtroom evidence, and regulatory law to directly confront legal theory, which is characteristic of some of Jasanoff's most recent work. This is well represented and captured in the essay "In a Constitutional Moment," the final piece in the volume. Invoking both STS and legal concepts, she analyzes the significant sociopolitical and technological transitions wrought by globalization in constitutional terms, drawing our attention to problems of citizenship, markets and global knowledge. Her essay pushes legal theory to be more constructivist and STS theory to be more cognizant of the law.

Constitutional moments bring us directly to the idea of public reason itself, the overarching conception for the volume, and the subject of its introductory essay. As Jasanoff conceives it, public reason is one response to the problem of trust in the "risk society", our current age of technological uncertainty, information excess, and proliferating expertise. Although governmental systems can and do take recourse to blanket denials or pure technical reason in the face of calls for accountability, they also provide public proofs of various kinds. Public reason then consists of "institutional practices, discourses, techniques and instruments through which modern governments claim legitimacy in an era of limitless risks— physical, political and moral." Structures of public reason are part of the larger architecture of political life and help constitute the bargain between citizens and their governing institutions. They also entail particular models of citizen reason and agency, public and private. In *Science and Public Reason*, Jasanoff illuminates a facet of political life that was omnipresent but somehow invisible.

The political stakes, therefore, of public reason are huge. It conditions forms of citizen subjectivity, imaginaries of the State, and possible routes of political engagement. The volume then is a script for scholarship and action. In an age of political guile and slick punditry—captured brilliantly by comedian Stephen Colbert's notion of "truthiness"—attending to public reason is a first step towards debating, reconstructing, and practicing norms of accountability. It may also be a path towards ensuring that public decision-making utilizes our best knowledge, not the ideological beliefs of extremists. In this sense, imagining public reason may also lay open important avenues for protecting and even reinvisioning democracy.

"When a poet's mind is perfectly equipped for its work," T.S. Eliot wrote in his essay on John Donne, "it is constantly amalgamating disparate experience." Anyone who is acquainted with Sheila Jasanoff or her work on science and democracy will immediately recognize such a mind, and these essays, as much as the book as a whole, are exemplars. A weaver of ideas, literatures, and experiences, she charts original and strange paths through seemingly familiar landscapes, and produces new order out of heterogeneous kinds. O.J. Simpson, 9/11, a *Daily Telegraph* headline, the BRCA 1 and 2 genes, the U.S. Constitution within its glass case, a formaldehyde rule-making, Earth hanging in space—this book manifests how disparate objects are brought together to generate a single narrative about technoscience and political culture. Such a mind is on exhibit in the book that follows. It is a gathering of seemingly disparate pieces, fitted together and reinterpreted to generate an exciting new whole.

Acknowledgements

It takes a leap of faith to convince oneself that writings which have already appeared in print are worth publishing again. Few would come to this conclusion on the basis of their own convictions. In my case, only the steady encouragement of close friends and colleagues over many years persuaded me to put this collection together. Even then it was a slow process. Indeed, almost a decade and one canceled book contract have gone by since I first conceived the unifying theme for this volume. It was July 4, 2003 when, with fireworks exploding in the distance, I wrote to a small group of fellow travelers suggesting that public reason was the connecting thread running through much of my work over the preceding twenty years. The further passage of time since then means that there are now newer pieces to set beside the old; more importantly, there is a longer perspective from which to discern patterns that were not entirely clear even then. I have tried to highlight these in a new introduction and an afterword which I hope will bring coherence to writings that have been read more for their topical interest than for the ideas that cut across them.

I would like to thank here the people whose invaluable support made this book possible. John Carson, Clark Miller, Ravi Rajan and Shiv Visvanathan, good friends since our paths first intersected at Cornell, were among the earliest proponents of this project. Their confidence that an audience would be found for the book was as crucial to its conception as their advice about what to include in its table of contents. Stephen Hilgartner's sage counsel made it possible to settle on a list that seemed both balanced and inclusive. Steve Rayner generously invited me to publish the resulting work in his edited series and persuaded me to stick with a title that had caused me much anxiety even though it fitted the book's purposes well.

There is no authorial debt quite so large as the one owed to readers of work in progress, and I have been fortunate during my Harvard years to find a cohort of exceptionally perceptive critics. The introductory essay benefited from several pairs of eyes that managed to combine sympathy and understanding with detachment. Stève Bernardin was the kindest imaginable cheerleader, pointing out and helping to correct serious organizational deficiencies while providing unswerving support for carrying the project through to completion. John Carson's as always trenchant editorial comments helped greatly to sharpen and clarify the arguments.

Rob Hagendijk, Gesa Lindemann and Andy Stirling raised my spirits with their warmly positive reception of the first chapter as well as the project as a whole. And David Winickoff not only shaped the table of contents, critiqued the introduction, and kept alive the flame of commitment, but offered a uniquely personal gift of confidence by volunteering to write a preface.

It has been a source of surprise and disappointment to me that the field of science and technology studies, despite its profound implications for contemporary politics and law, finds it hard to connect to work in those areas. This is fundamentally a problem of interdisciplinarity: we have built high discursive walls and exclusionary academic practices that make even the prospect of exchange seem daunting. It is rare to find multilingual intellects who can overcome the barriers, and rarer still to find one willing to play the role of interlocutor-in-chief while boundary-crossing work is taking shape. Ben Hurlbut is such a person, and I have been more fortunate than I can say in having the benefit of his vision to expand my horizons in thinking through this project. Needless to say, all of the friends named above have only helped to improve a work whose imperfections remain entirely my own.

A book's production presents logistical as well as intellectual challenges. I would like to thank Khanam Virjee for her enthusiastic support as Associate Editor at Routledge-Earthscan and Charlotte Russell for smoothly handling the details of paperwork, communication and design. Above all, I am grateful to Shana Rabinowich for providing her ever resourceful administrative assistance, from tracking down scattered publishers and texts to obtaining copyright clearances.

My family's presence as the warp and weft of my life makes all things seem possible. This collection, representing as it does the work of a lifetime, is fittingly dedicated to Jay Jasanoff, companion, chief enabler, husband and friend.

Credits

2. Product, Process, or Programme: Three Cultures and the Regulation of Biotechnology
   In Martin Bauer, ed., *Resistance to New Technology* (Cambridge: Cambridge University Press, 1995), pp. 311–331.

3. In the Democracies of DNA: Ontological Uncertainty and Political Order in Three States
   New Genetics and Society, Vol. 24, No. 2 (2005), pp. 139–155.

4. Restoring Reason: Causal Narratives and Political Culture
   In Bridget Hutter and Michael Power, eds., *Organizational Encounters with Risk* (Cambridge: Cambridge University Press, 2005), pp. 209–232.

5. Image and Imagination: The Formation of Global Environmental Consciousness
   In Paul Edwards and Clark Miller, eds., *Changing the Atmosphere: Expert Knowledge and Environmental Governance* (Cambridge, MA: MIT Press, 2001), pp. 309–337.

6. Contested Boundaries in Policy-Relevant Science
   Social Studies of Science, Vol. 17, No. 2 (1987), pp. 195–230.

7. The Songlines of Risk
   Environmental Values, Vol. 8 (1999), pp. 135–152.

8. Judgment under Siege: The Three-Body Problem of Expert Legitimacy
   In Peter Weingart and Sabine Maasen, eds., *Democratization of Expertise? Exploring Novel Forms of Scientific Advice in Political Decision-Making*, Sociology of the Sciences Yearbook (Dordrecht: Kluwer, 2005), pp. 209–224.

1 Reason in practice

For the world's most privileged citizens, life in the early twenty-first century offers abundant ease and enjoyment, together with unprecedented opportunities for personal growth and fulfillment. Yet in countries around the globe, even in the most mature democracies, politics today is marked by pent-up anger, cynicism, fear, and violence. From the United States, an unexpected cauldron of populist discontent, to Europe, the Arab world, and beyond, there is widespread loss of faith in good government and even in the idea of progress. It is as if societies have lost the knack, and the taste, for reasoning together to plan futures which all can see as serving their needs and interests. Crisis, however, brings opportunity, in scholarship no less than in politics. This troubled historical moment offers an unexpected vantage point from which to rethink our ideas of democracy and good government, and to do so with closer attention to two institutions that have transformed the modern world: science and technology. This is a moment which, through its very contradictions, invites us to be attentive to democracy's failures. It forces us to ask whether, prompted by the ascendancy of science and technology, issues that matter to publics have been prematurely taken out of politics—and, if so, how democratic nations might reinvent their practices of governance in the interests of building more just, inclusive and promissory futures. This collection of essays contributes to that project of reimagination.

The politics of demonstration

Little more than a century ago, Western intellectuals and social reformers saw the world as nicely progressing from superstition and ignorance to knowledge and reason. Science led the way, revealing indisputable facts about the natural world and ourselves in it. Those truths, self-evident to the founding thinkers of the Enlightenment, laid the basis for actions whose rightness could be taken for granted because they were consistent with the observable realities of nature. The idea of natural law was not strange to human minds: premodern societies depended on shamans and seers, priests, and prophets to ratify correspondences between nature's dictates and human institutions. Kings ruled by divine right; people went to temples to pray for children or for rain. Science, however, overturned habits of blind deference, offering a less fallible, more democratic means of creating harmony between nature and human aspirations. Here, finally, was a way of getting at nature's truths unmediated by power and influence. The experimental method, in particular, seemed to put scientists in direct conversation with the world as it is. Truth claims could be checked experimentally against phenomena that could in principle be observed by all (Dear 2006; Shapin and Schaffer 1985). The potential for public witnessing bypassed the risks of distortion by well-placed actors falsely claiming superior knowledge. Enlightened societies from the late eighteenth century onward became those in which science spoke truth to power—and power listened of necessity, to defend and demonstrate its own right to rule (Price 1965; Picon 2002).

Scientific ways of knowing gave rise to a politics of demonstration that modern nation states found supremely useful. Advances in science and technology—technoscience for short—made lives easier, healthier, more productive. In the hundred years after the industrial revolution, diseases yielded, distances were crossed, the air was cleaned, and the sheer slog of countless workaday lives gave way to rhythms that were far more comfortable, if also more humdrum. Armed with scientific knowledge and enabling technologies, human societies seemed poised to challenge the ancient ills of old age and sickness, penury, and hunger. Nirvana could be reached here on Earth; research and development, not prayer and meditation, held the answers. A sense of control over nature was born, especially in rich nations with the resources to exploit technoscientific advances. To the delight of enlightened rulers, technological power seemed easy at first to reconcile with democratic values (Ezrahi 1990). As long as state-supported scientific and technological developments delivered tangible public goods, accountability was served and the threat of despotism receded.

That optimistic alliance between science, technology and democracy proved short-lived. A hundred years of shocks and surprises rudely disrupted the original compact: two World Wars with millions dead; repeated genocidal conflicts; entrenched poverty and hunger; environmental pollution; epidemic diseases; states ruling by terror, prepared to turn guns on their own people rather than cede control; and from 1945 onward the fear of ultimate war, bringing nuclear annihilation. President John F. Kennedy's inaugural address of 1961 captured in its well-remembered cadences the contradictions of the unfolding technological future: "For man holds in his mortal hands the power to abolish all forms of human poverty and all forms of human life." The utopian promises of the Enlightenment retained their appeal. Yet offsetting them by mid-century were grimmer prospects, even the extinction of the species that had aspired to godlike knowledge and power. More science could no longer be counted on to deliver better lives when the same knowledge could be turned to good and evil uses—to manufacture pharmaceuticals or deadly toxins, generate nuclear power or make nuclear bombs, diagnose threats or impose dictatorial discipline. How to direct science and technology toward beneficial ends became an increasing preoccupation of postwar societies and governments. New social movements of the mid-twentieth century made it clear that state expectations from science and technology no longer mapped neatly and inevitably onto visions that citizens held for themselves.

The wheel of enlightenment took another implacable turn before the end of the millennium, introducing new disconnects between science and democracy. Knowledge in a sense became its own undoing, as a vast penumbra of what we do not know and cannot presume to control grew along science's moving frontiers (Beck 1992). Scientific research could no longer be counted on to provide an expanding array of reliable, documented, policy-relevant facts. Indeed, facts in the sense of uncontested claims turned out to be in surprisingly short supply as governments undertook more ambitious projects of national defense, public health, economic growth, agricultural production and global environmental sustainability. Nor could technology be relied on to validate political action through successful demonstrations in real time. Technology in operation proved far more unruly (Wynne 1988), more error prone, less predictable, and less easily transferable across geopolitical boundaries than optimists had proclaimed. Increasingly, technological systems seemed to develop lives of their own, overflowing the pilots, models and field tests that had once justified them (Callon et al. 2009).

Things went wrong, sometimes on catastrophic scales, from computer system crashes to global financial meltdowns to industrial disasters and climate change. The jolting nuclear accident at Japan's Fukushima Daiichi power plant in March 2011 carried all the trademarks of human overreaching: in a nation schooled to accept the state's expert assurances, an earthquake of unexpected severity set loose a tsunami of epic proportions, overwhelming an aging and ill-maintained plant's inadequate failsafe mechanisms. Political questions quickly surfaced in all such cases: who was at fault; who should have known; who should be compensated; and who held responsible?

One common response was denial. Accidents and disasters were often written off in official accounts as unintended consequences of well-intentioned choices. No one, this story went, could reasonably have foretold that rising fossil fuel use would lead to climate change, high dams would destroy riverine ecosystems, disease-preventing chemicals would give rise to insect and viral resistance, hormone replacement therapy in postmenopausal women would raise their risk of breast cancer, explosives would be commandeered by terrorists converting bodies into living bombs, or electronic social networks would create preconditions for both anti-despotic revolutions and crimes of violence. Defining such failures as "unintended" tacitly absolved technology and its human progenitors of responsibility and blame. No actors, after all, could be held to account for the unknowable. Without knowledge there can be no basis for logic or causal argument; to act against the unknown is to be like mad Hamlet discoursing with the "incorporeal air." Paradoxically, the theme of unintended consequences reaffirmed the naturalistic narrative of progress from which policymakers continued to draw their legitimacy (Wynne et al. 2007). The benefits of technology could be seen and known; these were real, reliable, calculable. Harms, by contrast, were deemed exceptional, systemic, recognizable only after the fact, and therefore relegated to the category of the unpredictable.

A second response, loved by bureaucrats and their expert advisers, was to seek refuge in rational calculation. Futures perhaps could not be completely known, but they could be assessed and managed under the increasingly important rubrics of risk assessment, cost-benefit analysis (Kysar 2010), and evidence-based policy. These too were exonerating discourses. They neatly divided the tasks of governing the future into a scientistic and supposedly apolitical realm of assessment and prediction, and a concededly political, but entirely separate, realm of political response and management (NRC 1983). Products, projects and scenarios could be modeled well enough according to this conceptual paradigm by experts with the knowledge and training to evaluate their strengths and vulnerabilities. Political managers could come in when calculation was complete, to demand safeguards whose costs would not be out of proportion to the benefits conferred by taking useful risks. Who bears the risks and who gains the benefits was not always on the discussion table.

To many observers this retreat to technical expertise only reinforced techno-logical society's "organized irresponsibility" (Beck 1988); it implied levels of control that seemed demonstrably overblown. The near meltdown at the Three Mile Island nuclear plant in 1979 eliminated U.S. public trust in the safe operation of nuclear power and ended the nation's supremacy in nuclear engineering. The calamity at Fukushima opened the way to doubts and questions whose full impli-cations for the nuclear industry would not be known for years. More fundamen-tally, from the standpoint of ruling institutions, the discovery that every seeming certainty carries at its margins a weight of unresolvable uncertainty challenged the foundational presumptions of enlightened governance. If a government's first duty is to find solutions to social problems, consistent with public interest and public demand, then a technoscientific enterprise that inexorably links knowledge to non-knowledge fails to deliver the legitimacy that it once so confidently promised.

Demonstration, under these challenging conditions, slipped out of the grasp of governments and became at once more democratic and more oppositional (Barry 1999; Callon et al. 2009). When governments unveiled new technoscientific programs, from the construction of railroads, runways or high dams to support for new and emerging technologies, people demonstrated their contrary views through active resistance. In the United States, politicians gained mileage from alliances with the religious right, which denied scientific doctrines from evolution to anthropogenic climate change. Elsewhere, genetically modified plants were uprooted from research plots, animal testing labs and nanotechnology centers were bombed, and people staged mass marches, sit-ins or blockades to prevent new construction projects. Seen as Luddite excess by political authorities, but as "uninvited participation" by more detached analysts (Doubleday and Wynne 2011), direct action by citizens signaled at the very least a breakdown in orthodox political communication and a demonstrable need for new forms of public accountability.

A new age of reason

Caught between the hammer of uncertainty and the anvil of unintended consequences, how can governments renegotiate the double contract of modern democracies—first, with the citizens who elect them and, second, with the science and technology that enable states to promise growth and employment? How can governments persuade skeptical and skittish citizens that theirs is not a world of magical realism in which massive technological intrusions into the material world can be authorized with no one to take responsibility for evil consequences? Citizens of advanced technological societies demand a modicum of certainty that the benefits of science and technology, especially when conducted with taxpayer support, will arrive as promised, and not bring danger or ruin (or, as in the case of the life sciences, moral breakdown) in their wake. Even when innovation is left largely to the private sector, as it mostly is in liberal democracies, governments must try to ensure that corporate profit motives will not expose publics to harms that are unlimited and uncompensated. How under these trying circumstances can states seek to retain public trust?

These dozen essays, culled from some twenty-five years of research and writing, cast the spotlight on one answer to the problem of trust in an age of uncertainty: public reason. The term public reason as I use it in this volume is not a matter of constructing principled arguments that obey universal rules of democratic delib-eration (Rawls 1971). Instead, my objective, grounded in the field of science and technology studies (STS), is to ask what ruling institutions do in practice when they claim to be reasoning in the public interest. Public reason, for me, is not simply the result of meeting exogenously defined criteria of logic or argument, though such rules matter: rather, it is what emerges when states act so as to appear reasonable. Reasoning comprises the institutional practices, discourses, tech-niques and instruments through which modern governments claim legitimacy in an era of limitless risks—physical, political and moral. Included here as well is an inquiry into the background conditions that lead citizens of democratic states to accept policy justification as being reasonable. What kinds of reasons sit best with which sorts of publics, and how does public reasoning relate to political culture and the authorization of expertise? More particularly, how does the fact that we live in information-soaked environments, constantly depending on others' exper-tise, affect the democratic ambitions of public reason? The attempt to answer these sorts of questions positions my work in conversation with related explora-tions in democratic theory, legal studies, and ethnographies of modernity.

A complete political theory of late modern democracy must include, in my view, alongside classical reflections on representation, participation, and voice, an explicit and sufficient account of the reasoning of state institutions. Sufficiency, for these purposes, means that we have to account for reason not only theoreti-cally, at the level of claims made on its behalf, but also empirically, as a political practice that connects the communicating state to its attentive citizens. In acting for or on behalf of citizens, governments operate with tacit understandings of what people are like, especially in their capacity to interpret facts and develop arguments (Jasanoff 2004a). By uncovering those presumptions, these essays speak to the construction of the political subject as a reasoning agent, not through the sciences of mind, brain and behavior, but through legal and institutional arrangements that presuppose certain ideals of human agency and autonomy. This volume therefore extends work in the history and sociology of the human sciences by exploring, through studies of public decision making, contemporary presumptions about the nature of rationality, both as an attribute of human minds and as a normative goal for social and political collectives.

Scattered in time and across disciplinary literatures, the essays collected here articulate a set of theoretical preoccupations that may not be immediately apparent to readers who have come upon these works singly or in isolation. Those unused to my methods of extracting broad theoretical ideas from the empirical details of everyday talk and practice may miss the forest for the trees, seeing topical case studies instead of an integrated exploration of abiding questions in democratic theory. Yet recurrent questions and gradually coalescing answers run through all of my work on science, technology, law and policy, whether the examples pertain to environmental risk, technological disasters, novel biological organisms, global environmentalism, the nature of evidence, or the legitimacy of administrative rulemaking.

Three organizing themes have guided my choice of research topics and analytic methods: first, a commitment to comparison, especially across national political cultures, as a means of elucidating entrenched but unacknowledged habits of reasoning in the public square; second, a focus on the practices of separating expert from commonplace modes of reasoning, especially in the production of what I call "regulatory science" (Jasanoff 1990); and third, a deep concern with the law as both site and instrument of shaping democratic accountability and forms of reasoning. The articles that follow are grouped for convenience under one or another of these three headings, but it is their interwoven character that I want to emphasize. The centrality of the law in particular—not as written text, but as a set of practices, a source of norms, a continuous historical narrative of what societies are about, and an instrument for stabilizing or destabilizing authority—is visible throughout these pieces. The essays also illustrate my attempts to bridge divides that have proved perennially troublesome for social analysis—between macro and micro, structure and agency, theory and practice, descriptive accuracy and normative theory. Necessarily, too, the works illustrate changes in my own thinking, notably from the structural modes of analysis that I followed in the 1980s to the need I see now to acknowledge the fluidity and performativity of reasoning while still remaining attentive to cultural stability and continuity.

Reason by comparison

Reason is a great naturalizer, and public reason naturalizes much that seems arbitrary in politics. Once we are persuaded of the reasonableness of an argument or action, it becomes the most natural thing in the world to accept it: of course, this is how things are; of course, this is how things should be. To make the contingency of reason visible, then, we must look as if through the eyes of visitors from other worlds, much like pre-colonial ethnographers who decoded the locally contingent and culturally specific assumptions that held together the complete, self-reinforcing logics of alien belief systems (Douglas 1986; Sahlins 1996). Even today, the anthropological project is directed toward making other people's beliefs transparent, accessible, and comprehensible. Many seemingly alien ways of making sense of the world would not seem strange, the anthropological texts instruct us, if we could but put ourselves inside the life worlds of those holding the odd beliefs. If you were a Zuni or a South Sea Islander, a faith healer or a customary law judge, an African woman with AIDS or a Hispanic mother in an Anglophone U.S. reproductive health clinic, you too would see the world in the ways they do. Their reason would become, however temporarily, your own.

It is harder to distance oneself from the processes of naturalization within one's own cultures of reason and reasonability; in short, it is easier to render the strange familiar than the familiar strange. To some extent, the ethnographic method works with respect to subcultures of specialized practice. Thus, both observation and participant-observation are important components in the methodological toolkit of science and technology studies, helping to destabilize the special kind of naturalization created by scientific and technical representation. The genre of laboratory studies, for instance, treats sites of fact and artifact making as if they are foreign cultural spaces, where work practices can be watched and recorded with the same meticulous neutrality that an ethologist brings to observing animal behavior (Latour and Woolgar 1979; Latour 1987; Bijker et al. 1987). But fruitful and provocative though such work has been, it tends to slide into the trap of behaviorism, more attuned to explicit and visible signals than to inarticulate norms and beliefs. Intersubjective phenomena, collectively endorsed beliefs, and above all moral and ethical self-understandings tend to get shortchanged in such studies. STS research has been more effective in showing how people build scientific instruments, medical standards or large technological systems than legal rules, ethical principles or regimes of administrative rationality.

Comparison across cultures offers one way out, especially using the methods of interpretive analysis: thick description (Geertz 1973), close reading of texts, observation of meaning-making in social practices and interactions (Goffman 1959), and attention to institutions, discourses, and histories. By seeing how other political cultures frame and resolve the quandaries of uncertainty and accountability, and how they uphold their own regimes of reason, we can become better observers of naturalizing moves in our own politics. Comparison thus solves the problem of the "view from nowhere"—that position of mythic neutrality that no analyst can achieve in practice. Instead, this method allows different, actual "somewheres" to be brought into productive contrast, revealing patterns and persistences that might otherwise remain unperceived.

I learned this from my first comparative study, in which my collaborators and I discovered unexpected differences between Europe and the United States in the seemingly straightforward project of regulating chemicals suspected of causing cancer (Brickman et al. 1985). The same scientific evidence about the same chemicals led to different assessments of risk across Britain, France, Germany, and the United States—the four countries in our study. Even the concern with carcinogens turned out to be anything but universal, with some national authorities declaring that these substances do not, and should not, constitute a "natural kind" for regulatory purposes. Trying to unravel these puzzling divergences led to decades of work in which I developed theoretical concepts to help explain why national decision making systems diverge when coming to terms with uncertain facts and extraordinary events.

One of my best known comparative essays is "Product, process, or programme: three cultures and the regulation of biotechnology" (reproduced as Chapter 2 of this volume). A study of the early years of controlling biotechnology in Britain, Germany, and the United States, this article shows how discrepancies in assessing what is at stake in regulating biotechnology emerged very early in national debates on the presumed risks of the new techniques. Specifically, genetic engineering and its suite of techniques were framed out of the field of regulatory concern in the United States, where scientific consensus held that there was nothing specially worrisome about the process of genetic modification (GM). American attention focused instead on the material results of genetic engineering, adapting existing regulations to bring new GM products under control. By contrast, most European nations, including Britain, viewed the process of gene manipulation as fraught with sufficient uncertainty to warrant parliamentary attention. German anxiety went deeper, fed by recollections of the disastrous programmatic alliance between science, technology and the state that had legitimated wartime abuses, from unethical human experimentation to the extermination of persons the Nazi state deemed genetically unfit (Gottweis 1998). National exercises in public reasoning concerning biotechnology, whether in legislative debates, court decisions, or risk assessment, were rooted in these original framings. Subsequent transnational controversies, such as the conflict between Europe and the United States over the safety and utility of genetically modified crops (Winickoff et al. 2005), can be traced back to these historically situated, institutionally sanctioned and discursively performed analytic frames.

Theoretically and methodologically, "Product, process, programme" charted new directions in comparative analysis for myself and others. As in my other work, a mix of close textual reading, especially of law and regulation, and interpretive analysis of parallel debates and controversies provided the basis for drawing robust comparative conclusions. This article marked an early elaboration of the theme of co-production that has been central to my work. In this case, an entire technology—incorporating not only its material features but associated imaginations of risks and benefits—was defined to harmonize with underlying visions of the state and its rights and obligations *vis-à-vis* citizens. The resulting nation-specific interweaving of *is* (what are the risks of biotechnology) and *ought* (under what conditions and constraints should biotechnology be carried out) exemplified a bioconstitutional moment of the kind that accompanies significant developments in the life sciences and technologies (Jasanoff 2003, 2011). At such moments, as further elaborated in this book's final essay, the meanings that a society accords to life, and the responsibilities that a state assumes for life's nurturing and protection, are reworked together through a process of simultaneous definition and articulation. These are moments of renewal for cultures of public reasoning, episodes in which tacit social commitments are challenged and, in the course of normal politics, typically reaffirmed.

Another comparative piece, "In the democracies of DNA: ontological uncertainty and political order in three states" (this volume, Chapter 3), analyzes the normative choices made in regulating new technologies from a co-productionist perspective: what sorts of novel biological processes and entities are allowed to come into the world, under what regimes of responsibility, and why? Using examples from the regulation of embryo research and agricultural biotechnology in Britain, Germany and the United States, this essay seeks to explain cross-national differences in the positions that states take with respect to the risks posed by borderline life forms: hybrid or hard to classify constructs that I refer to here as "monsters." The conditions under which such ambiguous forms of life are permitted to exist in each state depend on the felt capacity of its legal order to circumscribe the ethical and social risks of these novelties and to keep them from overflowing publicly enacted containment measures. Postwar Germany, fearful of state-sanctioned lawlessness and reliant on its Basic Law to set firm limits on state power, was least willing to tolerate the coming into being of ontologically suspect, risky entities that arouse political and moral anxiety. By contrast, the United States proved far more hospitable toward ontological experimentation, consistent with a faith in the market as a robust enough instrument for adjudicating between permissible and impermissible experiments. These examples show how deep-seated assumptions about the state's competence as the arbiter of collective norms can shape the pace and direction of biological research and development.

The legitimacy of public reason depends, as already indicated, not only on its logic and propositional content but also on the performance of reasoning in the public square. To be sure, the technical quality of the state's analytic exercises, such as risk assessment, cost-benefit analysis, and constitutional law (themselves historical accomplishments of no small significance), does matter; weak logics, unsupported by evidence and expertise, cannot sustain policy. But in forums ranging from high courts to the blogosphere the adequacy of reasoning is equally a function of the state's ability to give reasons convincingly. Curiously, in discussions of public reason, the publics for whom governments perform their rituals of rationality have received short shrift—frequently because these audiences are written off as know-nothings who do not understand science (Wynne 1995; Sunstein 2005). Yet in a functioning democracy there has to be a correspondence between what officials offer in the way of public justification and what is heard and respected by the citizens for whom such gestures are devised. That correspondence, I have argued, is anything but random. Just as cultures have routines and scripts, or folkways, that assign meaning to actions, events and relationships, so political cultures are characterized by relatively stable "civic epistemologies," or "public knowledge ways," that comprise preferred modes of producing public knowledge and conducting policy deliberation.

These preferences become most visible at moments of crisis, when the state has to explain why things went wrong and what it will do to prevent future breakdowns. In Chapter 4, "Restoring reason: causal narratives and political culture," I compare three massive failures that challenged a state's capacity to govern in the nation's interests: the 1984 Bhopal gas disaster in India; the "mad cow" crisis of 1996 in

Britain; and the September 11, 2001 terrorist attacks in the United States. This choice of cases underscores an important principle of interpretive methodology—more can be gained by comparing events that are similar in their potential to define or transform politics than in their topical specificity. This particular comparison sheds light on the dimensions of political order that each state seeks to immunize or hold beyond question, such as the authenticity of human experience in India, the perceived integrity of public officials in Britain, and the technical competence of policy analysis in the United States. By contrasting disparate national rituals of "restoring reason," these cases reveal much about the civic epistemologies that underwrite different styles of official justification in contemporary democracies.

But, as critics of my methods have been quick to note, cross-national comparison has limits. Even if nation states are powerful aggregators of collective preferences, capable of shaping their reasons to satisfy durable civic epistemologies, strong social forces may transcend national particularities, such as independence or environmental movements, economic globalization, transnational professional networks, electronic communications, or populist uprisings of the sort that swept across the Arab world in early 2011. Do national differences continue to matter in policy justification? Is there not a tendency for state-by-state differences to be swamped by tidal waves of knowledge and technological change that eventually bring about convergent standards of rationality and discourse? Are science and technology not, after all, the ultimate levelers of differences in public reason?

For any scholar steeped in the methods and findings of science and technology studies, the answer is clear. Big transformations do happen, and they may in time overcome local specificity, producing similar preferences worldwide for particular forms of evidence, expertise and argument. The European Union (EU) can be seen as one grand experiment in forging supranational norms of reasoning. Yet as the EU's travails in the early twenty-first century also illustrate, history cannot be so easily set aside. Imitation does not necessarily produce identity, in public reasoning or in policy outcomes. Formal discourses of reason, such as quantitative risk assessment or bioethics, may be borrowed from across borders and they may spread like wildfire, but they are re-embedded in nation-specific institutional contexts and reperformed by national actors playing to local civic epistemologies. It remains to be explored, not assumed, whether "the same" technical rationality works out similarly in disparate settings; typically, the answer is "no," as shown in some of my work on regulatory science discussed below.

Nor does the fact of globalization liberate scholars from the need to study how leveling happens, if and when it does. "In the middle of the 20th century," remarked the famous Brundtland report on sustainable development, "we saw our planet from space for the first time" (WCED 1987). Who, however, was this "we," how was the "planet" seen, was it indeed "for the first time," and whose interests did the new Earth images advantage or disadvantage? If the ontology of the planet changed significantly in the late twentieth century, through altered means of seeing and knowing, then what new moral and political orders were co-produced in those moments of enlightenment? These are some of the questions I explore in Chapter 5: "Image and imagination: the formation of global environmental consciousness."

Consistent with other studies of the formation of new scientific ideas and epistemes, this chapter highlights the complex work that had to be done to make the boast of "seeing the planet" a reality. The distanced vision that the Brundtland report celebrated was itself the product of Cold War tensions and the space race, for it was the astronauts of the Apollo program and their Soviet cosmonaut counterparts who brought home the now-familiar images of the Earth as a lonely planet surrounded by swirling clouds. Not only military competition but commercial enterprises wishing to advance their global ambitions carried the Earth images to viewers around the world, but even then the uptake of planetary thinking remained patchy. For the great majority of the Earth's residents, the thin overlay of a global environmental consciousness, fostered by space science and military technologies, and focused on incomprehensibly distant futures (Jasanoff 2010), failed to offset the concerns of the palpable present. The uneven circulation of allegedly global discourses of reason reveals the persistence of norms and imaginations that remain resolutely time and place-bound, and that provoke resistance when attempts are made to override local commitments in the name of such global abstractions as sustainability or human survival.

Expert rationality

The authority of governments today is inseparable from expertise. States have access to many sources of power—not least weapons and secrecy—but even those resources cannot be accumulated and kept up to speed without expert advice. We cannot imagine a central bank without economists, an environment ministry without scientists, a public health agency without medical specialists, or a police department without law enforcement professionals. The Cold War needed its physicists, its decision theorists, its intelligence experts, and its computer scientists (Edwards 1996). It is less clear, however, how states recognize who is an expert, mediate conflicts among experts, or persuade publics that they have enrolled the best available expertise into the tasks of governance. Little attention has been paid to the emergence of expertise as a phenomenon in modern government, and still less to the largely tacit theories that underpin rule by experts in democracies. Yet for all practical purposes, we live today in an "Expert Raj" (an imperium of experts) whose modes of acquiring authority, especially in global institutions, are as opaque to ordinary citizens as the self-legitimating claims of rulers in distant metropoles were to colonial subjects living in the peripheries of empire.

One way to approach this paradox of contemporary democracy is to look at crucial moments of emergence, conflict or reconceptualization in which the principles underlying trust in government by experts are exposed to public scrutiny. The production of expert rationality then emerges as a special kind of democratic problem-solving. I have shown that legitimation depends at such moments on invoking science, or more accurately public imaginations of science, in support of the state's planned actions. In turn, the recourse to science and expertise demands forms of boundary work that derive their persuasiveness from prior state—society relationships and the political and sociotechnical imaginaries they support (Jasanoff 1990; Jasanoff and Kim 2009). As we have seen, states tend to carry on during and after moments of crisis by appealing to well established, widely shared notions of why failures occur and what can be done to ensure that such things will not happen again. The rationality of experts emerges according to this line of analysis as never natural but always achieved, through institutionalized rules of the game that admit or preclude particular modes of asserting expertise.

Methodologically, my approach to studying such moments of de- and re-stabilization differs from classic studies of controversies and boundary work in STS. Unlike many subject-specific investigations of scientific disputes, aimed largely at revealing the interpretive flexibility of expert observations, my studies display the subtle ways in which such disagreements, and their settlements, repro-duce cultural preferences for particular types of evidence and modes of delega-tion. With regard to boundary drawing, what interests me again is not so much the work done in specific cases as the respects in which boundaries such as that between expertise and common sense shore up deeper collective commitments to forms of epistemic and political delegation (civic epistemologies). Investigating these regularities necessarily calls for sensitivity to history, familiarity with the details of legal and administrative processes, and awareness of the contexts in which controversies arise and achieve resolution.

My work on expertise began at a time of unprecedented turmoil in U.S. regula-tory politics. Ronald Reagan's election to the presidency in 1980 shook the founda-tions of the American regulatory state severely enough to earn the label "the Reagan Revolution." His administration is widely credited with policies that favored dereg-ulation and pushed forward a neoliberal ideology that remained in force long after the fall of the Iron Curtain in 1989. A less visible aspect of U.S. policymaking in those years was to redraw the institutional boundaries between science and politics established during the New Deal. The expansion of federal power under President Franklin D. Roosevelt had sharply increased the number and variety of agencies implementing new governmental mandates. Those bodies gained a reputation for combining specialist knowledge of matters within their jurisdiction with the experi-ence needed to make convincing political decisions, but they were prone to capture by the very interests they sought to manage. The 1946 Administrative Procedure Act ensured that executive expertise would be subject to public testing; no admin-istrative decisions would be made without giving the public an opportunity to ques-tion the agency's expert claims. Experts' reasons, in other words, would carry weight only if they satisfied interested and affected parties.

The 1960s and 1970s saw further increases in federal administrative power in the United States, with a spate of laws controlling risks to health, safety and the environment (Wilson 1980; Brickman et al. 1985). This period was also marked by the rise of new social movements and non-governmental organizations claiming to represent the public interest against unacceptable risk-creation by private capital. Now the threat of capture appeared distinctly to tilt against purely economic interests, and business and industry fought the emerging alliance between regulatory agencies and public interest groups by attacking the agencies' technical expertise. Whereas an earlier generation had ratified transparency and public explanation as appropriate controls on runaway power, the deregulators of the post-Reagan era returned to science as their resource of choice in challenging agency discretion. Arguments that regulatory agencies were misusing science drew strength from long centuries of cultural work that had established science, the voice of nature, as distinct from politics, the voice of society (Latour 1993). In the United States, appeals to sound science as the touchstone for good policy gained ground, coupled with charges that agencies, through non-scientific, subjective judgments, were introducing politics into science, thereby contaminating the only secure basis for public reason (Brickman et al. 1985). In this period of reaction, the boundary between science and politics had to be remade through institutional reforms. It became fashionable for opponents of regulation to demand that agencies should install additional scientific advisory committees, use only peer-reviewed science, and strictly separate scientific assessments from any consideration of values (NRC 1983).

I first reflected on the implications of these trends for public reason in "Contested boundaries in policy-relevant science," which I reproduce here as Chapter 6. That 1987 article focused on the raucous debate over the quality of science used by the Environmental Protection Agency (EPA), a lightning rod then and now for opponents of federal regulation and big government. Much of the contestation centered on whether EPA had used peer-reviewed science in its standard-setting. Interestingly, neither EPA's friends nor foes questioned the need for peer review; all agreed that review was essential for the production of reliable scientific knowledge. But behind the shared rhetoric were sharp disagreements about the meaning of "peer" in the domain of regulatory science. EPA's detractors insisted that reviewers should be impartial members of the scientific community with no relationship to the agency nor any active commitment to its mission. EPA, by contrast, viewed as good peers precisely those scientists who could interpret uncertain knowledge in the light of the agency's regulatory mission, and could thus bridge the gap between known facts and legally mandated actions. On the whole, experts chosen by the agency were more likely to be swayed by concerns for public and environmental health, in other words to espouse caution, while scientists with no experience of EPA's policy dilemmas were more likely to demand strict standards of proof and a higher bar for regulation. The apparent consensus on the value of peer review proved on examination to be a façade for tense boundary struggles over who should determine, and by what criteria, the proper balance between risk-taking and precaution.

A decade later, when risk assessment was securely established as a powerful discourse of public reason in the United States, I revisited the same contested territory in "The songlines of risk" (this volume, Chapter 7). By then, it was clear that risk is a defining framework for modern government, extending far beyond the regulation of hazardous products and activities. Social theorists had begun to view risk as an organizing force in society, capable of creating new social identities, solidarities and conflicts (Beck 1992). Governments for their part increasingly tied their claims to legitimacy to their capacity to diagnose, calculate and manage risks. But the seemingly universal modern preoccupation with risk conceals significantly different notions of individual agency and collective responsibility in hazardous situations. In channeling social anxieties about technology, this essay suggests, the technical discourses of risk resemble the "songlines" with which Australian aboriginals sing their land into being, producing varied imagined realities. Culturally specific models of agency and their implications for collective action are articulated in the performance of risk analysis, and yet they come to be seen as the natural and only possible order of things. It follows that centralized methodologies of risk analysis tend to reduce the diversity of standpoints and perspectives that might make policymaking more robustly democratic. The most effective way to denaturalize the songlines, then, is to hold them up against other, equally justifiable, ways of constructing reality.

In "Judgment under siege: the three-body problem of expert legitimacy" (this volume, Chapter 8), I turned to the problems of accountability that arise in a representative democracy from committing important policy decisions to anonymous experts. I import theories of delegation from the law into an analysis of what it would take to ensure that experts will act in the public interest. That task can be facilitated by distinguishing among the three "bodies" of the article's title, each of which calls for different principles of delegation: the "body" of the individual expert; the "body" of policy-relevant knowledge; and the "body" of advisers who assess available information in forms suitable for underwriting public policy. Western political systems, I show, have diverged in their respective efforts to legitimate these three bodies. Thus, in policy and practice, Britain pays most attention to the expert's individual virtues, the United States to the integrity of bodies of professional and technical knowledge, and Germany to the balanced composition of the expert bodies that advise the state.

Rounding out the section on expertise is an article that found unexpected resonance and has continued to be widely cited and reproduced since it was published in 2003, "Technologies of humility: citizen participation in governing science" (Chapter 9). The point of departure here is the gradual transformation in Western understandings of the relationship between knowledge and action. At the turn of the twenty-first century, many things that seemed self-evident about science even fifty years back no longer seem so. In particular, the image of an impersonal science, standing apart from human interests and values, and sternly committed to the delivery of truths, has given way to an awareness that science is frequently commissioned to serve political ends, is constrained by the limits of human imagination and capability, and, through its very ambition, extends the horizons of uncertainty while producing new knowledge. Prediction based on sciences exhibiting these properties has proved much less convincing than policymakers had hoped. Prudence calls for "technologies of humility" to take better account of uncertainties and unknowns in forecasting the future. Traditional methods of risk analysis—committed as they are to assessing the future on the basis of present knowledge—should be supplemented by analyses that are more attentive to history, to past failures of understanding, and to persistent inequality and injustice.

Law, science and public values

Analysts of science and technology have not by and large examined the intersections of law and science as sites of shared knowledge production and norms-making though these two institutions enjoy equal authority in modern democracies. Yet no account of public reason can ignore the foundational influence of law in shaping allowable forms of discourse in the public sphere, as well as dominant ideas about what kinds of claims are sufficient in justifying state action. Indeed, if science claims a monopoly on revealing truths, the law can claim a parallel monopoly on defining the nature of evidence. As a practical matter, neither science nor law could function without unswerving commitments to both truth *and* evidence, but arguably science has dedicated more energy to the accuracy of its representations of nature (truth), and law more to the persuasive demonstration of causality and relevance (evidence) for purposes of moral adjudication. How the law evaluates science for its own needs, and how it influences societal understandings of evidence, are therefore central to any adequate account of public reason.

Three essays in this volume were written during a period in which American politics and legal practice, though not the academic social sciences, became intensely aware of interactions between law and science. In 1993, the U.S. Supreme Court issued the first of three major rulings on the admissibility of scientific evidence, *Daubert v. Merrell Dow Pharmaceuticals, Inc.*, 509 U.S. 579 (1993). The lawsuits that precipitated this landmark decision reflected years of private sector frustration with jury verdicts that seemed systematically to privilege plaintiffs' interests in defiance of what companies insisted was reliable countervailing scientific evidence. Ostensibly designed to safeguard the integrity of science in the courtroom, the Supreme Court's evidence decisions of the 1990s removed decision making authority from juries and reassigned it to judges, who were enjoined to act as gatekeepers for scientific testimony. My writings on science and evidence in the post-*Daubert* era reflect in part an attempt to probe what this shift meant for making and evaluating knowledge in legal settings. Are lay judges demonstrably better than lay juries at distinguishing good science from bad? If so, how do they— as non-scientists—proclaim and defend their superior ability to discriminate? In part, too, I was concerned with *Daubert*'s implications for transforming the very ideas of lawfulness and legality: what impact would the mandated judicial deference to science have on the capacity of courts to render justice?

These questions seemed ripe for analysis by scholars trained in science and technology studies. *Daubert* and its progeny showed virtually no awareness that the practices of science and technology had been systematically researched for decades, nor of the results of such work. Even when the decisions referenced findings from the philosophy or sociology of science, these resources were mobilized idiosyncratically, with little attempt to probe their underlying logics. My book on expert advisory committees, for example, was cited in *Daubert* for the proposition, "Publication (which is but one element of peer review) is not a *sine qua non* of admissibility; it does not necessarily correlate with reliability" (509 U.S. at 593). Accurate as far as it goes, this sentence sidelined the book's most important argument: peer review, especially in the regulatory context, does not so much apply exogenous standards of good science as *create* the standards by which claims can be judged as falling inside or outside the bounds of good practice. A more reflective reading might have led the authors of *Daubert* to conclude something similar about adjudicating the admissibility of evidence—that is, admissibility criteria are remade within the course of *Daubert*-based proceedings rather than imported intact from some external storehouse of foolproof tests of scientific reliability (Jasanoff 1995).

The first of the law articles, "What judges should know about the sociology of science," originally published in the legal journal *Jurimetrics* (and included here as Chapter 10), sought to remedy this lack of self-awareness by rehearsing in accessible form some basic insights from social studies of scientific knowledge that might be useful for judges. The article reflects a relatively early stage in my thinking about law and science and thus has numerous shortcomings—including, importantly, that it does not consider the implications of sociology of technology (as opposed to sociology of science) for evidence decisions.

Methodologically, the article exemplifies a naively appealing model of interdisciplinarity: the presumption that there are stable, self-contained conceptual packages that can be moved without difficulty across branches of scholarship, in this case from sociology to law, enriching and amplifying both. This presumption, however, cuts against the grain of my own critique of *Daubert*, which similarly presumes that scientific criteria of validity can be straightforwardly applied to legal evidence. Nonetheless, the article marked an attempt to engage in cross-disciplinary writing, translating (or trying to translate) concepts from one domain of intellectual practice to another. The article's very simplicity may help explain its relatively wide circulation in both legal and STS literatures.

It soon became clear, however, that a different kind of exploration, more attentive to the complexities of adjudicatory practice and discourse, would be needed for a deeper understanding of ways in which law and science inflect and reinforce one another. Methodologically, such a move is consistent with the growing focus on the practical enactment of social ideas in STS as well as in other social sciences (Camic et al. 2011). Theoretically, too, the turn toward practice was compatible with the idea of co-production—the notion that knowledge and norms (*is* and *ought*) are not separable, as they are often taken to be, but are simultaneously defined through intertwined processes that put together new epistemic and social realities (Jasanoff 2004b). From a co-productionist standpoint, it is not enough to say that judges should learn some basic tenets of the sociology of science. That prescription reifies too many categories: science, law, judging, sociology. The challenge instead is to understand how the coupled working of law/science (a particular instantiation of Michel Foucault's famous dyad of power/knowledge) constitute, as it were, the cultural DNA of modern rationality. It is imperative to take apart the intricate machinery through which these two institutions co-construct such fundamental elements of public reason as expertise, objectivity, common knowledge, and common sense. Micro-investigation of legal processes becomes an indispensable technique for investigating how these cornerstones of democratic governance are defined in practice.

The next two articles carry out such investigations from different perspectives. These pieces show that, in a thoroughly modern twist on ancient natural law thinking, the law still depends on establishing epistemic bright lines, or matters of fact, with which to align its normative judgments. Facts must speak clearly as facts in order for the law to be seen as acting justly. Distinctions between acceptable and unacceptable expertise, the intellectual preoccupation of *Daubert* and the Supreme Court's other evidence rulings, are crucial to that line-drawing. But all rules need to be performed in order to have effect, and such performances bring beliefs and resources into play that the rulemakers did not necessarily imagine. Those background resources, as much as the formal rules themselves, give to any legal system its organic specificity.

In "Expert games in silicone gel breast implant litigation" (Chapter 11), I traced the interaction of rule and practice to show how the law constructed expertise in a specific post-*Daubert* context. Catalyzing the reform debate on law-science interactions in the mid-1990s were thousands of lawsuits against manufacturers by women who had undergone silicone gel breast implant surgery. At its peak, the litigation involved some 400,000 plaintiffs claiming to be suffering a host of disorders, from inflammation and painful hardening of breast tissue to "atypical" immunological dysfunctions caused by silicone seeping into their bodies from leaky implants. Their complaints spurred numerous epidemiological studies whose results by and large failed to support the claims of immune system damage. For many critics, the pro-plaintiff judgments in some of these lawsuits became paradigm examples of the legal system's tolerance for bad science (Angell 1996).

Much could be said about the co-evolution of multidistrict litigation, the science of silicone gel in women's bodies, and standards of acceptable evidence in this protracted conflict. In this article, I called attention to two aspects of that dynamic. First, shifting attention away from gatekeeping judges, I picked apart the strategies by which attorneys for the parties sought to enhance the credibility of their expert witnesses using the new rhetorical resources offered by *Daubert*. Second, I analogized that maneuvering to moves on a game board in which the objectivity of proffered testimony can be established along two tactically separable axes: either by embedding the expert witness within an authorizing community of fellow practitioners, acting in accordance with approved professional standards; or by representing the expert witness as a credible spokesperson for impersonal, hence mechanically objective, authority, such as accepted scientific theories, tests, or instruments. Incidentally to my main point in that article, but contradicting any overly neat periodicity (Daston and Galison 2007), the "game board" metaphor points to the coexistence of multiple strategies of producing objectivity in legal and political practices at any given historical moment.

Courtroom reasoning is a performance not only by specific actors (lawyers and expert witnesses) but for a specific kind of audience, composed of moral adjudicators (judges and juries) who themselves are witnesses to the efficacy of the performance. Perhaps most especially in criminal trials, these adjudicators must be made to feel as if they are seeing the alleged wrongdoing at first hand. "The eye of everyman" (this volume, Chapter 12), based on a close reading of transcripts from the notorious 1995 murder trial of the football star O.J. Simpson, calls attention to the central role of vision, especially judicial vision, in constructing moral authority in the courtroom. At one point in the Simpson trial, the prosecution asked the presiding judge, Lance Ito, to admit expert testimony on the reliability of video clips made at the crime scene. In denying this request, Ito displayed how tacit assumptions about the boundary between expert and lay understandings can determine the formal outcome of an admissibility decision. Video testimony, Ito ruled, does not need further explication by experts. This is something that untrained and unaided eyes can grasp and interpret well enough. The judge's own eyes provided the test: since Ito was able to make sense of the video, so should the "everyman" of the article's title. On another motion, however, Ito refused to let the defense retest the crime scene blood samples (in other words, to witness truth for themselves). He ruled that the results obtained by Cellmark, a private testing company using standard protocols, should satisfy both parties' needs. Here he came down on the side of expert vision, concluding that professional eyes are allowed to witness certain kinds of evidence without need for further cross-checking. Such contingent, issue-specific decisions within the same trial underscore the continuing centrality of the lay perspective, only that of judge rather than jury, in settling what counts as expertise, and who is held to possess it, in the post-*Daubert* courtroom.

The final essay in this volume stretches the canvas of legality to the broadest questions of legal authority and democratic governance, showing how concurrent changes in science and technology and in our basic moral intuitions produce unstated norms that are profoundly constitutive of ordered societies. As the title indicates, "In a constitutional moment: science and social order at the Millennium" was written in a time of historical transition when questions about the prospects for human solidarity seemed wide open for reconsideration. Globalization had eroded boundaries and brought once distant societies together, forcing renewed examination of concepts such as sovereignty and nationalism; and the September 11, 2001 terrorist attacks on the United States had not yet happened. In this article, I argued that constructivist approaches to exploring the nature of facts and objects within STS must be extended to include at one and the same time the normative envelopes—the emerging global constitutional orders—within which such things achieve recognition and are integrated into the social fabric. I called this move "constructive constitutionalism" and sketched how its analytic frontiers can be charted along three dimensions: debates about self and identity, importantly related to changes in the life and earth sciences; discourses of consumerism as they intersect with notions of citizenship, especially around innovation and emerging technologies; and tensions between democratic government and the rise of supranational expert authorities claiming new varieties of imperial knowledge.

Conclusion

Reason is achieved, not attained. That is the quickest way to sum up a body of work representing decades of research on a wide variety of issues arising in disparate institutional contexts within national legal and policy frameworks from three continents. That terse summation, however, provides the basis for several conclusions that cut against the grain of conventional wisdom about the nature of public reason, democracy, and modernity itself.

First, this volume shows that reason, as enacted in the practices, discourses and institutions of diverse political cultures, is not a universal category, and the achievement of reason is not—and cannot be—simply a matter of applying impersonal logic and principled argument to facts that decision makers everywhere could and should hold in common. Rather, the forms and techniques of public reasoning in any society run along culturally particular discursive tracks, laid down on historically contingent institutional foundations, and lubricated by repeated articulations for audiences attuned to specific modes of demonstration and argument. To satisfy democracy's evolving demands, reason requires continual reperformance conditioned by locally particular civic epistemologies—which themselves evolve in the course of history. The analogy to scripts and acting is apposite, except that players in national dramas of public reason are seldom as self-conscious about their role-playing as are actors performing on stage or screen. Part of the explanation for this dearth of self-understanding, I argue, is that specialized policy discourses, often drawing their power from the epistemic authority of science, corral the policy-maker's reasoned arguments away from alternative logics and sensibilities (different songlines), thereby rendering reflection more difficult.

Second, public reason is not only an epistemic but also a normative achievement. This follows from the theoretical framework of co-production, but the studies in this volume move beyond mere assertion that co-production happens to illustrate in fine empirical detail just how the commingling of *is* and *ought* takes place. Whenever and wherever reason underwrites and justifies power, it takes its color from culturally grounded understandings of how power ought to be rendered accountable. It is impossible to keep apart judgments of how to know the world in order to govern it from concomitant judgments about how best to govern the world as we know it. Thus, how a democratic society accommodates itself to rule by experts—whether by insisting on individual virtue or by demanding formal technical credentials, for instance—influences the composition of advisory committees, the form and frequency of knowledge controversies, and the means chosen to effect closure. In the process of undertaking rational analysis and action, political actors play out deeper imaginaries of what it means to behave rationally in public space.

Third, public reason is as much an achievement of law as it is of scientific and technical expertise. Reason, as a democratic norm, could not be attained without constant appeals to the law, which not only prescribes applicable procedural rules but also defines how knowledge should be collected, imparted, and debated for purposes of gaining public assent. The law, as discussed in many of the following selections, encodes dominant cultural understandings of the state's obligation to explain itself to citizens, as well as tacit views of what citizens are capable of knowing and learning. In this respect the law is a repository of beliefs about human nature that have been tested through experience, though not necessarily by science. These beliefs, in turn, reaffirm the civic epistemologies that characterize political cultures and give them their originality and distinction.

Fourth, making sense of public reason as a social and cultural achievement dissolves the boundaries between micro and macro, by showing that the grand abstractions of reason, such as expertise and objectivity, are constructed and reconstructed through small, mundane actions and inactions. Culturally distinctive styles of reasoning are reinforced in the micro-practices of powerful institutions, as when an advisory committee defines who is a peer for purposes of peer review, a judge decides where to draw the line between common sense and expert witnessing, or citizens ask for demonstrations of competence from government officials in order to restore public confidence. At such moments the legitimacy of the greatest institutional actors, including nation states and supranational agencies, is temporarily called into question. Challenges to reason serve, in effect, as moments in which the ideal of rational choice for the good of society must be asserted and performed yet again. Through repeated episodes of public reasoning, policy institutions affirm their right to exist, to be taken seriously, and to govern for the people.

These arguments offer a counterpoint to analyses of reason grounded exclusively in theory and principle. The thick descriptions of political culture provided in these essays undercut any simplistic or universal definitions of reason, rational action or modernity, displaying instead a series of intricate political struggles in which democratic aspirations are the only constants: aspirations to know and to learn, to govern wisely, to deliver universal justice, and to make sure that experts remain accountable to the people whose futures their reasoning helps shape. But in showing that reason is achieved through historically contingent social practices, and therefore never to be taken for granted, this volume also serves a normative function, that of enabling critique, revealing alternatives, and liberating the democratic imagination to soar above the constraints of the immediately possible. It feels right, then, to close this introduction with a comment from a friend who understood this broader point and provided much-needed encouragement for pulling together this collection:

> Moreover your work enables audiences to understand why the way forward with science and citizenship is one potentially full of opportunity, yet not self-evident—and it is self-evidence and inevitability that in a sense most need to be challenged to encourage civic participation.

References

Angell, Marcia. 1996. *Science on Trial: The Clash of Medical Evidence and the Law in the Breast Implant Case*. New York: Norton.

Barry, Andrew. 1999. "Demonstrations: Sites and Sights of Direct Action." *Economy and Society* 28(1): 75–94.

Beck, Ulrich. 1988. *Gegengifte: Die organisierte Unverantwortlichkeit*. Frankfurt: Suhrkamp.

Beck, Ulrich. 1992. *Risk Society: Towards a New Modernity*. London: Sage Publications.

Bijker, Wiebe, Thomas Hughes, and Trevor Pinch, eds. 1987. *The Social Construction of Technological Systems: New Directions in the Sociology and History of Technology*. Cambridge, MA: MIT Press.

Brickman, Ronald, Sheila Jasanoff, and Thomas Ilgen. 1985. *Controlling Chemicals: The Politics of Regulation in Europe and the United States*. Ithaca, NY: Cornell University Press.

Callon, Michel, Pierre Lascoumes, and Yannick Barthe. 2009. *Acting in an Uncertain World: An Essay on Technical Democracy*. Cambridge, MA: MIT Press.

Camic, Charles, Neil Gross, and Michèle Lamont, eds. 2011. *Social Knowledge in the Making*. Chicago: University of Chicago Press.

Daston, Lorraine and Peter Galison. 2007. *Objectivity*. New York: Zone Books.

Dear, Peter. 2006. *The Intelligibility of Nature: How Science Makes Sense of the World*. Chicago: University of Chicago Press.

Doubleday, Robert and Brian Wynne. 2011. "Despotism and Democracy in the UK: Experiments in Reframing Citizenship." In Sheila Jasanoff, ed., *Reframing Rights: Bioconstitutionalism in the Genetic Age*, pp. 239–262. Cambridge, MA: MIT Press.

Douglas, Mary. 1986. *Purity and Danger: An Analysis of Concepts of Pollution and Taboo*. London: Routledge & Kegan Paul.

Edwards, Paul. 1996. *The Closed World: Computers and the Politics of Discourse in Cold War America*. Cambridge, MA: MIT Press.

Ezrahi, Yaron. 1990. *The Descent of Icarus*. Cambridge, MA: Harvard University Press.

Geertz, Clifford. 1973. "Thick Description: Toward an Interpretive Theory of Culture." In *The Interpretation of Cultures*, pp. 3–30. New York: Basic Books.

Goffman, Erving. 1959. *The Presentation of Self in Everyday Life*. New York: Doubleday.

Gottweis, Herbert. 1998. *Governing Molecules: The Discursive Politics of Genetic Engineering in Europe and the United States*. Cambridge, MA: MIT Press.

Jasanoff, Sheila. 1990. *The Fifth Branch: Science Advisers as Policymakers*. Cambridge, MA: Harvard University Press.

Jasanoff, Sheila. 1995. *Science at the Bar: Law, Science and Technology in America*. Cambridge, MA: Harvard University Press.

Jasanoff, Sheila. 2003. "In a Constitutional Moment: Science and Social Order at the Millennium." In Bernward Joerges and Helga Nowotny, eds., *Social Studies of Science and Technology: Looking Back, Ahead*, pp. 155–180. Yearbook of the Sociology of the Sciences. Dordrecht: Kluwer.

Jasanoff, Sheila. 2004a. "Science and Citizenship: A New Synergy." *Science and Public Policy* 31(2): 30–34.

Jasanoff, Sheila, ed. 2004b. *States of Knowledge: The Co-Production of Science and Social Order*. London: Routledge.

Jasanoff, Sheila. 2010. "A New Climate for Society." *Theory, Culture and Society* 27 (2–3): 233–253.

Jasanoff, Sheila, ed. 2011. *Reframing Rights: Bioconstitutionalism in the Genetic Age*. Cambridge, MA: MIT Press.

Jasanoff, Sheila and Sang-Hyun Kim. 2009. "Containing the Atom: Sociotechnical Imaginaries and Nuclear Regulation in the U.S. and South Korea." *Minerva* 47(2): 119–146.

Kysar, Douglas. 2010. *Regulating From Nowhere: Environmental Law and the Search for Objectivity*. New Haven: Yale University Press.

Latour, Bruno. 1987. *Science in Action: How to Follow Scientists and Engineers through Society*. Cambridge, MA: Harvard University Press.

Latour, Bruno. 1993. *We Have Never Been Modern*. Cambridge, MA: Harvard University Press.

Latour, Bruno and Steve Woolgar. 1979. *Laboratory Life: The Social Construction of Scientific Facts*. Beverly Hills: Sage Publications.

National Research Council (NRC). 1983. *Risk Assessment in the Federal Government: Managing the Process*. Washington, D.C.: National Academies Press.

Picon, Antoine. 2002. *Les saint-simoniens: raison, imaginaire et utopie*. Paris: Lavoisier.

Price, Don K. 1965. *The Scientific Estate*. Cambridge, MA: Harvard University Press.

Rawls, John. 1971. *A Theory of Justice*. Cambridge, MA: Harvard University Press.

Sahlins, Marshall. 1996. *How "Natives" Think: About Captain Cook, For Example*. Chicago: University of Chicago Press.

Shapin, Steven and Simon Schaffer. 1985. *Leviathan and the Air-Pump: Hobbes, Boyle, and the Experimental Life*. Princeton, NJ: Princeton University Press.

Sunstein, Cass. 2005. *Laws of Fear: Beyond the Precautionary Principle*. New York: Cambridge University Press.

Wilson, James Q. 1980. *The Politics of Regulation*. New York: Basic Books.

Winickoff, David, Sheila Jasanoff, Lawrence Busch, Robin Grove-White, and Brian Wynne. 2005. "Adjudicating the GM Food Wars: Science, Risk, and Democracy in World Trade Law." *Yale Journal of International Law* 30: 81–123.

World Commission on Environment and Development. 1987. *Our Common Future*. Oxford: Oxford University Press.

Wynne, Brian. 1988. "Unruly Technology." *Social Studies of Science* 18: 147–167.

Wynne, Brian. 1995. "Public Understanding of Science." In Sheila Jasanoff, Gerald Markle, James C. Petersen, and Trevor Pinch, eds., *Handbook of Science and Technology Studies*, pp. 380–392. Thousand Oaks, CA: Sage.

Wynne, Brian, Ulrike Felt, et al. 2007. *Taking European Knowledge Society Seriously*. Report of the Expert Group on Science and Governance. Brussels: Commission of the European Communities.

2 Product, process, or programme

Three cultures and the regulation of biotechnology*

Introduction

The development of a multinational regulatory framework for biotechnology during the past twenty years provides an unparalleled opportunity to study the processes by which technological advances overcome public resistance and are incorporated into a receptive social context. Through the vehicle of regulation, states provide assurance that the risks of new technologies can be contained within manageable bounds. Procedures are devised to limit uncertainty, channel the flow of future public resistance, and define the permissible modalities of dissent. Regulation, in these respects, becomes integral to the shaping of technology. A regulated technology encompasses more than simply the 'knowledge of how to fulfill certain human purposes in a specifiable and reproducible way.'[1] Regulation transmutes such instrumental knowledge into a cultural resource; it is a kind of social contract that specifies the terms under which state and society agree to accept the costs, risks and benefits of a given technological enterprise.

The passage of biotechnology from moratorium[2] to market in just twenty years exemplifies this process of social accommodation. During this period, biotechnology moved from a research programme that aroused misgivings even among its most ardent advocates to a flourishing industry promising revolutionary benefits in return for negligible and easily controlled risks. The transformation occurred almost simultaneously and with remarkable speed throughout Europe and North America. To facilitate the commercialization of biotechnology, the United States, and the European Community and several of its member states, adopted laws and regulations to control not only laboratory research with genetically engineered organisms but also their purposeful release into the environment.[3] Risks that once were considered speculative and wholly unmanageable[4] came to be regarded as amenable to rational assessment in accordance with sound scientific principles. Apocalyptic visions and the rhetoric of science fiction yielded to the weightier discourse of expert advice and bureaucratic practice. The research community coalesced to persuade the public that the risks of biotechnology could be assessed in a reasonable way and that earlier fears of ecological disaster were mostly unfounded.

These changes in the status of biotechnology were all the more noteworthy because, as of the early 1990s, the risks of genetic manipulation remained largely hypothetical. Scientists and industrialists confidently proclaimed that no serious harm would befall ecosystems or human health if our daily bread were baked with genetically engineered, quick-rising yeast, if economically significant crop plants were fitted out with herbicide resistance genes, or if fruit farmers sprayed their orchards with gene-deleted bacteria designed to prevent frost formation. Unlike toxic chemicals, however, the products of the new biotechnology have not been around long enough to display their whole range of beneficial and adverse effects. Despite repeated allusions to Bhopal and Chernobyl by opponents of biotechnology, there is no reservoir of precedents into which one can readily dip for historical parallels to the production and use of laboratory-crafted living organisms – products not of nature but of human invention.

Nonetheless, as regulators in different countries approve new uses of biotechnology and reassure their publics that the risks are manageable, they are obliged to place believable outer limits on the technology's potentially harmful impacts. An important question for students of technology to ask is whether the resulting accounts of risk have diverged cross-nationally, conditioned by varying socio-political influences, as predicted by the social studies of science and as previously documented in studies of environmental regulation and risk management.[5] Were there observable differences in national regulatory responses to biotechnology and, if so, could they be traced to differences in national traditions of legal and administrative decision making? How, in turn, did the process of constructing the risks of biotechnology for regulatory purposes affect the opportunities for public participation and protest?

This chapter is based on a focused comparison of the way governmental authorities in Britain, Germany, and the United States conceptualized biotechnology as a regulatory problem in the specific context of releasing genetically modified organisms (GMOs) into the environment. Looking primarily at events in the decade from 1980 to 1990, I describe how public resistance and state response initially led to quite different understandings about risk in each national context, and hence to divergent characterizations of biotechnology as a policy issue. In all three countries, however, the dominant conception enabled regulators to devise strategies for managing uncertainty and neutralizing the most common forms of organized opposition. Although their techniques varied – legislation, bureaucratic reorganization and expert advice were differentially employed – regulators in each nation succeeded in rearranging a potentially limitless expanse of scientific unknowns into familiar paradigms of assessment and control. I conclude with some observations about what this analysis implies for mobilization against risk in advanced industrial societies.

Paradigms of control

In order to approve the deliberate environmental release of GMOs, regulators in the United States, Britain and Germany had to persuade their respective political constituencies that the risks of biotechnology, although novel, lay sufficiently close to their prior experience of technological risks to permit effective public control. Although the ultimate goal was the same everywhere, the strategy of public reassurance adopted in the three countries varied, especially in the willingness to admit that biotechnology poses novel or special risks to human well-being. 'Specialness' as it relates to the adverse impacts of biotechnology had been understood on at least three different levels since the 1970s. First, opponents of the technology argued that human intervention through genetic engineering would produce *physical risks* to health and the environment that were different in kind and magnitude from risks created by 'natural' processes of genetic combination and recombination. Secondly, some observers were persuaded that the widespread application of biotechnology in agriculture would create a variety of *social risks*, ranging from the commodification of nature to the elimination of family farms in the West and to severe economic dislocations in developing countries. Thirdly, the esoteric technical content of biotechnology was considered likely to increase the distance between expert decision makers and the lay public, thereby exacerbating the *political risk* – increasingly troubling in modern industrial societies – of excluding citizens from meaningful control over technologies that could transform their lives. As we shall see below, these three dimensions of risk, each entailing its own discourses of protest and legitimation, were emphasized to different degrees in the regulatory politics of the United States, Britain and Germany.

United States – a product-based approach

The first applications for conducting deliberate release experiments caught regulatory agencies in the United States without appropriate institutional mechanisms in place for conducting persuasive safety evaluations. The only supervisory body that researchers could turn to at the outset was the National Institutes of Health (NIH), which had been regulating laboratory experiments involving recombinant DNA (rDNA) molecules since the mid-1970s. Pursuant to guidelines first adopted in 1976 and substantially relaxed in 1978, all federally funded rDNA experiments had to be approved by NIH's Recombinant DNA Advisory Committee (RAC). Governmental control, in other words, was tied to the sponsorship of research, a scheme that proved increasingly vulnerable as biotechnology headed out of the laboratory toward commercial application.

The insufficiency of the NIH review process was dramatically exposed when two University of California scientists, Steven Lindow and Nickolas Panopoulos, sought permission to carry out a field test using the 'Ice-Minus' bacterium, a member of the *Pseudomonas* family that had been genetically engineered to increase the frost resistance of plants. The scientists advising the NIH reviewed the application, requested some modifications, and decided unanimously on the second round of review that the experiment was safe. Their conclusion, however, was set aside by a federal court of appeals, which blocked the experiment on the ground that NIH had not carried out a proper environmental impact assessment, as required by the US National Environmental Policy Act (NEPA). In *Foundation on Economic Trends v. Heckler*,[6] the court especially deplored NIH's failure to explain why a type of experiment that had been considered too risky to undertake under the 1976 guidelines could now be permitted to go forward with so little explicit consideration of its risks. The scientific community predictably saw this call for greater public accountability as an insupportable intrusion into safety evaluation by a 'technically illiterate' judiciary. All the same, *Heckler* threw into relief the fact that NIH's research-funding mission did not sit well with creating an appropriate institutional forum for airing lay concerns about the risks of commercial biotechnology.

The Ice-Minus episode among others forced the US government to regularize its procedures for controlling the commercial applications of biotechnology. In 1986 the president's Office of Science and Technology Policy (OSTP) published a *Coordinated Framework for the Regulation of Biotechnology*, identifying the responsibilities of the three agencies with most extensive jurisdiction over the new technology – the Environmental Protection Agency (EPA), the Food and Drug Administration (FDA), and the US Department of Agriculture (USDA). A Biotechnology Science Coordinating Committee (BSCC) was established to develop a common inter-agency approach to issues governed by the Coordinated Framework. In addition, each of the lead regulatory agencies developed new institutional capabilities for dealing with biotechnology. For example, EPA established a Biotechnology Science Advisory Committee (BSAC) to give advice on the scientific aspects of regulation.

These institutional arrangements reflected in the first instance a consensus across the US government that the authority contained in existing laws, aimed largely at controlling physical risks, was sufficient to regulate any novel problems associated with biotechnology. OSTP and the agencies participating in the Coordinated Framework persuaded Congress that regulations issued under the old laws would adequately clarify concepts and eliminate possible jurisdictional overlaps. This approach was consistent with the views of many scientists in research and industry that the risks of biotechnology were not in any sense special or unique, and that biotechnological products – pesticides, drugs, foods, and food additives – should not be treated any differently from similar products created by traditional biological or chemical processes.

While denying the need for new legal authority, the Coordinated Framework happily accepted the institutionalization of new scientific authority. The creation of an expert advisory committee, BSAC, at the individual agency level and a coordinating committee, BSCC, at the inter-agency level indicated that federal regulators viewed the task ahead primarily in scientific terms and were prepared to strengthen their institutional capabilities accordingly. OSTP's central role in developing the Coordinated Framework reinforced the view that regulating biotechnology was not a matter for broad participatory politics but for expert policy making at the highest levels of the executive branch. The object at every turn seemed to be to demonstrate that the mainstream forces of science – not activists like Jeremy Rifkin nor the assorted nay-sayers of the environmental movement – were in the driver's seat with respect to managing the emergent technology.

An influential report published by the National Research Council (NRC) in 1989 lent support to the US government's evolving position that commercial biotechnology should not be regarded as a specially risky enterprise in relation to human health and the environment.[7] On each of three issues where splits had developed among federal regulatory agencies,[8] the NRC report sided with the agencies that took the more benign view of biotechnology's hazards. Specifically, the NRC report concluded that

> (i) the *product* of genetic modification and selection constitutes the primary basis for decisions . . . and not the *process* by which the product was obtained; (ii) although knowledge about the process used to produce a genetically modified organism is important . . . the nature of the process is not useful for determining the amount of oversight; and (iii) organisms modified by modern molecular and cellular methods are governed by the same physical and biological laws as are organisms produced by classical methods.[9]

The message was obvious: mere use of biotechnological techniques did not make a harmless product dangerous; nor, conversely, were organisms produced by 'classical methods' safe simply because they were not genetically engineered. The report as a whole helped crystallize the conclusion that, for policy purposes, biotechnology was to be regarded as a supplier of familiar classes of products – not as a novel technological process threatening mysterious and incalculable harm to social well-being.

Elaborating on the theme of 'no special hazards', the NRC report on the whole belittled the possibility that GMOs would introduce uncontrollable risks into the environment. With respect to genetically modified plants, for example, the NRC committee concluded, first, that the potential for enhanced weediness was the most significant environmental threat. The committee then determined that this risk was likely to be low for a variety of reasons – for example, that the analogy between genetically modified crop plants and 'exotics' was 'tenuous' and that 'genetically modified crops are not known to have become weedy through the addition of traits such as herbicide and pest resistance.'[10]

As the last sentence suggests, the committee's emphasis throughout the report was on what was already known about genetic engineering and environmental release rather than what still remained unknown. For example, the report took pains to point out that molecular methods, whether used on plants or microorganisms, are highly precise and lead to modifications that can be fully characterized and understood.[11] This precision, the committee felt, provided sufficient safeguards against unpredictable behaviour by the resulting organisms. Assessing the social or political risks of biotechnology would have been out of place in a report that self-consciously disciplined uncertainty through technical language; indeed, no explicit discussion of social or political issues contaminated the apparent specificity of NRC's scientific analysis.

Debates concerning the 'scope' of regulation gave further evidence of US policymakers' reluctance to treat the risks of biotechnology as different in kind from those of more traditional biological manipulation. The 1986 Coordinated Framework, for instance, proposed two definitions for organisms requiring review: intergeneric organisms (that is, organisms formed by combining genetic material from sources in different genera), and pathogens.[12] During public comment, these proposals were severely criticized on the ground that they focused – inappropriately in the view of many scientists – on the process by which an organism was produced rather than on the probable riskiness of the product.

Arguments about the scope of regulation continued to divide official opinion for several years, with EPA's staff and scientists favouring a different approach from that of FDA and USDA. In 1990, EPA's biotechnology advisory committee proposed a quite inclusive and process-based definition of scope ('organisms deliberately modified by the introduction into or manipulation of genetic materials in their genomes'), from which it proposed to exclude all organisms that did not raise new risk assessment issues. The BSAC felt that this approach was broad enough to address potential risks, yet flexible enough to cover future developments in biotechnology. Critics complained, however, that EPA's formulation still displayed an excessive tilt toward process over product as the framing concept for regulation and that this stance contravened the recommendations of the NRC report.[13]

The existence of the NRC report allowed EPA's critics to legitimate their attacks on EPA's scope proposal through an appeal to scientific consensus. But 'science', as socially constructed in US regulatory debates, is often a double-edged sword, and it served as the discourse of choice for EPA's supporters as well. In particular, BSCC, the expert inter-agency coordinating committee that many saw as hostile to EPA, was itself attacked for straying beyond its charter, holding closed meetings, and impeding EPA's scientific inquiry. At the committee's December 1989 meeting, Margaret Mellon of the National Wildlife Federation expressed scepticism based on 'the composition of the BSCC – all high-level administrators, not scientists'.[14] Others accused the committee of unlawfully and heavy-handedly appropriating the review functions of the Office of Management and Budget (OMB), whose own intervention into issues of regulatory science had become a matter of considerable notoriety during the Reagan administration. By late 1990, these challenges led OSTP to rename the BSCC as the Biotechnology Research Subcommittee of the Committee on Life Sciences and to scale down its involvement in policy making.[15]

Confusion in regulatory circles, and associated boundary disputes over expertise and authority, rekindled interest in a legislative solution to managing biotechnology, but political pressure was insufficient to overcome a settled congressional reluctance to do anything that might endanger the US industry's competitive position. Instead, actions by the FDA and the White House, acting through OSTP, consolidated the policy position that only the characteristics of specific products were legitimate objects of regulatory assessment. Labelling theirs a 'risk-based' or a 'science-based' strategy of safety evaluation, these agencies continued to harp on the theme that any negative consequences of biotechnology could be adequately controlled product by product, without creating barriers against 'useful innovation'.[16]

The courts, which in the American political context might have provided an independent spur to a broader public debate on biotechnology, proved unusually quiescent throughout the period of policy development. In *Diamond v.*

Chakrabarty,[17] the US Supreme Court held by a narrow five-to-four majority that biologically modified microorganisms could be patented under an existing law whose operational language had been drafted 200 years before the advent of biotechnology. The decision on its face dealt with a narrowly legal question: whether living things constituted patentable subject matter under the Patent Act. Researchers and industry, however, found more grounds for rejoicing in the decision's subtext, for by relying on existing law the Court implicitly rejected the argument that the risks of biotechnology were so novel as to require special legislative attention. Even the *Heckler* decision, which some had taken to be a sign of awakening judicial activism in matters of biotechnology regulation, refused to require a programmatic evaluation of all deliberate releases, and it proved in any event to be an anomaly rather than a trend-setter with respect to later judicial decisions. Most subsequent challenges to proposals for environmental release from groups like Jeremy Rifkin's were curtly dismissed for lack of standing to sue.

Britain – biotechnology as process

Events in Britain suggested that the government was prepared to take a somewhat more expansive view of biotechnology's risks than were federal policy makers in the United States. Since 1978, laboratory work involving 'genetic manipulation' had been controlled through regulations issued under the Health and Safety at Work Act of 1974. Applications to conduct such activities had to be approved by the Genetic Manipulation Advisory Group (GMAG), replaced in 1984 by the Advisory Committee on Genetic Manipulation (ACGM)[18] to the Health and Safety Commission (HSC), Britain's lead agency for worker protection. Biotechnological work with environmental implications was further reviewed by the Department of the Environment, which obtained expert advice from its own interim Advisory Committee on Introductions. By the late 1980s, however, it became clear to British authorities that many biotechnological activities, including large-scale industrial production and deliberate releases into the environment, could not properly be controlled through the existing regulatory structure for occupational safety.[19]

Developments within the European Community provided additional impetus for Britain's decision to enact more formal statutory controls. In April 1990, the Community adopted two directives relating to biotechnology: one on contained experiments and one on deliberate release of GMOs. Recognizing the need for new legal authority to implement the latter directive, the British government introduced into the Environmental Protection Act of 1990 (the so-called Green Bill) a new Part VI governing GMOs. Meanwhile, environmental and health and safety authorities decided to replace their existing expert committees with a single new committee to review applications for releasing GMOs into the environment. The resulting interdepartmental Advisory Committee on Releases to the Environment (ACRE) held its first meetings in July 1990.

Debate on the Green Bill provided a focal point for environmentalists to demand more public participation in decisions about GMOs, and the government responded by agreeing to include an environmental representative on its new advisory committee on environmental release. The first person selected for this position was Julie Hill, a member of the Green Alliance, an environmental lobbying group spun off from the Liberal Party that had been particularly active in commenting on the Green Bill. Within Britain's normally closed and consensual policy culture, Hill's appointment marked at once a blow to tradition and a concession to long-standing regulatory practice. Asking an environmentalist to sit on ACRE affirmed the state's acceptance of the lay public's interest in biotechnology as significant enough to be represented in future negotiations over safety, but after the appointment, as before, the power to make decisions remained closely held within an expert advisory body.

Broadening the range of participation on ACRE appeared on the surface to be more responsive to the special social and political risks of biotechnology than comparable actions of the US government. It was almost as radical a move in the British context, according to one observer, as inviting Jeremy Rifkin to give advice on biotechnology might have been in America. Sceptics note, however, that the new committee was formed under the aegis of the HSC, the most partici-patory of Britain's regulatory agencies; under the Health and Safety at Work Act, HSC and its various operating committees are required to be constituted as 'tripar-tite' bodies, representing industry, labour, and local governments. Given this tradition of participation, it was perhaps easier for ACRE to accommodate a new interest (environmentalism) than it would have been for less broad-gauged scien-tific committees, such as those attached to the Ministry of Agriculture, Fisheries and Food.[20] Further, the move came at a time when the conservative government was seeking to expand its ties among moderate environmentalists. For British government and industry, the Green Alliance may well have represented environ-mentalism with a human face – a voice of reasoned dissent that could be internal-ized without seriously jeopardizing the evolution of technology. In constructing an appropriate advisory committee on deliberate releases, then, the government simultaneously constructed an official form of green participation that regulatory authorities were prepared to live with.

In Britain as in the United States, a well-timed report by a prestigious expert body helped reinforce the government's efforts to sort out its legal and institutional arrangements for dealing with biotechnology. The Royal Commission on Environ-mental Pollution (RCEP), a standing body charged with advising the government on environmental matters, decided that the time was ripe for a thorough evaluation of deliberate release, looking both at the possible consequences of releasing GMOs and at procedures for identifying, assessing and mitigating their risks.[21]

Issued in 1989, like its US counterpart, the Royal Commission's report was both more expansive in its treatment of impacts and more open in admitting uncer-tainty than the corresponding US document. Thus, instead of dwelling on benign past experiences and the precision of molecular techniques, the British experts emphasized how much was still unknown – and hence how little could be predicted with assurance about the likely behaviour of GMOs in the environment. With respect to genetically modified plants, for example, the RCEP report considered a broader range of possible risks than the NRC and seemed unwilling to dismiss any of these risk scenarios as wholly improbable. Thus, the RCEP felt that the historical experience with exotics could be highly relevant if a GMO were released into an environment where it was not native.[22] With respect to herbicide resistance, the Commission considered not only the possibility that the resistant gene might spread to weedy species, but also that the genetic engineering of plants resistant to herbicides could lead to greater use of environmentally damaging herbicides.[23]

The RCEP's stance, acknowledging the unpredictability of nature, was echoed in official British policy. In its guidance note on environmental release,[24] the ACGM subcommittee on releases spoke of possible differences between natural evolutionary processes and results obtained through genetic manipulation, noting for example that the release of a novel organism could involve the introduction of larger numbers than in the case of natural mutations. In sum, the subcommittee concluded as late as January 1990 that 'the deliberate release of novel types to foreign habitats could occasionally disturb the natural equilibrium of those habitats'.[25]

British authorities seemed to accept without question the Royal Commission's recommendation that all GMO releases, to start with, should be subject to regulatory scrutiny. Put differently, this amounted to accepting the principle (denied in America) that the process of genetic modification was an appropriate basis for defining the scope of policy action. Officials at both DoE and HSE acknowledged that risk categories might eventually be established that would either exempt some products from evaluation or subject them to reduced oversight.[26] But they indicated that any such relaxation would have to be based on actual experience, that is, on empirically observed data from earlier releases. These views were seconded by Dr John Beringer, the first chairman of ACRE, who thought that all GMOs should in principle be subject to review, although it might eventually be possible to move to a two-tier system of clearances for new GMOs – a 'fast track' for relatively familiar organisms and a slower track for all others.[27]

Having agreed to a case-by-case approach, British regulators were most concerned to ensure that the approval process would flow as smoothly as possible from the standpoint of the applicant. The creation of a single 'postbox'[28] in the form of ACRE bypassed the possibility of inter-agency differences of the kind that arose in America. This committee was to review all applications for release regardless of whether the product was a food, drug, pesticide or crop plant. Moreover, the risk assessment guidelines and notification procedures adopted by the ACGM subcommittee on deliberate release, ACRE's predecessor, were to serve as the blueprint for new interdepartmental regulations.[29] In particular, the guidance note outlined a risk assessment procedure, spelling out what information applicants should provide on an interdepartmental form to facilitate unified submissions. The instructions accompanying the form were symptomatic of the extent to which deliberate release in Britain had been redefined from an exercise in assessing uncertainty to a matter of following bureaucratic routine: 'Continuation sheets should be used wherever necessary. These should be in A4 format and clearly marked with the number of the item to which they relate.'[30]

Additional steps toward normalizing the regulatory treatment of biotechnology were taken with the publication of the Royal Commission's report on 'GENHAZ', a systematic approach to evaluating proposals for environmental releases of GMOs.[31] The Commission acknowledged that each release was likely to be unique, and hence that blanket exemptions were not warranted for any products of genetic modification. Nevertheless, the risk assessment procedure the Commission outlined provided reassurance on at least two levels. First, the proposed analytic approach was based on a method already in use in the chemical industry, a fact that tended to make biotechnology look more like another, less novel form of hazardous activity. Secondly, the procedure assumed that an experienced, interdisciplinary team of experts would be able to imagine the possible hazards of release, and hence to guard against potentially unacceptable consequences. This presumption essentially negated the possibility of significant hazards lying beyond the imaginative reach of the trained scientific mind.[32]

Germany – a programmatic view

The three major dimensions of biotechnology's risks – physical, social, and political – were perhaps most fully deconstructed, or thematized, in the German case, although public debate was slower to take shape in Germany than in Britain or the United States. The regulatory history of genetic engineering in Germany began in the early 1960s with a top-down decision by the federal government to target biology as an area for state-supported R & D. The biotechnology programme received a further boost with the creation in 1972 of the Federal Ministry for Research and Technology (BMFT), whose central mission was to channel funding toward designated 'key technologies'. Paralleling the work of NIH in the United States, BMFT supervised the German response to the Asilomar conference, where researchers first expressed concern about the risks of genetic manipulation. Guidelines closely modelled on NIH's were issued by a restricted, *ad hoc* committee of experts, including at first neither labour nor industry, though these interests were later represented in a twelve-member implementing commission.[33] Through the early 1980s, the strategy of containing regulatory debate within carefully structured expert committees ensured a relatively narrow focus on the physical risks of rDNA research and correspondingly muted attention to the social and political consequences of the new technology.

The rise of new social movements and the waning of previously controversial issues such as nuclear power opened the way for a more participatory politics of biotechnology by the mid-1980s.[34] The Green Party was first elected to the Bundestag in 1984 and soon created a working group on genetic technology. In the same year, an alliance between the Greens and the Social Democrats led to the formation of a parliamentary Commission of Inquiry *(Enquete-Kommission)* to examine the opportunities and risks associated with developments in genetic engineering. As the state's policy on biotechnology was subjected for the first time to systematic, institutionalized criticism, two views emerged concerning the novelty of the problem confronting policy makers. The Greens and the Social Democrats argued that the risks of biotechnology were sufficiently unsettling – uncertain, potentially catastrophic, perhaps irreversible – to require a new political order for their management and control. Key to this new order would be a more pronounced voice for the public, institutionalized through new forms of public participation. The Christian Democrats insisted, to the contrary, that biotechnology was amenable to control through established forms of assessment by technically trained experts.

Green opposition to biotechnology led in due course to litigation. In an unusual lawsuit against Hoechst chemical company, German environmentalists in Hessen challenged a planned facility for the production of genetically engineered insulin on the ground that the state had not sufficiently guaranteed the safety of biotechnology. Existing laws, they argued, could not be construed as providing an adequate basis for controlling risks whose unique characteristics required explicit legislative authorization, just as nuclear power had done a decade earlier. The administrative court of Hessen accepted this representation of uniqueness and, in a move that went beyond the actions of any US court, ordered the cessation of industrial biotechnological activity until a suitable legal framework was in place. Within a year, however, the German parliament set aside this inconvenient roadblock by passing the 1990 Genetic Engineering Law, a statute that critics denounced for repudiating the inroads made by participatory politics on the government's insulated, bureaucratic-technocratic structures of control.

By combining the functions of protection (*'Schutz'*) and promotion (*'Forderung'*) within a single law, the legislature affirmed the state's presumed capacity to undertake these potentially conflicting tasks without compromising the values or rights of its citizens, but early implementation of the law raised questions as to whether this optimism was justified. As a partial concession to public concerns, the law opened up participation on the government's key advisory committee and created a new public hearing process for deliberate release applications. These procedural innovations seemed responsive to the theme of political risk articulated during the controversy preceding the law's enactment. In practice, however, the first public hearings deteriorated into administrative wrangles and rhetorical stand-offs that led the government in 1993 to rescind the hard-won right to a hearing. The environmentalists' position on the safety evaluation committee, too, appeared likely to become bureaucratized, as the Greens, unable to pay for their representatives, considered replacing them with sympathetic government officials.[35]

The political construction of risk and resistance

I have argued thus far that the risks of biotechnology, particularly as regards their novelty, were construed in fundamentally different ways within the regulatory frameworks of three advanced industrial nations – the United States, Britain and Germany. The divergences during the 1980s are most strikingly apparent if one looks in retrospect at the dominant characterization of biotechnology as a regulatory problem in each country and the impact of this problem definition on later debates about risk. See Table 2.1 for a two-dimensional, and hence necessarily oversimplified, representation of the cross-national differences in the thematization of risk.

Table 2.1 Thematization of risk

	Physical	*Social*	*Political*
US product	High	Low	Low
UK process	Medium	Medium	Medium
Germany programme	Medium	Medium	High

The focus in the United States was increasingly on the *products* coming into the market-place and the physical risks they may pose to human health *or* the environment. In Britain, regulators appeared initially more prepared to accept the *process* of genetic modification as the frame for policy making, with concurrent attention to the physical and social dimensions of risk. But this acknowledgment of the technique's specialness was undercut to some degree by a bureaucratized hazard evaluation procedure that stressed routine and internalized possible opposition from environmentalists. German political debate on biotechnology was unique in taking as its domain the entire *programmatic* relationship between technology and society, as mediated by the state, a position that led to a full-blown discussion of risks. Eventually, parliamentary action, in the form of a special law on genetic engineering, confirmed that the state's programme of promoting and regulating biotechnology was sufficiently novel to require explicit legislative licence. (See Table 2.2 for a summary of the main forms of resistance in each country and the associated variations in the state's responses to public challenge.)

In the remainder of this chapter, I will argue, first, that these cross-national variations were consistent with previously noted features of each country's political culture and regulatory style; secondly, I will suggest that the divergent forms of political accommodation worked out in each country were similar in result – in each case, the selected policy initiative blocked significant avenues of public dissent and smoothed the way for a relatively untroubled further development of biotechnology.

The US case illustrates the well-known national preference for according science a central role in public decision making. US regulators have generally been more inclined to justify their actions with appeals to objective knowledge than their European counterparts. Extensive scientific records, mathematical modelling of risk and uncertainty, and detailed procedures for peer review and quality control, all bear witness to the US decision maker's need to enlist the impartial authority of science in support of costly and controversial policy decisions. Confronted with scientific uncertainty, American agencies are reluctant simply to admit ignorance and exercise subjective judgment. If an extrapolation must be made from limited data, it has to be according to prestated rules of decision that spell out technical methods for dealing with uncertainty.[36] More generally, science in the US frequently serves as a resource with which political adversaries seek to trump their opponents in the regulatory arena. Scientific disputes thus become a surrogate for unstated ethical or economic conflicts.

Table 2.2 Resistance and response

	Forms of resistance				State responses				
	Scientific debate	Legislative debate	Litigation	Party politics	Expert committees	Administrative rules	Legislation	Judicial action
US	yes	some	yes	no	new	yes	no	yes (pro-development)
UK	some	some	no	no	new/expanded	yes	expanded	no
Germany	no	yes	yes	yes	expanded	yes	new	yes (anti-development)

Not surprisingly, then, every major US player with a stake in biotechnology policy stated publicly that decisions in this area should be based on sound science. Competition among these actors to justify their positions in scientific terms under-scored the power of science as a legitimating rhetoric in politics. EPA, the most risk-averse of the US agencies (and, in the Reagan–Bush years, also the most politically vulnerable), created a new scientific advisory committee, BSAC, to shore up its credibility in the politics of regulation. When the White House tried to seize control of biotechnology policy, it created the BSCC, ostensibly to provide *scientific* coordination across the government, but in practice to serve as a coun-terweight to possibly recalcitrant regulatory agencies. BSCC, in turn, relied on the National Research Council for a still more authoritative exposition of the scientific principles that should govern the regulation of biotechnology. In due course, the NRC report provided scientific ammunition for OSTP scientists, Vice-President Dan Quayle's Competitiveness Council, and others who wished to challenge EPA's cautious regulatory approach.

Scientific pluralism, the result of scientific claims being produced by parties with competing claims to authority, is inevitably a feature of American regulatory poli-tics, showing that the effort to tame uncertainty through technical discourse does not necessarily resolve conflicts. The multiplicity of agencies (EPA, FDA, USDA, NIH) and committees (BSCC, BSAC, NRC study committee) with an active interest in biotechnology virtually guaranteed that multiple technical accounts of risk would proliferate in the public domain once decision making was narrowed to questions of physical risk and safety. The protracted battle over the scope of regulation was but one example of the fracture lines that arise when American political actors draw upon 'scientific principles' to justify their agendas with respect to risk.

The British style of policy making, in contrast to the American, tends to be informal, cooperative, and closed to all but a select inner circle of participants. Disputes are resolved as far as possible through negotiation within this socially bounded space, and the power of the judiciary is seldom invoked even for enforce-ment purposes. These differences have had an impact on the production and use of regulatory science (science used as a basis for policy),[37] which tends in Britain to be less diverse and less admitting of uncertainty than in the United States (Wynne and Mayer, 1993). Early attempts to manage the deliberate release of GMOs, however, showed British scientists and regulators as apparently more receptive than their US counterparts to admitting the special status of biotech-nology and to recognizing a broad range of possible hazards, from the ecological to the social and (to a lesser degree) political.

This finding seems inconsistent at first blush with observations previously made in the area of chemical regulation, where British experts consistently represented the risks as less severe than their counterparts in the United States. While American regulators often banned substances based on animal evidence alone, British health and safety authorities refrained from aggressive action except in cases where there was observable harm to human health. At a deeper level, however, Britain's seemingly higher tolerance for chemical risks and lower toler-ance for biotechnological risks can be traced to similar underlying views about what constitutes acceptable evidence for political action. The British policy maker's classic preference for empirical proofs, attested to by credible communities of experts, explains why so few of the risks of biotechnology were initially ruled out as improbable, just as it explains why chemicals were so often exonerated when they only damaged the health of test animals but showed no effect on humans. British caution over biotechnology proceeded from the fact that no one had yet had the opportunity to *see* how gene-altered organisms might behave in the environment, removed from the physical containment of laboratories. In the absence of direct evidence, it was easy for all sides to agree that experience alone could guide the making of regulations, including the establishment of risk criteria and classes of exemptions. Biotechnology thus classically lent itself to the case-by-case regulatory style favoured by policy makers in Britain; it was a style well suited in this instance to permitting incremental adjustments to the new technology.

Britain's sensitivity to the need for broader political representation in biotechnology policy was also consistent with that country's established practices for managing risks to health and safety. The framework of tripartite decision making in the field of worker protection was easily adapted to include a representative of the environmental community. Giving the 'greens' a formal role in ACRE at least temporarily neutralized the threat of public discontent. At the same time the move, which left the state in charge of choosing its environmental partner, seemed unlikely to upset the science–government–industry consensus that normally drives policy in Britain. Many observers of the British regulatory scene saw the expansion of ACRE as yet another instance of successful political cooptation whereby a potentially troublesome 'outsider' voice is brought into – and contained within – the channels of closed, consensual, and expert-dominated decision making.

Relations among science, technology and the state have historically been less transparent in Germany than in the other two countries, and public disputes among experts are something of a rarity in the regulatory arena. Yet, the German environmental movement scored early and relatively pronounced political success, winning representation in parliament at a time when British environmentalists were hardly visible as a national political force. Confrontations over technological risk in Germany have been intensely political, even violent at times, as in the case of anti-nuclear protests in the late 1970s and early 1980s. Again, these dynamics reproduced themselves with reasonable accuracy in the context of biotechnology. The German policy debate was most directly tied to the agendas of the major political parties. Perhaps in consequence, it was also most successful in forcing an open public discussion of the social and political ramifications of biotechnology, avoiding the strictly scientific framing that accounted for so much of the American discourse on risk. In a society where expertise is normally the prerogative of the few, insistence on the value implications of biotechnology (rather than exclusively on its technical uncertainties) powerfully legitimated citizens' claims that they should be accorded a wider role in the direction of the new technology. Yet, by enacting a comprehensive regulatory law, the state in the end re-established the very bureaucratic culture of risk management that had initially aroused public protest. The 1990 law permitted technology to develop without substantial fear of widespread citizen mobilization.

Conclusion

I have devoted much of this essay to the theme that political and regulatory culture counted in the way that members of three technological societies imagined, characterized, delimited, and controlled the products of their scientific ingenuity. In each country, an early phase of protest seemed at first to expand the vocabulary of resistance to a new and fearful technology. Contingent and culturally specific accountings of risk led in the 1980s to divergent national conceptualizations of the problem facing regulatory authorities. Cultural influences surfaced most strikingly in the science-centred definition of risk in the United States, in the political adaptation of existing expert bodies in Britain, and in the comprehensive legislative response to citizen mobilization in Germany.

The final twist to the story, however, becomes apparent only when we ask what these preliminary characterizations of risk meant in terms of the future of biotechnology. It is difficult to avoid the conclusion that all three countries, despite their culturally conditioned ways of constructing biotechnology as a policy issue, converged in their willingness to make the technology possible. In each country, the dominant political framing appeared to rule out one or more of the expected forms of public resistance, thereby ensuring that scientific uncertainty would not spill over into social and political unrest. Thus, in the United States, congressional and judicial inaction left the discussion of biotechnology's risks within a bureaucratic framework where the issue was most likely to be analysed in the relatively narrow terms of physical hazards. Moreover, the absence of legislation foreclosed new opportunities for judicial review and sharply restricted the dissenting public's least constraining avenue of access. Similarly, in Britain, despite an initially more expansive reading of biotechnology's uncertain consequences, decision making was soon channeled into a framework of carefully structured expert committees that provided assurance by internalizing dissent. Finally, legislation in Germany re-established a working state–industry partnership that formally bowed to citizen concerns but closed down the kind of open-ended political debate that had preceded the enactment of the genetic engineering law. In all three national settings, then, historical contingencies and political culture proved equally amenable to accommodating the determined thrust of biotechnology's forward movement. Explanations for this ultimate convergence lie in all probability in the theatre of international relations, where national protest politics confronted, and eventually succumbed to, the rhetoric and politics of global competitiveness.

Notes

* In Martin Bauer, ed., *Resistance to New Technology* (Cambridge: Cambridge University Press, 1995), pp. 311–31.
1 Harvey Brooks, "Technology, Evolution, and Purpose." *Daedalus* 109 (1980), p. 66.
2 In the mid-1970s leading molecular biologists declared a moratorium on research with recombinant DNA until the risks were properly explored and regulated. A scientific meeting at Asilomar in 1976 laid the conceptual basis for research safety guidelines that were formally adopted by the National Institutes of Health (NIH).

3 European countries that have legislated on this issue include Denmark, Germany and Britain. In the Netherlands, regulations governing deliberate releases were developed under the Environmentally Hazardous Substances Act. As noted below, on 23 April 1990, the European Community adopted a directive on the deliberate release of genetically modified organisms. Member states were required to implement the directive by the end of 1991.

4 The 1976 NIH guidelines prohibited deliberate release experiments. Just two years later, NIH decided that the prohibition could be waived on a case-by-case basis.

5 See, for example, Sheila Jasanoff, *Risk Management and Political Culture* (New York: Russell Sage Foundation, 1986).

6 *Foundation on Economic Trends v. Heckler*, 756 F.2d 143 (D.C. Cir. 1985).

7 National Research Council, *Field Testing Genetically Modified Organisms – Framework for Decisions* (hereafter referred to as *Field Testing*) (Washington, DC: National Academy Press, 1989).

8 Among the agencies participating in the Coordinated Framework, EPA's positions tended consistently to diverge from those of FDA and USDA.

9 Henry I. Miller, Robert H. Buris, Anne K. Vidaver, Nelson A. Wivel, 'Risk-Based Oversight of Experiments in the Environment,' *Science* 250 (1990), p. 490.

10 NRC, *Field Testing*, p. 52.

11 See, for example, NRC, *Field Testing*, Executive Summary, pp. 3–4.

12 *Federal Register*, 26 June 1986.

13 EPA Memorandum, p. 2.

14 'BSCC Urged to Hold More Meetings. Open Process', *Pesticide and Toxic Chemical News*, 27 December 1989, p. 7.

15 Jeffrey Merves, Congress and Administration Closer to Regulating U.S. Biotech Industry, *The Scientist*, 4 (22) (1990), p. 12.

16 See, for example, Office of Science and Technology Policy, 'Exercise of Federal Oversight Within Scope of Statutory Authority: Planned Introduction of Biotechnology Products into the Environment,' *Federal Register*, February 27, 1992, pp. 6753–6762. See also, David A. Kessler et al., 'The Safety of Foods,' *Science* 256 (1992), pp. 1747–49 and 1832.

17 *Diamond v. Chakrabarty*, 447 U.S. 303 (1980).

18 To deal with the issue of deliberate release, ACGM had created an Intentional Introductions Sub-Committee (IISC). ACGM's own name subsequently was changed to Advisory Committee on Genetic Modification.

19 Existing regulations were deemed defective not only because of their limited scope but because they referred to the no longer existent GMAG. See *The Impact of New and Impending Regulations on UK Biotechnology*, report of a meeting sponsored by the Department of the Environment, the Health and Safety Executive and the Bioindustry Association (hereafter cited as *Impact*) (Cambridge: Cambridge Biomedical Consultants, 1990, p. 12) (remarks of Richard Clifton, Health and Safety Executive).

20 I am indebted to Les Levidow for calling my attention to this point.

21 Royal Commission on Environmental Pollution, *The Release of Genetically Engineered Organisms to the Environment* (hereafter referred to as *Release of GEOs*), Thirteenth Report (London: HMSO, 1989). Although the Commission spoke of genetically engineered organisms (GEOs), the term genetically modified organism (GMO) eventually took over as the international standard term for organisms produced by genetic engineering. In this chapter, I follow the international usage.

22 RCEP, *Release of GEOs*, p. 21.

23 RCEP, *Release of GEOs*, p. 20.

24 ACGM, 'The Intentional Introduction of Genetically Manipulated Organisms into the Environment,' Guidelines for risk assessment and for the notification of proposals for such work, HSE Guidance Note 3 (revised), January 1990.

25 HSE Guidance Note 3, p. 5.

26 See comments of Richard Clifton and Douglas Bryce in *Impact*, pp. 15, 24.
27 Interview with John Beringer, London, July 1990.
28 Comments of Richard Clifton, *Impact*, p. 15.
29 HSE Guidance Note 3.
30 HSE Guidance Note 3, Interdepartmental Proposal Form, p. 1.
31 Royal Commission on Environmental Pollution, *GENHAZ* (London: HMSO, 1991).
32 Although GENHAZ looked like a further attempt to routinize biotechnology regula-
    tion, British industrialists were less than enthusiastic about this labour-intensive,
    cautiously empirical approach to safety assessment. As of the summer of 1993, it
    looked as though this Commission proposal would probably remain on the drawing
    board except for isolated trial applications. The European Commission's efforts to
    streamline regulation, somewhat on the U.S. model, seemed likely to swamp any
    distinctively national assessment efforts.
33 Sheila Jasanoff, 'Technological Innovation in a Corporatist State: The Case of Biotech-
    nology in the Federal Republic of Germany,' *Research Policy* 14 (1985), pp. 23–38.
34 See, generally, Herbert Gottweis, 'German Politics of Genetic Engineering and Its
    Deconstruction,' *Social Studies of Science* (in press).
35 Interview with Jens Katzek, German Bundestag, Bonn, July 1993.
36 Thus, in regulating chemical carcinogens, U.S. regulatory agencies have developed
    complex principles and mathematical models for extrapolating human risk estimates
    from animal data. British regulators have never adopted comparable analytical methods.
37 For an extended discussion of the properties of regulatory science, see Sheila Jasanoff,
    The Fifth Branch: Science Advisers as Policymakers (Cambridge, MA: Harvard
    University Press, 1990).

References

ACGM, Advisory Committee on Genetic Manipulation (1990). *The intentional intro-
    duction of genetically manipulated organisms into the environment. Guidelines for risk
    assessment and for the notification of proposals for such work*. HSE Guidance Note 3
    (revised), January 1990.
Brooks, H. (1980). Technology, evolution and purpose. *Daedalus* 109, 66.
Gottweis, H. (1995). German politics of genetic engineering and its deconstruction. *Social
    Studies of Science* (in press).
'Impact' (1990). *The impact of new and impending regulations on UK biotechnology*.
    Report of a meeting sponsored by the Department of the Environment, the Health and
    Safety Executive and the Bioindustry Association. Cambridge: Cambridge Biomedical
    Consultants.
Jasanoff, S. (1985). Technological innovation in a corporatist state: the case of biotech-
    nology in the Federal Republic of Germany. *Research Policy* 14, 23–38.
Jasanoff, S. (1986). *Risk management and political culture*. New York: Russell Sage
    Foundation.
Jasanoff, S. (1990). *The fifth branch: science advisers as policymakers*. Cambridge, Mass:
    Harvard University Press.
Kessler, D. A. et al. (1992). The safety of foods. *Science* 256, 1747–9 and 1832.
Merves, J. (1990). Congress and administration closer to regulating U.S. biotech industry.
    The Scientist 4(22), 12 November, p. 12.
Miller, H. I., Burris, R. H., Vidaver, A. K. and Wivel, N. A. (1990). Risk-based oversight
    of experiments in the environment. *Science* 250, 490.
NRC, National Research Council (1989). *Field testing genetically modified organisms –
    framework for decisions*. Washington, DC: National Academy Press.

OSTP, Office of Science and Technology Policy (1992). Exercise of federal oversight within scope of statutory authority: planned introduction of biotechnology products into the environment. *Federal Register*, 27 February, pp. 6753–62.

RCEP, Royal Commission on Environmental Pollution (1989). *The release of genetically engineered organisms to the environment*. Thirteenth Report. London: HMSO.

RCEP, Royal Commission on Environmental Pollution (1991). *GENHAZ*. London: HMSO.

Wynne, B. and Mayer, S. (1993). How science fails the environment. *New Scientist*, 5 June, pp. 33–5.

3   In the democracies of DNA

Ontological uncertainty and political order in three states[*]

Efforts to manage and control the development of biotechnology in its early decades exposed a paradox. When promoting innovation, states and private corporations characterized this technological sector as a singular, well-demarcated site for public policy, held together by its distinctive means of production (e.g., genetic manipulation), its unique property regimes (e.g., patents on life), its institutionally hybrid methods of collaboration (e.g., university-industry partnerships), and above all its ultimate goals with regard to living things (to improve on 'natural' entities by engineering them for greater purity, productivity, efficiency or novel characteristics). Yet, when it came to regulation, industry lobbying, governmental action, and public deliberation were all structured along so-called vertical lines, corresponding to specific commercial product categories. In the context of control, biotechnology was represented not as a revolutionary, transformative shift in our modes of industrial production, but as just one more incremental step, barely deserving a second glance, in humankind's long involvement with making nature more productive and pliant.

The trend toward regulating biotechnology by product classes emerged earliest and most explicitly in the United States, where policymakers from the 1980s onward repudiated legislation targeted at the process of genetic manipulation (Jasanoff, 1995). But the European Union, too, partly followed suit, moving away from the process-based approach that had characterized the directives on biotechnology adopted in 1990. At the most basic level, policy frameworks tended to distinguish 'red' biotechnology, directed toward pharmaceutical development, from 'green' biotechnology, aimed at agricultural production. After all, the reasoning went, the former focuses on questions of human health, and increasingly also on biomedical ethics, whereas the latter engages with questions of environmental risk and threats to biodiversity. These differences seemed to demand recourse to different domains of technical expertise, as well as engagement with different constellations of stakeholders. Reflecting these realities, most governments had long since placed regulatory authority over pharmaceuticals and agricultural commodities in different agencies or ministries (e.g., in the United States, the Food and Drug Administration for the former, and the Department of Agriculture for the latter). In the logic of modern governance, it seemed only natural to divide up the technical and political dimensions of regulating biotechnology among these pre-existing sectors of bureaucratic competence.

Public responses around the world, however, have questioned the conceptual bifurcation that treats biotechnology as unitary for production and promotion, but multiple for regulation. The logics and discourses of state action, driven by specialized expertise and bureaucratic rationality, do not map so neatly onto the logics of public approval and acceptance—especially in a culturally heterogeneous, global public sphere. From the bottom-up perspective of citizens who have to live in, and with, a world modified by biotechnology, there are cross-cutting questions of metaphysics, epistemology and ethics that unify the disparate areas of technological application. As research on public opinion has shown, there are features of accountability and reassurance that many people hope to find in the emerging regulatory structures for biotechnology, and those features are not constrained by the boundaries of traditional, product-oriented health and safety regulation (Marris et al., 2001). The very same features that have led biotechnology enthusiasts to embrace it as a revolutionary means of production have also persuaded many consumers and members of the public of the need for new forms of engagement with biotechnology's overall aims and purposes. Neither the timing nor the discursive format of regulatory proceedings offers scope for this kind of broadly normative engagement. In short, the interests of deliberative democracy are not wholly satisfied by policy institutions whose role and remit were molded primarily by concerns for safe and efficient product innovation.

Cross-national stand-offs over the commercialization of genetically modified (GM) crops, the patenting of gene fragments and higher life forms, and the divergent policy regimes that have developed around research with embryonic stem cells give tangible evidence of the conflicts that can arise if tacit public expectations with respect to the management of biotechnology are not met. These frictions, arising only after extensive state and private investments in research and product development, run counter to the interests of both scientists and the public in the free flow of scientific knowledge. They also disrupt the global commitment to free trade enshrined in the World Trade Organization. It seems clear that both national leaders and the publics they answer to would benefit from a deeper understanding of the conditions that have led their counterparts in other nations to substantially different conclusions about the pros and cons of biotechnology. Whether or not such understanding leads to greater convergence in public values or policy action, it should increase the intelligence and sophistication of the global debate on these issues.

The social sciences can contribute importantly to this kind of illumination through comparative, cross-national analysis of regulatory politics. It is widely recognized by now that public problems do not simply appear on policy agendas, as if placed there through the direct imprint of exogenous events. Rather, they are framed in particular ways by cultural commitments that predispose societies, no less than the individuals within them, to fit their experiences into specific types of causal narratives.[1] These narratives are grounded in longstanding institutional practices and ways of knowing that enable societies at once to conceptualize and find solutions to newly perceived threats to their security or well-being. Even the most technical issues are interpreted in the context of established, but varied, social approaches to defining and coping with public problems. These insights, largely derived from studies of domestic policy and politics, acquire added significance when translated into a comparative framework. By exposing underlying sources of variation, cross-cultural comparisons can help explain why national publics are more or less inclined to accept particular forms of technological change. At the same time, by grounding risk perception and regulatory behavior in the deeper matrix of political culture, comparative work resists dismissing the opposition to biotechnology as nothing more than an unreasoning fear of novelty, grounded in the public's ignorance of scientific facts.

This paper compares the regulatory uptake of biotechnology in three advanced industrial democracies—Britain, Germany and the United States—and shows that systematic differences have developed around several major applications of genetic manipulation. Four are described below: abortion, assisted reproduction, stem cells, and genetically modified crops and foods. Different policy choices with respect to each of these issues reflect in part the diverse capacities of each nation's regulatory institutions to deal with the scientific, social and ethical uncertainties around biotechnology. These institutional frameworks constitute in effect an apparatus of collective sense-making through which national governments and publics interpret what biotechnology both promises and threatens. More specifically, national regulatory approaches help to position the ontological novelties created by biotechnology either on the side of the familiar and manageable or on the side of the unknown and perhaps insupportably risky. Public responses to biotechnology are thus shown to be embedded within robust and coherent political cultures rather than being ad hoc and contingent expressions of concern that vary unpredictably from issue to issue.[2]

Sites of divergence: policy responses to biotechnology

In February 1997, newspapers in the United Kingdom carried stories about a historic victory on an unlikely frontier. Diane Blood, a 30-year-old public relations consultant from Nottinghamshire, had won permission to be inseminated with sperm taken from her dead husband, Stephen. British administrative and legal authorities had denied Diane the right to be inseminated with Stephen's sperm because it had been removed without his consent, at *her* request, while he was dying of bacterial meningitis. But lack of consent, the UK courts held on appeal, only barred insemination in Britain. Under European law, Diane could not be deprived of her right to take the sperm to another country, such as Belgium, whose laws permitted a pregnancy to be initiated under these circumstances. Diane eventually bore two children conceived through artificial insemination with her late husband's sperm in Brussels.

Though the main elements of the story are unambiguous, press reports on the February day when the news of Diane Blood's legal victory broke show that there were sharply different ways of interpreting what was at stake. *The Daily Telegraph*, a pillar of the British press, carried the headline, 'Widow wins fight to bear child of dead husband' (Marks, 1997). Accompanied by a picture of a young woman holding a baby, demurely dressed in black, a cross dangling at her throat, this headline emphasized the theme of kinship triumphant: a line of descent continued by a wife's determination to press the family relationship beyond her spouse's death, the normal biological point of no return. Observers of British culture may, without too great a stretch, see here the recurrent trope of the family tragedy, a potent device for stirring and uniting the national imagination, whether averted, as in this case, or more commonly not (the Soham murders of 2002, Princess Diana's death in 1997, the novels of Dickens or the tragedies of Shakespeare).

The same story appeared in the American-flavored, international newspaper, the *Herald Tribune*, under the headline, 'In UK Court Case, Widow Wins Right to Use Spouse's Sperm' (Associated Press, 1997). Here, too, the verb 'wins' signaled a hurdle overcomed, but the *Tribune*'s subtext was quite different from the *Telegraph*'s. Flanked by the picture of a smartly dressed, smiling young woman leaving the courthouse, surrounded by photographers, the predominant theme in this rendition was the individual's victory over forces that sought to curtail her right, as an autonomous consumer, to use a desired commodity—in this case, the 'spouse's sperm.' Again, it is tempting to discern here some familiar elements of the American cultural landscape: the emphasis on the lawsuit, the individual's right of reproductive choice, and the commodification of the part- ner's sperm to satisfy that felt right. The baby born to the woman in *this* story would be, one senses, very much a product of her own desires, not, as suggested in the *Telegraph*'s account, the realization of a couple's shared but tragically interrupted dream of family life.

The subtle semiotics of newspaper headlines offers an entry point to a more general argument. Even the most basic processes of life—in this case, the union of egg and sperm to produce new offspring—can be read in the context of modern biotechnology as telling very different stories, with contrasting moral and ethical implications. Through its capacity to generate new forms of life, biotechnology renders unstable the received boundaries between the natural and the unnatural. Children, for instance, can be conceived when their biological father is no longer living—violating the ancient taboo against necrophilia and the modern one against unconsenting parenthood. Complex social work, such as that done in Diane Blood's case by courts, fertility clinics, and daily newspapers, is needed then to reorder the instability, to put the new and potentially threatening entities and behaviors unchained by biotechnology back into places where they can be inter- preted and controlled. Let us turn to a more detailed exploration of the ways in which biotechnology's ontological exuberance has been managed in the political cultures of Britain, Germany and the United States.

Abortion: high principles, mundane practices

Abortion, the intentional termination of pregnancy, is an ancient means of controlling reproduction through artificial means, but it achieved new political visibility and salience in the later 20th century following the development of technologically assisted contraception and the associated rise of the women's movement. Abortion can be seen as one of the earliest forms of biotechnology, albeit not one productive of life: in freeing a woman of an unwanted pregnancy, abortion necessarily denies existence to the developing fetus. Because of its implications for research on embryos and stem cells, the legal treatment of abortion is a necessary starting point for reviewing cross-cultural divergences in regulating biotechnology. As we shall see, disparate legal regimes have developed around abortion in three countries that differ in their understandings of the ontological status of the fetus, their definition of the pregnant woman's interests, and their positioning of the state's role.

In the United States, abortion law was federalized by the deeply divisive 1973 Supreme Court decision in *Roe v. Wade* (1973) and reaffirmed several times, most authoritatively in *Planned Parenthood of Southeastern Pennsylvania v. Casey* (1992). *Casey* left standing the core element of *Roe*—the recognition of a woman's constitutional right to have an abortion—but it also recognized that the state has an interest in protecting the life of the unborn, and that this interest can assume priority once the fetus becomes viable, that is, capable of surviving outside the mother's womb. As long as *Roe* and *Casey* remain the law, states may regulate abortions only to the extent that they do not infringe upon the fundamental right guaranteed by these decisions.

In Britain, abortion is regulated by the 1967 Abortion Act, which permits the termination of pregnancy under stated conditions related to the physical or mental health of the woman, the well-being of her existing family, or the risk of giving birth to a handicapped child. Though abortions require the consent of two physicians, many concede that the clause covering risks to the woman's health has been interpreted so broadly as to authorize, in effect, abortion on demand in England and Wales. A provision of the 1990 Human Fertilisation and Embryology Act reduced the time limit for permissible abortions from 28 to 24 weeks. This change reflected a firm medical consensus in favor of the lower limit, according to sources I consulted at the time, and it happened with barely a ripple of debate about women's rights or the ontological status of the embryo.

In Germany, abortion law was caught up in the broader politics of reunification after the fall of the wall between former East and West Germany. While the country was divided, a more liberal legal regime had developed in the east, allowing virtually unrestricted abortions during the early months of pregnancy. This arrangement ran up against the Constitutional Court's holding that, under Germany's constitution, the Basic Law, the embryo must be accorded full human dignity from the moment of nuclear fusion between egg and sperm. Politically, too, the notion of abortion on demand was anathema to Chancellor Helmut Kohl's ruling Christian Democratic government. Under a compromise whose terms were not fully worked out until after reunification, Germany retained the 19th century law that declared all abortions to be criminal acts punishable by imprisonment. At the same time, lawful exceptions were made for pregnancy terminations to protect the health of the mother, provided she underwent appropriate counseling and was certified as being in compliance with statutory requirements.

On the surface, then, all three countries made legal accommodations permitting women more or less liberal access to abortions during the first three to six months of pregnancy, but the underlying rationales were vastly different, as were the grounds for loosening earlier, more restrictive laws. Only Germany felt it needful to adjudicate the ontological status of the embryo itself; the American pro-choice movement resisted repeated attempts to write such declarations into US law, while in Britain no attempt was made to clarify this issue, and access to abortion was based, as in Germany, on considerations of maternal and familial welfare. Only in America, by contrast, was abortion treated as an extension of a woman's constitutional right to personal liberty, and hence absolutely protected for a time against state intervention. In both European nations, welfare state concerns for health and family provided the basis for crafting a rationale for abortions, under authority delegated by the state to the medical profession.

Assisted reproduction

The birth of Louise Brown, the world's first test-tube baby, through in vitro fertilization (IVF) in 1978 opened a new era in technologically assisted reproduction. Just as the advent of the birth control pill changed the social context for abortion, so IVF reframed discussions of the nature of kinship and family that had begun decades earlier with the growing popularity of artificial insemination as a treatment for male infertility. Only, whereas artificial insemination problematized the notion of fatherhood, now it was the mother's taken-for-granted relationship to her child that became destabilized, producing extended legal and social ripples. Those ripples spread in varying patterns across the cultural norms and institutional structures for regulating reproduction and the family in three nations.

Family affairs are matters of state law in the United States, and so the issues raised by IVF surfaced first in state courts and legislatures. Curiously, though, the first public trial of the meaning of motherhood in the era of assisted reproduction involved little if any high technology. This was the case of Baby M, a girl born in 1986 in New Jersey to Mary Beth Whitehead, who had been artificially inseminated with sperm from William Stern. Together with his wife, Elizabeth, who for health reasons did not wish to conceive and give birth herself, William wanted to adopt the child that Whitehead, a married mother of two, carried to term. The case spilled into litigation when Baby M's 'surrogate mother' refused to give up the child and fled with her to Florida. Under court order, mother and daughter were returned to New Jersey, where the state's highest court held that the contract between Whitehead and the Sterns was unenforceable under applicable law and policy, but that the child's best interests demanded that custody be given to the Sterns.[3]

Since the mid-1980s, American women and their partners have experimented with many forms of IVF and surrogacy. Perhaps most controversial after Baby M was the use of so-called gestational surrogacy—a process in which an embryo created through IVF is implanted into a woman who carries the baby to term. In the widely discussed case of *Johnson v. Calvert*,[4] the California Supreme Court held that, in case of conflict, the couple intending to procreate, that, is the genetic parents of the child, would have priority over any rival claims of the gestational mother. In so holding, the court reinterpreted a provision of state family law that had defined a child's birth mother as its 'natural mother.' With this decision, California joined Belgium as one of the friendliest homes for uses of IVF and surrogacy. Couples wishing to have children may even contract with surrogates to carry children who are not genetically related to any of the parties to the agreement, although the California courts have ruled that the initiating couple may not thereby absolve itself of responsibility to care for the resulting baby.[5]

The value of IVF for prospective parents has risen with the development of prenatal diagnostic techniques that allow embryos to be screened for inherited genetic abnormalities and so be excluded from implantation. The same techniques can also be used to select embryos for sex and also for tissue matches with siblings in need of healthy bone marrow or other transplants. Under U.S. law, many of these services are provided in virtually unregulated fashion, with private clinics deciding which tests they will offer and to whom. Thus, sex selection to achieve 'family balance'—a euphemism for ensuring that couples will have the son or daughter they desire—is widely advertised by IVF clinics. In sum, U.S. law and practice treats a couple's desire to have children, and even children with certain predetermined characteristics, as the primary factor shaping the use and regulation of prenatal screening.

The contrast with Britain and Germany could hardly be starker, although the approaches taken in these two countries are not identical. In Britain, a 1990 law created the Human Fertilisation and Embryology Authority (HFEA) and charged it with licensing and monitoring all IVF and insemination clinics nationwide, as well as institutions undertaking embryo research and the storage of gametes and embryos. Issues such as prenatal screening or sex selection that are resolved in ad hoc and decentralized ways in the United States are subjected to central governmental control in the United Kingdom. Under this scheme, physicians and prospective parents have less latitude to decide what testing or screening services will be made available than do private clinics in the United States. Embryos produced through IVF, but not implanted, are stored and used under HFEA guidelines pursuant to the HFE Act; these preclude, for instance, the removal of an unconsenting husband's sperm as happened in the Diane Blood case. Surrogacy is also regulated by law, and discouraged. While surrogacy agreements are not illegal, they are not enforceable, and it is a crime to advertise for a surrogate. In practice, this means that most surrogacy arrangements in Britain occur within the family, through agreements between close kin rather than strangers united by contract.

Germany in 1990 enacted what remains the most restrictive European legislation pertaining to assisted reproduction. Under German law, surrogacy is banned and all IVF embryos must be implanted in the woman who supplied the ova. Only as many embryos may be created as are actually implanted, and in no case more than three. Hence, the kinds of disputes that have erupted in other countries over the ownership, use and moral status of embryos are essentially precluded from occurring in Germany. The law acts in effect as an ontological prohibition, keeping entities potentially disruptive of the moral order from ever coming into being. Prenatal genetic diagnosis is also banned by law, reflecting a continued German anxiety over technologies that may allow the selection of human beings according to criteria of relative worth. This regime is the very antithesis of the American one in its resistance to experimentation with technologically mediated reproductive choices.

Three national responses to IVF and associated prenatal testing techniques show once again how uncertainty is handled differently by each country's regulatory apparatus. Decentralized decisionmaking and a market-based approach to testing have produced in the United States a particularly hospitable climate for trying things out, with boundary-testing actions preceding, and provoking, the making of normative judgments. Britain's approach is more restrictive in setting uniform national guidelines for all matters to do with the human embryo, so that technology unfolds under the state's watchful and politically self-conscious supervision. Germany has sought to maintain a state of perfect legal and ethical clarity, and it has done so by legislating against border-crossing ontologies that could create uncertainty through unchecked social and ethical innovation.

Stem cells

The early years of the 21st century ushered in a surprising debate in many industrial nations. The question was whether and under what conditions states should support research using embryonic stem cells. Derived from very early human embryos, these undifferentiated cells have the capacity to develop into many types of specialized cells that could potentially be used to treat diseases of the heart, brain, nerves, or other organs and tissues. By the turn of the century, many biologists regarded stem cell research as the most promising of all frontiers in biomedicine. For the first time since the recombinant-DNA debates of the 1970s, however, governments hesitated to offer unrestricted support for a potentially revolutionary project in the life sciences. The reasons were closely tied to the framing of life itself as a political issue, and national policies toward embryonic stem cells diverged according to dominant framings in each country.

Michel Foucault famously called attention to the conversion of life, or *bios*, into the subject matter of political action, and more broadly governmentality, in modernity (Foucault, 1990 [1976], pp. 135–45; see also Agamben, 1998, pp. 1–8). But what would he have made of the strange forms that biopolitics took on the other side of an ocean at the dawn of a century he did not live to see? As deployed by the US religious right, the concept of 'life' is less an instrument for classifying or regulating populations than a device for keeping at bay unruly social movements or novel constellations of social life.

In May 2005, President George W. Bush threatened his first veto, noteworthy enough for a president comfortably in charge of the party that also controlled both houses of Congress. The subject was stem cells—a topic Bush had addressed in August 2001 at his first press conference as a first-term president. At stake was a congressional attempt to expand the domain of federally funded research on stem cells beyond the narrow limits laid down in 2001. The president had authorized research only with cell lines that existed before that date, and the number of available lines turned out to have been greatly overestimated. On May 24, the House of Representatives, by a vote of 238 to 194, expanded the zone of permitted research to include 'spare embryos' left over from IVF procedures, and the Senate appeared likely to follow suit. But Bush remained firm in his opposition, announcing a few days before the House vote: 'I'm a strong supporter of adult stem cell research, of course. But I made it very clear to the Congress that the use of federal money, taxpayers' money, to promote science which destroys life in order to save life, is—I'm against that ... And therefore, if the bill does that, I will veto it' (Stolberg, 2005).

Presidential rhetoric, resting on the underlying calculus of interest group politics, here took over the philosopher's work of ontological ordering. The newly popular trope 'science which destroys life in order to save life' implicitly casts the embryo, from the moment of fertilization, as a form of human life on a par with that of diseased adult patients. In using this language Bush and his supporters circumvented the decades-long legal battle to safeguard the *Roe-Casey* settlement that acknowledged women's constitutionally protected liberty rights without taking a stance on the biological status of the embryo. What had not been won in the courts by legal authority, nor indeed in biomedical research institutions under the authority of the life sciences, was thereby claimed as the victor's spoils of the electoral process. Fusing morality with the market, a presidential policy that most polls showed to be *inconsistent* with the majority's ethical wishes was presented as *consistent* with the majority's desire for wise stewardship of the taxpayers' money.

Britain's policy toward stem cell research, considered the most permissive in Europe, drew the ontological line around stem cells differently. Under the HFE Act, research on embryos is permitted in principle until the appearance, at roughly 14 days, of the primitive streak, a thickened line of cells signaling the division of the embryo into recognizable right, left, front and back parts, as well as the formation of the central nervous system and major organs. In other words, British law for all practical purposes does not regard pre-14-day-old embryos as being biologically continuous with fully developed human life. Stem cells derived before this cut-off point in embryonic development are therefore lawfully available for research. After that date, sharp developmental boundaries are seen as harder to sustain and research on embryos is correspondingly curtailed. An authorized regulatory structure, the HFEA, offers public reassurance that the moral order will be maintained and that science, once embarked on manipulating life at the early embryonic stage, will not slide down the slippery slope to treating *all* life as subject to genetic modification.[6] As yet, public faith in the HFEA's capacity to carry out its delicate mission has not eroded, even though science's remit has already expanded beyond the bounds foreseen in 1990, for example, through the inclusion of entities created by procedures other than the fertilization of egg and sperm within the statutory definition of an embryo.

In Germany, constitutional law underwrote essentially the same ontological settlement that was politically endorsed in the United States by a Republican administration out to consolidate its conservative religious support. The developing embryo is entitled in Germany to be accorded full human dignity, but that status is achieved through the principled application of law rather than the vagaries of presidential politics. Although German law does not allow the creation or destruction of embryos for research, the Bundestag voted in early 2002 to allow the importation of stem cells from abroad if they had been created before a stated cut-off date. This condition fulfills the generally accepted dictum that no embryo should be expended for German research, since the pre-existing stem cells were clearly created without those needs in mind. As in the two other cases, a line is drawn between ethically permissible and impermissible research, but, in the German case, the morally relevant line is that between ethics inside and outside the nation, not between embryonic and adult stem cells as in the United States nor between the pre- and post-14-day entity as in Britain. Accepting human life as a transcendental good, Germany has ruled how scientists may manipulate its earliest manifestations. Germany cannot, of course, legislate the same morality for other nations, but it *can*, it seems, maintain an internal order that provides no incentives for others to act in ways deemed ethically unacceptable in Germany.[7]

GM crops

The political reception of GM crops, and by extension GM foods, in the three countries seems at first sight to turn the picture with respect to stem cells on its head. In this case, it is the United States that has provided the most hospitable home for innovation and commercial production, whereas Britain has been most reluctant to allow the technology to develop, with Germany positioned somewhere between. But a closer look at each nation's accommodation with GM crops reveals underlying regularities.

By all reasonable measures, the United States is the world leader in the production and use of GM crops. US companies were prominently among the first to develop, test and market these plants. In 2000, barely five years after their first commercial introduction, the United States accounted for some two-thirds of the production of GM crops and almost 75% of the acres planted with these crops worldwide (Pew Initiative on Food and Technology, 2001). US research has continued to lead the search for new applications of crop biotechnology, for example, in designing a wave of 'agriceutical' products whose engineered properties straddle the line between conventional food and pharmaceuticals. Given the strong opposition to GM crops in Britain and elsewhere in Europe, as well as America's own history of concern about environmental and health risks (Brickman, Jasanoff & Ilgen, 1985; Vogel, 1986), many have wondered why the US public has greeted this new technology so complacently. Have Americans grown tired of being risk averse?

The answer, on examination, has less to do with public perceptions of GM products than with the state's reliance on and deployment of science as an instrument for quelling possible controversy. Early in the history of biotechnology, a convergence of views between university-based molecular biologists and corporate promoters of biotechnology led to the characterization of genetic modification as a process that should arouse no special regulatory concern. Under a 1986 White House policy known as the Coordinated Framework (Office of Science and Technology, 1986), US agencies decided to regulate biotechnology under a mosaic of existing laws that conferred, in the administration's view, adequate authority to ensure the safety of GM products. Modern biotechnology was represented for regulatory purposes as an extension of older techniques of biological manipulation, not as a radical break with past practices. To be sure, this position required advocates to maintain that the technology was at once familiar and revolutionary, a delicate balancing act that produced paradoxical sentences like the following from the Coordinated Framework: 'While the recently developed methods are an extension of traditional manipulations that can produce similar or identical products, they enable more precise genetic modifications, and therefore hold the promise for exciting innovation and new areas of commercial opportunity.' It was the theme of specificity, however, that carried the day for policymakers, overcoming arguments about unknowns and unknowables that might have justified a more proactive legislative response to biotechnology.[8]

British policies toward agricultural biotechnology were initially formulated along relatively permissive lines as in the United States, although experts in Britain were more cautious from the start about the environmental consequences of large-scale commercialization of GM crops.[9] The regulatory climate changed, however, in 1996. It was then revealed that the experts advising the Ministry of Agriculture, Fisheries and Food had erred in predicting that 'mad cow' disease would not be transmitted from cattle to humans and had also concealed their own uncertainties from the public.[10] In an environment of increased concern and distrust of experts, intensified by news flashes about possible health hazards from GM food, the British public massively turned away from these products, and the government realized that it had a crisis of confidence on its hands.

The state's response was to reconstitute the frayed institutions of governance that appeared to have lost the public's trust. This entailed, to start with, bringing a wider range of voices and opinions into the decisionmaking process, which the government proceeded to do first by constituting a new, broad-based advisory committee, the Agriculture and Environment Biotechnology Commission, and second by conducting, with the commission's assistance, a nationwide debate on the commodification of GM crops, entitled *GM Nation?* Shortly after that process, the government announced its first approval of a GM crop, a maize species modified to resist a chemical weed killer, glufosinate ammonium; two other GM crops were denied approval (Coghlan, 2004). Agricultural biotechnology companies, it seemed, had gained what they had wanted, but not on the terms they had successfully lobbied for in the United States. GM crop approvals would go forward much more cautiously in Britain, with a deeper, case-by-case exploration of uncertainties and greater sensitivity to possible adverse effects. Under such heightened scrutiny, there would clearly be no guarantee that crops deemed safe by US or other exporting nations would be accepted as safe for use in Britain.

The German response to GM crops produced no public outcry comparable to that in Britain. On this issue as in others relating to biotechnology, Germany sought to avoid controversy by opting for a legislative framework that reduced the risk of ontological mixing or impurity—thereby also minimizing the possibility of normative conflicts. Specifically, in June 2004 the Bundestag passed a stringent law on growing GM crops in Germany. Key provisions included restrictions on the amount of land to be planted with GM crops, a national register to keep track of these crops, and a requirement that farmers pay damages to non-GM growers whose fields are contaminated by GM varieties. The horror of unregulated things, so prevalent in the German legal order, came through in a parliamentarian's comments on the law: 'In the interest of farmers and consumers, we do not want genetically altered foods uncontrolled and initially unnoticed to sneak onto our grocery shelves' (Deutsche Welle, 2004b). It was perhaps a reaction, too, to the US situation, where polls showed that GM ingredients had found their way into the food chain without the knowledge or consent of most consumers.

Yet even the strictest of laws could not eliminate all unruly behavior. A German news service reported in May 2004 that unknown vandals had destroyed a research plot planted with GM crops in the eastern German state of Sachsen-Anhalt. In response, state authorities said that GM crops were being grown in secret on 29 plots throughout the country, but that the corn grown there would be used only in animal feed (Deutsche Welle, 2004a). Experimentation, it seemed, was not dead in Germany; only the conduct of it could not be disclosed by a government publicly committed to the ideal of transparency.

The politics of ontological ordering

We are now in a position to draw out some of the regularities in the three national responses to biotechnology, taking into account both the biomedical and the agricultural realms. Most generally, the differences seem to center on the institutional resources that each nation deploys in carrying out the task of ontological ordering that biotechnology, in its zeal for hybridity, inevitably requires. How should the novel entities produced through genetic and other biological manipulations be classified? Who will resolve the moral dilemmas associated with living things whose legal status is uncertain and whose impacts on the physical and social environment are impossible to predict with any certainty? In each country, questions such as these have arisen in connection with other technological developments, but perhaps never with quite the urgency generated at the fast-moving frontiers of biotechnology.

In comparing the three countries, we are struck first of all by the different degrees of tolerance for 'monsters,' or entities that threaten disorder by crossing the settled boundaries of nature or society. Experimentation, in human reproduction as well as in crop biotechnology, has been the order of the day in the United States, cautiously tolerated in Britain, and for the most part shunned in Germany. This variation in the acceptance of new entities—whether in kinship structures or in crops and food—is systematically linked to each nation's institutional arrangements for dealing with uncertainty. As summarized in Table 3.1 below, the American approach on the whole favors innovation and risk-taking, regulated by

Table 3.1 National strategies of normalization

US	UK	Germany
Monsters encouraged	Monsters permitted	Monsters forbidden
Market-regulated innovation	Expert-regulated innovation	Law-regulated innovation
Decentralized norms	Centralized norms	Centralized norms
Winner-take-all settlement of controversy	Consensual settlement of controversy	Reasoned (principled) settlement of controversy
Judicial accountability	Parliamentary and administrative accountability	Legislative accountability

the laws of the market, leaving complaints and grievances to be sorted out after the fact by the courts. By contrast, both Britain and Germany have opted for more cautious legislative solutions, allowing innovation to proceed only within a normative framework arrived at by law. But whereas Britain countenances a certain amount of ambiguity, leaving it to expert bodies to offer case-specific clarification, Germany has preferred to reduce the scope of both administrative and technological discretion by crafting unambiguous and strictly enforceable legal norms. In Germany, if the laws are properly adhered to, there *can* be no ontologically confusing frozen embryos, nor GM crops that exist unrecorded, outside a national register.

Only the Bush administration's seemingly unshakeable aversion to embryonic stem cell research seems to counter the national drive toward biotechnological innovation in the United States, but what we see here is not an anomalous societal turn away from risk-taking. Patently, many Republicans, beginning with President Ronald Reagan's widow and including staunch conservatives like Senator Orrin Hatch of Utah, back a more relaxed approach toward stem cell research. They, like the majority of Britons, are prepared to accept early embryos as biologically and morally different from growing children and adult human beings. Not for them, nor for most Democrats, the easy elision of developmental and cognitive differences reflected in George Bush's reference to 'science which destroys life in order to save life.' Commonsensical empiricists in the Anglophone world, on either side of the Atlantic, find it difficult to equate a blob of cells on the point of a pin with a thirteen-year-old child suffering from juvenile diabetes or a 60-year-old victim of Parkinson's disease.[11]

In the US stem cell debate, one sees the laws of the market setting the high-visibility terms of national political ideology rather than the lower-order conditions for technological innovation. The exaltation of 'life,' be it in the four or five-day embryo or in a persistently vegetative woman kept 'alive' with a feeding tube,[12] is the discursive ploy of a president who failed to win the popular vote in his first term and won only a slim majority in his second. The administration's stance on this issue has less to do with the metaphysics or morality of borderline life forms than with the simple calculus of keeping a winning coalition in place. It is the expedient adoption of a rhetoric that plays particularly well to America's anti-abortionists, one of the coalition's most volatile, yet indispensable, components. In this case, it is important for those in power to sell the rhetoric of 'life' directly to their consuming publics, as a transcendental *political* commodity; that goal overrides a laissez faire economy's normal indulgence toward researchers and pharmaceutical companies who wish to sell a technologically configured and commodified 'life' to *their* markets, in the form of remedies for disease.

Concluding reflections

A decade ago, I wrote that policy institutions in the United States, Britain, and Germany had chosen to frame the risks of biotechnology in different ways: the first as a stream of *products*, the second as a unique and innovative *process*, and the third as a collaborative *program* between science, technology and the state (Jasanoff, 1995). Ten years later, the further unfolding of politics and policy around biotechnology allows us to see with greater clarity how such framings of risk and safety are sustained in practice. In the United States, where the market is the dominant form of social ordering, it is no accident that biotechnology has been construed as a stream of products, the goods that the market is best positioned to deliver and regulate. In Britain, where the state regulates innovation by creating a shared empirical culture of taken-for-grantedness, it again seems natural to focus on, and be seen to master, a process that visibly remakes life in forms not yet well understood by experts or publics. And German attentiveness to possibly dangerous programmatic alliances between technological innovation and the state is coupled to a postwar legal and political order that is exceptionally resistant to the idea of ungoverned or ungovernable spaces and to categories that defy the controlling capacity of the law.

Political culture, then, is intimately linked to the ways in which nations choose to govern the uncertainties that necessarily accompany technological innovation. Yet as I have suggested throughout this paper varying national approaches to regulation and control carry specific, non-negligible consequences for democratic politics. In particular, regulatory choices invariably affect the degree to which publics can unpack and deliberate on the underlying purposes of innovation. Which of the brave new worlds opened up by biotechnology are worth our collective investment? Which, perhaps, will produce lives we will regret living with, or living at all? These questions are not equally open for consideration in each of the three risk management regimes reviewed in this paper.

Not surprisingly, opportunities for deliberating on the aims of innovation have been most conspicuously absent in the United States, the country most hospitable to the fact of innovation. Farmed out to public intellectuals and, lately, to presidential ethics commissions of uncertain legitimacy and purpose, the task of reflecting on the directions of biotechnological advancement has largely been excluded from the public sphere. In Britain, the shock of the 'mad cow' crisis, coupled with turn-of-the-century pressures for political reform, converted expert ignorance and uncertainty into a more political issue than ever before. The result was a more thorough exploration of the environmental consequences of agricultural biotechnology and a higher standard of proof for GM crops and foods than in the United States. But questions of what *is* have to date occupied the British political imagination more than questions of what *ought* to be, and *GM Nation?* remains as yet an ad hoc experiment in deliberation rather than a marker of radical institutional change. Only in Germany has the temptation to privatize ethical deliberation been successfully resisted and the normative and political questions surrounding biotechnology have been extensively debated in the public sphere. But the response has been to erect high, some would say unacceptably high, barriers against social and technological creativity. Obsessed with the need for clarity, German institutions have displayed relatively little tolerance for the kinds of progress that may result from confronting disorder and learning systematically to accommodate it.

All this is consistent with the observation that human understandings of nature and social adaptations to nature are profoundly interlinked—indeed co-produced (Jasanoff, 2004). This deep interpenetration of the social and natural stands in the way of easy prescriptive solutions for the normative problems that confront us today in relation to biotechnology. Cross-national comparison may not alter that picture radically, since one can no more graft another nation's political forms onto one's own than successfully transplant pieces of human identity. Yet, to the extent that comparison enlarges our awareness of alternative possible worlds, it may aid the cause of reflection in a time of bewildering socio-technical change.

Notes

* *New Genetics and Society*, Vol. 24, No. 2 (2005), pp. 139–55.
1 On the sociological process of framing, see Goffman (1974). Useful extensions of framing to domains of public policy may be found in Schon & Rein (1994), Medrano (2003), Jasanoff (2005).
2 In recent work, I have defined political culture as the 'systematic means by which a political community makes binding collective choices. The term encompasses structured modes of action, such as litigiousness in the United States, but also the myriad unwritten codes and practices with which a polity supplements its formal methods of assuring accountability and legitimacy in political decisionmaking. Political culture in contemporary knowledge societies includes the tacit, but nonetheless powerful, routines by which collective knowledge is produced and validated. It embraces institutionalized approaches to reasoning and deliberation. But equally, . . . political culture includes the moves by which a polity, almost by default, takes some issues or questions out of the domain of politics as usual' (Jasanoff, 2005, p. 21).
3 *In the Matter of Baby M*, 109 N.J. 396 (1988).
4 For an interpretation of the case, see Hartouni (1997), pp. 85–98.
5 *In re Marriage of Buzzanca*, 61 Cal.App.4th 1410 (1998).
6 On the UK debate over the slippery slope, see Mulkay (1997); see also Jasanoff (2005), pp. 155–7.
7 For a compelling ethnographic exposition of this argument, see Sperling (forthcoming).
8 For more on the problematic status of biotechnology's newness, see Jasanoff (2001), pp. 34–50.

9 For a more detailed discussion of this point, see Jasanoff (2005), pp. 56–8.
10 These failures were extensively documented in *The BSE Inquiry Report* (2000).
11 On the importance of visual perception in drawing ontologically significant bounda-ries, see Jasanoff (2005), pp. 152–5, 196.
12 The case in question was that of the brain-dead woman Terry Schiavo, which attracted extraordinary media and political attention in March 2005. By signing a bill allowing Schiavo's parents access to the federal courts, George Bush joined the fundamentalist Christian right in its ultimately unsuccessful attempt to keep Schiavo artificially fed and hydrated, as she had been for 15 years. Fascinating in its own terms, the case cannot be discussed in detail within the scope of this article.

References

Agamben, G. (1998) *Homo Sacer: Sovereign Power and Bare Life* (Stanford, CA: Stanford University Press).

Associated Press (1997) In UK court case, widow wins right to use spouse's sperm, *Herald Tribune*, February 7, p. 5.

Brickman, R., Jasanoff, S. & Ilgen, T. (1985) *Controlling Chemicals: The Politics of Regulation in Europe and the United States* (Ithaca, NY: Cornell University Press).

The BSE Inquiry Report (2000) (http://www.bseinquiry.gov.uk/) [accessed: May 2005].

Coghlan, A. (2004) Britain gives go-ahead for first GM crop, *New Scientist*, 9 March (http://www.newscientist.com/channel/life/gm-food/dn4754) [accessed: May 2005].

Foucault, M. (1990 [1976]) *The History of Sexuality*, Vol. 1 (New York: Vintage).

Goffman, E. (1974) *Frame Analysis: An Essay on the Organization of Experience* (Cambridge, MA: Harvard University Press).

Hartouni, V. (1997) Breached birth: Anna Johnson and the reproduction of raced bodies. In *Cultural Conceptions: On Reproductive Technologies and the Remaking of Life*, pp. 85–98 (Minneapolis, MN: University of Minnesota Press).

Jasanoff, S. (1995) Product, process, or programme: three cultures and the regulation of biotechnology. In Bauer, M. (ed) *Resistance to New Technology*, pp. 311–31 (Cambridge: Cambridge University Press).

Jasanoff, S. (2001) Ordering life: law and the normalization of biotechnology, *Politeia*, XVII(62), pp. 34–50.

Jasanoff, S. (ed) (2004) *States of Knowledge: The Co-Production of Science and Social Order* (London: Routledge).

Jasanoff, S. (2005) *Designs on Nature: Science and Democracy in Europe and the United States* (Princeton: Princeton University Press).

Johnson v. Calvert (1993) 5 Cal. 4th 84.

Marks, K. (1997) Widow wins fight to bear child of dead husband, *The Daily Telegraph*, February 7, p. 6.

Marris, C., Wynne, B., Simmons, P. & Weldon, S. (2001) *Public Perceptions of Agricul-tural Biotechnologies in Europe (PABE)*. Final Report of the PABE Research Project, Contract number: FAIR CT98-3844 (DG12 – SSMI), Lancaster University, December.

Medrano, J. D. (2003) *Framing Europe: Attitudes toward European Integration in Germany, Spain, and the United Kingdom* (Princeton, NJ: Princeton University Press).

Mulkay, M. (1997) *The Embryo Research Debate: Science and the Politics of Repro-duction* (Cambridge: Cambridge University Press).

Office of Science and Technology Policy, Coordinated Framework for Regulation of Biotechnology (1986) 51 *Federal Register* 23302, 26 June.

Pew Initiative on Food and Biotechnology (2001) Genetically modified crops in the United States, Factsheet (http://pewagbiotech.org/resources/factsheets/display.php3?Factsheet ID = 1) [accessed May 2005].

Planned Parenthood of Southeastern Pennsylvania v. Casey (1992) 505 US 833.

Roe v. Wade (1973) 410 US 113.

Schon, D. A. & Rein, M. (1994) *Frame/Reflection: Toward the Resolution of Intractable Policy Controversies* (New York: Basic Books).

Sperling, S. (forthcoming) Reasons of conscience: Stem cells, bioethics and German citizenship. PhD dissertation, Princeton University.

Stolberg, S. G. (2005) In Rare threat, Bush vows veto of stem cell bill, *New York Times*, 21 May, p. 1.

Vogel, D. (1986) *National Styles of Regulation: Environmental Policy in Great Britain and the United States* (Ithaca, NY: Cornell University Press).

Welle, D. (2004a) GM crop trials underway throughout Germany, 5 May (http://www. dw-world.de/dw/article/0,1191060,00.html) [accessed: May 2005].

Welle, D. (2004b) Bundestag passes stringent law on genetically modified crops, 6 June (http://www.dw-world.de/dw/article/0,1240112,00.html) [accessed: May 2005].

4   Restoring reason

Causal narratives and political culture[*]

Do human societies learn? If so, how do they do it, and if not, why not? The American activist singer and song writer Pete Seeger took up the first question in the 1950s (Seeger 1955)[1] in a song whose concluding lines circled hauntingly back to its opening and whose refrain – 'When will they ever learn?' – gave anti-war protest in the 1960s a musical voice. Seeger's answer was, apparently, 'never'. Like many a pessimist before and since, Seeger saw human beings as essentially fallible creatures, doomed to repeat history's mistakes. But modern societies cannot afford to stop with that unregenerative answer. The consequences of error in tightly coupled, high-tech worlds could be too dire (Perrow 1984). If we do *not* learn, then it behoves us to ask the next-order questions. Why do we not? Could we do better?

For social analysts, part of the challenge is to decide where to look for answers. At what level of analysis should such questions be investigated? Who, to begin with, learns? Is it individuals or collectives, and if the latter, then how are knowledge and experience communicated both by and within groups whose membership remains indeterminate or changes over time? Organizational sociologists from Max Weber onwards have provided many insights into why collectives think alike. Especially illuminating is the work on group socialization, routinization and standardization (Bowker and Star 1999; Vaughan 1996; Short and Clarke 1992; Clarke 1989; Bourdieu 1980; Foucault 1979; Weber 1946). This literature focuses on the inculcation of disciplined habits and practices among a group's human members, leading to common styles of thought and modes of behaviour. To these observations, studies of technological systems have added a material dimension. Theorists of the left, from Karl Marx to more recent scholars such as David Noble (1977) and Langdon Winner (1986a), have looked to the power of capital (or other hegemonic formations such as colonialism and the state) to explain the design of obdurate technological systems that constrain group behaviour. Everyday metaphors – such as 'built-in', 'path-dependent' or 'hard-wired' – underscore a widespread popular awareness that material structures can shape a society's developmental trajectories in ways that seem, for all practical purposes, inevitable.

The problem from the standpoint of learning is that the better we get at creating and, secondarily, explaining stability in groups and systems, the harder it seems to make or to account for change. If human collectives are bound by deeply

socialized practices and rituals, and rigidly constrained by the technological infrastructures of their lives, how can they break out of those iron cages to craft safer,
more supple and more sustainable forms of life? How, more particularly, do new
ideas find toeholds and footholds, let alone *take* hold, in settings configured by
and for outworn modes of thinking and knowing, as well as their material embodiments? To make progress, it would seem, we need more dynamic models of the
ways in which people arrive at common understandings of their condition, about
what works as well as what has failed to work. How are such shared beliefs about
the causes of success and failure constructed in advanced technological societies?
And if we penetrate to the heart of that puzzle, can we also ask how systematic
beliefs and forms of life may be *re*constructed to let in new interpretative
possibilities?

Put differently, stories about learning are, at one and the same time, epistemological stories. They are narratives of how people acquire trustworthy knowledge
from experience – and how they either fit new knowledge to old mindsets or transform their cognitive habits, individually and collectively, so as to arrive at radically
altered understandings. In modern life, moreover, those understandings encompass
not only how people wish to order their relations with each other but also how they
go about living with the products of their technological inventiveness.

In this chapter, I look at the nation state as an important analytic unit within
which to explore the problem of such collective learning. There are several reasons
for this choice. First, we know from several decades of cross-national research
that risk issues are framed for public policy through nation-specific institutional
and political forces that influence what is seen as potentially harmful and how
such harms should be avoided (Jasanoff 1995; Jasanoff 2005; Vogel 1986).
Accordingly, learning about risk often happens within a framework structured by
the dynamics of national politics. Second, the cultures or styles of decision making
within nation states affect the production of policy-relevant knowledge and
discourse and thereby set the habits of thought and language that shape the possibility of learning. For example, the vulnerability of US decision makers to legal
challenge is associated with a preference in that country for seemingly objective
and rational analytic tools, such as quantitative risk assessment (Porter 1995;
Jasanoff 1986). But these techniques, in turn, frame which risks U.S. decision
makers are likely to take note of and the parameters within which they will seek
prevention or remediation (Winner 1986b: 138–54). Third, in a time of growing
recognition that not only elites but broader publics, too, are key players in processes of learning, the nation state offers a critically important site for examining
how citizens make sense of threats and disasters. Public ways of knowing, which
I have elsewhere termed civic epistemologies (Jasanoff 2005), are constituted,
displayed, and reaffirmed within the decision-making processes of states,
including those aimed at the management of risk and prevention of harm.

To illustrate these points, I adopt a comparative approach, looking at three
episodes of learning following technological catastrophes in India, Britain and the
United States. On the surface, the examples chosen from each country have little
substantively in common: a chemical disaster in India (Bhopal), a food safety

crisis arising from industrial agriculture in Britain ('mad cow' or BSE) and a terrorist tragedy exposing vulnerabilities in civil aviation and urban infrastructure in the United States (9/11). They are, however, comparable in other salient respects that bear on learning. Each was perceived as a problem of national proportions with international ramifications, calling for solutions at national and supranational levels. Each precipitated years of public inquiry into the causes of what had happened, as well as public efforts to prevent similar disasters from occurring in the future; in that respect each event was a site of learning, as well as a site of memory.[2] In each case, the power of the state was invoked in distinctive ways to organize the search for truth, with important implications for the 'truths' that were revealed in the process. In each, too, policy closure of a formal kind was achieved, although the underlying narratives of cause and responsibility remained significantly, and stubbornly, more open-ended.

Through a comparison of these three national policy-learning exercises, I hope to show that civic epistemology is, in a sense, foundational to contemporary polit-ical cultures and helps define the trajectories of learning within a given polity. I focus my analysis on one aspect of learning only: the efforts to determine a causal agent or agents in each instance, since identifying causes is a prerequisite to any subsequent efforts to target solutions and remedies. Who, or what, in short was held responsible for the breakdowns that precipitated each crisis or catastrophe, and how did those findings, and their ambiguities, shape subsequent policy responses? I relate the answers to these questions, in turn, to the cultures of knowl-edge making that steered national learning processes towards particular conclu-sions. A point that emerges from this comparison is that the particularity of national civic epistemologies lies, in part, in the boundary that each framework constructs between factual and moral causes or, put differently, between respon-sibility and blame.

India: Bhopal gas disaster

On the night of 3 December 1984, barely a month after the traumatic assassination of Prime Minister Indira Gandhi, India experienced the worst industrial accident ever recorded. The scene of the disaster was a pesticide plant run by Union Carbide in Bhopal, the capital of the central Indian state of Madhya Pradesh. Water seeping into a storage tank of liquid methyl isocyanate (MIC) – no one knew exactly how – released the chemical in a lethal gaseous form over the sleeping city. Though exact casualty figures will never be known, up to 3,500 people were estimated to have died from the immediate effects of toxic exposure and as many as 150,000 people were permanently injured or disabled.

A tragedy of this magnitude necessitated prompt remedial action by the state and the Indian government did respond quickly. Action was complicated, however, by the heterogeneity of the network within which the events unfolded, a network that joined together in an unprecedented web of cross-national interactions, corpo-rate entities, legal systems, medical experts, regulatory authorities and countless local victims (Jasanoff 1994; on technological networks, see Bijker et al. 1987).

At the level of physical causation, the story was clear to all: deadly toxic gas escaping from an identified source had killed or injured large numbers of people living in the vicinity. At a systemic or moral level, responsibility was much harder to assign.

In the days, months and years that followed the disaster, the Indian government and other affected actors had to come to grips with the complexity of the ties that bound them, and these efforts led to vastly divergent causal accounts. To what extent, for instance, was legal ownership relevant to liability and how did it intersect with blame? Union Carbide, the parent company, disavowed responsibility for events occurring at a facility managed by its Indian subsidiary, almost half-owned by the Indian state, and entirely overseen by local staff and personnel. Whose neglect or failure, moreover, had precipitated the tragedy? Union Carbide officially maintained that it was an act of sabotage by a disgruntled employee – a theory that absolved the company of any legal or moral liability (Kalelkar 1988). At the opposite extreme, many Indian critics blamed a global power structure that permitted uncaring multinationals like Union Carbide to perpetrate 'genocide' on unsuspecting citizens of developing societies (Visvanathan 1985). Which of these views prevailed, if either, clearly had huge implications for future policy.

Medical science, too, failed to deliver univocal answers to important issues of causation. In the chaos following the gas release, both affected bodies and their specific afflictions remained unrecorded. MIC's irritant properties at very small doses were well known, and thousands of instantaneous deaths provided sombre evidence of the chemical's lethal potency at higher exposure levels. But the long-term effects on people who had been more peripherally affected remained unestablished for decades. Because MIC was dangerous to handle, no studies had been done on its effects at low doses on the nervous system, the respiratory tract, vision or digestion, let alone on the psychological effects of being a gas survivor. Then, too, national and local medical authorities clashed with the victims in interpreting their symptoms and tendering appropriate remedies. A bitter technical confrontation erupted within days of the accident, centring on whether MIC had broken down into cyanide in victims' bodies, causing symptoms that sufferers claimed were alleviated by the antidote thiosulfate (Jasanoff 1994: 185–7). Experts sent in by the Indian government denied the victims' claims of cyanide poisoning and debunked community efforts to act on an officially discredited theory. Ensuing governmental action to block thiosulfate distribution and to arrest and detain physicians offering the treatment left a legacy of distrust that persisted into the present century.

Legal disputes growing from the disaster proved as thorny as they were inconclusive. An initial descent on Bhopal of prominent American trial lawyers, scenting huge damage awards, prompted the Indian government, under the so-called Bhopal Act, to assume the sole right to represent all claimants under an extended *parens patriae* doctrine. A New York federal court refused to allow the case against Union Carbide to be tried in the United States, as India had requested, on the ground that adequate justice could be done by the Indian legal system, even though no industrial accident on remotely this scale had ever troubled the subcontinent's courts. The complex legal skirmishes led in 1989 to an out-of-court settlement of $470 million by Union Carbide, brokered by the Indian Supreme Court. It was closure of a kind – indeed, even a vindication of sorts for Bhopal victims if measured against the substantially smaller $180 million settlement in May 1984 in the Vietnam veterans' lawsuit against manufacturers of Agent Orange (Schuck 1986). But from the victims' social and psychological standpoint the closure was anything but settling. In exchange for money, the Indian government dropped all criminal charges against the company, thereby permanently foreclosing what many saw as the only morally supportable response to Union Carbide's negligence. The settlement swept under the carpet the political economic critique that had framed the accident as a natural consequence of deep structural imbalances in the world. For those who saw both the state and the multinational corporation as shoring up the corrupt structures of global inequality, the mere transfer of millions of dollars from one to another equally non-accountable actor brought cold comfort. Money alone could not remedy what some saw as a moral catastrophe.

The Bhopal disaster, then, opened up a nested set of possible causes – from individual malice to corporate negligence and from state failure to global political economy – without leading to a broad societal consensus on any one of these. The lack of resolution was poignantly in evidence during a field trip to Bhopal that I made with a colleague in the summer of 2004, almost twenty years after the original catastrophe.[3] By sheer coincidence, only in the week of our visit did the Indian government release the last instalment of the Bhopal settlement, ending years of confrontation over whether state authorities or victims were entitled to increases in the fund through interest accumulation and fluctuating exchange rates. Local newspapers reported that the payouts would produce a short-term increase in sales of cell phones, scooters and other consumer goods, while patient groups maintained that the funds were barely sufficient to cover the long-term costs of medical treatment and rehabilitation.

The funds will be paid out in due course, but the sense of justice denied still burns strong in many of Bhopal's gas-affected citizens, some of whom were children when the disaster happened. The recently fenced-in plant sits abandoned, in a densely populated, still unmodernized part of the city, home to grazing cows and memorialized only by a nondescript stone statue of a female figure near its entrance gate. At community centres and health clinics run by veteran activists, people whose lives were permanently scarred by the events of 1984 wait for a fuller redress that may never come. One of our informants stated that, for him, this case would not truly close until Warren Anderson, Union Carbide's chief executive in 1984, served at least one symbolic day behind bars. Another activist leader focused on corporate responsibility from a different angle, describing the strategies that he and his associates were following to hold Union Carbide's new owner, Dow Chemical, responsible for environmental damage caused by the plant. *These* claims, he insisted, had not been formally extinguished by the 1989 settlement and his group was pursuing political and legal opportunities in India and the United States in an effort to bring Union Carbide, through Dow, to book for offences that had never been properly accounted for.

To the extent that Bhopal victims' groups continue to assert successful claims against the Indian state, it is not so much through official recognition of their health and safety claims as through the authenticity of their suffering. Twenty years after the precipitating events, after several changes of government and the assassination of Rajiv Gandhi, during whose prime ministership the Bhopal settlement was negotiated, victims' demonstrations seem still to have power to elicit responses from the state. One activist leader described, for example, a successful hunger strike that he and two colleagues had conducted in Delhi to persuade the government that the Bhopal Act did not pre-empt private litigation against Dow for environmental damage around the Union Carbide plant. What proved compelling in this case was not a factual demonstration of how bad things are in Bhopal, but the expressive voice of a community which, through the uniqueness of its experience, gained and retains moral claims on a nation's conscience – regardless of any divergences in their reading of the 'facts'.

The tragic open-endedness of the Bhopal case so many years later speaks to features of public knowledge making in India that we will return to later in this chapter. For now, let us flag chiefly the lack of anything approaching a definitive epistemological resolution: a time and place when all the major participants came together to agree on a common understanding of what had actually happened and what should be done on the basis of that shared knowledge. In the absence of such a moment of truth, multiple narratives of responsibility and blame continue to flourish in Bhopal, on the look-out for new external audiences or events to legitimate them. Yet this very lack of resolution can be seen as a form of learning – not the kind that necessarily leads to regulatory change or institutional reform, though both did happen in the disaster's wake (Jasanoff 1994), but rather the kind that, through its very incompleteness, reveals the impossibility of taming a cataclysmic event through necessarily imperfect managerial solutions. The open-endedness of learning at Bhopal offers in this sense its own redemption, by negating the possibility of forgetfulness.

Britain: BSE, food safety and the restoration of trust

If Bhopal burst upon the stage of world history in a single night of death and destruction, Britain's bovine spongiform encephalopathy (BSE or 'mad cow') crisis crept slowly into public consciousness over the course of much of a decade. The earliest signs of trouble appeared in the mid-1980s. Cows began to sicken mysteriously; they staggered and drooled as if gone mad and eventually died. The epidemic had affected 160,000 animals by 1996. This was bad news enough for the export-oriented British beef cattle industry, but regulators sensed the shadow of something worse around the corner. If whatever ailed the cows were to cross the species barrier and infect people, Britain might be faced with a public health disaster of unprecedented proportions. The Ministry of Agriculture, Fisheries and Food (MAFF), the agency responsible for both agricultural productivity and food safety regulation, took up the dual challenge for policy: to diagnose and stop the spread of illness in cattle and to allay the incipient official concern that people, too, might be at risk from BSE.

The second issue presented MAFF with a basic logistical difficulty. How could the ministry launch an inquiry into a public health hazard of potentially epidemic scale (beef was, after all, Britain's staple meat) without causing mass panic and so destroying an industry already burdened by the direct costs of coping with BSE in cows? Faced with this dilemma, MAFF followed the traditional British strategy of containment. A small, trusted body of experts, headed by Oxford Vice Chancellor Sir Richard Southwood, an eminent zoologist and policy adviser, was convened to recommend what actions should be taken both to assess the risks to public health and to stop the spread of infection. The committee was alarmed at the rapid and uncontrolled industrialization of animal husbandry, including the 'unnatural' practice of feeding ground meat and bone meal to cattle that most probably had caused the spread of BSE. Yet the face the state turned towards the public was one of calm reassurance, with both advisers and officials stating that the risk of disease transmission from cows to humans was too small for concern. The infective agent might have jumped the species barrier once, from sheep to cows, but the Southwood committee saw little need to worry about a second jump from ruminants to human beings (MAFF 1989).

MAFF's confidence, together with that of its advisers, that BSE would not affect humans, and could be controlled in cattle through incremental restrictions on possibly infected cuts of meat, turned out to have been misplaced. An empiricist culture of governance, never too happy with speculative judgements, could not write off the possibility of harm without seeking further evidence. British authorities began to monitor suspicious cases of human death from an illness known as Creutzfeldt-Jakob disease (CJD) and by 1996 enough instances of a new variant (vCJD) had been found to persuade them that the unthinkable had happened: 'mad cow' disease had crossed into people and it was essential to make that news public. On 23 March, Stephen Dorrell, the Secretary of State for Health, announced to Parliament that ten deaths from vCJD had been identified in Britain. Against earlier expert predictions, it appeared that as many as several hundred thousand unsuspecting Britons might now be at risk of an irreversible and fatal degenerative brain disease caused by the same infectious agent as BSE.[4] The panic that MAFF had so assiduously sought to prevent suddenly gripped not only Britain but also the European Union and Britain's non-European trading partners, most of whom immediately banned imports of British beef. Within Britain, too, the giant food industry took potentially contaminated beef off the shelves and turned to safer sources, such as Argentinian meat for use in McDonald's hamburgers. The episode cost the UK public sector alone £4 billion. More important, if less tangible, was the ensuing 'civic dislocation' (Jasanoff 1997) that caused citizens to turn away from government as a source of credible health and safety information and made the restoration of trust an urgent priority for Labour following its decisive electoral victory in 1997.

If neither Union Carbide nor the Indian state had wanted to resolve the multiple factual conflicts around the Bhopal gas disaster, the same could not be said of Tony Blair's new Labour government and BSE. The government promised a full public inquiry, Britain's favoured mechanism for ascertaining the facts after any major breakdown or controversy. A lengthy process headed by Lord Phillips of Worth Matravers, a Law Lord, concluded in 2000 that MAFF and its technical advisers had made substantial errors of judgement, on the basis of imperfect understandings of the facts and of available policy options (Lord Phillips 2000). The inquiry identified MAFF's culture of secrecy (exceptional even in British terms) as an underlying problem that had prevented timely disclosure of risks and aggressive pursuit of scientific knowledge and policy alternatives. These findings dealt a final blow to a ministry that had for years been under fire for its lack of transparency and close ties to agribusiness. MAFF was dissolved, its responsibilities were transferred to other bodies, such as the expanded Department of Environment, Food and Rural Affairs, and a new advisory committee, the Food Standards Agency, was formed to provide more transparent, consumer-oriented advice to government on matters of food safety.

From the standpoint of public knowledge making, however, what interests us most is the Phillips inquiry's strategy for determining who was to blame for the BSE fiasco. Was it a failure of knowledge and competence, and if so of individuals or institutions? The committee was on surest ground when it concluded that MAFF and its advisers had acted contrary to widely accepted principles or easily accessible public knowledge – put differently, when people seemed to have violated canons of common sense. Thus, in one instructive passage, the committee said:

> . . . we do not consider that the [Southwood] Working Party correctly applied the ALARP [as low as reasonably practicable] principle. Animals with BSE that had developed clinical signs of the disease were to be slaughtered and destroyed. No steps were to be taken, however, to protect anyone other than babies from the risk of eating potentially infective parts of animals infected with BSE but not yet showing signs. It is true that infectivity of the most infective tissues – the brain and spinal cord – rises significantly shortly before clinical signs begin to show. It is also true that there were reasons to think that babies might be more susceptible to infection than adults. *But we do not consider that these differences justified an approach that treated the risk from eating brain or spinal cord from an animal incubating BSE as one in respect of which there were no reasonably practical precautions that need be taken.*
> [my emphasis]

To empiricist judicial minds, trained in common law notions of reasonableness, it seemed obvious that infectivity could never be contained within strict physical demarcations (brain and spinal cord), any more than some beef-eating populations (adults in this case) could be declared absolutely unsusceptible to risk. Responsible experts, the inquiry concluded, should have known that risk in a population extends across a continuum, from zero to certain harm, with corresponding opportunities for graduated precautionary action. It was plainly unreasonable, then, to target for protection only the high end of the risk continuum: babies exposed to brain and spinal cord tissue from infected but pre-symptomatic cattle. Other consumers, too, should have been provided for under the accordion-pleated principle of 'as low as reasonably practicable' risk reduction. MAFF's advisers had not acted commonsensically enough.

When it came to assigning individual responsibility, however, the committee was noticeably more hesitant. Expert bodies might be held accountable to widely accepted public health principles, such as ALARP, just as they might be expected to craft regulatory responses carefully fitted to the uncertainties of the situation. But individual public servants could not be deemed at fault for errors of fact or judgement so long as they were acting in good faith, according to their best understanding of their duties. The following observations from the Phillips inquiry are instructive [paragraph numbers indicated; my emphasis throughout]:

- It is inevitable that an Inquiry such as ours focuses on what went wrong. The main point of having the Inquiry is to find out what went wrong and to see what lessons can be learned from this. *This can be harsh for individuals. Their shortcomings are put under the spotlight. The overall value of the contributions that they have made is lost from view.* We do not wish our Report to produce this result . . . (Lord Phillips 2000: 1245).
- Those who were most active in addressing the challenges of BSE are those who are most likely to have made mistakes. As was observed in the course of the Inquiry, 'if you do not put a foot forward you do not put a foot wrong.' In this context we think it right to single out for mention Mr Meldrum. Mr Meldrum was Chief Veterinary Officer in Great Britain for almost the whole of the period with which we are concerned. He involved himself personally in almost every aspect of the response to BSE. *He placed himself at the front of the firing line so far as risk of criticism is concerned* (Lord Phillips 2000: 1250).
- *We are satisfied that where Mr Meldrum perceived the possibility of a significant risk to human health he gave this precedence over consideration of the interests of the livestock industry* (Lord Phillips 2000: 1256).
- We have criticized the restrictions on dissemination of information about BSE in the early stages of the story, which were motivated in part by concern for the export market. We suspect that this may have reflected a culture of secrecy within MAFF, which Mr Gummer sought to end with his policy of openness. *If those we have criticized were misguided, they were nonetheless acting in accordance with what they conceived to be the proper performance of their duties* (Lord Phillips 2000: 1258).
- For all these reasons, while we have identified a number of grounds for individual criticism, we suggest that *any who have come to our Report hoping to find villains or scapegoats, should go away disappointed* (Lord Phillips 2000: 1259).

Evident in these quotations is a firm commitment to protecting public servants against undue censure for honest mistakes. This protectiveness is understandable in a political culture that values learning from experience – in which both experts and civil servants have traditionally risen to power and influence not merely, nor mainly, on the strength of technical credentials, but by showing that they have served the public interest to the best of their abilities (Jasanoff 1994, 2005). It would not do, in this context, to make 'villains or scapegoats' of people who may have displayed intellectual shortcomings, but only through having placed themselves 'at the front of the firing line' of criticism, or who may have been misguided, but were acting throughout 'in accordance with what they conceived to be the proper performance of their duties'. To penalize such people simply because of mistakes would be to deprive the state of a cadre of dedicated public servants that the nation could ill afford to lose. Unlike some national elites, who stand *above* the people in skills and knowledge, British public servants ideally stand *for* the polity. They are people in and out of government who not only possess the virtue of selflessness but who, through experience and service, have earned the right to see and know for the wider public – who embody, in other words, their nation's civic epistemology, its capacity for generating reliable collective knowledge.

A change of government and a major public inquiry led in Britain to serious institutional redesign, most notably through the dissolution of a long-established ministry. At the same time, as we will see below, it left untouched core beliefs about the best way to preserve trust in government and to construct credible public knowledge for purposes of collective action.

United States: 9/11, aeroplanes and the failure of intelligence

The terrorist attacks of September 11 (2001) on the United States were, on one level, vastly different in kind from the methyl isocyanate and BSE disasters. Although the death toll of nearly 3,000 was close to the loss of life sustained in Bhopal, the event that came to be known as 9/11 was universally seen, unlike the two earlier tragedies, as having been caused by intentional human malice. The nineteen young Muslim terrorists who were among the dead that day were bent on killing Americans and destroying major symbols of American economic and political might, the twin towers of New York's World Trade Center, the Pentagon, and possibly the White House or the Capitol. The attacks were immediately compared with the Japanese assault on Pearl Harbor that brought the United States into the Second World War. Framed as an act of war, 9/11 led in turn to military retaliations against Afghanistan, the prime training ground of the Al-Qaeda terrorist network, and Iraq, a country inimical to US interests in the world but not connected, according to official findings, with the 9/11 attacks.

Yet contained within the script of 9/11 was what we may with little stretch of the imagination view as a 'normal' technological disaster in the sense discussed by Perrow (1984). It involved the use of commercial airliners as weapons aimed at large buildings – thereby subverting the normal operations of two of modernity's most foundational technological systems, transportation and urban infrastructure. Unsurprisingly, the 9/11 Commission's sweeping remit under its authorizing statute of 2002 included a look at the security of commercial aviation. One of the Commission's prime tasks was to determine how four aeroplanes could have been hijacked from three US airports and crashed into national landmarks, and how to keep such incidents from occurring again. Indeed, the final report's first chapter is entitled, in words drawn from the first transmission from the hijacked American Airlines Flight 11, ' "We have some planes" ' (9/11 Commission 2004). The chapter offers a blow-by-blow reconstruction of what happened on board each of the four doomed airliners and how aviation authorities had tracked but failed to intercept the planes.

True to the practices of a country in which open information is believed to be the cornerstone of political empowerment and rational policy making, the 9/11 Commission identified problems in the US intelligence system as the major reason for the surprise attacks. The report highlighted many institutional deficits that had prevented information from being shared in timely fashion and so had kept the big-picture threat of Al-Qaeda from emerging with the kind of clarity that might have prompted preventive action. Important among these deficiencies, the report concluded, were the organizational barriers that kept two of the nation's foremost intelligence-gathering outfits, the Federal Bureau of Investigation (FBI) and the Central Intelligence Agency (CIA), from effectively sharing information related to terrorism. To counter those failures of coordination, the Commission recommended the appointment of a single national intelligence director, whose job would be to pull the intelligence capabilities scattered among fifteen separate federal agencies into a functioning, organic whole. It was neither the processes of information collecting, nor the nature of the information collected, that the Commission blamed. The fault was attributed instead to the absence of a single synthesizing institution that could absorb the available information and convert it into a credible, reliable assessment of the risk of terrorism.

Here and there in the report are suggestions that the Commission understood the difficulty of building such an all-seeing, or all-knowing, eye within the government. In a chapter called 'Foresight – and Hindsight', the Commission noted that the failures that had led to 9/11 included not only those of policy, capabilities and management, all of which presumably could be corrected through familiar changes in organization and governance, but also those of imagination, a far more difficult virtue to cultivate inside the routines of administrative practice (9/11 Commission 2004: 339). Observing that '[i]magination is not a gift usually associated with bureaucracies', the chapter went on to say:

> It is therefore crucial to find a way of routinizing, even bureaucratizing, the exercise of imagination. Doing so requires more than finding an expert who can imagine that aircraft could be used as weapons. Indeed, since Al Qaeda and other groups had already used suicide vehicles, namely truck bombs, the leap to the use of other vehicles such as boats (the *Cole* attack) or planes is not far-fetched.
>
> (9/11 Commission 2004: 344)

But here we confront a paradox. If it did not take *much* imagination to conceive of what happened on 9/11, why did the Commission identify lack of imagination as a key factor leading to the attacks? And if the use of aircraft as weapons could have been foreseen so easily, why did the relevant authorities fail to exercise the modest amount of imagination needed to forestall that event?

The answer that emerges on the page following the above quote is telling: for imagination is here reduced, for all practical purposes, to routine administrative analysis. The Commission identifies four fairly uncontroversial analytic steps that the Counterterrorism Center (CTC) might have taken but did not: analysis from the enemy's perspective; development of tell-tale indicators; requirements for monitoring such indicators; and identifying systemic defences within terrorist-controlled aircraft. None of these elements is presented as new or path-breaking. Indeed, they had become standard, the Commission suggests, in the years after Pearl Harbor, and CTC's error lay in not using them well or at all. The methods 'did not fail', the report concludes, 'they were not really tried' (9/11 Commission 2004: 347–8). The alleged failure of imagination, then, was little more than a failure to do conventional risk assessment in the national security arena, in accordance with long-established codes of practice.

The irony of this move – beginning with an ambitious attempt to chart new conceptual territory but returning to fighting yesterday's war on yesterday's terms – did not go unnoticed. A commentary on the 9/11 report by Judge Richard Posner, an acerbic social critic and one of America's foremost apostles of the free market, blamed the Commission for proposing a solution that did not follow from its own analysis (Posner 2004). His own suggestions, based as he said on the Commission's findings, were more modest, specifically targeted and often technological. For example, with regard to airline safety, Posner called for better passenger and baggage screening, secure cockpit doors and override mechanisms to enable hijacked planes to be controlled from the ground. He also recommended more effective border controls, including biometric screening, and improved building evacuation plans, which he felt had received too little attention.

At bottom, however, Posner's disagreements with the Commission rested on ideological foundations. Accusing the Commission of 'herd thinking' and a lean towards centralized planning, Posner charged that the proper solution to 9/11 was not a unified intelligence system of questionable efficacy that aggrandized the state. Consistent with market principles, Posner's view seemed to be that the bottom-up forces of individual or small-scale entrepreneurship would do better at producing robust collective defences than top-down state coordination of all information sources:

> The Commission thinks the reason the bits of information that might have been assembled into a mosaic spelling 9/11 never came together in one place is that no one person was in charge of intelligence. That is not the reason. The reason or, rather, the reasons are, first, that the volume of information is so vast that even with the continued rapid advances in data processing it cannot be collected, stored, retrieved and analyzed in a single database or even network of databases. Second, legitimate security concerns limit the degree to which confidential information can be safely shared, especially given the ever-present threat of moles like the infamous Aldrich Ames. And third, the different intelligence services and the subunits of each service tend, because information is power, to hoard it.
>
> (Posner 2004: 11)

Posner concluded that, ultimately, there is very little a society can do to prevent truly novel risks like 9/11; it is therefore wasteful to engage in too much front-end planning to keep such surprises from happening.

In this respect, Posner's dissent from the Commission's conclusions echoes what another market libertarian, the late political scientist Aaron Wildavsky (1988), had said almost two decades earlier about the futility of advance planning against environmental and other hazards. In both Posner's and Wildavsky's esti-mation, post-hoc determinations of causality, coupled with precisely targeted remedies, will serve society better than trying to predict harms in advance and predicting erroneously. Underlying both positions is a deep, and thoroughly American, suspicion of the state and its capacity to see, or know, for the people; in a culture committed to the discourse of transparency, the state arguably has no privileged position from which to see any differently than its individual members, who can see well enough for themselves.

Causal analysis and civic epistemology

What light do these three national disasters, and subsequent attempts to make sense of them, shed on our initial question: do human societies learn and, if so, how do they do it? As we have seen, all three events gave rise to long, costly, anguished efforts to identify the causes of tragedy and affix responsibility accord-ingly. For this purpose, it proved necessary in all three cases to produce bodies of communal knowledge that would underwrite and make plausible the causal anal-ysis that the state wished to embrace for itself and to have its citizens endorse. In this section we ask how each effort reflected or reinforced established national approaches to public knowledge making or, in other words, each nation's charac-teristic civic epistemology. To what extent were the explanations given for each event stamped or shaped by cultural commitments to particular ways of knowing?

As I have argued elsewhere (Jasanoff 2005), the credibility of governmental actions in contemporary knowledge societies depends crucially on the public evaluation of competing knowledge claims and the consequent production of reliable public knowledge. The concept of civic epistemology acknowledges the centrality of this dynamic. It refers to the mix of ways in which knowledge is produced, presented, tested, verified and put to use in public arenas. These public knowledge-ways, moreover, are not universal but are grounded in historically conditioned practices that may vary from one national context to another. Seen in this light, civic epistemology is a constitutive element of political culture. In any functioning political community, including importantly the nation state, we can identify distinctive, shared understandings among citizens and rulers about what makes some sorts of knowledge claims or modes of reasoning seem more credible than others; public explanations, in turn, achieve robustness by meeting entrenched, institutionalized, cultural expectations about how to produce authori-tative knowledge.

Cross-national comparisons, conducted thus far mostly among Western coun-tries, have shown five dimensions of possible variation in the practices of civic epistemology: (1) the dominant styles of public knowledge making; (2) the methods of ensuring accountability; (3) the practices of public demonstration; (4) the preferred registers of objectivity; and (5) the accepted bases of expertise (Jasanoff 2005). Reviewing our three cases of causal analysis in the light of these factors reveals interesting contrasts that resonate with and extend earlier comparative research. These contrasts are summarized in Table 4.1 and elaborated in greater detail below.

The organization of post-disaster inquiries in each country conformed to well-known national *styles of public knowledge making*. In India, the state took early control over medical and legal fact-finding following a disastrous accident, but, significantly, was unwilling or unable to establish a process for making those facts authoritative.[5] In the absence of a definitive public inquiry, multiple accounts of suffering and blame continued to circulate, prompting, as we have seen, new claims and counter-claims as much as two decades after the original tragic event. Factually as well as morally, the Bhopal disaster refused to close; indeed, it spawned a tradition of social protest that promised to outlast the immediately affected generation and to reframe a case of failed industrial risk management as a question of global inequity and injustice. In Britain, by contrast, a judicial inquiry presided over by a Law Lord produced a consensual account of the facts and broad agreement on the institutional changes needed to prevent a recurrence – most particularly, the disbanding of the seriously discredited MAFF. Unlike the BSE inquiry, which followed an adjudicatory model, the US 9/11 Commission drew its authority from bipartisan representation and a politically negotiated unanimity. Not surprisingly, the Commission's primary policy recommendation, the centralization of intelligence gathering, took the form of a managerial fix that sidelined politics and values and quickly won the approval of both major political parties.

The methods for ensuring *accountability* in public knowledge production varied as much across the three cases as did the inquiry processes. In Bhopal, the company,

Table 4.1 Civic epistemology: a comparative overview

	India	*Britain*	*US*
Form of post-disaster inquiry	Social protest	Judicial inquiry	Bipartisan national commission
Public knowledge making (style of)	Contentious; movement-based	Embodied; service-based	Pluralist; interest-based
Public accountability	Fluid assumptions; political	Assumptions of trust; relational	Assumptions of distrust; legal
Demonstration	Elite knowledge vs. authentic experience	Common sense empiricism	Socio-technical experiments
Objectivity (strategy for)	Contested; view from somewhere	Negotiated; view from everywhere	Analytic; view from nowhere
Expertise (basis for)	Institutional or political position	Experience	Formal analytic methods

the government and the victims were sceptical about each other's approaches to fact-finding and this mutual suspicion never resolved itself. Union Carbide continued to insist on the sabotage theory, although the victims ridiculed it; the government continued to deny some of the victims' health claims and pegged compensation to administrative classifications rather than to subjective assessments of harm; and the victims continued to insist that they and their offspring had been irreparably damaged in ways not fully accounted for by official medical experts or financial reckonings. In marked contrast, the BSE inquiry produced a relatively uncontested version of the facts and a correspondingly uncontroversial allocation of responsibility. It held accountable institutional actors who, like MAFF or the Southwood working party, had failed to act on the basis of common knowledge and common sense. On the other hand, the inquiry exonerated individuals who, like Mr Meldrum, had made mistakes while sincerely carrying out their duty. For the 9/11 Commission, accountability was more a matter of following the appropriate analytic routines so as to ascertain objective facts; inexcusable error lay in agencies like the CTC not using information to the fullest and not pushing analysis far enough to uncover in-principle knowable truths.

Participants in knowledge making in all three countries relied on different forms of public *demonstration* to legitimate their particular epistemologies. In India, the company and the government used formal legal procedures to reach a settlement designed to make further fact-finding unnecessary. But the settlement never completely assuaged the victims' sense of injury and as late as 2004 activist groups were still staging acts of conscience such as hunger strikes to win benefits from the state. Victims who never experienced the consolation of a day in court won instead a lifelong hearing in the courts of public opinion, in India and beyond. In Britain, the risk of interspecies BSE transmission was publicly admitted only after epidemiological research uncovered evidence of a new pathology. Similarly, British authorities proved reluctant to set upper bounds on the number of possible human infections until they had accumulated several years of data on proved and probable incidents of vCJD. On both issues, certainty was achieved only on the basis of proofs that everyone found persuasive. In the United States, the two 9/11 explanations that gained widest support were, on one hand, the massive failure of intelligence and, on the other, the lack of suitable technological fixes such as biometric passports and better baggage screening. Both are consistent with a civic culture in which breakdowns in social order are frequently framed as technological failures. By the same token, technology, whether social (like intelligence gathering) or material, is the preferred American means of problem solving and US rulers frequently gain support by demonstrating, through public socio-technical experiments, that their policies work (Ezrahi 1990).

National strategies for establishing the *objectivity* of official fact-finding also differed among the three cases. In post-Bhopal India, the major actors each claimed primacy for their own forms of knowledge, but on divergent grounds. Thus, the Indian government used its experts to produce official counts of death and injury, but these were disputed by the victims and their representatives, who preferred to rely on subjective experience backed by community-based clinical observations.

Union Carbide also stuck by the opinions of its own experts, particularly on the issue of sabotage, implying that neither Indian officialdom nor the victims could be trusted to produce an unbiased appraisal of the facts. If the Indian knowledge claims represented a view from *somewhere* – that is, from a partisan political standpoint – post-BSE Britain took pains to construct the view from *everywhere*, a consensual account that brooked no real dissent. Discernible within the inquiry findings, moreover, was an acceptance of some truths as self-evident, for example when the committee agreed that infectivity rises shortly before clinical signs of disease appear and that babies are likely to be more susceptible to infection than adults. Statements such as these bear the stamp of a culture that readily accepts the possibility of communal vision. The 9/11 Commission, too, forged a common position, but it did so by sticking close to a dry reconstruction of the events and carefully excluding areas of possible partisan contention. The faults it found, similarly, were those of inadequate analysis and information processing rather than of moral or political short-sightedness (as in Bhopal) or of ignoring obvious facts (as in the BSE case). This approach to objectivity corresponds most nearly to what the philosopher Thomas Nagel (1989) has termed the 'view from nowhere' – that is, a view that is self-consciously shorn of interest or positional bias.

Finally, the three case studies of causal learning illustrate different notions of what constitutes legitimate *expertise*. In the aftermath of Bhopal, it became clear that the major parties were willing neither to trust each other's experts nor to accept any adjudication of the relative merits of their claims as dispositive. There was, in short, no shared credibility economy (Shapin 1995) in which experts for the warring interests could negotiate their cognitive differences and arrive at a common understanding. Expertise remained irretrievably tied to the parties' institutional positions; valid knowledge, then, was not knowledge detached from political engagement but knowledge gained as an extension of politics.

The BSE case, by contrast, displayed at many levels Britain's cultural commitment to a transcendental notion of embodied expertise – that is, expertise acquired through experience, with the expert's standing deriving not only from superior technical abilities but also from a proven record of public service (Jasanoff 1997). Lord Phillips, Sir Richard Southwood and Mr Meldrum all conformed to this image of the expert who stands above special interests, and the inquiry committee's refusal to identify any 'villains or scapegoats' indicated a deep reluctance to question the merits of that kind of expertise. Individuals may have erred when they acted outside the bounds of common sense, but they were not held, for that reason, morally blameworthy. For the 9/11 Commission, which similarly blamed no individuals personally, the chief failure lay in the system's inability to process information in accordance with appropriate frameworks of analysis. Experts, under this reading, were people possessing the necessary technical skills to read the tea leaves of passing events. Their job was to foster, through impersonal analysis and appropriate organizational routines, the sort of preventive imagination that the Commission found so sadly lacking in the disastrous lead-up to 9/11.

Conclusion: learning cultures

Bhopal, the BSE crisis and 9/11 were disasters on a scale that engaged entire nations in processes of collective self-examination and efforts at preventive learning. I have suggested that these efforts unfolded within, and were constrained by, the national traditions of producing and evaluating public knowledge that I have termed civic epistemologies. These institutionalized ways of coming to terms with communal experience are a feature of contemporary political cultures. They at once provide the means of sense making in tangled circumstances and discipline, to some extent, the kinds of reasoning that are considered robust or plausible within a functioning political community. The causes identified and the people or institutions held responsible in each case reflected national commitments to holding still, or *not* questioning, certain features of each nation's political culture, along with a willingness to undertake some forms of institutional reform or policy change.

The cases help us address a major problem identified at the beginning of this chapter: how do we account for learning within extremely stable organizational settings, including nation states, that devote considerable energy and resources to withstanding change? The answer has to do, in part, with the heterogeneity of 'culture' as displayed in these cases. Civic epistemology, in particular, is not a seamless way of knowing shared by all participants in a political community. Far from it. In India, for instance, all those who grappled with the consequences of Bhopal were engaged in producing public facts; yet their notions of how to make facts count and be authoritative were, and remained, apart. There was, to be sure, a formal financial settlement of claims, but this did not constitute closure with respect to the moral narratives of suffering and blame that continued to circulate in India long after the events of December 1984. Events as much as two decades after the date of the accident suggest that the state and its citizens recognized the power of moral arguments to spill over and outlast resolutions reached solely on the basis of factual determinations or administrative convenience.

Britain and the United States both appointed official bodies to inquire into the causes of the BSE fiasco and 9/11 respectively, but while both processes effectively shifted the ground from moral blaming to institutional failure, neither succeeded in fully closing off alternate readings of the events. Closure on facts and evidence was perhaps most complete in Britain, but even in that relatively consensual environment disagreement quickly appeared over the adequacy of the government's policy response. Criticism of the Food Standards Agency and the later vehement controversy over genetically modified crops suggest that state and citizens remained sharply divided over crucial aspects of how to produce authoritative knowledge and robust explanations in areas of high uncertainty. In the United States, Posner's dissent from the 9/11 Commission points to a similar persistence of multiple epistemologies within a single political system. Posner's argument centred, after all, on the state's capacity to serve as a consolidated nerve centre for anti-terrorist intelligence. In questioning the feasibility of that role, Posner spoke for critics from the right and left of the political spectrum who place more faith in local knowledge and decentralized action than in centralized managerial solutions based on seeing like a state (Scott 1998).

Learning from disaster emerges out of these stories as a complex, ambiguous process – conditioned by culture, yet not easily forced into univocal, totalizing, national narratives. It is in the raggedness of accounting for tragic experience that the possibility of cultural reinvention ultimately resides. Comparisons of the sort undertaken here help reveal the cracks in the paving stones of culture from which creative gardeners can coax into bloom new shoots of understanding and self-awareness.

Notes

* In Bridget Hutter and Michael Power, eds., *Organizational Encounters with Risk* (Cambridge: Cambridge University Press, 2005), pp. 209–32.

1 'Where Have All the Flowers Gone?' was arguably Pete Seeger's best-known song. It was inspired by a Ukrainian folk song quoted in Mikhail Sholokov's epic 1928 war novel *And Quiet Flows the Don*. The opening lines were:

> Where have all the flowers gone, long time passing?
> Where have all the flowers gone, long time ago?

2 Historians use the term 'site of memory' to refer to places, including the imaginative spaces of works of art and literature, where communities repose, and reify, their memories of significant past events. While this is not the place for a fuller discussion of history and memory, I note that the construction of memory is integral to the process of learning and that public policy – which is often based on an authoritative analysis of past events – therefore can be seen as an important site of memory in modern societies.

3 I was accompanied by Stefan Sperling, whose anthropological perspective has greatly enriched my own policy analytic interpretation of the lack of closure in Bhopal. We are particularly indebted to Abdul Jabbar and Satinath Sarangi for their time and generosity in offering personal interviews, supporting materials and introductions to others in the gas-affected communities of Bhopal.

4 By the end of 2002, 129 people would be diagnosed with confirmed and probable cases of the disease (Andrews et al. 2003).

5 Some of the Indian government's difficulties may relate to the complexities of being embroiled in transnational litigation against Union Carbide, but other considerations had to do with avoiding potential liability for what had happened under its watch in Bhopal. These issues bear more detailed investigation than I am able to provide within the limits of this chapter. For additional perspectives, see Jasanoff (1994).

References

9/11 Commission. 2004. Final Report of the Commission on Terrorist Attacks upon the United States. W.W. Norton.

Andrews, N. et al. 2003. "Deaths from variant Creutzfeldt-Jakob Disease in the UK." *Lancet* 361: 751–52.

Bijker, W., T. Hughes and T. Pinch (eds.). 1987. *The Social Construction of Technological Systems*. MIT Press.

Bourdieu, P. 1980. *The Logic of Practice*. Stanford University Press.

Bowker, G. C. and Star, S. L. 1999. *Sorting Things Out: Classification and Its Consequences*. MIT Press.

Clarke, L. 1989. *Acceptable Risk? Making Decisions in a Toxic Environment*. University of California Press.

Ezrahi, Y. 1990. *The Descent of Icarus: Science and the Transformation of Contemporary Democracy*. Harvard University Press.

Foucault, M. 1979. *Discipline and Punish: The Birth of the Prison*. Random House.

Jasanoff, S. Forthcoming. *Designs on Nature: Science and Democracy in Europe and the United States*. Princeton University Press.

Jasanoff, S. 1997. "Civilization and Madness: The Great BSE Scare of 1996." *Public Understanding of Science* 6:221–232.

Jasanoff, S. 1995. "Product, Process, or Programme: Three Cultures and the Regulation of Biotechnology." In M. Bauer, ed., *Resistance to New Technology*, Cambridge University Press, pp. 311–331.

Jasanoff, S. 1994. *Learning from Disaster: Risk Management after Bhopal*. University of Pennsylvania Press.

Jasanoff, S. 1986. *Risk Management and Political Culture*. Russell Sage Foundation.

Kalelkar, A. 1988. "Investigation of Large-Magnitude Incidents: Bhopal as a Case Study." http://www.bhopal.com/infoarch.htm (visited October 11, 2004).

Ministry of Agriculture, Fisheries and Food (MAFF). 1989. *Report of the Working Party on Bovine Spongiform Encephalopathy* (Southwood Committee Report). HMSO.

Nagel, T. 1989. *The View from Nowhere*. Oxford University Press.

Noble, D. F. 1977. *America By Design: Science, Technology and the Rise of Corporate Capitalism*. Oxford University Press.

Perrow, C. 1984. *Normal Accidents: Living with High Risk Technologies*. Basic Books.

Phillips, Lord. 2000. *The Inquiry into BSE and variant CJD in the United Kingdom*. http://www.bseinquiry.gov.uk.

Porter, T. 1995. *Trust in Numbers: The Pursuit of Objectivity in Science and Public Life*. Princeton University Press.

Posner, R. 2004. "The 9/11 Report: A Dissent." *New York Times, Sunday Book Review*. August 29.

Schuck, P. 1986. *Agent Orange on Trial: Mass Toxic Disasters in the Courts*. Harvard University Press.

Scott, J.C. 1998. *Seeing Like a State*. Yale University Press.

Seeger, P. 1955. "Where have all the flowers gone?"

Shapin, S. 1995. "Cordelia's Love: Credibility and the Social Studies of Science." *Perspectives on Science* 3(3):255–275.

Short, J. F. and L. Clarke (eds.). 1992. *Organizations, Uncertainties, and Risk*. Westview Press.

Vaughan, D. 1996. *The Challenger Launch Decision: Risky Technology, Culture, and Deviance at NASA*. University of Chicago Press.

Visvanathan, S. (with R. Kothari). 1985. "Bhopal: The Imagination of a Disaster." *Lokayan Bulletin* 3:48–76.

Vogel, D. 1986. *National Styles of Regulation*. Cornell University Press.

Weber, M. 1946. *From Max Weber: Essays in Sociology* (trans. and ed. H.H. Gerth and C.W. Mills). Oxford University Press.

Wildavsky, A. 1988. *Searching for Safety*. Transaction Books.

Winner, L. 1986. "On Not Hitting the Tar-Baby." In *The Whale and the Reactor: A Search for Limits in an Age of High Technology*, pp. 138–154.

Winner, L. 1986. *The Whale and the Reactor: A Search for Limits in an Age of High Technology*. University of Chicago Press.

5 Image and imagination

The formation of global environmental consciousness*

As the mood of the West turned retrospective and millennial in the final years of the twentieth century, it became clear that the images by which Western societies were defining the meaning of this stretch of history had shifted their form and emphasis—from pictures of division and conflict for the first three-quarters of the century to those of interconnectedness at its end. War and destruction dominate the frames through which we look at most of the past hundred years: the disjointed march of troops from nowhere to nowhere on the battlefields of the Great War, the emaciated bodies and charred cities of the second and wider World War, the eruptions of American firepower in the fields and villages of Vietnam, and the mass evacuations that presaged the killing fields of Cambodia. These images have not faded from our collective consciousness. Rather, they have gained secondary and tertiary currency through the commemorative efforts of contemporary historians, novelists, filmmakers, and museologists, all intent, it seems, on finding at this emotionally charged calendrical moment the appropriate visual languages to memorialize the century's vast conflicts.[1] One need think only of the controversies surrounding the U.S. Vietnam memorial and their resolution through Maya Lin's inspired and reflective roll call of names, the attack against perceived revisionism in the *Enola Gay* exhibit at the U.S. National Air and Space Museum (Harwit 1996), Stephen Spielberg's embrace of black-and-white cinematography in his 1993 opus *Schindler's List,* and the lengthy, emotional debates about how best to commemorate the Holocaust in Berlin, the once and future capital of reunified Germany.

Sometime during the last three decades of the century, however, images of connection, of dissolving boundaries, began to supplement, and at times crowd out, division in our visual and imaginative space. President Richard Nixon's controversial visit to China in 1972 was perhaps a starting point, providing compelling television footage of one of the world's most committed cold warriors visiting the shrines and monuments of the very nation he had fought so doggedly to isolate from communion with the West. The watershed year of 1989 brought additional stirring images, with the fall of the Berlin wall on November 9 signaling the official end of bipolar tensions and, to some, even "the end of history" (Fukuyama 1992). And on January 1, 1999, months before war-torn Kosovo gripped the television screens, the pictures of a new common currency, the

Euro—as yet available only in virtual form—made concrete the extraordinary, voluntary ceding of sovereignty through which eleven European nations sought to erase the scars and trenches of the two world wars that had split their continent.[2]

One image perhaps more than any other has come to symbolize the Western world's heightened perceptions of connectedness at the end of the millennium: that of the earth suspended in a void, captured by the cameras of the U.S. space program beginning with the Lunar Orbiter in 1966 and culminating with *Apollo 17*, the last mission to land men on the moon.[3] The image confronts Americans today at every turn, from the revolving globe used as a background for so many televised, and now networked, news programs to the logo that wordlessly asserts the global reach of credit cards, airlines, automobile manufacturers, telephone companies, bookstores, academic programs, and virtually every other product or service that travels. It is also an image that catches the spirit of contemporary environmentalism, one of late modernity's signature social movements. The picture of the earth hanging in space not only renders visible and immediate the object of environmentalists' concern, but it resonates with the themes of finiteness and fragility, and of human dependence on the biosphere, that have provided growing impetus for environmental mobilization since the 1960s. It is as well a deeply political image, subordinating as it does the notional boundaries of sovereign power in favor of swirling clouds that do not respect the lines configured by human conquest or legislation. It is in this respect a fitting emblem of Western environmentalism's transnational ambitions.

While many have pointed to the image of Earth from space as an artifact that fundamentally altered human consciousness, there have been few systematic attempts to explore how, when, or to what extent such a transformation occurred, let alone how this potent visual resource interacted with other, more commonly recognized political forces (for example, scientific knowledge, economic interests, or hegemonic power) in the formation of shared environmental awareness (for an exception, see Sachs 1994). There are several reasons why it is important to fill this gap. To begin with, the televised distribution of standardized visual symbols, and visual language more generally, is creating a global communicative resource whose political implications demand closer exploration. Images may transcend cultural lines in ways that words cannot, thereby helping to create communities of meaning and shared responses or demands that cut across ordinary linguistic and governmental divides. More generally, there is growing interest in the social sciences in the power of visual representation to sway both belief and action (Scott 1998). Sight moreover, like any sense, is now seen as something that has to be manipulated and disciplined in order for people in the aggregate to see things in the same ways.[4] The politics involved in constructing common vision has accordingly begun to draw attention.

This chapter, then, is a study of the reception of the image of planet Earth in American and, through U.S. mediation, international environmental politics. At a theoretical level, this project can be seen as contributing to the interpretive turn in international relations theory by attempting to understand better the role of ideas in promoting transnational cooperation and conflict (Keohane 1988; Haggard and

Simmons 1987; Haas 1990b; Litfin 1994). More specifically, it extends earlier work on epistemic communities by probing, within visual culture, one possible source of shared beliefs about the environment.[5] At the same time, the project also fits comfortably within the core research agenda of science and technology studies: it explores the creation of new knowledge about nature and its diffusion to varied audiences through technologically mediated visual representations.[6] The chapter's organization reflects these paired objectives. I begin by reviewing major strands in international relations theory and science and technology studies that deal with image making and its power to foster shared social and political awareness. I then successively discuss the emergence of Earth consciousness in postwar politics, the early history of responses to the image of planet Earth, and its later thematization and uptake in the discourses of risk, politics, economics, and ethics. The chapter ends with reflections on the merits of the planetary image as a resource for global action to protect the environment.

Common vision, concerted action

What makes people from different societies believe that they should act to further common goals, even if these goals require them to sacrifice or postpone perceived economic and social interests? In a world in which political will has classically been exercised through national institutions, how can we account for the rise of transnational coalitions, such as the contemporary environmental movement, that seem to articulate their objectives in defiance of the positions of nation states? How, more generally, do people form commitments to collective action on a global scale, and from where do they derive notions of an international common good that are strong enough to override the intense but parochial pull of national self-interest?

A promising place from which to begin addressing these questions is Benedict Anderson's influential work *Imagined Communities* (1991), which sought to explain how nationality became modernity's most compelling social identifier. Why, Anderson asked, has nationality proved to be such a peculiarly robust form of ideology, resisting for instance Marxism's brave attempts to reclassify world politics in terms of shared class allegiances? Why are people willing to go to war, courting death in defense of nationhood, and why do they agree to do this even when, as in the case of Indonesia, the entity that commands their loyalty is a loosely connected string of islands with no plausible claims to linguistic or cultural unity? Rejecting geographic determinism as inadequate, Anderson defined the nation as "an imagined political community—and imagined as both inherently limited and sovereign" (Anderson 1991, 6). The move from physical to imagined demarcations proved intensely liberating to theoreticians of the state. Anderson and his many followers were able to probe the mechanisms by which people come to think that they belong to something so invisibly put together as a nation, and which, in short, endow the concept of nationhood with meaning. The turn to "imagined communities" made it possible to encompass within a single theoretical frame such disparate manifestations of nationhood as Austria-Hungary,

Indonesia, and the ultimately failed construct of postpartition Pakistan, its brackets not firmly enough welded through a shared Islamic faith to withstand the divisive force of intervening Hindu India.

Print capitalism plays a central role in Anderson's story of nationalism. Newspapers, he argued, exerted a profound pull on social imagination, making it possible for people in far-flung places to read about and react to the same events at the same time. The printed page became the instrument through which people who previously had no connection with each other could now *imagine* that they were part of a single community, experiencing and participating in a single national drama. Readers were bound together by the newspaper's inbuilt clock, which inexorably marked off the days (and, through morning and evening papers, even times of days), juxtaposed happenings from around the world in a collage of adventitiously related events, and rendered them obsolete the very next day with another collection of stories, equally random though united by the same seemingly inevitable logic.

Anderson originally ascribed to the controllers of the printed page an almost unlimited capacity to mobilize nationalism, but in the book's second edition he added a chapter, more Foucauldian in inspiration, on three other institutions of power—the census, the map, and the museum—through which modern states have tried to discipline their citizens' nationalistic imaginations. Through these institutions, enterprising states could manufacture or erase boundaries and histories, connections and divisions. A telling exercise in image making occurred at the fifteenth anniversary celebration of Cambodia's independence in November 1968, in honor of which

> Norodom Sihanouk had a large wood and papier-mâché replica of the great Bayon temple of Angkor displayed in the national sports stadium in Phnom Penh. The replica was exceptionally coarse and crude, but it served its purpose—instant recognizability via a history of colonial-era logoization. "Ah, our Bayon"—but with the memcry of French colonial restorers wholly banished. French-reconstructed Angkor Wat, again in "jigsaw" form, became . . . the central symbol of the successive flags of Sihanouk's royalist, Lon Nol's militarist, and Pol Pot's Jacobin regimes.
>
> (Anderson 1991, 183)

Nationalism as "logoization," imagination overwritten by image making—all possible, so Anderson argued, through a means of production that permitted images to be removed from context, made infinitely reproducible, and so implanted in people's minds as seedlings of national fellow-feeling.

This account of political community building strikingly resonates with work in science and technology studies that attempts to explain how scientific representations of the natural world acquire a hold on people's beliefs. No one perhaps has done more to illuminate this process than Bruno Latour, the French ethnographer and philosopher of science, for whom the investigation of scientific knowledge in the making has long been coextensive with trying to understand what gives scientific images and inscriptions their special persuasive power (Latour and Woolgar 1979). In one of his best-known expositions of the subject, Latour argues that the difference between "savage," or prescientific, and "civilized," or scientific, knowledge lies not so much in how people perceive reality but in the ability of modern science to *circulate* its perceptions by rendering them "mobile, flat, reproducible, still, and of varying scales" (Latour 1990, 45). Latour called the resulting inscriptions "immutable mobiles" because—unlike the *objects* that science observes (countries, planets, microbes)—*representations* of them (maps, photographic plates, Petri dishes) can move around in fixed forms created by the exertions of scientists.

To this point, there is a startling family resemblance between Anderson's logoized nations and Latour's immobilized inscriptions: both move, both can be mobilized, both are torn away from the specific circumstances of their production, gaining greater power through this erasure of history and context. Yet the two writers are profoundly at odds in their understanding of the forces that create mobility. For Anderson, capital is the prime mover. Without its support, states could not control the printing presses that produce the maps and images that impress themselves, in turn, on the awaiting minds of protonationalist citizens. Latour turns this argument on its head, insisting that it is the mundane craftsmanship of visualization that moves things and people, and so gives rise to power. In passages that read almost as if they were written to counter Anderson, or equally Foucault, Latour says that we continually misunderstand the relationship between science and power

> because we take for granted that there exist, somewhere in society, macroactors that naturally dominate the scene: Corporation, State, Productive Forces, Cultures, Imperialism, "Mentalités," etc. . . . Far from being the key to the understanding of science and technology, these entities are the very things a new understanding of science aad technology should explain. The large-scale actors to which sociologists of science are keen to attach "interests" are immaterial in practice so long as precise mechanisms to explain their origin or extraction and their changes of scale have not been proposed.
>
> (Latour 1990, 56–57)

"Capitalism," for Latour then becomes a special case of accumulation—that of money:

> Thus capitalism is not to be used to explain the evolution of science and technology. It seems to me that it should be quite the contrary. Once science and technology are rephrased in terms of immutable mobiles it might be possible to explain economic capitalism as another process of mobilization and conscription.
>
> (Latour 1990, 59)

Latour's commitment therefore is to elaborating the details of scientific practice (not, characteristically, of science funding), the workaday routines of sampling and observation, recording and classification through which an entire Amazonian forest, for example, can be transformed into a tractable, movable catalog of soil types and plant varieties, and ultimately even a theory of causation to explain whether the forest is advancing or retreating (Latour 1995).

Does the aggregated power of money control the technologies of representation, which then function as levers of ideology? Or does mastery of the craftwork of representation cumulatively give rise to power, lodged, as Latour (1990, 59) memorably puts it, in "centers of calculation" that in effect *make* the world by circulating particular interpretations of it? Or is the relationship between image and imagination altogether more complex, requiring visual stimuli to resonate with cultures of interpretation that help define their ultimate meanings in time and place? Let us turn to an actual case. In this chapter we will investigate more exactly how a single image, that of planet Earth, became an inhabitor of Western consciousness and an icon, more particularly, of U.S. environmentalism. In doing so, we will not (following a typically Latourian program) seek chiefly to retrace the networks of rocket and satellite production, nor the labyrinths of the military-industrial establishment, that importantly enabled the making of the original image. Rather, we will focus on a less easily encapsulated dimension of the story, that of the image's transmission, uptake, and interpretation within disparate communities of discourse and action.[7] Unlike Anderson and Latour, both of whom link their studies of power primarily to the technologies of image making and circulation, I aim to look more closely at the imagination of the viewers—and the self-conscious consumers—of this potent symbol of human and natural interconnectedness. Without the participation of these ordinarily unsung actors, images would not be invested with the meanings that motivate political action.

Viewing Planet Earth

American commentators have frequently written of the transforming impact of the picture of Earth suspended in space, as captured on film by successive *Apollo* mission astronauts. The late astronomer Carl Sagan, whose televised program *Cosmos* won him something akin to cult status in the 1980s, was one of those who helped to popularize this theme:

> While almost everyone is taught that the Earth is a sphere with all of us somehow glued to it by gravity, the reality of our circumstance did not really begin to sink in until the famous frame-filling *Apollo* photograph of the whole Earth—the one taken by the *Apollo 17* astronauts on the last journey of humans to the Moon.
>
> (Sagan 1994, 5)

Sagan selected a particular image as his icon, the one that shows Earth in the round, with no clouds concealing (to a culture familiar with conventions of mapping) the readily imaginable outlines of states in Arabia and the horn of Africa.[8] Environmentalists as a rule are inclined to agree with Sagan's judgment about the importance of that image. Writing in 1990, the ecologist Daniel Botkin said:

> It is more than 20 years since the phrase "spaceship Earth" was coined and made popular and 20 years since the Apollo astronauts took this famous photograph of the Earth from space—a blue globe, enveloped by swirling white clouds, against a black background—creating an image of a small island of life floating in an ocean of empty space.
>
> (Botkin 1990, 5)

A remarkably similar point was made some years earlier by the World Commission on Environment and Development (WCED) in its influential report, *Our Common Future*:

> In the middle of the 20th century, we saw our planet from space for the first time. Historians may eventually find that this vision had a greater impact on thought than did the Copernican revolution of the 16th century, which upset humans' self-image by revealing that the Earth is not the centre of the universe. From space, we see a small and fragile ball dominated not by human activity and edifice but by a pattern of clouds, oceans, greenery, and soils. Humanity's inability to fit its activities into that pattern is changing planetary systems fundamentally.
>
> (World Commission on Environment and Development 1987, 308)

The idea of a "scientific revolution" held particular appeal for others who commented on the *Apollo* picture. Laurence Tribe, at one time a critic of technology's instrumental rationality and later a constitutional scholar at Harvard Law School, remarked that this image—"the earth as a dramatically finite and surprisingly delicate blue-green globe" (Tribe 1973, 620)—had ushered us toward "the fourth discontinuity." This was a moment that displaced the human ego by making it conscious of the physical limitations of the place it inhabits. This decentering effect, Tribe and others have said, was on a par with three great intellectual discontinuities of the past: the Copernican revolution, which displaced the earth from the center of the universe; the Darwinian revolution, which displaced human beings from the pinnacle of the tree of creation; and the Freudian revolution, which exposed the workings of the unconscious mind and made humankind aware that we are not, after all, masters in our own house.

Continuing the theme of scientific revolutions, some suggested that the picture of our lonely planet brought about nothing less than a paradigm shift in ways of thinking about how the world works. Lynton Caldwell, a leading figure in the new environmentalism of the 1970s, explicitly took this position:

> The change from the belief that the sun, moon, and stars revolved around the earth to the Copernican view of the earth's place in the solar system was a paradigm shift. The change marked by [the aftermath of *Apollo*] is from the

view of an earth unlimited in abundance and created for man's exclusive use to a concept of the earth as a domain of life or biosphere for which mankind is a temporary resident custodian. . . . The newer view sees it as an ultimately unified system . . . that may supply man's needs as long as he observes the system's rules.

(Caldwell 1990, 21)

Elsewhere, Caldwell linked the image to the internationalization of environmental policy:

The first landing on the moon on 20 July 1969 and pictures of the Earth from outer space brought to many people a realization that their environment had many of the characteristics of a closed system. "Spaceship Earth" became a metaphor, and "Only One Earth" was the motto of the 1972 United Nations Conference on the Human Environment.

(Caldwell 1992, 67)

Another author, Joseph Campbell, suggested that the making and broadcasting of the *Apollo 17* trip had "transformed, deepened, and extended human consciousness to a degree and in a manner that amount to the opening of a new spiritual era" (Campbell 1972, 239).

All these observations credit the planetary image with inducing a sudden, radical, and far-ranging shift in political consciousness, as human beings redefined their understanding of what it means to live together on the earth. But the widespread acceptance of this reading by environmentalists runs counter to much of what we know about cultural responses to imagery. Whether in the history of science or in the history of art, it seems that images become persuasive only when ways of looking at them have been carefully prepared in advance, through the creation of a stylized visual idiom or an interpretive tradition that knows how to respond to particular types of images (see, for example, Jones and Galison 1998; Alpers 1983; also Sachs 1994). The meaning of pictures is inseparable from the context that supplies the idioms of interpretation. What, then, were the historical, political, and cultural circumstances in which the vision of Planet Earth acquired its now-canonical readings? Did the image give rise to demonstrably new forms of understanding about the environment and associated concepts of governance, or did it simply reinforce older habits and patterns of political association?

Narrative traditions

Many of the themes invoked in connection with the *Apollo* image predated the photographs that gave them unforgettable embodiment. In particular, reflections on the earth's finiteness, its fragility, its limited resources, the interconnectedness of its physical and biological systems, and the flimsiness of its geopolitical boundaries were all current in Western thought and writing well before the astronauts of *Apollo 17* brought back the most famous icon of the floating planet.[9] Thus, the maverick American engineer and inventor R. Buckminster Fuller (1969), who prided himself on having viewed the earth imaginatively before there were astronauts, coined the term *Spaceship Earth* to describe humanity's flight on a superbly designed, self-contained vehicle lacking only an intelligible operating manual.[10] Fuller's metaphor quickly became popular in enlightened political circles. The influential British economist and environmentalist Barbara Ward (1966; see also Ward and Dubos 1972) borrowed the term, finding it a congenial hook on which to hang her own ideas about transnational harmony, sustainable development, and the need for global redistribution of wealth. Ward's friend and philosophical ally, the noted liberal Democrat Adlai Stevenson, then U.S. Ambassador to the United Nations, observed in a speech before the UN Economic and Social Council in July 1965, "We travel together, passengers on a little spaceship, dependent on its vulnerable resources of air and soil; all committed for our safety to its security and peace; preserved from annihilation only by the care, the work and, I will say, the love we give our fragile craft" (Stevenson 1979, 821).

Although Fuller and others spoke of the earth as a spaceship, it was the University of Michigan economist Kenneth Boulding who explicitly connected the planet's roundness with a global imagination of the environmental predicament (Boulding 1966, 3–14). Air travel, Boulding observed, had begun to accustom people since World War II with "the notion of the spherical earth and a closed sphere of human activity" (Boulding 1966, 3).[11] The sense of the planet as an enclosed system had gradually replaced the image of the frontier, with its wide open spaces and promise of endless resources. The new era, Boulding argued, would require a new kind of economic discipline: a "spaceman economy," in which "man must find his place in a cyclical ecological system," replacing the earlier "cowboy economy," which countenanced "reckless, exploitative, romantic, and violent behavior," especially with respect to resource consumption (Boulding 1966, 9).

Others, too, had begun to note that the triad of population, consumption, and pollution might place irreversible stresses on the planet's health. Among the earliest and most influential voices in the United States was that of Rachel Carson, whose 1962 book *Silent Spring* offered a part-scientific, part-elegiac exposition of how the indiscriminate use of chemical pesticides was silencing bird populations throughout North America and gravely threatening all earthly life (Carson 1962). The Club of Rome, a prestigious association of scientists and intellectuals, went further. Using newly developed techniques of computer modeling, its controversial report, *The Limits to Growth*, predicted a sudden and drastic collapse of the Earth's economic, social, and environmental systems (Meadows et al. 1972). Despite many methodological criticisms, the report's catastrophist vision persisted as one of the enduring themes of modern environmentalism (Cotgrove 1982; Ashley 1983; Bloomfield 1986).

Perceptions of the earth as a closed system inspired less calamitous scientific stories as well. Most widely discussed perhaps is the so-called Gaia hypothesis, originated in the early 1970s by James Lovelock, a physicist working for the National Aeronautics and Space Administration (NASA), and further developed with Lynn Margulis, a microbiologist known for her theory of the origins of eukaryotic cells. Versions of the hypothesis range from a weak (and uncontroversial) form that merely posits complex linkages between biological and nonbiological activity at the earth's surface to stronger claims that the earth's atmosphere maintains a steady state for the express purpose of sustaining life, and that biological organisms actively manipulate their environment to this end (Lovelock 1979; Margulis and Lovelock 1976; Schneider 1991). It is not the validity or theoretical coherence of Lovelock's and Margulis's scientific ideas that is significant for our purposes, but rather their integrative, planetary vision. An outgrowth of NASA's interest in the possible existence of life on Mars, the Gaia hypothesis illustrates how the technology of space exploration fostered a global science of biogeochemical interactions. Even before the space age allowed humanity actually to look the earth in the face, scientific imaginations were constructing narratives on a global scale about what was happening at the earth-atmosphere interface.

If the conquest of flight ushered in an age of environmental claustrophobia, it also made geopolitical divisions seem more vulnerable. By the late 1940s, the world's major powers were already arrayed into the sharp dualities of the Cold War. The earth as a globe dominated the visual renditions of this new political dispensation. The standard view adopted by the superpowers looked down on the world from the North Pole. From this standpoint, image makers were free to decide only how much of the Southern Hemisphere they would include in their field of vision. A 1947 report sponsored by the Council on Foreign Relations, for example, displayed the polar perspective as adapted from an official chart used by the U.S. Air Force. The map was cut off at the 30th parallel, showing the top of north Africa and fringes of Iran and India, but nothing at all of Latin America. "Strategists," the report observed, "term the area between the 30th and 65th parallels the key zone since all modern wars have started there" (Baldwin 1947). The same projection appears as a logo to this day on publications of Harvard University's Belfer Center for Science and International Affairs, an institution whose identity was molded during the Cold War. Image and imagination, still powerfully fused, deny the emergence of a more complex, less bipolar political order.

Yet the implications of the global perspective have always been thoroughly ambiguous. The view from the pole could be read, on one hand, as an invitation to strengthen state sovereignty. A 1948 report by the President's Air Policy Commission took just this tack, using the polar projection to underscore the threat of aerial war. Surveying the world from a position near Point Barrow, Alaska, and looking 7,000 miles along the earth's surface in all directions, the Commission graphically illustrated the emergence of "a new element through which this country may be attacked—the air." The report called for a stronger air force as "the best conceivable defense" against air attack (President's Air Policy Commission 1948, 11). But the polar gaze equally supported messages of peaceful coexistence in the postwar world, as evidenced by the United Nations logo adopted in the same period. Although the North Pole again occupied the image's center, no nation, however far from the central viewing point, was excluded from the UN's encompassing vision. Even Australia appears outlined in full at the outer margins of the UN world.

Finally, no account of the interpretive conventions that have grown up around the earth image would be complete without the voices of the astronauts who saw as eyewitnesses what the rest of humanity experienced only through pictures and television. Unwitting seers, confronting a vision for which little in life had prepared them, these observers tell what it was like to see the earth before anyone else had appropriated the images. Some were stirred to uncharacteristic eloquence. William Anders, a member of the December 1968 *Apollo 8* mission that for the first time saw the earth whole, set the tone for many later interpreters. Imagining the earth as a "little Christmas-tree ornament against an infinite black backdrop of space," Anders commented on its "fragility and finiteness":

> I find it somewhat ironic that we went up there for the moon, but probably it was the Earth and the perspective of it that most impressed hard-bitten test pilots like us—and I guess the rest of the world—the most. Because the pictures of the first Earthrise and the first full Earth floating in space, I think, have been a major contribution in helping people get a better feeling for the Earth's place in our lives and in the universe. You realize that Earth is about as physically significant as one grain of sand on a beach. But it's our only home.
>
> (In Folger, Richardson, and Zimmer 1994, 38)

One recognizes in Anders's groping phrases some familiar strains of contemporary environmentalist discourse: fragility, finiteness, insignificance, the unavoidable dependence of human life on this planet ("our only home"). Yet barely three and a half years later, when NASA was winding up the first phase of lunar exploration, the "hard-bitten" edge was back, and some members of the *Apollo 17* crew seemed able to take the spectacular earthscape for granted. Eugene Cernan records the following conversation with his fellow-traveler Harrison "Jack" Schmitt:

C: "Oh, man—Hey, Jack, just stop. You owe yourself 30 seconds to look up over the South Massif and look at the Earth."
S: "What? The Earth?!"
C: "Just look up there."
S: "Aaah! You've seen one Earth, you've seen them all." (Chaikin 1994)

If even astronauts on the moon could so quickly accustom themselves to one of the twentieth century's grandest displays, then it hardly seems probable that the rest of humanity, preoccupied with innumerable local cares and conflicts, was drawn by the image to an all-new, enduring global ecoconsciousness. Did its mere dissemination—as capitalist logo or scientific "immutable mobile"—compel people to reimagine their political affiliations on a worldwide scale? Not so. As we will see, connections between the global image and an imagined global community evolved along more intricate pathways, as human actors and institutions strove in disparate ways to assimilate, or exploit, the photographic evidence of their common destiny. Associated shifts from local or national to global environmental thinking—although they *can* be documented—have been neither seamless nor smooth, but rather subtle, sporadic, partial, and unevenly distributed among the world's political communities.

Varieties of global experience

Global environmental consciousness, I am suggesting, did not coalesce all at once in response to a striking visual stimulus, but took shape gradually in diverse domains of social and political practice during the final decades of the twentieth century. Strands of increasing global awareness can be traced in the discourses of risk, politics, commerce, and ethics. In each context, we observe a selective uptake of themes prevalent in older narratives of earthwatching, but reinforced and given new persuasive power through association with the *Apollo* photographs.

Framing risks globally

Most observers of American environmental politics agree that something happened to alter its character in the decade roughly marked by the publication of *Silent Spring* in 1962 and the celebration of the first Earth Day, a nationwide event involving some 300,000 citizens, on April 22, 1970. Often termed the *new environmentalism*, the movement born in this period of ferment diverged from earlier forms of environmental activism in its focus on people and their habitats rather than on the preservation of nature for its own sake. It was founded, according to one analyst, on "a broader conception of the place of man in the biosphere, a more sophisticated understanding of that relationship, and a note of crisis that was greater and broader than it had been in the earlier conservation movement" (McCormick 1989, 48).

Its targets, however, were initially local. They concerned first and foremost the effects of pollution on common people's homes and lives. Rachel Carson's ground-breaking vision, as noted earlier, took as its central theme the harms caused by pervasive use of chemical pesticides. Although she imagined a whole world deprived of birdsong (her book began with a fable of poisoned landscapes and dying animals and vegetation), some of her most telling vignettes involved ordinary citizens reporting on changes in their immediate surroundings: the disappearance of robins in one town, the decimation of swallows in another. These local insults added up to a problem of concededly national proportions. In 1970, President Nixon ordered the creation of the Environmental Protection Agency largely on the ground that a new organization was needed to coordinate a nation-wide fight against pollution. But local issues continued to predominate in environmental politics. In 1978, for example, toxic chemicals found in the basements of homes in the Love Canal area of Niagara Falls, New York, precipitated an intense flurry of pollution-centered legislative and regulatory activity (see for example Levine 1982). This and similar episodes fueled the era's most powerful form of environmental mobilization, the NIMBY, a social movement whose tightly bounded, *local* imagination was synonymous with the slogan "not in my backyard." Chemical pollution of communities remained a guiding theme of U.S. environmentalism well into the 1980s.

It was not until the later 1980s that a global conception of environmental protection rooted itself in Western consciousness. Almost imperceptibly, the causes and extent of environmental degradation (for example, deforestation, desertification, ozone depletion) began to be defined across political domains far larger than individual communities and even more encompassing than nation states. Attention began to shift from end-of-pipe controls on specific polluting facilities to questions of prevention and lifestyle change. A new term—*sustainability*—came into common use in policy discourse, bridging what had previously seemed an irreconcilable contradiction between environmental protection and human development. Appropriately enough, the book that heralded this new era was not the work of a single author with a distinctively personal vision, but of an international committee of experts, the World Commission on Environment and Development, chaired by Norway's prime minister Gro Harlem Brundtland. Both in its title and by explicit reference (as quoted above), *Our Common Future* conveyed, and helped crystallize, a sense of the whole human condition, framed by the planetary image and global in its prescriptive scope. No longer would it be sufficient for environmental activism to concentrate its energies primarily on the invasion of individual backyards by chemical pollution.

Global environmental politics

From NIMBY to a global politics of the environment, however, was no easy step. The transition arguably began with the age of space exploration, but its progress is not yet complete. That the earth image impels many observers to "think globally" has been apparent ever since the early satellite launches. Barbara Ward, for example, imagined the solidarity that U.S. astronauts must feel with their Soviet counterparts and speculated that their feat would erase the Cold War's central political conflict:

> When the astronauts spin through more than a dozen sunrises and sunsets in a single day and night; when the whole globe lies below them with California one minute and Japan the next; when, as they return from space, they feel spontaneoulsy, with the first Soviet spaceman: "How beautiful it is, *our* earth"; it is inconceivable that no modification of consciousness or imagination occurs, no sense that quarrels are meaningless before the majestic yet vulnerable reality of a single planet carrying a single human species through infinite space.
>
> (Ward 1966, 146)

Her comments interestingly foreshadowed Anders's testimony that the earth is "as physically significant as one grain of sand" and yet "it's our only home."

Perhaps self-consciously echoing Anders, Ward and her distinguished environ-mentalist colleague Rene Dubos published a book in 1972 with the title *Only One Earth*. This became the official theme of that year's Stockholm conference on the environment. Carl Sagan in turn gave the image an explicitly political spin, while reiterating the theme of humanity's insignificance:

We are too small and *our statecraft too feeble* to be seen by a spacecraft between the Earth and the Moon. From this vantage point, our obsession with nationalism is nowhere in evidence. The Apollo pictures of the whole Earth conveyed to multitudes something well known to astronomers: on the scale of worlds—to say nothing of stars or galaxies—humans are inconsequential, a thin film of life on an obscure and solitary lump of rock and metal.

(Sagan 1994, 5–6; emphasis added)

The World Commission on Environment and Development similarly juxtaposed the transitory geopolitical constructions of the globe against an enduring ecolog-ical view: "From space, we see a small and fragile ball dominated not by human activity and edifice but by a pattern of clouds, oceans, greenery, and soils" (World Commission on Environment and Development 1987, 308).

While astronauts, astronomers, and international experts identified the earth image with coexistence and political interdependence, the use and enjoyment of environmental resources remained for many other actors tightly bound to national interests. A case in point was President Ronald Reagan's astonishing and emphatic rejection of the draft Law of the Sea (LOS) convention following his election in 1980. Here was an accord governing the oceans that had enjoyed bipartisan support in the Nixon, Ford, and Carter administrations and had seemed virtually ready for adoption by the late 1970s. It presented U.S. negotiators with an appar-ently uncomplicated trade-off: increased navigational freedom, simplifying and counteracting a patchwork of jurisdictional claims by coastal states, in return for a decrease in the right to mine seabed resources, including manganese nodules, which developing countries saw as the common heritage of mankind (Sebenius 1984). For those committed to the negotiation, the two issues were inextricably linked. Concession on seabed mining was the necessary price for avoiding the expanding territorial ambitions of coastal states. Yet as the negotiations went on for decades, fissures appeared in the U.S. position corresponding to changing perceptions of costs and benefits among some of the parties to the negotiation. American mining interests, in particular, came to believe that the draft treaty was penalizing them more than was warranted by corresponding gains on the side of navigation. As support crumbled for a comprehensive solution, combining navi-gation and mining, a new Republican administration began to think the unthink-able and pulled the United States out of the almost-completed negotiations.

The fate of the LOS conference in the 1980s can be seen in retrospect as a triumph of persistent nationalist claims to global environmental resources over a nascent internationalist worldview. This point was well understood by Richard Darman, vice chair of the U.S. delegation to the 1977 session of the third LOS conference and a perceptive participant-observer of the treaty process. In an article in *Foreign Affairs*, Darman argued that the conference was being driven, to the detriment of U.S. interests, both pragmatic and ideological, by a community of

> internationalist lawyer-codifiers. The internationalists' tendency to favor collective over individual action is combined with the codifiers' tendency to wish to see the world in neat static terms. Above and beyond practical considerations, there is an aesthetic antipathy toward the "disaster" of nonuniformity, and a general distrust of the possible benignness of self-regulating, dynamic processes.
>
> (Darman 1978, 381)

Darman conceded that foiling the internationalist vision of a single regime for navigational and seabed governance carried a risk. The oceans occupying two-thirds of the earth's surface might be "carved up" along geopolitical lines in ways that would benefit developed countries over developing ones. Political boundaries would in effect be drawn where none had previously existed. This, in turn, would create a problem of equity that might affect U.S. strategic interests. But this issue, Darman urged, should be addressed on its own terms through mechanisms such as loan guarantees and technology transfer. International equity did not require the United States to recognize the oceans as the common property of humankind or to countenance the development of new international institutions whose mandates would inevitably erode national sovereignty. Equity problems, in other words, could be redressed without having to accept the case for global ownership or control of the oceans.

When the Clinton administration signed a revised LOS convention in July 1994, the official explanation declared a victory for free-market principles over objectionable centralized planning and for sovereignty over loss of national control. A government fact sheet on LOS posted on the World Wide Web notes that the United States has won a guaranteed seat on key committees, increased power to block adverse decisions, and credit for exploration already undertaken by American companies (U.S. Department of State 1996). Clearly, framing the seas as an economic resource ran counter to the planetary imagination. A view founded on the necessity—even the rightness—of competition among nations blocked the emergence of transnational management institutions and a genuinely global politics of resource allocation.

A similar resurgence of national sovereignty can be observed under the Convention on Biological Diversity (CBD), even though this treaty, too, was initially conceived as an instrument for effectuating allegedly global environmental interests. By the late 1980s, alarm about rapid, worldwide extinctions of species and associated activism by leading biologists had created a demand for international action to protect the earth's scarce biological resources (Takacs 1996). In response, the United Nations Environment Program (UNEP) initiated in 1988 a series of expert and intergovernmental deliberations with the aim of preparing a legal instrument for the conservation and sustainable use of biodiversity. Consistent with these goals, the convention sought to address economic and social concerns along with scientific ones. The experts convened by UNEP were asked to take into account "the need to share costs and benefits between developed and developing countries" as well as "ways and means to support innovation by local people."

The text of the CBD was adopted in Nairobi in May 1992 and opened for signature in June of the same year at the United Nations Conference on Environment and Development (the Rio "Earth Summit"). It entered into force in December 1993, ninety days after the thirtieth ratification. From the beginning, however, international efforts to balance conservation against development, equity against economics, and global management against national sovereignty proved to be highly contentious. A test of the convention's attempted global framing of biodiversity arose in 1999 at a meeting in Cartagena, Colombia, to approve an international biosafety protocol governing genetically modified organisms. Acrimony between developing countries and major grain exporters caused the meeting to break down without any agreement being reached. A new round of negotiations in Montreal in early 2000 proved more productive, although the agreement reached there represented more a working conpromise among contrary interests than a global accord on basic presumptions. As in the case of LOS, environmentalism's global ambitions bowed to pressure from economic interests defined at the national level.

One of the few environmental regimes in which the political ideal of "One Earth" arguably has come closer to fruition is that governing climate change (popularly better known as "global warming"). Here, there has been a convergence between the *scientific* construction of a problem that transcends national boundaries (see Miller 2001) and a *normative* construction that recognizes the rights of developing as well as developed countries to be protected against the worst consequences of greenhouse-gas accumulation in the atmosphere. Even on the scientific side, considerable work was needed to define climate change as something other than the sum of local weather patterns—in other words, as a problem of "whole-earth" dimensions. Prerequisites included the formation of the Intergovernmental Panel on Climate Change and its hard-fought acquisition of credibility as a body capable of representing the best scientific judgment with respect to climate change. This evolutionary story stands markedly at odds with the conventional account of the earth image as herald and harbinger of a sudden paradigm shift in environmental consciousness. The emergence of climate change as a global phenomenon, moreover, coincided, as we will see, with the appearance of an ethical discourse that had no precursor in the politics of either LOS or biodiversity.

Commerce's global ambition

U.S. environmentalists were not alone in sizing up the symbolic potential of the earth image. The picture of the planet became almost an instant classic in the visual repertoire of advertising, at first retaining its connections to themes of environmental stewardship, but gradually shedding these in favor of something more like "universalism" or simply "global reach."[12] Commerce, environment, and the earth in space were first linked together in 1968 in the *Whole Earth Catalog*, an entrepreneurial venture that both articulated and capitalized on the values of the new environmental movement. The cover picture showed the North American land mass almost entirely obstructed by a large white cloud; below appeared the caption "THE UNIVERSE: from planet Earth on a sunny day." Inside, the *Catalog*'s offerings emphasized environmental restoration, community building, simplicity, authenticity, and medical self-help. Supplements published over the next five years all carried the same cover picture accompanied by the same message. A new version planned for the millennium continued several themes of the late 1960s. Consumers were still offered "tools for producing knowledge, reporting and broadcasting the news as you see it, and creating communities according to your own values and ideals" (Rheingold 1994).

Contemporary advertisers of services and products no longer link globality so explicitly to environment-friendly lifestyles. Instead, the planetary symbol tends to stress the deployer's capacity to move people and products (and, in the case of television, images) effortlessly around the globe. Not surprisingly, the picture has become an important property for CNN, the cable news service that built its empire by bringing viewers face to face with events from the furthest reaches of the earth—with an immediacy prized equally in the White House and in the head-quarters of some of the United States's most intransigent enemies. Not only for CNN, but for many other advertisers, it is the imagined shrinking of time and distance between the consumer and the object of consumption that has become the image's most alluring message.

Advertisements also illustrate the infinite interpretive flexibility of an image that has achieved iconic status throughout Western culture. Just as the Mona Lisa, the world's most famous painting, has been adapted, interpreted, and sometimes subverted, to suit every taste,[13] so too has the planet's portrait been manipulated in varied ways to create a universally accessible visual counterpoint to messages of persuasion and seduction. One commonplace strategy is to focus on the part of the globe on which the advertiser's commercial activities are specifically targeted. Another is to superimpose the image on something else—for example, a burning, spherical candle or a pair of clasped hands—thereby hybridizing the instantly comprehensible sign of global interconnection with other, less normalized messages (energy crisis, regional business partnerships, company logos, and the like), which then are empowered to travel, as it were, on the shoulders of the earth.

These advertising pictures do not claim the power of direct representation, the seemingly literal transcription of a new reality celebrated by environmental writers and scientists. Consider, once again, Sagan's evocative reading of the *Apollo 17* image, in which he first zoomed in on its dense, geopolitical meanings before pulling back (as noted above) to a more abstracted, apolitical, indeed dehumanized gaze:

> There's Antarctica at what Americans and Europeans so readily regard as the bottom, and then all of Africa stretching up above it: You can see Ethiopia, Tanzania, and Kenya, where the earliest humans lived. At top right are

Saudi Arabia and what Europeans call the Near East. Just barely peeking out at the top is the Mediterranean Sea, around which so much of our global civilization emerged. You can make out the blue of the ocean, the yellow-red of the Sahara and the Arabian desert, the brown-green of forest and grassland.

(Sagan 1994, 5)

In commercial discourse, by contrast, Earth has no fixed, human-made coordinates. It is, as often as not, a dream image, as in an advertisement for Thai Airways, which shows an incredibly remote planet held at the eye of a huge silvery needle against a black velvet sky and a ribbon of deep purple, the advertiser's signature color. Through their very ubiquity, however, these modified pictures reinforce the status of the underlying "original" image as a common cultural resource; they appear and disappear as figments of our common imagination, even as they cater to our culturally calibrated desires.

A planetary ethics

Modern environmentalism includes at its core a widely acknowledged, if only imperfectly realized, ethical imperative to renegotiate human beings' relationship with nature in the light of new scientific understandings. More than a generation ago, Boulding observed in his article on Spaceship Earth that we were as yet "very far from having made the moral, political, and psychological adjustments which are implied in [the] transition from the illimitable plane to the closed sphere" (Boulding 1966, 4). Now, more than two decades after the first landing on the moon and the first photographic portrayals of the earth from space, it is possible to identify at least three strains of ethical discourse that appear specifically to derive their force from a global, as opposed to a national or local, framing of humanity's environmental predicament.

The first is a gradual extension of the precautionary principle into transnational environmental policy. This legal precept originated in German law as one of five fundamental principles governing environmental decisions. Briefly stated, the precautionary principle asks for restraint on human activities that could harm the environment when there is not enough evidence to determine for sure whether such harm will occur. American environmental law has opted on the whole for a seemingly more pragmatic, risk-based approach that allows development to proceed when the benefits are calculated to exceed the probable harm.[14]

With respect to environmental hazards of global scope, however, the utilitarian calculus of risks and benefits is harder to sustain than in the context of localized pollution problems from a waste dump or chemical factory. Uncertainties loom larger, and, within the contested frameworks of global politics, practices of analysis and reassurance cannot be as readily stabilized through well-worn channels of expert deliberation. The result has been to introduce what some international theorists have termed a *bias shift* away from problem solving toward a set of actions geared more toward prevention (Ruggie 1986). For example, as Karen Litfin has argued, the Montreal accord on the control of ozone-depleting substances would not have adopted nearly so stringent a set of targets had it not been for the discovery of the Antarctic ozone hole, which atmospheric science had not predicted and for which there was no obvious nonanthropogenic explanation (Litfin 1994).

The second strand of an emergent global ethical discourse centers on the idea of sustainability and more specifically on concepts of stewardship for future generations. The World Commission on Environment and Development built the norm of stewardship into its very definition of sustainability in *Our Common Future*, endorsing only those patterns of development that would leave future generations no worse off than their forebears in the present. Lynton Caldwell, for one, explicitly ties this shift to the *Apollo* image, which in his telling induced a move "from the view of an earth unlimited in abundance and created for man's exclusive use to a concept of the earth as a domain of life or biosphere for which mankind is a temporary resident custodian" (Caldwell 1990, 21). The elaboration of intergenerational ethics as a legal principle likewise rests on a recognition of "the planet" as the appropriate spatial framing for sustainable environmental action. Edith Brown Weiss's important treatise on the legal foundations of intergenerational ethics begins on a note familiar to all earthwatchers: "The human species inhabits a small, relatively new, and so far as we know, unique planet— Earth. It is also a fragile planet" (Weiss 1989, 1).

The third ethical strand has to do with the obligations of the developed North to the developing South in matters of environmental policy. The recognition of such an obligation is not in itself new, as is evident from our earlier discussion of the Law of the Sea negotiations. Thus, even while espousing a position of unilateralism and national self-interest, Darman rejected the prospect of a highly inequitable regime for exploiting global seabed resources. Ethics, however, was embedded within the discourse of rational choice, where it became simply one more item to tote up along with other national interests. Acting ethically was no more important in principle than respecting the needs of the mining industry or of commercial shipping. Efforts to treat equity as a higher-order variable within LOS proved unsuccessful. Indeed, in his analysis of the U.S. withdrawal from LOS, the negotiation theorist James Sebenius has argued that developing nations' attempt to promote a supervening, *transnational* ethical discourse—that of the New International Economic Order (NIEO)—was a prime reason for the formation of a "blocking coalition" and the eventual breakdown of the conference (Sebenius 1991).

Claims about equity have received a more sympathetic hearing under regimes that have (unlike LOS and CBD) successfully constructed environmental problems on a transnational level, most notably ozone and climate change. Thus, an Indian environmental group, the Centre for Science and Environment, successfully deconstructed the tacit normative assumptions incorporated within early efforts to create objective measures of the "global warming potential" of greenhouse gases (Agarwal and Narain 1991). Perhaps more important, the very kinds of equity arguments that were rejected by Northern nations when put forward by the South under the label *NIEO* now seem to carry greater moral as well as political weight. Terms like *vulnerability* and *equity* have entered the language of global environmental accords. Both the ozone and climate change regimes explicitly recognize the special economic and ethical claims of developing nations through legal provisions ensuring delayed implementation, funding, and technology transfer. It is tempting to conclude that framing pieces of the natural world in global terms—such as the *ozone hole* or *climate*—has facilitated an ethical discourse that also operates at the global level, without needing to be subordinated to the older calculus of national interests.

Seeing things together

The power of words to compel action has been a subject for philosophical and political analysis from Plato down to modern times. The power of images may be no less profound, especially in this era of mass visual communication, but it has yet to receive the same sustained scrutiny from social theorists. My object in this chapter has been to trace the complex pathways by which one image—that of planet Earth—has come to inhabit our political consciousness as an icon of global environmentalism.

A closer look at the image's reception suggests that its connections with environmental thought and action have been anything but straightforward. The picture, to begin with, picked up and reinforced themes of the earth's fragility and finiteness that had begun to percolate through policy discourses decades before the space age began. In this way, it may have subtly helped to shift the perception of environmental risk from issues of purely local scope to longer-term concerns for human survival. Yet although it was appropriated early on to support arguments for global environmental governance (witness the "Only One Earth" theme of the 1972 Stockholm conference), such thinking failed to move entrenched national interests in resource management regimes ranging from seabed mining to the protection of biodiversity. The image's widespread exploitation by commercial enterprises has underscored its iconic properties but arguably blunted its moral and political connotations. Possibly the most important consequence to flow from the planetary image is the visual anchor it has provided for emerging, globally articulated ethical concepts, such as the precautionary principle, sustainability, and intergenerational equity.

Global stewardship remains nonetheless a deeply contested concept. Battles over the Law of the Sea and biodiversity throw into sharp relief some of the dangers that people around the world—from the South as well as the North—perceive in allowing environmental risks, and their control, to be framed globally. The idea of international governance, especially in matters of natural resource management, carries for many the threatening specters of bureaucratic inflexibility, loss of sovereignty, and even new forms of colonial domination drawing their legitimacy from science. The planetary image, moreover, conveys a serene (some might say contemptuous) disregard for the human condition. Not only does it appear to erase the territorial claims of nation states, but it also renders invisible the day-to-day environmental insults suffered by billions of the world's poorest citizens: dirty air, polluted water, inadequate sanitation, infectious diseases, damaged crops, loss of green spaces, and the decay of built environments. Indeed, people themselves are eliminated from this image of environmentalism, as in some of the darker fantasies of ecofascism. As a dazzling offshoot of the twentieth century's most destructive technological impulses, the photograph that preeminently symbolizes planetary togetherness ironically undermines its own authority in the eyes of skeptics. It promises an imagined community as encompassing as the earth itself, but is this a community in which those without the power to patrol the heavens, to map and perhaps to devastate the earth, can ever meaningfully participate?

I would like nevertheless to end this chapter on a note of mild optimism. Seldom in the course of preparing an academic publication have I encountered so much spontaneous interest among my U.S. conversation partners as in discussing the topic of this piece. Almost everyone I spoke with, it seemed, had his or her own favorite associations with the Earth image; many admitted to possessing a variant of it on some prized but mundane object, such as a T-shirt, a tote bag, or a poster. If general circulation models and integrated assessments belong to the "high" scientific language of global environmentalism, then for most Americans the picture of planet Earth surely belongs to its vernacular. It is not, if it ever was, an arcane "immutable mobile" that simply extends the dominance of instrumentally rational ways of perceiving the environment. Nor is it a decontextualized, impersonal logo through which an unscrupulous, hegemonic power is asserting its reach across the globe. Thoroughly domesticated and sustaining multiple meanings, the image may, after all, rekindle an associationism through which America's too self-centered political culture can embrace in imagination those billions of others who also regard the Earth as their only home.

Notes

* In Paul Edwards and Clark Miller, eds., *Changing the Atmosphere: Expert Knowledge and Environmental Governance* (Cambridge, MA: MIT Press, 2001), pp. 309–37.
1 For the appearance of memory as a major theme in historiography, see Nora 1987. On war and memory, see Fussell 1975 and Winter 1995. Representations of the two world wars multiplied in both high and popular culture in the last decades of the century, as exemplified by Michael Ondaatje's *The English Patient* (in both novel and film versions), Pat Barker's *Regeneration* trilogy, and Stephen Spielberg's *Schindler's List* and *Saving Private Ryan*. For a comparative account of attempts to memorialize World War II in Germany and Japan, see Buruma 1995.
2 As of January 1999, only four (Britain, Denmark, Greece, Sweden) of fifteen members of the European Union had not joined the European Monetary Union.
3 There are, in fact, a large number of pictures of the earth from space, as documented and archived by NASA's Johnson Space Program; these may be viewed at NASA's website. The most famous (as discussed below) is the *Apollo 17* picture of the whole planet, showing the horn of Africa and Saudi Arabia. Its popularity can be attributed to several factors, including the size and fullness of the planet, the absence of clouds, and the clarity and color of the visible land masses. Like all of NASA's pictures, this one is not covered by copyright and can be downloaded from the web.
4 For instance, in a courtroom, the jury's ability to see things is framed by the judge and discursively constituted by expert witnesses. See, in this regard, Goodwin 1994 (writing about the videotape in the Rodney King trial) and Jasanoff 1998.

5 See, for example, Haas 1989, 1990a. See also my own argument that political analysis needs to take more seriously the ways shared epistemes are created and achieve standing in the political realm, in Jasanoff 1996, 173–197.
6 Representation has long been a topic of major interest in science and technology studies and there is a vast literature dealing with scientific representations in particular. For an introduction, see Lynch and Woolgar 1990.
7 By focusing on *regimes* of interpretation, I do not mean to suggest that individual perceptions are unimportant. There is clearly interesting research to be done on ways in which people in varying national or social surroundings have made sense of the image of the earth. This type of ethnographic work, however, lies outside the scope of this chapter.
8 One can only speculate on the reasons for this particular choice. It is, as noted, one of the relatively few earth images that shows the full globe relatively unencumbered by clouds. It therefore conforms well to the ways in which cultures familiar for some five centuries with the artifacts of mapping, both spherical and two-dimensional, *expect* to see the earth.
9 It should be noted that representations of the earth seen as if from a distant vantage point were not unknown in the Western mapping tradition. For example, the *Celestial Atlas of Harmony*, a magnificent series of engravings by the seventeenth-century Polish cartographer Andreas Cellarius, displays the earth set amidst the other bodies of the solar system as conceived by the astronomers Ptolemy, Copernicus, and Tycho Brahe. In several of these illustrations, the earth appears as a delicately suspended, beautiful, blue-green globe.
10 Fuller noted that few people actually sense themselves to be in a spaceship because most have seen only small portions of the earth's surface; even veteran pilots, he observed, had not viewed more than about one-hundredth of the earth. In a bow to Fuller, *Spaceship Earth* is the name given to the giant geosphere (a full rather than a half-sphere or geodesic dome) that marks the entrance to the Future World exhibit at Walt Disney World's Epcot Center in Florida.
11 Boulding (1966, 3) specifically contrasted the new visual perception of the earth as a sphere with the earlier imaging of earth as "an illimitable cylinder, essentially a plane wrapped around a globe."
12 This change in meaning may help to account for the image's widespread use as a symbol of the new millennium in the final years of the twentieth century. A detailed exploration of this phenomenon would be rewarding, but it unfortunately cannot be attempted within the scope of this chapter.
13 "She has also been used to advertise cheese, oranges, gramophone needles, cigars and ladies' shoes in Italy, Spain, Holland and England. Her name is an unfailing password everywhere. The German post office has issued the painting on a stamp. At the same time, she has given rise to many iconoclastic manifestations on postcards or cartoons, but they were friendly jokes and could also be taken for tokens of admiration" (Ottino della Chiesa 1985, 105).
14 To be sure, the precautionary principle also requires a balancing of caution against other desired policy objectives. Nonetheless, the principle's very framing places a greater emphasis on prevention than the discourse of risk analysis. For a persuasive critique of risk-based environmental regulation, see Winner 1986, 138–154.

References

Agarwal, Anil and Sunita Narain. 1991. *Global Warming in an Unequal World*. New Delhi: Centre for Science and Environment.
Alpers, Svetlana. 1983. *The Art of Describing: Dutch Art in the 17th Century*. Chicago: University of Chicago Press.

Anderson, Benedict. 1991. *Imagined Communities*. London: Verso (revised and expanded second edition, Verso, 1991).

Ashley, Richard K. 1983. "The Eye of Power: The Politics of World Modeling." *International Organization* 37(3): 495–535.

Baldwin, Hanson W. 1947. *The Price of Power*. New York: Harper and Brothers.

Bloomfield, Brian P. 1986. *Modelling the World: The Social Constructions of Systems Analysis*. Oxford: Blackwell.

Botkin, Daniel. 1990. *Discordant Harmonies: A New Ecology for the Twenty-First Century*. New York: Oxford University Press.

Boulding, Kenneth E. 1966. "The Economics of the Coming Spaceship Earth," in Henry Jarrett, ed., *Environmental Quality in a Growing Economy*. Baltimore: Johns Hopkins University Press.

Buruma, Ian. 1995. *Wages of Guilt*. London: Vintage.

Caldwell, Lynton K. 1990. *International Environmental Policy: Emergence and Dimensions*. Durham, NC: Duke University Press.

Caldwell, Lynton K. 1992. "Globalizing Environmentalism: Threshold of a New Phase in International Relations," in Riley Dunlap and Angela Mertig, eds., *American Environmentalism: The U.S. Environmental Movement, 1970–1990*. Philadelphia: Taylor and Francis.

Campbell, Joseph. 1972. *Myths to Live By*. New York: Viking Press.

Carson, Rachel. 1962. *Silent Spring*. New York: Fawcett Crest.

Chaikin, Andrew. 1994. "The Last Men on the Moon." *Popular Science* 245(3): 70–74, 88.

Cotgrove, Stephen. 1982. *Catastrophe or Cornucopia: The Environment, Politics and the Future*. Chichester, UK: Wiley.

Darman, Richard G. 1978. "The Law of the Sea: Rethinking U.S. Interests." *Foreign Affairs* 56(2): 381.

Folger, Tim, Sarah Richardson and Carl Zimmer. 1994. "Remembering Apollo: Astronauts Recall Their Flights to the Moon." *Discover* 15(7): 38.

Fukuyama, Francis. 1992. *The End of History or the Last Man*. New York: Free Press.

Fuller, R. Buckminster. 1969. *Operating Manual for Spaceship Earth*. Carbondale: Southern Illinois University Press.

Fussell, Paul. 1975. *The Great War and Modern Memory*. New York: Oxford University Press.

Goodwin, Charles. 1994. "Professional Vision." *American Anthropology* 96: 606–633.

Haas, Peter M. 1989. "Do Regimes Matter? Epistemic Communities and Mediterranean Pollution Control." *International Organization* 43: 377–403.

Haas, Peter M. 1990a. "Obtaining International Environmental Protection through Epistemic Consensus." *Millennium* 19(3): 347–364.

Haas, Peter M. 1990b. *Saving the Mediterranean: The Politics of International Cooperation*. New York: Columbia University Press.

Haggard, Stephan and Beth A. Simmons. 1987. "Theories of International Regimes." *International Organization* 41: 491–517.

Harwit, Martin. 1996. *An Exhibit Denied: Lobbying the History of Enola Gay*. New York: Copernicus.

Jasanoff, Sheila. 1996. "Science and Norms in International Environmental Regimes," in Fen O. Hampson and Judith Reppy, eds., *Earthly Goods: Environmental Change and Social Justice*. Ithaca, NY: Cornell University Press, 173–197.

Jasanoff, Sheila. 1998. "The Eye of Everyman: Witnessing DNA in the Simpson Trial." *Social Studies of Science* 28(5–6): 713–740.

Jones, Caroline A. and Peter Galison. 1998. *Picturing Science, Producing Art*. New York: Routledge.

Keohane, Robert O. 1988. "International Institutions: Two Approaches." *International Studies Quarterly* 32: 379–397.

Latour, Bruno. 1990. "Drawing Things Together," in Michael Lynch and Steve Woolgar, *Representation in Scientific Practice*. Cambridge, MA: MIT Press.

Latour, Bruno. 1995. "The Pédofil of Boa Vista," trans. Bart Simon and Katria Verreson. *Common Knowledge* 4(1): 144–187.

Latour, Bruno and Steve Woolgar. 1979. *Laboratory Life: The Construction of Scientific Facts*. London: Sage.

Levine, Adeline. 1982. *Love Canal: Science, Politics, and People*. Lexington, MA: Lexington Books.

Litfin, Karen T. 1994. *Ozone Discourses: Science and Politics in Global Environmental Cooperation*. New York: Columbia University Press.

Lovelock, James E. 1979. *Gaia, A New Look at Life on Earth*. Oxford: Oxford University Press.

Lynch, Michael and Steve Woolgar. 1990. *Representation in Scientific Practice*. Cambridge, MA: MIT Press.

Margulis, Lynn and James Lovelock. 1976. "Is Mars a Spaceship, Too?" *Natural History* June/July, 86–90.

McCormick, John. 1989. *Reclaiming Paradise: The Global Environmental Movement*. Bloomington: Indiana University Press.

Meadows, Donella H., D. L. Meadows, S. Rauderg and W. W. Behrens. 1972. *The Limits to Growth*. New York: Universe Books.

Miller, Clark. 2001. "Challenges in the Application of Science to Global Affairs: Contingency, Trust, and Moral Order," in C. Miller, and P. Edwards, *Changing the Atmosphere: Expert Knowledge and Environmental Governance*. Cambridge, MA: MIT Press.

Nora, Pierre, ed. 1987. *Les lieux de mémoire*. Paris: Gallimard.

Ottino della Chiesa, Angela. 1985. *The Complete Paintings of Leonardo da Vinci*. Introduction by Leopold D. Ettlinger. Harmondsworth, UK: Penguin Books.

President's Air Policy Commission. 1948. *Survival in the Air Age*. Washington, DC: U.S. Government Printing Office.

Rheingold, Howard. 1994. "Introduction," in H. Rheingold and S. Brand, *The Millennium Whole Earth Catalog: Access to Tools and Ideas for the Twenty-First Century*, 1st ed. (San Francisco: Harper San Francisco). Available at http://www.rheingold.com/texts/mwecintro.html.

Ruggie, John G. 1986. "Social Time and International Policy: Conceptualizing Global Population and Resource Issues," in M.P. Karns, ed., *Persistent Patterns and Emergent Structures in a Waning Century*. New York: Praeger.

Sachs, Wolfgang. 1994. "Satellitenblick. Die Ikone vom blauen Planeten und ihre Folgen für die Wissenschaft," in Ingo Braun and Bernward Joerges, eds., *Technik ohne Grenzen*. Frankfurt: Suhrkamp, pp. 305–346.

Sagan, Carl. 1994. *The Pale Blue Dot*. New York: Random House.

Schneider, Stephen, ed. 1991. *Scientists on Gaia*. Cambridge, MA: MIT Press.

Scott, James C. 1998. *Seeing Like a State*. New Haven: Yale University Press.

Sebenius, James K. 1984. *Negotiating the Law of the Sea*. Cambridge, MA: Harvard University Press.

Sebenius, James K. 1991. "Designing Negotiations Toward a New Regime: The Case of Global Warming." *International Security* 15(4): 110–148.

Stevenson, Adlai E. 1979. "Strengthening the International Development Institutions," in Walter Johnson, ed., *The Papers of Adlai E. Stevenson*, Volume VIII. Boston: Little, Brown, and Company.

Takacs, David. 1996. *The Idea of Biodiversity: Philosophies of Paradise*. Baltimore: Johns Hopkins University Press.

Tribe, Laurence. 1973. "Technology Assessment and the Fourth Discontinuity: The Limits of Instrumental Rationality." *Southern California Law Review* 46: 617–660.

U.S. Department of State. 1996. "Fact Sheet: US Oceans Policy and the Law of the Sea Convention," Bureau of Public Affairs, March 19. Website produced by Electronic Research Collections. Available at http://dosfan.lib.uic.edu/ERC/environment/fact_sheets/960319.html.

Ward, Barbara. 1966. *Spaceship Earth*. New York: Columbia University Press.

Ward, Barbara and Rene Dubos. 1972. *Only One Earth: The Care and Maintenance of a Small Planet*. New York: Norton.

Weiss, Edith Brown. 1989. *In Fairness to Future Generations: International Law, Common Patrimony, and Intergenerational Equity*. Dobbs Ferry, NY: Transnational Publishers and United Nations University.

Winner, Langdon. 1986. *The Whale and the Reactor: A Search for Limits in an Age of High Technology*. Chicago, IL: University of Chicago Press.

Winter, Jay. 1995. *Sites of Memory, Sites of Mourning: The Great War in European Cultural History*. New York: Cambridge University Press.

World Commission on Environment and Development. 1987. *Our Common Future*. Oxford: Oxford University Press.

6   Contested boundaries in policy-relevant science[*]

Recent advances in the sociology of scientific knowledge have emphasized the influence of social factors on the content of science. Facts are accepted as authoritative not necessarily because they can be empirically verified, but because they are validated through processes of informal negotiation and can be ranged into frameworks of shared assumptions and inferences. Social processes colour the extent to which pieces of scientific knowledge are perceived as certain, leading to differences in the interpretation of the same facts by scientists of different disciplinary training.[1] In areas of high uncertainty, political interest frequently shapes the presentation of scientific facts and hypotheses to fit different models of 'reality'.[2] The language in which scientists represent and legitimate their claims varies in accordance with the audience to which the representations are made.[3] Accordingly, one's impressions of the reliability of scientific knowledge can differ depending on whether one looks at the public language of science or at the private language in which scientists communicate their assessments of certainty to each other.

Though the sociology and philosophy of science both attest to the indeterminacy of knowledge, science has for several centuries maintained its authoritative status as provider of 'truths' about the natural world. To discover some of the reasons, one can turn to further insights from the sociology of science, especially in the work of those who have made the structure of the scientific community their special study. A widely accepted line of explanation emanating from the Mertonian school stresses the shared norms that foster cohesiveness in science, even though its practitioners come from divergent geographic, cultural or linguistic backgrounds.[4] Other scholars have called attention to the restrictive processes of entry into science, which involve not only an esoteric professional training but screening by numerous 'gatekeepers', such as senior academic colleagues or editors of professional journals.[5] Cohesion within science is also fostered by 'invisible colleges', 'research circles' or other informal networks that control the diffusion of scientific knowledge.[6] All of these mechanisms have helped to professionalize science, thereby enhancing the prestige and authority of its practitioners. Finally, the process of peer review, devised by scientists to validate each other's discoveries, reinforces the position of science as an autonomous social institution requiring no external control. Peer review procedures reaffirm not only that scientists maintain strict checks on the quality of each other's work, but that only professional scientists are qualified to pass judgement on the truth or significance of knowledge claims made by other scientists.

Much of the authority of science in the twentieth century rests as well on its success in persuading decision-makers and the public that the Mertonian norms present an accurate picture of the way science 'really works'. Unlike politics, science is 'disinterested' and 'objective' and, unlike religion, it is 'sceptical'. Accordingly, alone among major social institutions, science is believed capable of delivering a true picture of the physical world. Scientists have been quite successful in protecting this claim of exclusivity, jealously guarding their power to define the public image of science, and warding off competing claims by rival disciplines, particularly religion and various manifestations of 'pseudo-science'. Recent studies by Gieryn and others have drawn attention to significant 'boundary' disputes between science and other claimants to cognitive authority, and have underscored the pivotal role of language in establishing claims about the nature of science.[7]

The authority of science is seriously jeopardized when scientists are called upon to participate in policy-making. Administrative decision-making often requires a probing of the areas of greatest indeterminacy in science. Regulation of risks to health and the environment, in particular, involves issues at the frontiers of current scientific knowledge, where consensus among scientists is most fragile. Both science and regulation seek to establish facts. But the adversarial processes of rule-making employed in the United States presume that 'truth' emerges from an open and ritualized clash of conflicting opinions[8] rather than from the delicate and informal negotiations that characterize fact-finding in science. US administrative proceedings tend to 'deconstruct' the views held by scientific experts.[9] This is most clearly evident in formal rule-making, where lawyers use adjudicatory procedures to illuminate areas of weakness in expert testimony, including bias and uncertainty. Even in informal rule-making, however, agencies engage in considerable deconstruction of science in order to persuade reviewing courts that they have considered all possible viewpoints and arrived at a reasoned conclusion. In such settings the exercise of informed professional judgement, central to the performance of science, is not enough to establish an expert's credibility. An administrative process structured according to the rules of law depreciates views that cannot be supported by legally accepted forms of proof, such as empirical observations or published scientific authorities.

Although science is subjected to extreme deconstruction in the US regulatory process, the legitimacy of American regulatory decisions uniquely depends on rational justification, in scientific as well as in economic and legal terms.[10] This means that regulators must eventually present the public with a convincing scientific rationale for actions dealing with technological hazards, marshalling the supporting data and rejecting contrary evidence as persuasively as possible. In the US regulatory system, this public reconstruction of the scientific basis for regulation is one of the key responsibilities of the administrative agencies. Regulations must be backed by the issuing agency's own reading of the scientific evidence, with conflicts and uncertainties resolved in light of the agency's prior experience and its governing legal mandate. Through judicial review the agency head is held accountable for shortcomings in the scientific analysis as well as for the social and political consequences of regulation. Therefore, although scientists are often heavily involved in the early stages of decision-making, the scientific story presented to the public is finally a creation of the political process, and its ultimate test of validity occurs in the courtroom.

Governmental regulation of risk in the United States thus creates a partial overlap between the processes of scientific and legal inquiry and gives rise to competing claims of authority between science and government, particularly concerning the right to interpret the findings of science. Adherence to the Mertonian norms, coupled with a long tradition of critical peer control, has given scientists an assured basis for claiming cognitive authority. The policy process, however, simultaneously casts doubt on the disinterestedness and the certainty of science. These revealed weaknesses provide grounds for political decision-makers to assert that they have a right to engage in interpreting science, especially in areas that are controversial. A partial removal of cognitive authority to the legal and political arena is seen as the only way of assuring that the interpretation of indeterminate facts reflects the public values embodied in legislation as well as the norms of the scientific community.

With increasing governmental control over science and technology in recent decades, scientists and regulators have both acquired higher stakes in controlling the boundary between policy and science. Policy-makers have an overriding interest in responding flexibly to changing political currents. To the extent that science can be represented as indeterminate, requiring judgement rather than fact-finding, political decision-makers absolve themselves of the need to toe the line on any particular scientific orthodoxy. Emphasizing the indeterminacy in science also gives regulators a better chance of withstanding judicial review, since courts have traditionally been more deferential towards decisions based on discretionary judgements ('policy') than to those based on empirical findings ('science').

For scientists, however, there are serious risks in allowing policy-makers to expose the cognitive indeterminacy of science. The process of deconstruction tends to exaggerate the extent to which science deviates from the Mertonian norms. It suggests, for example, that scientists frequently disagree in their inter-pretation of data, that experts can be found to support virtually any reading of the evidence, and that the choice among different interpretations is ultimately either arbitrary or else coloured by political interest. Such themes, frequently sounded in regulatory controversies, challenge the view of science as a disinterested search for truth. They are profoundly detrimental to the scientist's self-image, a point that is perhaps under-rated in sociological analyses of reward structures in science. At the same time, exposés of uncertainty and disunity in science undermine public confidence and raise troublesome questions about whether scientists really deserve the symbolic and material rewards they have claimed from society in this century. Scientists, especially those whose work impinges on policy, thus have much to lose unless they can safeguard the classic normative view of science against charges of excessive indeterminacy.[11] To shore up their claims to cognitive authority, scientists have to impose their own boundaries between science and policy, thereby coming into potential conflict with policy-makers pursuing opposing interests.

In this paper I argue that many of the boundary disputes between science and policy are played out in the realm of language. The discourse of risk regulation has provided fertile ground for the creation of new linguistic labels whose primary function is to delimit the boundary between science and the political process. However neutral on their face, these terms are politically charged because they are used to explain or justify the allocation of power and prestige between the institutions of science and government. More generally, boundary-defining language not only serves the immediate interests of social and political groups, but, through the creation of new conceptual categories, opens the way for extending those interests to new or larger domains. The use of such language is an important strategic tool not merely for scientists and political officials, but for all other societal interest groups, such as industry and environmentalists, who have a stake in the way power is distributed among centres of scientific and political authority. A study of the way these disparate interest groups use boundary-defining terms about policy-relevant science reveals their essentially contested character.[12] Subtle shifts in meaning and reference correspond to efforts by each group to ensure that risk disputes are controlled by the institutions most sympathetic to their political interests.

In spite of their competing interests in defining the boundary between policy and science, there are certain rhetorical benchmarks on which all parties agree. It is universally accepted, for example, that 'science' should not be influenced by politics and that judgements as to what constitutes 'good' science should be left to scientists. All agree, as well, that scientists should not be involved in making 'policy'. Scientists themselves are quick to acknowledge that policy concerns should be addressed through the administrative process, *after* science has provided all the relevant evidence to the agencies. But while no one doubts that science should be done by scientists and policy by policy-makers, the problem for each interest group is to draw the dividing line between science and policy in ways that enlarge its own control over social decisions.[13] Competition among these groups leads to differing definitions of the point at which the autonomy of science ends and the role of political decision-making begins.

This paper examines three contested boundaries that have acquired special visibility in the regulatory discourse of the 1980s. The first concerns the attempt to define 'science' itself by distinguishing it from related concepts such as 'trans-science' or 'science policy'. The second boundary is the uncertain dividing line between 'risk assessment' and 'risk management' around which much of the American regulatory debate has been organized in recent years. The third is the notion of 'peer review', a term used only lately in relation to science in the policy environment, but already endowed with different readings by different political interests. While the first two disputes cover roughly the same terrain – how to distinguish science from policy – the debate about peer review seems to break new ground, namely, the selection of procedures for deciding scientific controversies relevant to policy. I suggest, however, that the new rhetorical emphasis on peer review, as well as the varying meanings assigned to the term, reflect the same political conflicts that underlie the other two boundary disputes. Talking about peer review instead of science policy or risk assessment thus represents a kind of rhetorical frame-shifting that is not untypical in political discourse.

Beyond trans-science

Regulatory problems demanding cooperation between scientists and public officials have been part of the political agenda in the industrialized countries for well over a century. The industrial revolution brought in its wake a variety of health, safety and environmental problems that required legislative or judicial attention, and experts played a growing role in shaping governmental responses. Until the 1960s the cooperation between experts and public decision-makers appeared fairly unproblematic. Scientists provided government with technical information and advice, while administrators and judges formulated legal or policy decisions. Few asked whether the scientists were performing purely scientific assessments or whether their deliberations were entirely free from political influence.

For science in the policy context, the age of innocence ended in the early 1970s. The environmental movement gathered momentum, focusing attention on hitherto unsuspected risks to health and the environment. The United States, along with most other industrial nations, enacted a spate of new legislation in order to prevent cancer, birth defects, degradation of the environment, loss of wildlife and depletion of natural resources. These preventive policies placed unprecedented demands on the capacity of science to predict future harm. Fed by images of impending environmental disaster, the public turned to science for more sophisticated methods of identifying and measuring risk. Science responded with a new emphasis on toxicological testing and increased use of predictive mathematical models. But this shift of scientific attention to the unknown, and possibly unknowable, effects of technology highlighted the intuitive, subjective and uncertain underpinnings of much of the advice that scientists provide to government. Moreover, the increasingly adjudicatory style of decision-making in the United States forced scientists to articulate their reservations about their technical assessments and generated questions about the coherence or reliability of policy-relevant science.

An important turning point for the relationship between scientists and regulators came in 1972 with the publication of Alvin Weinberg's article on 'Science and Trans-Science'.[14] In this article, Weinberg alerted both the scientific and the regulatory community to the existence of a grey zone between science and policy, characterized by questions 'which can be asked of science and yet which cannot be answered by science'.[15] Weinberg called this grey area 'trans-science', a term which, like C. P. Snow's 'two cultures', struck an unexpectedly responsive chord among a wide audience. It seemed to capture a distinction that many had been groping for in trying to understand policy controversies based on science. But subsequent elaborations of Weinberg's analysis suggest that the versatility of the term 'trans-science' helped assure its popularity. 'Trans-science' became a skeleton key by which different interest groups could attempt to unlock different doors in keeping with their specialized political objectives.

The concept of 'trans-science' served a strategically crucial purpose for scientists interested in reaffirming their professional authority. It suggested that the cognitive indeterminacy uncovered by the regulatory process was not intrinsic to science, but rather lay beyond or outside science. Conversely, an important corollary of Weinberg's analysis was that science proper is untouched by the uncertainties and expert conflicts that necessarily occur in trans-science. Thus, while regulators could be allowed considerable leeway to probe, and even decide, trans-scientific issues, science itself should remain the undisputed preserve of scientists, to be performed, evaluated and tested in accordance with the internal norms and procedures of the profession. Weinberg himself was careful to draw out some of the policy implications of his boundary-defining terminology, particularly in relation to the structure of the decision-making process. The following passage is especially revealing:

> If the question is unambiguously scientific, then the procedures of science rather than the procedures of law are required for arriving at the truth. Where the questions cannot be answered from existing scientific knowledge or from research which could be carried out reasonably rapidly and without disproportionate expense, then the answers must be trans-scientific and the adversary procedure seems therefore to be the best alternative.[16]

In other words, the deconstructionist techniques of establishing truth might be perfectly appropriate for trans-science, but they are out of place within the halls of genuine science.

A recent revisitation of the same boundary problem by Weinberg reveals even more clearly his desire to shield science against the taints of subjectivity, bias and disharmony that it acquires in the policy environment:

> No one would dispute that judgments of scientific truth are much affected by the scientist's value system when the issues are at or close to the boundary between science and trans-science. On the other hand, as the matter under dispute approaches the domain of science, most would claim that the scientist's extrascientific values intrude less and less.[17]

The passage illustrates an unswerving commitment to the Mertonian ideal of science, a position Weinberg underscores by blisteringly attacking the sociologists of knowledge who, in his view, have presumed to project a contrary image:

> At least the more extreme of the sociologists of knowledge claim that using traditional ways of establishing scientific truth – by appealing to nature in a disciplined manner – is *not how science really works*. Scientists are seen as

competitors for prestige, pay, and power, and it is the interplay among these conflicting aspirations, *not the working of some underlying scientific ethic,* that defines scientific truth. To be sure, these attitudes toward science are not widely held by practicing scientists; however, they ... nevertheless exert important influence on other institutions ... that ultimately influence public attitudes toward science and its technologies.[18]

Weinberg's concern quite clearly is that the uncertainties uncovered by the regulatory process will provide ammunition for those wishing to impugn the existence of an 'underlying scientific ethic' or to present a misleading picture of 'how science really works'. To guard against such attacks on 'the core of science',[19] Weinberg is prepared to concede a great deal of ground at the boundary between science and trans-science. His article on trans-science had already concluded that this boundary is 'elusive'. In his more recent work, as noted below, Weinberg appears willing to admit that much of the so-called 'science' of probabilistic risk analysis – an increasingly important source of conflict in regulatory proceedings – should be relegated to the trans-scientific side of the boundary. Indeed, Weinberg goes so far as to suggest that one should 'define a new branch of science, called regulatory science, in which the norms of scientific proof are less demanding than are the norms in ordinary science'.[20]

For non-scientific actors in the regulatory process, what is at stake in the boundary dispute between science and policy is not so much the image of science or the scientist as the question of institutional power. In a given regulatory proceeding, who should determine how the boundary is drawn between science and trans-science? And once this line is established, who should decide the controversial trans-scientific issues and by what procedures? Weinberg's original article seemingly viewed the boundary-defining function as a prerogative of scientists. In discussing the scientist's place in the 'republic of trans-science', Weinberg commented that 'though the scientist cannot provide definite answers to trans-scientific questions . . ., he does have one crucially important role: to make clear where science ends and trans-science begins'.[21]

A somewhat different position has been advanced by administrative lawyers, who have viewed Weinberg's analysis as a rationale for expanding the role of law and legal processes in decision-making at the frontiers of scientific knowledge. Within the growing body of legal scholarship on science and the regulatory process, Thomas McGarity's work on discretionary decision-making in the Environmental Protection Agency (EPA) and the Occupational Safety and Health Administration (OSHA) has proved particularly influential.[22] McGarity was drawn to an exploration of the boundary between science and policy through a study of efforts by the federal agencies to control chemical carcinogens in the 1970s. This regulatory endeavour presented the agencies with seemingly intransigent technical problems. Federal regulators recognized that the existence of a cancer risk to humans can seldom be established by means of direct evidence, since there is a paucity of reliable epidemiological data linking specific chemicals to cancer. As a result, regulatory determinations that a chemical may pose a cancer risk depend mainly on secondary evidence, such as animal tests and studies of a compound's capacity to induce mutations. But the interpretation of such data is fraught with uncertainty and expert disagreements, and the regulatory outcome seems to depend less on science than on the institutions and procedures that are used to resolve the proliferating technical conflicts.

Over the past fifteen years a number of federal agencies have taken up the challenge of creating a principled framework for regulating carcinogens. EPA and OSHA took the lead on this issue in the 1970s because of their pre-eminent role in controlling toxic substances. Later their efforts were paralleled or supplemented by the initiatives of the Interagency Regulatory Liaison Group (IRLG), which was active during the Carter administration, and by the Office of Science and Technology Policy (OSTP).[23] The approaches taken by each of these agencies have differed in form and scope. EPA and IRLG issued their principles of carcinogenic risk assessment in the form of relatively flexible guidelines, while OSHA attempted to cast its generic cancer policy in the shape of more formal regulations. OSTP tried to steer clear of making policy judgements in its risk assessment principles, whereas the other agencies acknowledged that policy determinations were needed in order to bridge areas of uncertainty. With regard to science, however, all of these frameworks adopted a basically deconstructionist approach. As a result, the number and complexity of principles used to define the process of risk assessment have increased over time. The agencies have become more and more sensitive as well to the need to characterize the uncertainties in carcinogenic risk assessment, and have developed elaborate methodological caveats for dealing with uncertain issues.

McGarity's analysis of carcinogen regulation by OSHA and EPA focused on a class of issues which he described as 'science policy' because 'both science and policy considerations play a role in their resolution'.[24] It is useful to look at his detailed elaboration of the science policy concept, since it too has gained currency in the discourse of health and safety regulation. Under the heading of science policy, McGarity included three broad types of issues: first, questions that are cast in scientific terms, but are inherently unanswerable by science for practical or moral reasons;[25] second, questions that cannot be answered because of insufficient scientific data, but are theoretically subject to resolution given adequate time and resources; and third, questions characterized by expert disagreements about either the interpretation of scientific studies or the inferences drawn from them. A careful reading of Weinberg's work suggests that he was well aware of such differences in the typology of 'unanswerable' questions and meant to subsume them all within the phrase trans-science.[26] Thus, it is difficult to argue that in purely conceptual terms McGarity's phrase 'science policy' marks a clear advance over the notion of trans-science. Nevertheless, the newer label continues to be widely used in discussions of science-based regulatory decisions. The explanation seems to lie largely in the term's connotations, which carry different rhetorical and strategic implications than those associated with the term 'trans-science'.

Perhaps the most significant feature of the phrase 'science policy' is that it has prescriptive overtones that are favoured by analysts trained in administrative law.

Science policy, after all, can be regarded as just another specialized subfield of policy which can be governed by the normal institutional and procedural controls of American administrative law. This point of view dominates McGarity's own writing. For example, he recognizes as clearly as Weinberg that the boundary between science and science policy is likely to be disputed, so that 'the regulator will need a mechanism for deciding whether an issue is in fact a science policy issue'.[27] The mechanism McGarity proposes, however, is 'direct oral testimony with cross-examination', a legalistic solution, which leaves ultimate authority for distinguishing between science and science policy in the hands of a judge or administrator rather than under control of scientific experts.

In his essay on EPA and OSHA, McGarity examined the procedures that might be appropriate for resolving science policy questions. In keeping with the author's disciplinary biases, the article unquestioningly assumed that these procedures should be derived from the existing framework of administrative law, a framework that favours a principled, judicially reviewable mode of decision-making. The focus of McGarity's analysis was a comparison of two different approaches to deconstructing the scientific basis of policy decisions: the innovative 'generic' procedures developed by EPA and OSHA in the late 1970s and the classic adjudicatory model of establishing the truth in disputes over scientific facts. The former approach sought to resolve certain issues relating to chemical carcinogenicity at a generic level, while the latter aimed at establishing the effects of particular substances through individualized, trial-type proceedings. The important point here is that McGarity considered *all* science policy issues as suitable for resolution through one or the other approach, each calling for a public deconstruction of scientific evidence followed by reconstruction according to established judicial or administrative rules. The open question for McGarity was merely how to choose between the two processes. Should the procedures adopted by the agencies be generic or particularized, informal or adjudicatory?

The strategic importance of these assumptions became clearly apparent in a controversy over formaldehyde, which EPA attempted to regulate during the ill-fated administration of Anne Gorsuch.[28] Formaldehyde met EPA's and OSHA's principal generic criteria for treating chemical substances as potential human carcinogens. An inhalation study in rats showed that formaldehyde is an undisputed animal carcinogen, producing nasal tumours in a high percentage of the exposed rodents at high doses. The compound also responded positively in a variety of tests for detecting mutagenicity. Nevertheless, John Todhunter, then EPA's assistant administrator for toxic substances, determined that formaldehyde did not present a significant cancer risk to humans. He reached this conclusion by assessing the properties of formaldehyde that seemed to weigh against a finding of carcinogenicity: negative bioassays in mice and other animals; negative results in studies using routes of administration other than inhalation; the absence of positive epidemiological findings; and the apparent reversibility of cell damage caused by exposure to formaldehyde at low doses or for short durations. These pieces of evidence led Todhunter to argue that the effects of formaldehyde on rats should be regarded as species-specific, hence not inherently problematic from the standpoint of human health.

In building his case on formaldehyde, Todhunter exercised the US administrator's privilege of picking and choosing from the scientific record those bits of data that best supported his policy decision. The problem, however, was that a backdrop of prior EPA rule-making constrained Todhunter's freedom to exonerate formaldehyde from the suspicion of carcinogenicity. In particular, EPA's pre-existing guidelines for assessing carcinogenic risk indicated that regulators should attach much greater weight to positive than to negative studies when evaluating conflicting data on carcinogenicity. Todhunter's deviations from this cardinal principle drew outraged reactions from environmentalists, Congress and members of the scientific community.[29] One vocal and highly effective critic, Nicholas Ashford, took the administrator to task for his mishandling of science policy.[30] By invoking this concept Ashford defended a particular approach to decision-making which, in the case of formaldehyde, might well have led to a different regulatory outcome from that intended by Todhunter.

Ashford's definition of 'science policy' highlighted the policy component of decisions at the borderline of science and policy:

> The term 'science policy' denotes issues that are grounded in scientific analysis but for which technical data are insufficient to support an unequivocal scientific conclusion. The ultimate resolution of these issues depends on determinations of social policy.[31]

This definition suggests that disagreements within science – signalled by the absence of unequivocal conclusions – suffice to characterize disputed technical issues as science policy. Having emphasized the non-technical dimensions of science policy, Ashford also stressed the need to maintain traditional administrative values in making science policy decisions, for example, openness and adequate public notice, especially when departing from prior agency propositions.[32] Such procedural requirements, Ashford charged, were violated by Todhunter's private and unilateral decision to downplay the cancer risk presented by formaldehyde.

This argument sounds compelling if one accepts the major premises underlying Ashford's and McGarity's analyses of science policy: that issues characterized by insufficient data or expert disagreements should not be classified as pure science but as science policy; that procedures for dealing with such issues should be defined by agencies rather than scientists; and that regulators should control decisions about whether particular issues should be categorized as science or science policy. It follows reasonably from these assumptions that changes in science policy should be made in accordance with the legal requirements that apply to administrative policy-making in general.

Ashford went even further. He suggested that policy considerations can override science altogether in resolving disputes about science policy:

In appropriate circumstances, of course, the agency may depart from scientific opinion on science policy issues. These issues do, after all, involve policy determinations, and accordingly should be made by the governmental entity charged with reflecting the will of the people through the execution of a congressional mandate.[33]

Such assumptions, however, have by no means gained universal acceptance. In particular, the chemical industry, which stood to lose most heavily from a strict application of the generic policies developed by EPA and OSHA, never agreed that the key technical issues in regulating carcinogens should be characterized as 'science policy'. Instead, industry spokesmen have always argued that carcinogen regulation is based on 'science', and that agencies should be careful not to subvert this science through technically naive or politically motivated administrative rules. Consistent with this position, the American Industrial Health Council (AIHC), a trade association formed to consolidate the chemical industry's opposition to generic regulation of carcinogens, vociferously attacked the government's proposed policies for identifying and classifying carcinogens, including OSHA's cancer policy and EPA's proposed generic approach to regulating airborne carcinogens. AIHC charged that science and policy are impermissibly mingled in all attempts to regulate carcinogens generically. OSHA's cancer policy attracted especially adverse comment. AIHC denounced it as an attempt to 'freeze science' through a 'cookbook approach' to reading scientific evidence.[34] As industry saw it, even controversial issues, such as the interpretation of animal data or techniques for extrapolating risk from high to low doses, were essentially scientific in character and should have been addressed by scientists rather than administrative agencies.

The formaldehyde controversy sheds interesting light on the scientific community's response to such partisan debates about the proper way to resolve disputes at the boundary of science and policy. One might expect *a priori* that scientists would hesitate to accept the full implications of Ashford's position, particularly his suggestion that social policy considerations should, if necessary, take precedence over scientific opinion in making regulatory choices. Given the institutional interests of science, one might expect scientists to find AIHC's rhetoric rather more appealing, since it caters to the image of science as an élite and apolitical source of cognitive authority. Yet in the debate over the carcinogenicity of formaldehyde a number of US scientists with impeccable professional credentials sided with Ashford and the environmentalists rather than with Todhunter and the chemical industry. Their use of language indicates how they reconciled this position with appeals to the authority of science.

Testifying before Congress in 1983, Bernard Weinstein of Columbia University expressed his conviction that the regulation of potential carcinogens 'must be firmly rooted in scientific principles'.[35] As examples of such principles, however, he cited many of the generic propositions adopted by EPA, OSHA and IRLG for assessing carcinogenic risk. Weinstein thus underplayed the policy content of the cancer principles and focused instead on the claim that they were all grounded in sound science. He stressed that there was no scientific support for deviating from any of these principles, as Todhunter apparently had done, and concluded that 'our understanding of the mechanism of action of environmental carcinogens ... is in a sufficient state of flux that it would be premature to alter the existing, well-established guidelines for detecting potential carcinogens'.[36]

Unlike Weinstein, Norton Nelson of New York University, who testified at the same set of hearings, referred to the principles as the federal government's 'cancer policy'. But Nelson left little doubt that he regarded this 'policy' essentially as an expression of scientific consensus. He noted that the principles underlying cancer testing and evaluation at EPA had found wide acceptance not only in the United States but among other national and international institutions concerned with regulating carcinogens.[37] From this vantage point, Nelson criticized Todhunter's analysis of formaldehyde as a striking departure from the prevailing scientific consensus, calling it 'the sort of a document that one would not expect an objective scientist to produce'.[38] Nelson admitted that advances in understanding the biology of cancer causation had created the need for a thorough revision of federal cancer policies. But he emphasized that such review and updating should be undertaken collegially by an accredited scientific body, preferably the National Academy of Sciences, so as to produce a more up-to-date consensus. Thus, both Nelson and Weinstein implicitly redefined the problematic issues in carcinogen regulation as fundamentally scientific. They were then able to challenge Todhunter's analysis of formaldehyde seemingly on the basis of science alone (and on their personal authority as scientists). Neither scientist endorsed the unpalatable notion that the dispute was a matter of science policy on which science had little definitive guidance to offer.

Risk assessment and risk management

Some federal agencies, including EPA, were regularly performing risk assessments for chemical carcinogens by the late 1970s. Over the next few years, support for the concept of risk assessment widened, helped along by pressure from the chemical industry and the anti-regulatory temper of the Reagan administration. Critiques of the generic approach to carcinogen regulation provided much of the intellectual justification for the spread of risk assessment methodologies. Industry alleged that generic procedures slighted scientific evidence in the interests of a heavy-handed and overly conservative policy of risk management. According to this view, generic policies were fundamentally flawed because they overlooked some of the key factors bearing on the degree of risk, most notably the relationship between dose and response and the extent of public exposure to particular toxic substances. As a result, generic policies were incapable of distinguishing between chemicals posing relatively high and comparatively trivial risks to human health. Industry argued that these systematic errors could be corrected only through comprehensive assessment of the quantitative as well as the qualitative dimension of chemical risks.

Supporters of risk assessment won a major legal victory in a lawsuit challenging the new occupational safety and health standard proposed by OSHA for benzene, a substance known to cause leukaemia in humans exposed to high doses. Acting in accordance with its generic cancer policy,[39] OSHA classified benzene as a high-risk substance and proposed to reduce workplace exposure to the lowest feasible level. Also consistently with the cancer policy, OSHA declined to perform a quantitative risk assessment for benzene. The petroleum industry objected to the proposed standard on several grounds and took the agency to court. The case was ultimately decided by the Supreme Court, where a plurality of the Justices held, in effect, that OSHA's failure to carry out a risk assessment rendered the proposed standard invalid.[40] According to the plurality opinion, OSHA's governing statute required the agency to demonstrate that there was a significant risk to workers at or below the existing exposure limit prior to issuing a new standard. The agency had conspicuously failed to make such a showing.

In industry's political agenda, however, the demand for formal risk assessment was part of a larger strategy to remove risk assessment from the control of agency scientists and bureaucrats, whom industry regarded on the whole as captive to pro-regulatory interests. AIHC, in particular, issued a series of position papers calling for a new institution to take over the task of doing risk assessments for the regulatory agencies.[41] Specifically, AIHC argued that the scientific integrity of risk assessment could be preserved only by delegating the task to a panel of independent scientists, preferably under the auspices of the National Academy of Sciences (NAS). The thrust of the proposal was to remove all marginally scientific issues involved in carcinogen regulation to the jurisdiction of an expert panel that would have little day-to-day contact with the legal and political dimensions of the regulatory process. But the proposal's political force derived from its appeal to the institutional authority of science, an appeal that many found reassuring after the endless scientific uncertainties laid bare by regulatory deconstruction.

Congress responded to AIHC lobbyists by asking NAS to study mechanisms for improving the quality and credibility of the science used in risk decisions. The National Research Council's Commission on Life Sciences formed a committee to examine risk management practices in the federal government, with the following main objectives in view:

> To assess the merits of separating the analytic functions of developing risk assessments from the regulatory functions of making policy decisions.

> To consider the feasibility of designating a single organization to do risk assessments for all regulatory agencies.

> To consider the feasibility of developing uniform risk assessment guidelines for use by all regulatory agencies.[42]

The focus on separating science from policy and on institutional reorganization both catered to the chemical industry's interest in removing much of the responsibility for interpreting technical information from the control of individual agencies.

One might well wonder at this point what had happened to the insights about policy-relevant science captured by Weinberg or McGarity. Political demand for separating science and policy seemed to deny the existence of any ambiguous border area where the two kinds of issues are inextricably joined. In fact, aware-ness of the fuzzy boundary between science and policy soon surfaced within the NAS committee. The problem was clearly laid out in a working paper by Lawrence McCray, project director for the risk management study.[43] McCray pointed out that experts familiar with carcinogenic risk assessment saw all but a handful of the analytical steps as involving a mixture of science and policy. Users of the technique agreed that very little in a typical risk assessment could be labelled as pure science. McCray's findings decisively influenced the committee, which ulti-mately refused to endorse a single, central board for regulatory risk assessment. Conceding that policy choices are involved in risk assessment,[44] the committee concluded that it was unrealistic to separate this process institutionally from the process of deciding how to manage risks.

Yet the NAS report also made numerous rhetorical bows to the notion that science can be separated from policy through sufficiently rigorous analysis. The idea was implicit in the committee's decision to characterize regulation in terms of two distin-guishable processes: risk assessment ('the characterization of the potential adverse health effects of human exposures to environmental hazards') and risk management ('the process of evaluating alternative regulatory actions and selecting among them').[45] The terminology alone suggests that the scientific and technical aspects of decision-making can be isolated from the socio-political ones. The report played further on this theme by exhorting the agencies to keep the two processes conceptually distinct:

> We recommend that regulatory agencies take steps to establish and maintain a clear conceptual distinction between assessment of risks and consideration of risk management alternatives; that is, the scientific findings and policy judgments embodied in risk assessments should be explicitly distinguished from the political, economic, and technical considerations that influence the design and choice of regulatory strategies.[46]

In a similar vein, the report noted:

> Even the *perception* that risk management considerations are influencing the conduct of risk assessment in an important way will cause the assessment and regulatory decisions based on them to lack credibility.[47]

> Before an agency decides whether a substance should or should not be regu-lated as a health hazard, a detailed and comprehensive written risk assessment should be prepared and made publicly accessible. This written assessment should clearly distinguish between the scientific basis and the policy basis for the agency's conclusions.[48]

> A frequent deficiency of agency risk assessments is the failure to distinguish between scientific and policy considerations in risk assessment.[49]

These remarks and recommendations all point to a powerful reluctance on the part of at least some NAS committee members to admit that science and policy might, at the boundary, be very difficult to distinguish from one another.

In all, the NAS report left the agencies in something of an intellectual quandary. They were instructed to distinguish as far as possible between the assessment and the management of risk. At the same time, they were informed that the two stages are inextricably linked, making any formal institutional separation of the two functions impractical. In view of its indecisiveness, it is not surprising that the report failed to impose consistency on the use of the key terms 'risk assessment' and 'risk management' by the policy community. In spite of the NAS committee's assertions to the contrary, agency officials saw some advantages in treating risk assessment as a wholly scientific enterprise, at least for rhetorical purposes. Emphasizing the objectivity of the procedure offered a means of persuading the public that regulatory decisions are based on a core of rational analysis and of enhancing public confidence in the impartiality of agency decisions.

This analysis may help explain an early insistence on the objectivity of risk assessment by William Ruckelshaus, twice the administrator of EPA, and the person credited with restoring the agency's credibility following Gorsuch's tenure in that office. Ruckelshaus conceded that in an imperfect world risk assessment may be influenced by extraneous factors such as the pressure of the regulatory timetable and limitations on the agency's resources. Nevertheless, he argued in a widely publicized address to the National Academy of Sciences that:

> Despite these often compelling pressures, risk assessment at EPA must be based only on scientific evidence and scientific consensus. Nothing will erode public confidence faster than the suspicion that policy considerations have been allowed to influence the assessment of risk.[50]

These remarks, of course, ran directly counter to the NAS committee's judgement that the analytical choices an agency makes in risk assessment must be influenced in part by policy considerations, especially the all-important decision about how conservative the agency wishes to be in determining a risk to public health.

As an experienced administrator, Ruckelshaus could not long ignore the fact that his speech to the National Academy was based on an unrealistic view of the objectivity of risk analysis. Indeed, EPA's own staff scientists maintained a much more sceptical view of the process, characterizing it as no more certain than a circumstantial murder trial, and possibly no better than pulling numbers out of thin air.[51] Ruckelshaus eventually withdrew from his endorsement of a formal separation between risk assessment and risk management, conceding that values influence the former as well as the latter. Characteristically, the alternative he put forward derived from the traditions of the American administrative process and accorded a central role to the deconstruction of science:

I think we need to dig up. We have to expose the assumptions that go into risk assessments. We have to admit our uncertainties and confront the public with the complex nature of decisions about risk.[52]

Following this analysis, Ruckelshaus and others have suggested that the agencies should be less concerned with the process of risk assessment and more with the transmission of their analytical efforts to the public. These views have led to greater emphasis on 'risk communication' – in other words, on the processes by which administrative agencies publicly reconstruct their scientific rationale for regulating risk.

In spite of Ruckelshaus's public turnaround, the notion that risk assessment can be compartmentalized as an objective, value-free exercise continues to hold powerful appeal. Yet the contrasting view that risk assessment is subjective and highly discretionary also has many adherents. As a result, inconsistent descriptions of the process are sprinkled throughout the policy literature. A recent report written for the Secretary of Health and Human Services (HHS) on assessing and managing toxic substances illustrates the phenomenon.[53] The report begins by stressing the fluid and hybrid character of risk assessment:

> The process of risk assessment, a process that is still very much in transition or evolution, is often a mixture of scientific facts, consensus, assumptions, and science policy decisions (i.e., policy statements made by agencies to resolve points of current controversy).[54]

But a later passage provides a curiously contradictory description:

> The actual process of assessing the risk should remain independent of the value judgments that are necessarily associated with the broader issues of managing the risk. Insuring the quality and independence of the scientific component of risk-management decisions is vital to the public's ability to weigh properly the social and philosophical values intrinsic in such decisions.[55]

Here the thrust is again towards analytically separating risk assessment from risk management and keeping science distinct from social and philosophical values in decision-making about risk.

It appears, then, that recasting the discourse of health and safety regulation in terms of risk assessment and risk management has not resolved the basic dilemmas that arise in the process of using science for policy. True, the phrase 'risk assessment' connotes a form of inquiry that is more like science than policy. Yet everyone concedes that there are elements of science policy or trans-science in risk assessment, and, if McCray's analysis is valid, such elements may even predominate over those that are purely scientific. If risk assessment involves a mix of scientific and policy considerations, then the use of the term fails to resolve the institutional questions posed by Weinberg and others. Who should carry out such analyses and under what formal constraints? What, in particular, is the role of science in risk assessment, and how should responsibility for providing authoritative assessments of risk be allocated among the scientists, policy-makers and political interest groups?

The NAS report gave the regulatory agencies some pragmatic guidance in answering these questions. As mentioned earlier, it put to rest the idea that all risk assessments should be performed by a central scientific panel independent of the regulatory agencies. This means that the agencies retain primary responsibility for developing risk assessment methodologies and applying them to specific cases. The NAS report also recommended that guidelines for drawing inferences from risk data be developed uniformly for all federal agencies by a single expert board,[56] but there appears little likelihood that an independent board along the lines recommended by the National Academy will be constituted in the foreseeable future.

With significant institutional reform ruled out, the development of risk assessment guidelines has been taken over by agencies having a particular interest in this area. For example, in March 1985 the Office of Science and Technology Policy issued a lengthy document to serve as 'a framework for regulatory agencies in assessing cancer risks from chemicals',[57] and, in November 1984, EPA issued its own proposed guidelines for assessing carcinogenic risk.[58] The OSTP document sought to reflect the current scientific consensus on carcinogenic risk assessment, and therefore explicitly disavowed all attempts to formulate policy. By contrast, EPA needed risk assessment guidelines for use in its various regulatory programmes and thus adopted positions with clear policy implications. In its final guidelines the agency included phrases (for example, 'the agency takes the position that') to indicate more clearly where it was making a policy decision.[59]

The EPA and OSTP guidelines represent more advanced thinking on the subject of chemical carcinogenesis than did the generic policies of the 1970s. But it would be difficult to argue that these initiatives fundamentally altered the balance of power between scientists and policy-makers with respect to carcinogen regulation. Both sets of guidelines called for a principled analysis of the uncertainties in the data. Disclosing these uncertainties, however, tends to place considerable discretion in the hands of the ultimate political decision-maker who chooses how to act in the fact of uncertainty. Moreover, at least in the case of EPA's guidelines, there are indications that the agency will exercise its discretion so as to err on the side of safety. In keeping with this philosophy, for instance, EPA proposes to use the linearized multistage model for high to low dose extrapolations when there is no information to preclude this choice. It is widely recognized that this model provides an upper limit to the risk, but not necessarily a realistic estimate of the actual risk.

OSTP arguably helped to increase the scientific community's control over carcinogenic risk assessment through its efforts to draw up guidelines acceptable to a broad cross-section of scientists. OSTP unquestionably consulted widely with non-governmental scientists in preparing its report, which was incorporated by reference into EPA's guidelines. An unintended side-effect of OSTP's efforts, however, was to heighten the political competition over those aspects of risk assessment that OSTP could not resolve as a matter of scientific consensus. In particular, a controversy developed between EPA and the Office of Management and Budget (OMB) over the content of EPA's risk assessment guidelines. In May 1986 Wendy Lee Gramm, head of OMB's Office of Information and Regulatory Affairs, announced that her staff was 'considering developing more specific guidance for performing risk assessments'.[60] Lacking any technical expertise in the area, OMB nevertheless seemed prepared to overrule EPA's proposals, although these were developed following extensive public comment and review by the agency's Science Advisory Board. OMB's assertion of control over risk assessment dramatically negated the view that federal decision-makers are prepared to accept risk assessment as an apolitical, largely scientific exercise.

The chemical industry too has played an active role in the politics of risk assessment. An important test of industry's attitudes to regulatory risk assessment came in 1983 when the manufacturers of urea-formaldehyde foam insulation (UFFI) took the Consumer Product Safety Commission (CPSC) to court over the agency's proposal to ban this product as a potential human carcinogen. A focal point of the lawsuit against CPSC, which was eventually decided in industry's favour on other grounds,[61] was the claim that CPSC's approach to assessing the carcinogenic risk of UFFI was scientifically unsound.

It is worth noting some key features of the strategy adopted by industry to discredit CPSC's decision. UFFI manufacturers were dissatisfied not merely with the quality of CPSC's risk assessment, but with the agency's decision to attempt a quantitative assessment at all on the basis of the available toxicological data. Industry argued, in effect, that formaldehyde should not be treated as a potential carcinogen, let alone be subjected to formal risk assessment. The crux of industry's complaint was that CPSC's decision on UFFI violated scientific norms. By mounting an all-out challenge to CPSC's scientific methods and assumptions, the UFFI manufacturers called into question the agency's competence to resolve issues at the borderline of science and policy. These dynamics suggest that industry's real concern in the area of chemical regulation remains the allocation of power between government agencies and the scientific community, since the latter is seen as more likely to interpret science in ways favourable to industry's interests.

The questions raised by the UFFI manufacturers provided some of the impetus for a further review of the scientific data on formaldehyde at a 'consensus workshop' sponsored by EPA and attended by experts from Europe and the United States.[62] The UFFI lawsuit thus achieved one of its immediate goals: moving the debate on formaldehyde to a more 'scientific' forum. At issue in the workshop was the correct interpretation of the conflicting data on formaldehyde and the advisability of assessing the compound's carcinogenic potential solely on the basis of the positive animal studies. While no one has questioned the workshop's usefulness as a consensus-building exercise, the proceedings were less effective from the standpoint of providing guidance to EPA. There was no consensus on one of the issues most relevant to the agency's regulatory task, namely, the method that should be used to extrapolate the risk to humans from the available animal evidence. In end effect, then, the workshop was a reminder that, at least in the US policy system, there are limits to scientific consensus formation as an approach to resolving science policy disputes.

While the chemical industry and its supporters worry that risk assessment leaves too much discretion within the hands of the regulatory agencies, some scientists at least are concerned that the process places undue emphasis on 'cognitive dissonance'[63] within science. Weinberg's articulation of these fears is particularly illuminating. He has argued that current attempts by policy-makers to obtain estimates of risk at low exposures transcend the limits of science. By proposing to recognize a new discipline called 'regulatory science', Weinberg asks in effect that scientists be protected against the deconstructive processes of regulatory risk assessment.

> I should think that a far more honest and straightforward way of dealing with the intrinsic inability of science to predict the occurrence of rare events is to concede this limitation and not to ask of science or scientists more than they are capable of providing. Instead of asking science for answers to unanswerable questions, regulators should be content with less far-reaching answers ... Furthermore, because these same limits apply to litigation, the legal system should recognize, much more explicitly than it has, that science and scientists often have little to say, probably much less than some scientific activists would admit.[64]

The distinction between 'scientists', who presumably understand the limits of science, and 'scientific activists', who refuse to do so, reinforces Weinberg's basic thesis that substantial areas of probabilistic risk assessment do not fall within the domain of science as defined by its professional practitioners.

Peer review: rhetoric and reality

Recognizing the need for scientific legitimacy, the US policy process has cast around for ways of ensuring that science is used in ways that will enhance public confidence. In the early 1970s, complaints by environmentalists about the closed character of expert decision-making led to a tremendous expansion of opportunities for public participation, so that democratic values could be injected into conflicts about the interpretation of science. Federal laws such as the Federal Advisory Committee Act, which mandates more openness in the deliberations of expert bodies, are typical legacies of that period. By the late 1970s, however, a different note entered into the critique of the federal government's analysis of science. Objections stemming from regulated industries rather than from consumer and environmental activists centred on the 'bad science' allegedly emanating from the agencies.[65] Critics argued that the science used in regulation was flawed, first, because policy considerations were permitted to taint the evaluation of science, and second, because the agencies lacked sufficient scientific competence. Industry-led efforts to distinguish science from policy (or risk assessment from risk management) were, in part, a response to the first problem; the second has been addressed mainly through demands for more 'peer review' of agency science.

Peer review in the regulatory process derives legitimacy primarily from the fact that this procedure has long been used within science to ensure the validity of new findings and interpretations. Moreover, peer review already has a well-established role in the allocation of research funds by federal granting agencies like the National Science Foundation and the National Institutes of Health. Since regulatory agencies also base many of their decisions on science, it seems reasonable to require that this science too should routinely undergo peer review. The underlying assumption is that the discipline of peer review will help hold governmental science to the same standards as science practised outside government. Timely review, so runs the argument, can help prevent such fiascos as the repudiation of EPA's study of health damage at Love Canal by a blue-ribbon commission appointed to pass on the study's scientific merit.

The structural features that define and motivate peer review in other settings, however, are largely absent in the regulatory context. In the case of both journal articles and grant proposals, for example, there is rarely any question as to what should be reviewed. In regulatory science the reviewable products are much harder to identify. Should agencies submit new test protocols or interpretive guidelines for review, or only completed studies? Should risk assessments be reviewed or only the primary data on which assessments are based? Given the indeterminate character of the 'science' used in agency decisions, the selection of peers, too, becomes a problematic issue. For scientific activity unrelated to policy-making, there is a general agreement that 'peers' are those with relevant disciplinary training and sufficient technical competence to evaluate the matter under review.[66] In the case of risk assessment, by contrast, it is not even agreed that we are dealing with science in any conventional sense, let alone with science bounded by recognized disciplinary contours and practised by identifiable colleges of scientific peers.

Because of the complicated interplay of science and policy in risk regulation, there is as yet no consensus on how to structure peer review within the policy process. Every agency that makes substantial use of scientific information has institutionalized some interactions between its own staff and scientists unaffiliated with the agency. These review procedures range from highly formal, legally controlled relationships, such as that between EPA and its Science Advisory Board (SAB), to less structured, *ad hoc* arrangements for examining the scientific basis of regulatory decisions. The potential impact of any kind of regulatory review is, of course, much greater than that of ordinary scientific review. Regulatory decisions carry broader socioeconomic consequences than the research of any individual scientist. Further, rejected articles or grant applications can usually find other sponsors, whereas an unfavourable decision by a regulatory agency can rarely be overturned except through litigation or, exceptionally, through appeals to Congress.

As a highly visible and influential process, regulatory peer review has attracted unfavourable notice from those dissatisfied with policy decisions about risk. Objections focus on the selection of scientific peers. A case in point was the controversy over FDA's use of a so-called Public Board of Inquiry (PBOI) to review the safety of the artificial sweetener aspartame. FDA was criticized for selecting two of the three PBOI members from the Massachusetts Institute of Technology (MIT), thereby permitting an over-representation of a single institutional viewpoint, as well as for putting a nutritionist on the board.[67] One observer, whose own work included research on aspartame, argued that the scientific disputes about the substance could better have been resolved by trained neuropathologists. But as Vincent Brannigan has noted in his case study of the aspartame PBOI, there was no agreement among the interested parties as to how these scientific issues should be defined.[68] Hence, it is hardly surprising that there were disagreements about the kind of expertise that should have been represented on the board.

Congress has criticized FDA in the past for wasteful and unnecessary use of advisory committees to resolve issues that were within the competence of the agency's in-house staff.[69] Such a complaint was recently raised in connection with FDA's regulation of Zomax, an anti-inflammatory drug that not only poses a cancer risk to humans, but has been associated with serious allergic reactions and a number of deaths. In March 1983 Zomax was temporarily removed from the market by its manufacturer, but a subsequent FDA proposal to remarket the drug triggered an investigation by the House Committee on Government Operations.[70] The committee found fault with several aspects of FDA's decision-making on Zomax, including the referral of the remarketing issue to the agency's Arthritis Advisory Committee. Congressional investigators believed that FDA failed to meet its own scientific prerequisites for such a referral, since the agency had not received any substantially new information about the drug's chronic effects on health.

In spite of the conflicts and problems associated with regulatory peer review, it is, in the words of one experienced EPA official, a 'growth industry'.[71] Within EPA, for example, demands for SAB's approval of scientific assessments have grown substantially in recent years. In 1981 SAB was reviewing only 15–20 issues a year. The number had risen to 54 for 1985 alone. One reason for the increased popularity of peer review clearly is the desire of political decision-makers to shield themselves against challenge by exhausting all available forms of scientific review. More and more EPA analysts, for example, are turning to SAB because they are aware that SAB's approval could carry weight with both the media and the courts. But regulatory peer review has also won the support of scientists and of private interest groups with quite different stakes in the policy process. Approval by such disparate groups suggests that peer review has a strategic importance extending well beyond concerns for improving the scientific basis of regulatory decisions.

Industry's advocacy of peer review is perhaps easiest to understand in strategic terms. Regulated industries have always insisted that errors in risk management policy arise through the failure of administrative agencies to use 'good science'. A logical next step is to demand that agencies adopt the procedure that scientists themselves use for quality control within their own disciplines. Institutionally, peer review serves industry's interests by transferring some of the discretionary authority to interpret indeterminate science to expert bodies that do not necessarily share the policy biases of federal regulators. The demand for peer review can thus be seen as a natural extension of the same interests that led industry to propose an independent scientific board to carry out risk assessments for all the regulatory agencies.

More puzzling is the readiness of some politicians and public interest activists to embrace the concept of peer review, as they did during the controversy over Todhunter's decision to discount the risks of formaldehyde. At a hearing in the House of Representatives, Todhunter was taken to task by Congressman Gore for not subjecting his analysis of the formaldehyde cancer data to peer review.[72] Ashford's critique of federal policies on formaldehyde also charged that Todhunter committed a procedural error by not undertaking peer review.[73] On the face of it, this apparent endorsement of scientific peer review seems inconsistent with Ashford's special sensitivity to the policy component of risk management decisions.

A closer analysis of the language used by Gore and Ashford, however, indicates that both were using the term 'peer review' differently from industry representatives such as AIHC. As conceived by industry, peer review involves the exposure of scientific analyses done by agency staffs to the scrutiny of scientists situated outside the agencies. Gore and Ashford, by contrast, included within their definition of peer review the internal review of administrative decisions by the agency's own technical staff.[74]

Some of Gore's most pointed questioning of Todhunter focused on the administrator's decision not to consult scientists in the Office of Toxic Substances (OTS) or CAG about his analysis of formaldehyde. Todhunter claimed that there was no need for him to do this because his memorandum represented a policy rather than a scientific decision, and thus was inappropriate for scientific review.[75] This excuse, however, failed to convince Gore, who insisted that Todhunter's decision was 'science'. In critiquing the administrator's action, Gore used the terms 'peer review' and 'staff review' interchangeably:

> However, you speak for the agency on the science question, and if you are going to unilaterally change the science that the agency uses to arrive at a decision, *without peer review, without staff review*, and then you have your judgment called into question by scientists of the eminence of those on the prior panel, then what does that do to the scientific process at EPA?[76]

Ashford, too, collapsed the notions of internal and external review procedures in commenting that 'Todhunter's memorandum was not reviewed by his scientific peers inside or outside the agency'.[77]

Both Ashford and Gore must have recognized that more internal review in the formaldehyde case would very likely have built pressure for overruling

Todhunter's assessment. In underplaying the compound's possible carcino-genicity, Todhunter had rejected most of EPA's existing guidelines for assessing chemicals with a carcinogenic potential. Scientists in CAG or OTS, many of whom were involved in developing those guidelines, had a stake in seeing them consistently applied and might well have opposed Todhunter's analysis if called upon to comment on the controversial memorandum. At the very least, their views would have created a record requiring explicit rebuttal, and consultation with EPA's own scientists might even have made Todhunter more sceptical about the analysis advanced by the formaldehyde industry.[78]

Given their professional and political interests, one would expect the scientific community to prefer external peer review over the kind of agency-internal review advocated by Ashford and Gore in the formaldehyde case. Outside review is much more consistent with the image science seeks to project of itself as an autonomous and politically incorruptible institution. In a congressional hearing following the formaldehyde controversy, Norton Nelson firmly endorsed the expected scientific viewpoint. The immediate object of his remarks was the cancer policy guidelines then under consideration at OSTP. Although these had been informally circulated to independent scientists for review, Nelson did not believe that the final product would achieve scientific credibility:

> I have no doubt that there are scientists in the Federal establishment that can do quite as well in terms of the science as scientists outside of the federal establishment, but I do not believe that the credibility required in this important issue can be achieved by cancer policy formulated within a purely administrative framework of OSTP and the federal agencies.[79]

Nelson suggested that for 'credible and technically competent advice' on a revised cancer policy the federal government should turn to an authoritative scientific body, preferably the National Academy of Sciences. Until such advice was forth-coming, Nelson considered it prudent to abide by the cancer policy developed during the Carter administration by the Interagency Regulatory Liaison Group:

> The IRLG document, which has been, I believe, disavowed by the present administration, is a perfectly good statement of many of the policies for cancer control. What I am asking is, why should we not stay with the accepted principles and policies which were established until we have undertaken an appropriate review, which I think is very important?
> And that review should be done, I sincerely believe, under auspices outside the federal structure.[80]

In using the term 'review', Nelson was referring to the scientific re-evaluation of particular policy-relevant fields (cancer testing, carcinogen risk assessment) rather than to the peer review of any specific document. However, while criticizing OSTP's efforts as inadequate, he held up as a model the guidelines developed by IRLG, another administrative agency within the 'federal structure'.

Congressman Ritter of Pennsylvania, a Republican with party loyalties to the Reagan administration, was quick to seize on the apparent contradiction in Nelson's testimony and to shift the debate to the issue of peer review:

> Dr Nelson, you mentioned that the current governmental attempt to try to refine or at least expose some possibilities of coming to grips with a policy on cancer, that somehow it was not under the correct auspices; was not proper. I should like to point out that the IRLG, which you seem to hold in very high esteem, was also a governmental body, an interagency body.
>
> It did not bring in peer review. It had a rotating membership. As a matter of fact, the very roughest first document from the OSTP review went out to peer review to people like yourself and members of the environmentalist community.
>
> You know, people have said that the IRLG review occurred behind closed doors and was not open to extensive peer review.[81]

Under Ritter's insistent questioning, the issue became not whether OSTP was the right kind of agency to rewrite federal cancer policy, but whether IRLG had conducted a form of peer review that Nelson, as a scientist, would approve. Unable to equate IRLG's practices with the ordinary norms of scientific peer review, Nelson beat a somewhat lame retreat:

> Well, I am somewhat familiar with the development of that document . . . It had extensive participation from outside scientists. I think I would agree with you that it should have had outside peer review. It did not.[82]

The formaldehyde case, then, illustrates the fluidity of the concept of peer review, showing how such a concept can be redefined to suit varying objectives by those with a stake in controlling the discourse of regulation. The Ritter-Nelson exchange indicates how the inherent ambiguity of the word 'review' (review of a scientific field, review of a document) facilitates such manipulation. Of course, this kind of verbal game-playing is easiest with terms that are fairly new in the political discourse. Certainly, the notion of peer review was not widely used in the regulatory context before the 1980s and, as noted earlier, its procedural correlates remain unclear in this setting. Legislative action, such as the adoption of a uniform federal peer review law, could narrow down the uses of the term by rendering certain readings either impossible or implausible. Congress, however, has shown little inclination to propose uniform procedures for regulatory decision-making, and has already mandated several different forms of statutory peer review. Moreover, the preceding discussion suggests that the identification of 'peers' and the structuring of a review process will always be more politically sensitive in the regulatory arena than in the areas of scientific publication or research funding. For these reasons, regulatory 'peer review' may remain a contested concept for the foreseeable future.

Conclusion

The three 'contested boundaries' I have discussed reveal a problem that was largely overlooked in the early attempts to define trans-science or science policy. The lines between science, policy, and the areas where the two are mixed are difficult to draw not merely because science is indeterminate, but because the effort to make such distinctions is politically charged. How one characterizes an issue on the spectrum between science and policy bears on the way it is ultimately decided, both institutionally and procedurally. If an issue is understood to be scientific, then it can legitimately be resolved by expert panels working with criteria that were never exposed to the full deconstructionist force of the administrative and legal process. Alternatively, if policy elements predominate over scientific ones in a borderline issue, then it is more appropriate to let agency officials and the courts provide the authoritative reading of the disputed technical data, using procedures taken from their respective traditions. The outcome of regulation in a particular case often depends critically on the way decision-making authority is allocated among scientific and political or legal institutions. The classification of issues at the boundary of science and policy, and the procedures used to resolve them, also have a potentially grave impact on the public image of science. Hence scientists, private interest groups and members of the policy establishment all have a stake in the definition of science and non-science, and the vocabulary used by all of these parties remains subject to manipulation or 'essentially contested'.

For scientists, the primary interest in these boundary disputes is to draw the lines between science and policy in ways that best preserve the authority and integrity of science. Scientists have an institutional stake in reducing public interactions between science and the administrative process, since these interactions emphasize the indeterminacy and lack of consensus within science, thereby weakening science's (and the scientist's) claim to cognitive authority. The cases discussed in this article suggest that scientists can adopt two fundamentally different rhetorical strategies to cope with this problem. One approach, perhaps best articulated by Weinberg, is to separate out the areas of maximal uncertainty and conflict and to declare them something other than 'real' science. Weinberg's own proposals for relabelling these boundary areas have included 'trans-science' and, more recently, 'regulatory science'.

Weinberg's approach, though protective of the institutional interests of science, avoids addressing some of the procedural issues of greatest concern to policymakers. In particular, merely identifying areas where science does not have all the answers fails to settle who should decide questions in these boundary regions, and by what methods or procedures. Scientists actively engaged in the policy process, whether as advisers or as advocates, have not been able to overlook this difficulty. Their response, exemplified by the positions of Weinstein and Nelson at the cancer policy hearings, has been in some respects almost the opposite of Weinberg's. Both Weinstein and Nelson emphasized, and perhaps exaggerated, the extent of scientific consensus underlying the federal cancer policies developed in the 1970s. Both urged more or less explicitly that revisions in these policies should be undertaken only by accredited scientific organizations using scientific modes of decision-making. In the context of cancer policy, then, Weinstein's and Nelson's remarks were calculated to draw the protective veil of science over many of the disputed issues which others might relegate to the domain of 'regulatory science' or 'science policy'. This approach, too, can be seen as furthering the interests of science, but by enlarging rather than minimizing the role played by science in decisions about risk.

In essence, the position adopted by Nelson and Weinstein with respect to cancer policy is similar to that of scientists in many European regulatory frameworks, where experts wield considerable influence and there is relatively little public debate about the proper limits on their range of inquiry. European officials and the public tend to accept as 'science' any issues that their technical advisory committees are prepared to treat as scientific. There is apparently little concern that policy issues will illegitimately be decided by scientists under the guise of technical decision-making. In the United States, however, the public deconstruction of science has progressed to a point where such trust in expertise is almost unthinkable. Once a policy-relevant area of science has been exposed to deconstruction, as in the case of carcinogen risk assessment, it is virtually impossible to make further decisions in the area without a degree of openness and adversarial debate that is uncommon in European policy systems.

A regulatory process centring on the deconstruction of science threatens the legitimacy of political as well as scientific decision-making. If it is seen that science cannot provide definitive answers to questions about risk, then policy-makers cannot fall back on unassailable technical justifications of their regulatory choices. In the regulatory controversies of the past ten years, especially those involving toxic chemicals, public interest groups have generally argued that in these circumstances regulators should be free to choose among different scientifically plausible interpretations of the evidence, guided primarily by their understanding of their statutory mission. But the strategy of highlighting the indeterminacy of science and the extent of administrative discretion leaves decision-makers vulnerable to charges of using science in arbitrary and capricious ways. The chemical industry has been aggressive in pursuing this line of attack. Its insistence on 'good science' and its complaints about the technical competence of the federal agencies are consistent with the broader objective of removing as much discretionary power as possible from regulators, who are viewed as captive to environmental interests. Administrators, such as Ruckelshaus, have vacillated between these two positions, hoping, on the one hand, that scientific deliberations will lead to clean, credible resolutions of policy dilemmas, but recognizing, on the other, that such solutions are seldom within the reach of science.

I have suggested here that terms like 'science policy', 'risk assessment' and 'peer review' are used in the regulatory discourse not only for conceptual clarity, but also to advance particular views about the nature of science and its relation to policy. The fluidity of these concepts arises from fundamental social disagreements about the extent to which science and scientists should control decision-making at the frontiers of knowledge. Since these boundary-defining terms affect the allocation of power, their meaning cannot be established independently of the political process. This makes for a certain untidiness in the discourse of risk regulation. Meanings attached to key terms tend to change over time and in the usage of different political groups. New terminology springs up as groups wishing to exert more authority over the interpretation of science find persuasive labels to justify their claims. In a pluralistic society, however, such uses of political rhetoric are entirely familiar, and will trouble only those who expect science to provide rational, apolitical paradigms for the evaluation of risk.

Notes

* *Social Studies of Science*, Vol. 17, No. 2 (1987), pp. 195–230.

1 See, for example, T. J. Pinch, 'The Sun-Set: The Presentation of Certainty in Scientific Life', *Social Studies of Science*, Vol. 11 (1981), 131–58.

2 D. Nelkin (ed.), *Controversy* (Beverly Hills, CA: Sage Publications, 2nd edn, 1984); R. Brickman, S. Jasanoff and T. Ilgen, *Controlling Chemicals: The Politics of Regulation in Europe and the United States* (Ithaca, NY: Cornell University Press, 1985).

3 M. Mulkay, 'Norms and Ideology in Science', *Social Science Information*, Vol. 15 (1976), 637–56.

4 R. K. Merton, 'The Normative Structure of Science', reprinted as Chapter 13 in *The Sociology of Science* (Chicago: The University of Chicago Press, 1973), 267–78.

5 D. Crane, 'The Gatekeepers of Science: Some Factors Affecting the Selection of Articles for Scientific Journals', *The American Sociologist*, Vol. 32 (1967), 195–201.

6 For a review of the literature pertaining to such structures, see D. E. Chubin, 'Beyond Invisible Colleges: Inspirations and Aspirations of Post-1972 Social Studies of Science', *Sociometrics*, Vol. 7 (1985), 221–54.

7 T. F. Gieryn, G. M. Bevins and S. C. Zehr, 'Professionalization of American Scientists: Public Science in the Creation/Evolution Trials', *American Sociological Review*, Vol. 50 (1985), 392–409; see also Gieryn and A. E. Figert, 'Scientists Protect Their Cognitive Authority: The Status Degradation Ceremony of Sir Cyril Burt', to appear in G. Böhme and N. Stehr (eds), *Sociology of the Sciences Yearbook*, Vol. 10 (1986).

8 In the US legal system, Judge Bazelon of the DC Circuit Court of Appeals has been a noted advocate of open and broadly participatory procedures in decision-making about science. In his view 'the healthiest thing that can happen is to let it all hang out, warts and all'. Statement by D. L. Bazelon, in Office of Technology Assessment, *Impacts of Neuro-Science*, Background Papers (1984), Appendix C, 29.

9 I am indebted to a private communication from B. Wynne for this use of the term 'deconstruct'.

10 See, for example, R. Brickman, 'Science and the Politics of Toxic Chemical Regulation: US and European Contrasts', *Science, Technology and Human Values*, Vol. 9 (1984), 107–11.

11 What is at stake for such scientists is not merely the public characterization of their discipline, but their own status within the scientific profession. To the extent that the public perceives policy-relevant science as not 'real science', its practitioners are in danger of being perceived as not 'real scientists'. This is not a purely theoretical worry, since scientists who participate too actively in policy formulation (for example, as agency employees or professional expert witnesses) often do get read out of the professional scientific community. The boundary work that scientists engage in to determine which policy advisers are true scientists and which are not is a topic that deserves further study, though it lies beyond the scope of this article.

12 For a study of essentially contested terms in the political process, see W. E. Connolly, *The Terms of Political Discourse* (Princeton, NJ: Princeton University Press, 2nd edn, 1983).

13 There are at least two approaches to this kind of line-drawing. One can either try to distinguish science from policy in substantive terms or to differentiate the class of scientists from the class of policy-makers. Following the latter approach, science can be redefined as that which is done by acknowledged scientists. In general, this paper focuses on the former (or substantive) approach to defining the science-policy boundary.

14 A. Weinberg, 'Science and Trans-Science', *Minerva*, Vol. 10 (1972), 209–22.

15 Ibid., 209.

16 Ibid., 215.

17 A. Weinberg, 'Science and Its Limits: The Regulator's Dilemma', *Issues in Science and Technology*, Vol. II, No. 1 (Fall 1985), 67.

18 Ibid. (emphasis added).

19 Ibid.

20 Ibid., 68. One may wonder whether the practitioners of what Weinberg characterizes as 'regulatory science' would accept this distinction. This inquiry, however, is not pursued further in this paper.

21 Ibid., 220.

22 T. O. McGarity, 'Substantive and Procedural Discretion in Administrative Resolution of Science Policy Questions: Regulating Carcinogens in EPA and OSHA', *The Georgetown Law Journal*, Vol. 67 (1979), 729–810; see also McGarity, 'OSHA's Generic Carcinogen Policy: Rule Making Under Scientific and Legal Uncertainty', in J. D. Nyhart and M. M. Carrow (eds), *Law and Science in Collaboration* (Lexington, MA: Lexington Books, 1983), 55–104.

23 For more detailed accounts of these developments, see S. Jasanoff, 'Science and the Limits of Administrative Rule-Making: Lessons from the OSHA Cancer Policy', *Osgoode Hall Law Journal*, Vol. 20 (1982), 536–61; M. E. Rushefsky, 'Assuming the Conclusions: Risk Assessment in the Development of Cancer Policy', *Politics and the Life Sciences*, Vol. 4 (1985), 31–66. Comparative studies of carcinogen regulation illuminate the degree to which risk assessment in the United States depends on the deconstruction of science: see, for example, S. Jasanoff, *Risk Management and Political Culture* (New York: Russell Sage Foundation, 1986).

24 McGarity, 'Substantive and Procedural Discretion', op. cit. note 22, 732.

25 Ibid., 733.

26 Weinberg, op. cit. note 14, 210–11.

27 McGarity, 'Substantive and Procedural Discretion', op. cit. note 22, 747.

28 Appointed to head EPA early in President Reagan's first term, Anne Gorsuch was forced to resign in 1983, along with many of the agency's top political appointees, following widespread charges of legal violations and administrative misconduct. The episode left EPA badly battered, and morale at the agency was at an all-time low when William Ruckelshaus succeeded Gorsuch as EPA Administrator.

29 See US House of Representatives, Committee on Science and Technology, *Hearing on Formaldehyde: Review of Scientific Basis of EPA's Carcinogenic Risk Assessment* (hereafter cited as *Formaldehyde Hearing*), 97th Congress, 2nd Session (May 1982).

30 N. A. Ashford, C. W. Ryan and C. C. Caldart, 'Law and Science Policy in Federal Regulation of Formaldehyde', *Science*, Vol. 222 (25 November 1983), 894–900.

31 Ibid., 895.

32 The principle that agencies must provide open and rational explanations for departures from prior policies is, of course, well established in US administrative law. See, for example, *Motor Vehicle Manufacturers Association v State Farm Mutual Auto Insurance Co.*, 463 US 29 (1983).

33 Ashford et al., op. cit. note 30, 895.

34 See Brickman et al., op. cit. note 2, 187–217.
35 US House of Representatives, Committee on Energy and Commerce, Subcommittee on Commerce, Transportation and Tourism, *Control of Carcinogens in the Environment* (hereafter cited as *Carcinogens Hearing*), 98th Congress, 1st Session (March 1983), 7.
36 Ibid., 16.
37 Ibid., 70.
38 Ibid., 71.
39 The generic cancer policy was not formally issued until after OSHA promulgated the exposure standard for benzene. However, OSHA relied on the conceptual framework of the cancer policy in developing the benzene standard.
40 *Industrial Union Department, AFL-CIO v American Petroleum Institute*, 448 US 607 (1980).
41 See, for example, AIHC, 'AIHC Proposal for a Science Panel' (mimeo, March 1981); 'Comparative Analysis of HR 6521 (Wampler Bill) and Science Panel Proposal' (March 1980); 'Proposals for Improving the Science Base for Chronic Health Hazard Decision-Making' (Scarsdale, NY: AIHC, December 1981).
42 National Academy of Sciences, *Risk Assessment in the Federal Government: Managing the Process* (Washington, DC: National Academy Press, 1983), 2.
43 L. E. McCray, 'An Anatomy of Risk Assessment: Scientific and Extra-Scientific Components in the Assessment of Scientific Data on Cancer Risks', in National Academy of Sciences, *Risk Assessment in the Federal Government: Managing the Process*, Working Papers (Washington, DC: National Academy Press, 1983), 83–101.
44 'The risk assessment process requires analytic choices to be made that rest, at least in part, on the policy consideration of whether to be more or less conservative when determining possible public health risks': NAS, op. cit. note 42, 139.
45 Ibid., 18.
46 Ibid., 7.
47 Ibid., 49.
48 Ibid., 153.
49 Ibid., 164.
50 W. D. Ruckelshaus, 'Science, Risk, and Public Policy', *Science*, Vol. 221 (9 September 1983), 1027–28.
51 C. Peterson, 'How Much Risk is Too Much?', *Washington Post* (4 February 1985), 8.
52 W. Ruckelshaus, 'Risk in a Free Society', *Risk Analysis*, Vol. 4 (1984), 157–62.
53 Department of Health and Human Services, *Risk Assessment and Risk Management of Toxic Substances* (April 1985).
54 Ibid., 21.
55 Ibid., 29.
56 National Academy of Sciences, op. cit. note 42, 166–67.
57 OSTP, 'Chemical Carcinogens: Notice of Review of the Science and Its Associated Principles', *Federal Register*, Vol. 50 (14 March 1985), 10371–422.
58 EPA, 'Proposed Guidelines for Carcinogen Risk Assessment; Request for Comments', *Federal Register*, Vol. 49 (23 November 1984), 46294–301. The guidelines were published in final form almost two years later: see *Federal Register*, Vol. 51 (24 September 1986), 33992–4003.
59 *Federal Register*, Vol. 51 (24 September 1986), 34001.
60 See E. Marshall, 'OMB and Congress at Odds over Cancer Risk Policy', *Science*, Vol. 233 (8 August 1986), 618.
61 *Gulf South Insulation v Consumer Product Safety Commission*, 701 F.2d 1137 (5th Cir. 1983).
62 See National Center for Toxicological Research, Report on the Consensus Workshop on Formaldehyde, Little Rock, Arkansas (3–6 October 1983).
63 Weinberg, op. cit. note 17, 67.
64 Ibid., 68.

65   See citations at note 41 above.

66   I. Mitroff and D. Chubin, 'Peer Review at the NSF: A Dialectical Policy Analysis', *Social Studies of Science*, Vol. 9 (1979), 199–232.

67   V. Brannigan, 'The First FDA Public Board of Inquiry: The Aspartame Case', in Nyhart and Carrow, op. cit. note 22, 181–202.

68   Ibid., 189.

69   US House of Representatives, Committee on Government Operations, *Report on Use of Advisory Committees by the Food and Drug Administration*, 94th Congress, 2nd Session (January 1976).

70   US House of Representatives, Committee on Government Operations, *Report on FDA's Regulation of Zomax*, 98th Congress, 1st Session (December 1983).

71   Interview with Terry Yosie, EPA, Washington, DC (June 1985).

72   *Formaldehyde Hearing*, 141–43.

73   Ashford et al., op. cit. note 30, 897.

74   This usage corresponds to the notion of peer review employed by Congress in the Federal Insecticide, Fungicide, and Rodenticide Act (FIFRA). The statute authorizes peer review of EPA studies relating to pesticides by scientists working within or outside the agency. Elsewhere, however, Congress has provided that scientific advisory committees must not include scientists employed by the federal government.

75   Todhunter was here caught in a double bind, though he apparently did not realize it. If his decision on formaldehyde was 'scientific', then it presumably would have benefited from peer review, as urged by Ashford and Gore. If, however, it was a policy decision, as Todhunter himself claimed, then it clearly went against EPA's established guidelines for carcinogenic risk assessment. As an individual agency official, Todhunter did not have the authority to deviate unilaterally from these guidelines. He should have announced his proposed policy changes openly and submitted them to public comment in accordance with standard US administrative practice. This he failed to do. Thus, whether Todhunter called the decision science or policy, it was procedurally defective.

76   *Formaldehyde Hearing*, 141 (emphasis added); also similar language on 143.

77   Ashford et al., op. cit. note 30, 897.

78   Todhunter was criticized by Norton Nelson of New York University for an overly pro-industry orientation in his analysis of the scientific data on formaldehyde: see *Formaldehyde Hearing*, 29.

79   *Carcinogens Hearing*, 72.

80   Ibid., 73.

81   Ibid., 84.

82   Ibid.

7 The songlines of risk[*]

In the world's industrial nations, 'risk' has become *the* organising concept that gives meaning and direction to environmental regulation. The stated purpose of most environmental legislation today is to reduce the likelihood of harm from our myriad ingenious technological activities to levels that are either demonstrably safe, or – if safety is an unattainable goal – then at least to levels that can be shown to be reasonable. Agencies implementing environmental laws increasingly are required to justify their actions on the basis of risk assessment, often done in quantitative form; in turn, scientists are called upon to satisfy the regulators' needs with reliable methods of detecting, measuring, and representing risks to human health and the environment.

Although risk assessment in one form or another provides the cornerstone for much environmental regulation, it would be a mistake to think that either policy-makers or technical experts can claim a complete monopoly on the concept of risk. In a time when Brent Spar, BSE (bovine spongiform encephalopathy or 'mad cow disease'), climate change, and the ozone hole have come to symbolise the tribulations of high-tech living, it is hardly possible for ordinary citizens to get along without their own working models of risk. Where do risks come from, who is to blame for them, and how can they be mastered, coped with, or altogether avoided? Just as, a century or so ago, the idea of *progress* helped to name an optimistic era, so today *risk*, by its very pervasiveness, seems to be the defining marker of our own less sanguine historical moment. European social theorists have taken the lead in arguing that the social circumstance which matters most in our intolerably jumbled modern condition is risk: all of us who inhabit the earth at the end of the 20th century – rich and poor, high and low, young and old – live equally in the embrace of the 'risk society' (Beck 1992).

Risk, at any rate, is impossible to ignore for anyone professionally concerned with the making and evaluation of environmental policy. Since the early 1970s, risk has been the focal point worldwide of countless legislative inquiries, guidance documents, court decisions, workshops, symposia, newspaper and television reports, and, of course, published articles and books. New journals, professional societies, research centres, and specialised university departments have been formed to enable systematic research and scholarly debate about risk. In the United States alone, more than a dozen studies of risk have been commissioned over the past fifteen years from the prestigious National Academy of Sciences. Through its policy arm, the National Research Council (NRC), the Academy has issued reports on particular sources of risk, such as pesticides (NRC 1987) or genetically modified organisms (NRC 1989), as well as on the practices and procedures of risk assessment (NRC 1983, 1994, 1996). The 1990 amendments to the U.S. Clean Air Act not only called for a technical review of risk assessment methods by the NRC, but also demanded that a joint presidential and congressional commission be formed to evaluate the conduct of risk assessment and risk management under federal environmental laws (Risk Commission 1997).

How much, then, can we claim to have learned from all this activity? What, in particular, have social scientists done to deepen our understanding of how risk functions in regulatory programmes or in societal relationships more broadly? And how might such work point the way toward more effective control of environmental hazards? In this paper, I would like first to offer a necessarily abbreviated overview of three major critical traditions that have emerged from the intensive social and political analysis of environmental risk. I will point out some of the strengths and weaknesses of these positions and show how they complement or extend one another. Much of the research I draw on for this purpose was based on national experiences with risk analysis and risk management, and to some extent on comparisons among national regulatory approaches. Yet, environmental hazards today have causes and consequences that often cut across national boundaries. These unruly problems strain the capacity of national and international decisionmakers to craft credible responses to risk. I will end with some reflections about the implications of social scientists' understandings of risk for the management of environmental hazards on a global scale.

Risk and social knowledge

Social critiques of risk-based environmental regulation can usefully be separated into three strands that differ along two significant dimensions: first, in their theoretical stance with respect to the nature of environmental knowledge, and, second, in their prescriptions for linking knowledge to political action (Jasanoff 1998). The first of these positions, which has tended to dominate governmental and scientific discussions of risk, espouses a positivist (or realist) theory of knowledge and a bureaucratic-rationalistic policy orientation. Risk, for critics of this school, is a tangible by-product of actually occurring natural and social processes. It can be mapped and measured by knowledgeable experts, and, within limits, controlled. If ruling institutions fail to achieve this mission, it is chiefly because their knowledge and competence are unequal to the task or because they lack the political will to take unpalatable action.

A second line of explanation, grounded in the sociology of scientific knowledge, looks upon environmental knowledge as a social construct and proposes a liberal, and pluralistic, solution to the problem of meshing knowledge with action. Risks, according to this point of view, do not directly reflect natural reality but are refracted in every society through lenses shaped by history, politics, and culture.

Faced with the same 'facts' about nature, Americans, for instance, fear cancer more than the British, the French tolerate nuclear power better than their German neighbours, and Americans are more receptive to biotechnology than Danes, Norwegians or Germans. In the light of such variations, the attempt to regulate risk solely on the basis of expert knowledge looks reductionist and conceptually inadequate. Constructivist analysis suggests that more attention needs to be paid to the connections between risk and culture, and it asks for increased negotiation and stakeholder engagement so that different perspectives on risk can be uncovered and accommodated. As we shall see, this approach has begun to gain ground in some recent, high-level U.S. proposals concerning risk and regulation.

The third, and in some ways most challenging, line of social analysis also takes its inspiration from constructivist theories of knowledge, but its focus is on the ways in which the concept of risk mediates between knowledge and power. Risk analysis, according to this approach, is first and foremost a specialised language and set of practices – in formal terms, a discourse (Foucault 1972) – that serves to channel power in society. The decision to frame environmental problems in terms of *risk*, for example, rules out other possible ways of talking about harms to human beings and the environment. Risk-talk implicitly empowers some people as experts and excludes others as inarticulate, irrelevant or incompetent (Winner 1986). Some examples may help to give these ideas greater concreteness.

The theory of bureaucratic failure

Industrial accidents, policy stalemates, discoveries of latent health and environmental hazards, the spiralling costs of clean-up and prevention – such problems continually beset even the best-planned programs of environmental regulation, and no literate citizen in an industrial society can be wholly oblivious to them. As commonplace as the failures is the explanatory impulse that lays the blame on faulty institutions. Rational courses of action, according to realist critics of regulation, are usually discoverable through inquiry, but corruption, incapacity, incompetence, political pressure, or lack of will get in the way of satisfactory institutional performance.

In the United States, this position has perhaps been most forcefully and articulately championed by Justice Stephen Breyer, a distinguished federal judge and former administrative law professor whom President Clinton appointed to the Supreme Court. In a cycle of lectures delivered at Harvard University in 1992, Breyer blamed a three-fold pathology for the perceived failures of environmental regulation of the preceding decades. First, he said, agencies are guilty of 'tunnel vision', which has led them to regulate negligible risks at enormous social and political cost. Second, he criticised a random agenda-setting process which has been driven too much by irrational public fears and thus has skewed national priorities. Finally, he blamed political pressures and faulty institutional design for inconsistent results in environmental risk management.

Breyer's proposed solution flowed with admirable logic from his three premises. In brief, he wished to establish within the executive branch of the U.S.

government 'a specific kind of group: mission oriented, seeking to bring a degree of uniformity and rationality to decision making in highly technical areas, with broad authority, somewhat independent, and with significant prestige. Such a group would make general and government-wide the rationalising efforts in which EPA [the U.S. Environmental Protection Agency] is currently engaged' (Breyer 1993: 61). This centralised risk assessment body would depend for its success on the traditional bureaucratic virtues of rationality, expertise, insulation, and authority.

Rationality was Breyer's *summmum bonum*; he cited with dismay a well-known scatter diagram created by a team of American social psychologists (Slovic et al. 1985) to show that the public tends to elevate unknown and unfamiliar risks over more familiar ones – regardless of their actual statistical frequency. Breyer's urge to insulate rational analysis from mere superstition and public misunderstanding corresponded well with the prevailing doctrine of the 1980s that technical risk assessment should be cleanly separated from political risk management – a doctrine authoritatively set forth by the National Research Council (NRC 1983). The NRC proposed that risk decisions could be carried out in a linear, and largely non-intersecting, sequence of steps, from research to the assessment, characterisa-tion, and management of risk.

The concept of an insulated 'superagency' for risk seemed to fly in the face of democratic politics and met with considerable public resistance. Breyer's answer was that democracies need authoritative decisions, and that public respect for government depends, 'in part, upon an organization's successful accomplishment of a mission that satisfies an important societal need. (Consider the rebound of confi-dence in the military during the 1980s)' (Breyer 1993: 63). Doing appointed public tasks well, Breyer argued, was central to creating a 'politics of trust'. After all, even a closed organisation like the military had been able to maintain public confidence through effective performance of its ordained mission. That people might differ in their assessments of success and failure in risk management – not to mention in their ideas of 'need' and 'mission' – seemed undreamt of in the judge's philosophy.

A closer look at the experiences of the Environmental Protection Agency, an organisation Breyer lauded, might have shaken the judge's confidence in closed expert decisions. By the early 1980s, repeated court challenges and ideologically motivated attacks had profoundly undermined EPA's hard-earned credibility. Scientific controversies, in particular, became so bitter that it became necessary to shore up the agency's claims to expertise with new forms of public accountability. True, EPA had to seek legitimation through layers of external scientific advice, but it could not do so without also increasing the transparency of the advisory process (Jasanoff 1992). Insulation, as EPA administrators learned over time, was not an especially successful formula for garnering public respect in the maelstrom of American politics.

Risk as a social construct

A very different view of why environmental risk management fails emerges from research on the social foundations of scientific knowledge. Studies of scientific controversies about risk have revealed the complex processes by which reliable knowledge about the environment is constructed. Consensus on such 'facts' as the risks of formaldehyde or DDT arises not from demonstrated deaths, disability or environmental damage, but from repeated confrontations among disparate scientific observations, their interpretation by experts and stakeholders, and the ingrained moral and social commitments of decisionmaking institutions (Jasanoff 1986; Johnson and Covello 1987; Irwin and Wynne 1996).

In democratic policy environments, the knowledge that environmental regulators would like to live by is always vulnerable to deconstruction – that is, to being pulled apart so that the underlying assumptions or value judgments are exposed to public review and criticism (Jasanoff 1986, 1987). Moreover, when environmental values are sharply divided, scientific information and expert discourses alone offer insufficient protection against the scepticism of people representing different social positions or interests. The degree to which scientists' assumptions are questioned or contested depends in large part on the ability of relevant state institutions, such as courts, regulatory agencies, and expert advisory bodies, to set credible limits on the scope of technical debate. In cases where such boundary drawing proves ineffectual, experimental methods, instruments, models, interpretations, and even scientists' personal integrity may be relentlessly questioned by the media and the lay public – sometimes to the point where contested claims no longer support policy action. Environmental science, in this sense, bears within it the seeds of its own unmaking.

Faced with the prospect of endless controversy and deconstruction, policy institutions in some countries have accepted the need for early, possibly repeated, consultation with multiple viewpoints in the processes of environmental regulation (Power and McCarty 1998). We shall return below to two such proposals that have emerged from recent U.S. policy deliberations. These new approaches mark a step forward in acknowledging that technical analysis and political deliberation should not be placed in separate compartments, as suggested in the 1983 NRC study. Rather, these elements should be recoupled through appropriate institutional and procedural arrangements.

A dangerous discourse

It has been difficult enough for regulatory agencies to recognise that risks in the modern world do not flow deterministically from conditions fixed by nature. A realisation that is only gradually dawning on policy institutions is that even the dominant framings of environmental problems do not represent neutral readings of reality. A policy-shaping conceptual framework such as *risk* builds upon underlying social models of agency, causality, and responsibility. Such frames in turn are intellectually constraining in that they delimit the universe of scientific inquiry, political discourse, and possible policy options (Jasanoff and Wynne 1998).

How does our attitude toward regulatory failure change if we shift attention from bureaucratic incapacity and the socially constructed character of knowledge to the problem framings presupposed by risk analysis? What additional insights do we gain if we pause to ask how the techniques of risk assessment, especially of the formal, mathematical kind, deal with the uncertainties and indeterminacies of human interactions with the environment. What does the very choice of these methods tell us about the choosers' underlying social relationships and their views about the distribution of power and responsibility in society? And what alternative conceptions of the good society are given up or set aside when environmental policy is founded on widespread use of formal risk analysis?

To see how ideas about environmental risk may indeed encode tacit normative and political judgments, let us embark first on a slight literary detour. Bruce Chatwin, the famed travel writer and novelist, wrote an account of his journeys in Australia that was at the same time a brilliantly suggestive meditation on the nature of reality and our perceptions of it. In *The Songlines*, Chatwin described the ancestral myth of the 'Dreamtime' among Australian aboriginals. This was the time in which 'each totemic ancestor, while travelling through the country, was thought to have scattered a trail of words and musical notes along the line of his footprints' (Chatwin 1988: 13). These 'Dreaming-tracks lay over the land as "ways" of communication between the most far-flung tribes'. They were not merely ways of communication, however, but also ways of constructing reality through particular modes of singing. In a marvellously evocative passage, Chatwin (1988: 14) interrogated his Russo-Australian friend and informant Arkady:

> Aboriginals could not believe the country existed until they could see and sing it – just as, in the Dreamtime, the country had not existed until the Ancestors sang it.
>
> 'So the land', I said, 'must first exist as a concept in the mind. Then it must be sung? Only then can it be said to exist?'
>
> 'True.'
>
> 'In other words, "to exist" is "to be perceived"?'
>
> 'Yes.'
>
> 'Sounds suspiciously like Bishop Berkeley's Refutation of Matter.'
>
> 'Or Pure Mind Buddhism', said Arkady, 'which also sees the world as an illusion.'

Formal risk assessment, I would like to propose, is the 'songline' of contemporary risk society's anxiety about its own technological achievements. Threats dimly conceived in the mind must be sung in this melody to exist and be perceived, as well as predicted and controlled. The commitment to risk assessment by both conservatives and liberals in American politics shows how deeply this particular form of analysis influences our very ability to think coherently about environmental harms. What are the distinctive elements of this songline? I want to dwell briefly on three: causation, agency, and uncertainty.

Causation

In the world of regulatory risk assessment, causation generally is viewed as a linear and mechanistic phenomenon. Asbestos causes cancer and dioxins cause birth defects in animals, but perhaps not in humans. The classical model of cancer risk assessment used by most U.S. federal regulatory agencies still conceives of risk as the result of individual or population exposure to single substances that are suspected of causing cancer. Regulators, of course, have learned over the years to add a lot of complexity to this causal picture. The old single-hit model of carcinogenesis has been replaced by one that views cancer more realistically as a multi-stage process; the new theory is mathematically expressed by differentiating, among others, the initiation stage from the stage of promotion. The notion that risk can be adequately represented as a single number has been largely discredited. We now recognise that risk is distributed over populations of varying composition and susceptibility, exposed for variable lengths of time, and by multiple pathways (NRC 1994). Quantitative models have grown increasingly sophisticated in their ability to combine and manipulate all these discoveries about people's varying encounters with environmental threats. The numbers generated by risk assessment appear to be getting better, although they may also be getting harder for ordinary people to interpret.

But how accurately does this picture in fact represent the totality of what is known even about such relatively well understood risks as environmentally induced cancer? A closer look immediately reveals how partial and selective are some of the most up-to-date models of risk assessment. A focus on analysing particular substances, for example, may overlook the importance of others. The American biochemist Bruce Ames and his associates have argued for years that most industrial chemicals are of far less concern as health risks than identical or similar substances to which we are exposed by 'nature' through our diets (Ames et al. 1987). This work has attracted an ideological following and much controversy, but this should not keep us from acknowledging that Ames and others are trying to impose on risk assessment an alternative, and in some ways more comprehensive, picture of the chemical induction of cancer – one that does not treat all 'causes' as if they fall on the 'artificial', or industrially produced, side of human exposure to chemicals in the environment.

The work of Ames and his colleagues tends to exonerate many of the chemical bad actors that have occupied the regulatory process for twenty-five years. But, as environmental groups have been quick to point out (Tal 1997), adding 'natural' causes to our ideas of causation should not necessarily reduce concern about exposure to industrial pollution or chemical products. We need only note a few of the ways in which quantitative risk assessment models simplify the world so as to lower the regulators' overall perception of risk. The impact of multiple exposure routes and possible synergistic effects is rarely captured in routine risk assessments. Behavioural patterns that may aggravate risk for particular subpopulations (a well-known example is smoking among asbestos workers) are similarly downplayed or disregarded. Aggregated risk figures may ignore specially vulnerable groups, such as children or the elderly. Socio-economic factors that tend to concentrate risk from many sources for poor, minority, and disenfranchised populations are only now beginning to get a harder look under intensifying pressure from the environmental justice movement (Bullard 1993; Greenberg 1993). Only an impoverished notion of causation could keep us from recognising the legitimacy of such criticisms, even though they are difficult to incorporate into models of quantitative assessment.

Agency

A second issue that bears investigation in this connection is the conception of agency that underlies the songlines of risk assessment. Implicit in this mode of analysis is the notion that risk originates in the inanimate world, although human behaviour can exacerbate its intensity. That this is only a simplifying assumption tends to fade from view because imputing risk to inanimate objects generally increases our sense of control and social order. It is easier, after all, to manage things than people, even when it is known that people are part of the problem. Thus, the U.S. gun lobby offers a complex understanding of agency through its bumper-grabbing slogan, 'Guns don't kill people, people kill people.' But as British regulators learned from the massacre of schoolchildren at Dunblane, it is the gun control advocates who have the advantage of simplicity: if guns are taken away, it no longer matters whether psychopaths or criminals can be effectively disciplined.

The gun lobby's troublesome sociological insight could be generalised just as readily to most of the environmental risks that we seek to characterise through mathematical modelling. Organisational sociologists have been writing for years about the complicated ways in which the physical and human elements of techno-logical systems interact to produce risky conditions and periodic disasters (Turner 1978; Perrow 1984; Clarke 1989). More recently, the French sociologists Michel Callon and Bruno Latour have taken this reasoning even further, dissolving the perceived solidity of the boundary between animate and inanimate actors (Callon 1986; Latour 1992). For these analysts, any artifact, be it a door stop or a bicycle or a refrigerator filled with chlorofluorocarbons, is not simply a *thing* with hard and fast contours: it is a physically stabilised, congealed embodiment of an entire history of social assumptions, conventions, interests, and cultural practices. The stability of artifacts, moreover, may be contingent or illusory.

The force of such insights is most often recognised in the wake of major disas-ters. The Rogers Commission appointed to investigate the Challenger disaster in the United States provides an example. One Commission member, the late physi-cist Richard Feynman, caught the media headlines with his celebrated demonstra-tion that a part used in the booster rocket, a rubber o-ring, froze at the temperature of freezing water (Gieryn and Figert 1990). The Commission as a whole, however, understood that blame could not be fixed on a malfunctioning inanimate object. People, too, were responsible for the disaster, because the decision to launch under suboptimal weather conditions had been, after all, a human act. The

Commission ultimately blamed a management structure that failed to convey engineers' concerns to the uppermost reaches of political decisionmaking (Challenger Commission 1986).

Subsequent sociological analysis has shown that even this conclusion unduly simplified the relationship between humans and non-humans. In Diane Vaughan's (1996) painstaking reconstruction of the events, no single agent was necessarily to blame. Responsibility (if this is a useful term at all) was distributed up and down through a political and cultural system that kept each significant actor or group of actors unaware of the decision's full complexity, and hence ignorant of all the possible points at which such a delicately coupled technological system could fail. Yet, in the conduct of environmental risk assessment – the formal prediction of future harm – things are generally deemed risky or safe in and of themselves. Whether for analytic simplicity or through deeper cultural conditioning, risk assessors seem to forget the permeability of the human and material spheres and the interchangeability of 'thing-causes' and 'people-causes'.

Uncertainty

My third observation about the Dreamtime that gave birth to environmental risk assessment has to do with the nature of uncertainty and social perceptions of it. Quantitative risk assessment has made great strides in the past ten years or so in its ability to conceptualise and mathematise uncertainty. This is an important and powerful method of organising what is known, what is merely surmised, and how sure people are about what they think they know. Quantified approaches can represent – often in very useful and understandable forms – the zones of uncertainty that should be most worrying when regulators attempt to manage risk.

Yet, these abstract and reductive techniques also give rise to some well-founded concerns. Social critics of modernity, such as the German sociologist Ulrich Beck (1992), have argued that modelling the world represents a form of domination and control that is deeply misleading; it is founded on the untenable premise that a perfectly objective, god's-eye view can be attained through scientific inquiry (see, for example, Ashley 1983). Others have suggested that the project of controlling nature by such means only induces alienation and apathy in those who are not prepared, for moral or historical reasons, to accept modernity's founding presumptions (Irwin and Wynne 1996; Jasanoff and Wynne 1998). But there are reasons to worry about risk assessment even if one does not reject outright the scientific management of nature.

Scepticism about the rationality of such analytic tools as quantitative risk assessment flows in part from cross-national, comparative, and historical research on the foundations of public policy (Jasanoff 1986; Porter 1995). What clearly emerges from these investigations is the socially embedded character of much that we do not know, as well as of much that we claim to know, about the interactions of nature and society. Uncertainty about the environment, in particular, increasingly appears as a very special form of politics. It is a social admission that there are things about our condition that we do not know (simple ignorance), but it is also an affirmation that we have the means and the will to find out more about those things that we label 'uncertain'.

Translating 'uncertainty' into formal quantitative language washes out the concept's cultural and political origins. To restore the cultural dimension, it is helpful to compare the discussion of uncertainty in different national settings. Let us consider for this purpose, two interesting and nearly contemporaneous papers about environmental uncertainty, the first by the British analysts Brian Wynne and Sue Mayer (1993), and the second by the American ecologist Simon Levin (1992), written when he was president of the Ecological Society of America. In their article, Wynne and Mayer challenged British scientists to be more open and humble in admitting their uncertainties about events in the natural world – to admit in effect that there are things that science does not have the means to know. Levin, on the contrary, asked his fellow ecologists to be bolder about characterising uncertainty and thus to draw parts of the unknown back into the grasp of science. Only in this way, Levin argued, could his community of experts help ensure that decisions in the face of uncertainty would be made with 'proper scientific input'. The differences in these divergent expectations of science are not accidental. They reflect, in ways that are beyond the scope of this paper, long-standing cultural traditions about the appropriate way to legitimate political decisions in Britain and the United States (see, for example, Ezrahi 1990; Jasanoff 1986). The point to note for now is simply that there *is* a political dimension to ways of thinking about uncertainty; yet, experts and policymakers are seldom aware of the deep-seated political and cultural biases that may influence their approaches to grappling with the unknown.

Risk and regulation in global perspective

How does the preceding discussion bear on the risks of global magnitude that are now confronting people on the earth: climate change, deforestation, marine pollution, loss of biodiversity, and new epidemics, to name just a few? I have tried to show thus far that risk concepts are not simply neutral descriptions of nature, but are culturally and politically conditioned ways of interpreting both our relationship to the world around us and our obligations to others on the planet. What conclusions can we draw from what we have learned about the socially embedded character of the risk concepts that are currently being deployed to deal with environmental debates at the international level?

There has been a tendency in elite decisionmaking circles to take for granted that science's planetary perspective on environmental risks will resonate in the same way with all people everywhere in the world. Globalisation, in this view, should present no special or different regulatory challenges from the ones we already know within national regulatory contexts. The chief difficulties that people foresee are those of developing the will and the technical capacity to implement potentially costly solutions to transnational problems (Skolnikoff 1993; Haas et al. 1994). At the cognitive level, many believe that the task of globalisation is already complete. Let me first document and then question these convictions – and, finally, come back to a possible way around the conflicts that I foresee.

The fourth discontinuity

Many people associate the birth of the modern environmental movement with the picture of earth suspended alone in space, as first seen by the Apollo astronauts. In the basic texts of modern environmentalism, author after author alludes to the transformative impact of this single image. Here is a typically lyrical passage from the ecologist Daniel Botkin (1990: 5):

> It is more than 20 years since the phrase 'spaceship Earth' was coined and made popular and 20 years since the Apollo astronauts took this famous photograph of the Earth from space – a blue globe, enveloped by swirling white clouds, against a black background – creating an image of a small island of life floating in an ocean of empty space.

A remarkably similar point was made by the World Commission on Environment and Development (WCED) in its influential report, *Our Common Future*:

> In the middle of the 20th century, we saw our planet from space for the first time. Historians may eventually find that this vision had a greater impact on thought than did the Copernican revolution of the 16th century, which upset humans' self-image by revealing that the Earth is not the centre of the universe. From space, we see a small and fragile ball dominated not by human activity and edifice but by a pattern of clouds, oceans, greenery, and soils. Humanity's inability to fit its activities into that pattern is changing planetary systems fundamentally.
>
> (WCED 1987: 308)

The idea of a 'scientific revolution' has never been far from the minds of those who commented on the Apollo picture. Laurence Tribe, a one-time critic of technology policy and later a constitutional scholar at Harvard Law School, noted the role of this image – 'the earth as a dramatically finite and surprisingly delicate blue-green globe' (Tribe 1973: 620) – in ushering us toward 'the fourth discontinuity'. This was a moment that displaced the human ego by making it conscious of the physical limitations of the place that it inhabits. This decentering effect, Tribe and others have said, was on a par with three great intellectual discontinuities of the past: the Copernican revolution, which displaced the earth from the centre of the universe; the Darwinian revolution, which displaced human beings from the pinnacle of the tree of creation; and the Freudian revolution, which exposed the workings of the unconscious mind and made humankind aware that we are not, after all, masters in our own house.

Continuing the theme of scientific revolutions, many environmentalists have suggested that the picture of our lonely planet brought about nothing less than a paradigm shift in ways of thinking about how the world works. Lynton Caldwell (1990: 21), an eminent environmentalist and policy analyst, is one exponent of this position:

> [T]he change from the belief that the sun, moon, and stars revolved around the earth to the Copernican view of the earth's place in the solar system was a paradigm shift. The change marked by [the aftermath of Apollo] is from the view of an earth unlimited in abundance and created for man's exclusive use to a concept of the earth as a domain of life or biosphere for which mankind is a temporary resident custodian . . . The newer view sees it as an ultimately unified system . . . that may supply man's needs as long as he observes the system's rules.

There is wide agreement, then, that *Apollo* confronted us with a unique historical moment – a moment defined by such radically new ways of seeing the earth that science was forced, in effect, to adopt a new environmental paradigm. Some have referred to this as the ecological epistemic paradigm, which stresses the interconnectedness of all of the earth's living and non-living systems (Haas 1990).

But the new paradigm raised many new questions and left some old problems profoundly unsettled. Chief among the uncertainties was the place of human beings in the biosphere. Hints of disagreement on this point can be found even in the passages quoted above. Take, for instance, from *Our Common Future* the observation that 'Humanity's inability to fit its activities into that pattern is changing planetary systems fundamentally.' Looking upon the earth's bounded periphery, the World Commission was apparently inclined to regard humanity as an unwanted disturbance in the balance of the biosphere. In contrast, Caldwell's designation of our species as a 'temporary resident custodian' grants more active agency to human beings, but imposes on them duties, increasingly recognised in the work of ethicists and international lawyers (Weiss 1989), to care for the inherited planetary system and to pass it on intact to future generations. These two views of humankind – interloper versus custodian – clearly imply very different moral obligations in relation to the biosphere. They point as well toward different kinds of limitations on the rights of human societies to use, alter, and manage the environment.

The scientific theory of ecological interconnectedness leaves unanswered some fundamental questions about what human beings are entitled to do with their environment. This is because the ecological paradigm focuses on the physical constraints of the biosphere without paying much attention to the economic, aesthetic, moral or spiritual dimensions of our relationship to the world around us.

There is another picture, somewhat less well-known than the *Apollo* image, that shows a night-time view of the earth's major population centres. It is one way – and a very compelling one – in which the ecological view of the biosphere has been visually represented. It was published some years ago in a special issue of *Scientific American* entitled 'Managing Planet Earth'. In his introductory essay for that volume, ecologist William Clark (1990: 1) of Harvard University explained the picture's significance in the following terms:

> The global pattern of lights created by today's civilisations is not unlike the pattern of exuberant growth that develops soon after bacteria are introduced to a nutrient-rich petri dish. In the limited world of the petri dish, such growth is not sustainable. Sooner or later, as the bacterial populations deplete available resources and submerge in their own wastes, their initial blossoming is replaced by stagnation or collapse.

This is a powerful analogy, and quite consistent with the premises of the ecological paradigm in emphasising the physical and biological limits on human existence. But notice what the analogy does *not* explicitly talk about: it does not say whether it is better – *before* reaching the point of stagnation or collapse – to have the lights in clusters, as they currently are in the world's major industrial regions, or evenly divided all over the earth's surface; nor does it say whether the lights are any more or less threatening for environmental sustainability depending on how they have been powered – with natural gas, solar panels, windmills, or nuclear energy.

Seeing things globally

The notion of the 'fourth discontinuity' is founded ultimately on a view of risk and scientific discovery that looks suspiciously like Justice Breyer's. It assumes that reasonable people the world over will perceive environmental threats and challenges in the same way, especially if they are shown how to look at them by science. This perspective on risk and its scientific representation asserts itself with the confidence of a supreme artist. Just let science show people the truth, and they will acknowledge its power and agree to live by it. Vincent Van Gogh wrote with just such confidence to his beloved brother Theo about the pictures that he would not sell in his lifetime. His sunflower paintings in particular, Van Gogh imagined, captured the essence of these blossoms in a way that might change how others would see them. He wrote in this vein to Theo both while and after he was painting them:

> I have three canvases on hand: first, three huge flowers in a green vase, with a light background; the second, three flowers – one gone to seed, one in flower, and the third a bud, against a royal blue background. This has a 'halo'; that is, each object is surrounded by a glow of the complementary colour of the background against which it stands out. The third, twelve flowers and buds in a yellow vase. This last is, therefore, light on light, and I hope will be the best.
>
> (Stone 1969: 379)

Later, he urged his brother to exhibit the paintings, saying that, while other artists might claim to have mastered other flowers, 'the sunflower is mine in a way' (Stone 1969: 407).

It is of course true that for many 20th-century citizens Van Gogh did forever transform the experience of seeing sunflowers, but the mistake is to think that this happened simply through the miracle of his painting. Even a little reflection brings to light the other ingredients in the story that had to come together in order for millions to appreciate Van Gogh's genius: his legendary lack of success in his lifetime, his madness and suicide (which resonated well with emerging modern myths of the alienated artist), his sister-in-law's careful tending of his memory, and the rise of a museum culture that brought these paintings to the masses. Nor should one forget that Van Gogh, for all his rebelliousness, was working within a culturally grounded painterly tradition that had taught artists to paint and people to see paintings in particular ways. His letters are full of detailed technical commentary on his own work and that of his fellow artists. His obsession with paint, light, and colour shines through even in the short sunflower passage quoted above.

If it takes all this weight of history and tradition to make people appreciate great works of art in the same way, then what work will it take to forge a common vision of problems in the global environment? There is a disquieting answer to this question and it centres on the use of force. The critic and cultural historian Paul Fussell (1975) describes in his unforgettable account of the Great War how sunrise and sunset became for British soldiers in the trenches the emblems of nature, continually contrasted with the horrors and ironies of war. As Van Gogh was born into an active painterly tradition, so these young men from every class of society had been educated in a literary tradition that ran from Shakespeare to Ruskin and the Romantics. This tradition had given them a vocabulary for the expression of 'sky-awareness', itself a culturally transmitted taste among country-loving Britons. But it was the discipline of the trenches that fundamentally reshaped the soldiers', and eventually their whole culture's, experience of this aspect of nature.

It was one of the war's cruel reversals, according to Fussell (1975: 52), 'that sunrise and sunset, established by over a century of Romantic poetry and painting as the tokens of hope and peace and rural charm, should come to be exactly the moments of heightened ritual anxiety'. This was the time when enemy lines were most distinctly revealed to each other, the Germans in the morning and the British in the evening. Dawn, Fussell adds, 'never recovered from what the Great War did to it'; this once-peaceful time accumulated 'the new, modern associations of dawn: cold, the death of multitudes, insensate marching in files, battles, and corpses too shallowly interred' (Fussell 1975: 63). We recognise this as the dawn of 20th-century poets, from T.S. Eliot to Philip Larkin.

Fussell's story makes us quail anew before Justice Breyer's vision of bureaucratically rational risk assessment. Is centralised authority, aiming for military precision and control, really the way to override historical and cultural differences in the perception and management of environmental risk? Should regulators in fact emulate the military in order to gain the public's trust? Even if top-down authority disciplines multitudes of people into common ways of seeing hazards, will the resulting agreement be worth the costs entailed? Is there any other way forward?

Fortunately, a very different conception of the risk-based regulatory process has begun to emerge from recent studies by several significant policy institutions, including the U.S. National Academy of Sciences and the Presidential/Congressional Commission on Risk Assessment and Risk Management (Power and McCarty 1998). Three aspects of the new approach are especially worth noting: (1) each study advocates the intertwining of analysis (science) with deliberation (politics) from the very earliest stages of the process; (2) both emphasise feedbacks and recursion, so that initial problem frames can always be revisited and redrawn in the light of experience; and (3) both accept the idea that closure comes from the needs of decisionmaking, not from a search for ultimate scientific resolution. The older linear model of risk assessment/risk management has not been abandoned, but it is now part of an entirely more complex process, one that is cyclical and grounded in, not separate from, the rhythms of deliberative politics.

To conclude, then, I have suggested that the social sciences have deeply altered our understanding of what 'risk' means – from something real and physical if hard to measure, and accessible only to experts, to something constructed out of history and experience by experts and laypeople alike. Risk in this sense is culturally embedded and has texture and meaning that vary from one social grouping to another. Trying to assess risk is therefore necessarily a social and political exercise, even when the methods employed are the seemingly technical routines of quantitative risk assessment. Judgments about the nature and severity of environmental risk inevitably incorporate tacit understandings concerning causality, agency, and uncertainty, and these are by no means universally shared even in similarly situated western societies.

Against this background, it makes very little sense to regulate risk on the basis of centralised institutional authority, insulation from public demands, and claims to superior expertise. Environmental regulation calls for a more open-ended process, with multiple access points for dissenting views and unorthodox perspectives. Like science itself, any particular approach to understanding risk needs to acknowledge its own provisional status, in all humility, 'lest one good custom should corrupt the world' (Tennyson 1930: 327).

Note

* *Environmental Values*, Vol. 8 (1999), pp. 135–52.

References

Ames, Bruce N., Renae Magaw, and Lois Swirsky Gold. 1987. 'Ranking Possible Carcinogenic Hazards'. *Science* **236**: 271–280.

Ashley, Richard K. 1983. 'The Eye of Power: The Politics of World Modeling'. *International Organization* **37**: 495–535.

Beck, Ulrich. 1992. *The Risk Society: Towards a New Modernity*. London: Sage Publications.

Botkin, Daniel. 1990. *Discordant Harmonies: A New Ecology for the Twenty-First Century*. New York: Oxford University Press.

Breyer, Stephen. 1993. *Breaking the Vicious Circle: Toward Effective Risk Regulation*. Cambridge, MA: Harvard University Press.

Bullard, Robert D., ed. 1993. *Confronting Environmental Racism: Voices from the Grass-roots*. Boston: South End Press.

Caldwell, Lynton Keith. 1990. *International Environmental Policy: Emergence and Dimensions*. Durham, NC: Duke University Press.

Callon, Michel. 1986. 'Some Elements of a Sociology of Translation: Domestication of the Scallops and the Fishermen of St. Brieuc Bay'. In John Law, ed., *Power, Action, and Belief: A New Sociology of Knowledge?*, pp. 196–233. London: Routledge and Kegan Paul.

Chatwin, Bruce. 1988. *The Songlines*. London: Penguin Books.

Clark, William C. 1990. 'Managing Planet Earth'. In *Managing Planet Earth*, Readings from *Scientific American*, pp. 1–11. New York: W.H. Freeman.

Clarke, Lee. 1989. *Acceptable Risk? Making Decisions in a Toxic Environment*. Berkeley: University of California Press.

Ezrahi, Yaron. 1990. *The Descent of Icarus: Science and the Transformation of Contemporary Democracy*. Cambridge, MA: Harvard University Press.

Foucault, Michel. 1972. *The Archeology of Knowledge and the Discourse on Language*. New York: Pantheon.

Fussell, Paul. 1975. *The Great War and Modern Memory*. New York: Oxford University Press.

Gieryn, Thomas F. and Anne E. Figert. 1990. 'Ingredients for a Theory of Science in Society: O-Rings, Ice Water, C-Clamp, Richard Feynman, And the Press'. In Susan E. Cozzens and Thomas F. Gieryn, eds., *Theories of Science in Society*, pp. 67–97. Bloomington, IN: Indiana University Press.

Greenberg, M. 1993. 'Proving Environmental Inequity in Siting Locally Unwanted Land Uses'. *Issues in Science and Technology* 4: 235–252.

Haas, Peter M., Robert O. Keohane, and Marc A. Levy, eds. 1994. *Institutions for the Earth: Sources of Effective International Environmental Protection*. Cambridge, MA: MIT Press.

Haas, Peter M. 1990. *Saving the Mediterranean*. New York: Columbia University Press.

Irwin, Alan and Brian Wynne, eds. 1996. *Misunderstanding Science?* Cambridge: Cambridge University Press.

Jasanoff, Sheila. 1998. 'The Political Science of Risk Perception'. *Reliability Engineering and System Safety* **59**: 91–99.

Jasanoff, Sheila. 1992. 'Science, Politics, and the Renegotiation of Expertise at EPA'. *Osiris* **2**: 195–217.

Jasanoff, Sheila. 1987. 'Contested Boundaries in Policy-Relevant Science'. *Social Studies of Science* **17**: 195–230.

Jasanoff, Sheila. 1986. *Risk Management and Political Culture*. New York: Russell Sage Foundation.

Jasanoff, Sheila and Brian Wynne. 1998. 'Science and Decision Making'. In Steve Rayner and Elizabeth L. Malone, eds., *Human Choice and Climate Change*, pp. 1–87. Columbus, OH: Battelle Press.

Johnson, Branden B. and Vincent T. Covello. 1987. *The Social and Cultural Construction of Risk*. Dordrecht: Reidel.

Latour, Bruno. 1992. 'Where Are the Missing Masses? The Sociology of a Few Mundane Artifacts'. In Wiebe E. Bijker and John Law, eds., *Shaping Technology/Building Society*, pp. 225–258. Cambridge, MA: MIT Press.

Levin, Simon. 1992. 'Sustaining Ecological Research'. *Bulletin of the Ecological Society of America* **73**: 213–218.

National Research Council (cited as NRC). 1996. *Understanding Risk*. Washington, DC: National Academy Press.

National Research Council. 1994. *Science and Judgment in Risk Assessment*. Washington, DC: National Academy Press.

National Research Council. 1989. *Field Testing Genetically Modified Organisms: Framework for Decisions*. Washington, DC: National Academy Press.

National Research Council. 1987. *Regulating Pesticides in Food: The Delaney Paradox*. Washington, DC: National Academy Press.

National Research Council. 1983. *Risk Assessment in the Federal Government: Managing the Process*. Washington, DC: National Academy Press.

Perrow, Charles. 1984. *Normal Accidents*. New York: Basic Books.

Porter, Theodore M. 1995. *Trust in Numbers: The Pursuit of Objectivity in Science and Public Life*. Princeton, NJ: Princeton University Press.

Power, Michael and Lynn S. McCarty. 1998. 'A Comparative Analysis of Environmental Risk Assessment/Risk Management Frameworks'. *Environmental Science and Technology* **32**: 224A–231A.

Presidential Commission on the Space Shuttle Challenger Accident (cited as Challenger Commission). 1986. Report of the Presidential Commission on the Space Shuttle Challenger Accident. Washington, DC: US GPO.

Presidential/Congressional Commission on Risk Assessment and Risk Management (cited as Risk Commission). 1997. *Framework for Environmental Health Risk Management*. Washington, DC: Presidential/Congressional Commission.

Skolnikoff, Eugene. 1993. *The Elusive Transformation: Science, Technology, and the Evolution of International Politics*. Princeton, NJ: Princeton University Press.

Slovic, Paul, Baruch Fischhoff, and Sarah Lichtenstein. 1985. 'Characterizing Perceived Risk'. In R.W. Kates, C. Hohenemser, and J.X. Kasperson, eds., *Perilous Progress: Managing the Hazards of Technology*, pp. 91–125. Boulder, CO: Westview Press.

Stone, Irving, ed. 1969. *Dear Theo: The Autobiography of Vincent Van Gogh*. New York: Signet.

Tal, Alon. 1997. 'Assessing the Environmental Movement's Attitudes Toward Risk Assessment'. *Environmental Science and Technology* **31**: 470A–476A.

Tennyson, Alfred, Lord. 1930. *Idylls of the King*. New York: Macmillan.

Tribe, Laurence. 1973. 'Technology Assessment and the Fourth Discontinuity: The Limits of Instrumental Rationality'. *Southern California Law Review* **46**: 617–660.

Turner, Barry A. 1978. *Man-Made Disasters*. London: Wykeham.

Vaughan, Diane. 1996. *The Challenger Launch Decision: Risky Technology, Culture, and Deviance at NASA*. Chicago: University of Chicago Press.

Weiss, Edith Brown. 1989. *In Fairness to Future Generations: International Law, Common Patrimony, and Intergenerational Equity*. Dobbs Ferry, NY: Transnational Press.

Winner, Langdon. 1986. *The Whale and the Reactor: A Search for Limits in an Age of High Technology*. Chicago: University of Chicago Press.

World Commission on Environment and Development. 1987. *Our Common Future*. Oxford: Oxford University Press.

Wynne, Brian and Sue Mayer. 1993. 'How Science Fails the Environment'. *New Scientist*, 5 June: 33–35.

8 Judgment under siege

The three-body problem of expert legitimacy[*]

The 2004 U.S. presidential election will be remembered for many things: the close margin of George W. Bush's victory in the electoral vote (he would have lost to the Democratic candidate, John Kerry, if only the state of Ohio had swung the other way); renewed questions about the viability of the electoral college; the inaccuracies of exit polling; and the stark division of the country's voting map into the "red" states of America's heartland and the "blue" states of its more cosmopolitan periphery. More curiously, it was also an election that pitted one perception of the relationship of science and government against another. On Kerry's side were multiple Nobel laureates and other leaders of the scientific community, vocally asserting that the Bush administration had betrayed science in the pursuit of crass political objectives.[1] These advocates cited the administration's lack of support for embryonic stem cell research, which many saw as the next great frontier in biomedicine; they also pointed to a series of White House actions manipulating or suppressing scientific data – on environment, public health, and defense – that the government had deemed inconsistent with its overall political strategy.[2] Against these charges, Republican representatives either issued denials or claimed a superior ethical sensibility, most explicitly so in George Bush's statement in the second presidential debate, "We've got to be very careful in balancing the ethics and the science . . . because science is important, but so is ethics, so is balancing life."[3]

This was not the way relations between science and government were scripted to work in mature democracies. For more than fifty years, cooperation, not friction, has been the order of the day in dealings between science and the state in technologically advanced nations. Indeed, the political scientist Etel Solingen predicted that there would be "happy convergence" between the goals of the state and its scientific communities, when there is "a high degree of consensus between state structures and scientists, who enjoy internal freedom of inquiry and relatively comfortable material rewards" (Solingen 1993: 43). More empirically minded researchers have shown that it is in the state's interest to sponsor scientists as a separate "estate" to assist in matters of policy formulation and implementation (Price 1965), a "brain bank" to draw on for policy legitimation (Boffey 1975), or a skilled and specialized labor force available to lend its authority to the state in times of national need (Mukerji 1989).

These findings are consistent with the vision of a new social contract between science and the state put forward by presidential adviser Vannevar Bush at the end of the Second World War: in exchange for continued governmental support and freedom to define their research priorities and methods, scientists would provide the public with beneficial discoveries and a trained workforce (Bush 1945). Put succinctly, the contract provided money and liberty in exchange for knowledge and technical skills. In reality, the liberty offered to science was never complete; state support always came with strings attached, and the strings have both multiplied and tightened over the years, so that science today operates within a thick web of social constraints. Vannevar Bush's hope of weaning American science from dependence on military aims, and so liberating scientists from national security controls, for example, turned out to be illusory (Dennis 1994, 2004). Other state priorities, from environmental protection to enhanced university-industry collaboration, have shaped both the content and structure of governmental funding programs. And ethical concerns have led to varied restrictions on the use of federal funds for animal, human and biotechnological research, as well as a host of accounting and reporting mechanisms to force science to explain itself better to its public sponsors (Stokes 1997; see also Kevles 1998; Guston 2000).

Yet in a liberal democratic order, in which the state must continually expose itself to "attestive witnessing" by citizens (Ezrahi 1990), scientists' cooperation in national projects remains an invaluable resource, and states for the most part have been unwilling to risk serious breaks with organized science for the sake of short-term political gains. Rancorous partisan politics of the sort that surfaced in the 2004 presidential election is therefore unprecedented in the annals of recent science and seems contrary to the spirit of the postwar social contract. If scientists and their expertise are of such immense value, then mere party politics ought not to disrupt the peaceful coexistence of science and the state. Why, then, have relations between science and the party in power soured of late? Why, more specifically, have tensions arisen around biomedical funding, for decades one of the most pampered and cosseted areas of U.S. science policy?

In addressing these questions, I argue that the implicit contract between science and the state has subtly shifted focus in recent decades. Although public support for science remains of paramount concern to researchers and research institutions, the politics of science no longer centers solely on the size of appropriations. Only by continually reaffirming its utility in expanding domains of application can science assert sustained claims on the public till. At stake, therefore, is a deeper right to define how, when, by whom, and to what extent science will be integrated into the solution of public problems, and who, indeed, will frame those problems in the first place. These questions straddle the line between science and politics, or truth and power, and attempts to answer them entail inevitable boundary conflicts over where the role of science ends and that of politics or policy begins (on boundary conflicts involving science see Gieryn 1999). Precisely this sort of boundary struggle can be discerned in George Bush's desire to locate the stem cell controversy in the domain of "ethics" and "balancing life" – areas of acknowledged political supremacy rather than in "science."

As the stakes have shifted, so too has the content of the decisions for which the state relies on science. Across a wide range of contemporary policy issues, uncertainty and ignorance militate against the design of unambiguous technical solutions. Broadly characterized by the label of "risk" (Beck 1992), the threats that states are asked to mitigate on behalf of their citizens require the assessment of complex trajectories of social, technological and environmental change. There is typically no single, universally agreed upon, correct outcome to these sorts of assessments. Incoherence, not consensus, is the normal epistemological condition in many domains of policy-relevant knowledge.

In offering opinions on such contested and indeterminate issues, scientists can no longer stand on firmly secured platforms of knowledge. The questions contemporary policymakers ask of science are rarely of a kind that can be answered by scientists from within the parameters of their home disciplines. Scientists instead are expected to function as experts, that is, as persons possessing analytic skills grounded in practice and experience, rather than as truth-tellers with unmediated access to ascertainable facts. Accordingly, the technical expert's attributes often include, but are rarely limited to, mastery of a particular area of knowledge. What politicians and society increasingly expect from experts in decisionmaking processes is the ability to size up heterogeneous bodies of knowledge and to offer balanced opinions, based on less than perfect understanding, on issues that lie within nobody's precise disciplinary competence. Judgment in the face of uncertainty, and the capacity to exercise that judgment in the public interest, are the chief qualifications sought today from experts asked to inform policymaking. In these circumstances, the central question is no longer which scientific assessments are right, or even more technically defensible, but whose recommendations the public should accept as credible and authoritative. That question leads immediately to a second-order query: whose judgment should we trust, and on what basis?

All this has important consequences for democracy. So long as scientists were called upon mainly to provide specialized information – or, in the familiar phrase, to "speak truth to power" – there was no need to worry unduly about their political accountability. Peer pressure, it was assumed, would keep scientists honest; deviations from standards of professional rectitude would be uncovered and corrected by communities whose central function was to discover the truth and make it public. The shift from science to expertise, and from knowledge to judgment, confounds this easy expectation. Holding persons accountable for speaking the truth is different from holding them accountable for exercising judgment. And yet, as I show below, the discourses and practices of accountability have not yet caught up with the changing role of experts in the political process. Accountability measures in many societies still focus on one or possibly two of the three bodies that are relevant to the effective integration of science and politics: the bodies of knowledge that experts represent ("good science"); the bodies of the experts themselves ("unbiased experts"); and the bodies through which experts offer judgment in policy domains ("balanced committees"). The democratization of expertise demands, I suggest, renewed attention to the third of these bodies – namely, the institutions of advice-giving. It is this neglected level of analysis that I foreground in this paper, arguing that attempts to ensure data quality and lack of bias are not alone enough to serve the needs of democratic governance; measures are also needed for securing the legitimacy of expert advisory bodies.

To this end, I begin by briefly discussing the disjunction between the rhetoric of scientific disinterestedness in U.S. science policy and the reality of science's thickening ties to society. I then use two phases of the American debate on the peer review of regulatory science to show how a reductionist rhetoric of "good science" – encompassing only the first of the three relevant bodies – continues to dominate the U.S. framing of the problem of expert legitimacy. That framing, I show, is deeply resistant to counter-discourses emanating both from academic research in science and technology studies (STS) and from national regulatory practice. One consequence of that framing, in turn, is to blur the lines of expert accountability, drawing attention away from the institutional setting of advice-giving and concealing the need for public review of expert judgments.

Contrasting the American approach with that of Britain and Germany, I next illustrate how partial vision is not unique to the United States: these political cultures have also dealt selectively with the three-body problem, each highlighting one body at the expense of the others. I conclude by discussing the need for a richer theorization of the authority of policy-related expertise. Through that work we can begin to supplement, and compensate for, the weaknesses of accountability systems that reduce the three-body problem of expert legitimation to one or another of its constitutive elements.

The disinterestedness of science: rhetoric and reality

It is tempting to dismiss the scientific community's opposition to the Bush administration in 2004 as the complaints of a disappointed suitor. As the veteran science journalist Daniel Greenberg has documented, scientists dependent on the state for research support now constitute a powerful lobby, no less insistent in their demand for public funds than the beneficiaries of any other entitlement program (Greenberg 2001). This dependence, according to Greenberg, has bred a variety of deplorable behaviors in the scientific community, ranging from overselling the promises of research to outright fraud. Scientists, on this account, have lost faith in an administration that has not simply poured funds into new research frontiers identified by their communities, from climate change to embryonic stem cells. Political success has eroded what Greenberg sees as science's historically pristine ethical position – a position famously characterized by the sociologist Robert Merton as including the virtues of openness, communal sharing of results, and lack of interest in the financial or political consequences of inquiry (Merton 1973).

The overt political positioning of prominent scientists and scientific organizations in the 2004 U.S. presidential campaign was certainly a stark reminder that the years of ivory-tower science, guided by the Mertonian norms, are definitively over. With active state encouragement,[4] scientists in the United States and around the world have become avid entrepreneurs, not only in the search for nature's secrets but also in tirelessly seeking support for their work before and after the phase of discovery. The resulting multi-level engagement of scientists with politicians, venture capitalists, journalists, the mass media, patent lawyers, the courts, and the public renders almost fantastic any residual notions of science's disinterestedness and detachment from society.

But the messiness of today's interactions between science and society is not news to academic observers of that relationship. At no point in the growth of modern science was detachment from society the norm (see, for instance, Shapin and Schaffer 1985; Golinski 1992; Jardine 1999; and for the modern period, Kevles 1987). Rather, science and other powerful social institutions – church, state, corporations, the media – have long engaged in negotiations about the nature and limits of the patronage that scientists enjoy, and the associated constraints on their liberty. Science's vaunted detachment, in other words, is a partial thing, achieved through societal interactions that are necessarily political. Galileo had to submit his beliefs formally to the strictures of the Catholic Church. Today, the controls on science are more subtle, if more pervasive: they relate, for the most part, not to scientists' substantive beliefs on particular issues, but to the means with which they are allowed to pursue certain lines of inquiry, the conditions under which their advice is sought, and the extent to which research trajectories are subordinated to political imperatives such as war or national security, environmental protection, or finding cures for life-threatening disease.

Clearly, then, it is both simplistic and ahistorical to claim that science became politicized for the first time at the turn of the 21st century, for arguably there never has been a time when the work of science was wholly distinct from the work of politics.[5] To be sure, substantial qualitative and quantitative changes have occurred in the performance of science and in its social, political, and economic links to society. Some have argued that the increased density of science-society interactions, particularly in the conduct of research, constitutes in and of itself a break with the past. European science policy scholars, in particular, have suggested that purely curiosity-driven, basic, or "Mode 1" research is a thing of the past. Instead, they say, we have entered the era of "Mode 2" science, characterized by wide-ranging interdisciplinarity, growing public-private collaboration, the rise of application-driven sciences, and increased demands for social accountability (Gibbons et al. 1994; Nowotny et al. 2001). These observations have rightly been seen as significant for the organization and funding of science, but their implications go further. Thoroughgoing changes in the production of science cannot but affect the foundations of scientific authority. As long as scientists could claim objective access to nature's laws, on the basis of observations unbiased by personal or political interests, that alone was sufficient to underwrite their expertise. With science more and more being produced in the service of social ends, the possibility of bias is far more evident, and the grounds of expert authority correspondingly in greater need of rearticulation.

Yet if the practices of science have evolved in the ways that scholars have documented, the political rhetoric around science has not kept pace, particularly in the

United States. One looks in vain for explicit acknowledgment that expert deliberations are a site of hybrid judgment, combining technical and normative considerations. Instead, virtually all public pronouncements on the role of science in policy home in on the need for untainted science and the associated need to defend science from the corrupting encroachments of money and politics. Thus, the United States charged the European Union with maintaining an illegal and *unscientific* moratorium against the importation of genetically modified crops and foods in its 2004 case in the World Trade Organization (Winickoff et al., in press). In a related vein, Europe's commitment to the precautionary principle has been widely decried by U.S. critics as a politically motivated opt-out from the intellectual rigor of *scientific* risk assessment – not taken on board as a valid normative response to uncertainty. U.S. scientists for their part have also tended to frame disputes over policy-relevant science in the black and white language of purity and deviance, whose logic is to represent scientists as accountable only to their own specialist peers. The Union of Concerned Scientists, for example, focused its February 2004 pre-election campaign on the need to restore scientific integrity in policymaking.

This lag between reality and rhetoric does not advance the cause of democracy. If science has always been in some deep sense political, then it is not the *fact* of science's embeddedness in politics that should any longer be of primary concern, but rather the *nature* of that embedding and its implications for accountable governance. When an American administration withholds research funds from a promising area of biomedicine, or denies the validity of the scientific consensus on climate change, the problem is not the threat that is thereby posed to the mythic purity of science. Of greater importance is the tacit change that such disagreements signal in the rules of the game by which science and politics have previously ordered their relations vis-à-vis each other. There is an apparent retreat from politicians' earlier deference to scientists' judgments on basic elements of science policy: when is it in the public's best interests to fund a promising line of research; and when is contested knowledge robust enough to justify policy action? Put differently, what seems to have eroded in the Bush era is not so much the integrity of science itself as scientists' influence over decisions at the nexus of science and politics – above all, over how to deliberate and how to act when knowledge and understanding are incomplete. It is that shift in the seat of judgment that calls for analysis.

Occurring largely outside the purview of formal legal and political institutions, such struggles over the institutional division of power between science and politics raise important questions for governance and political theory. At a time when the vast majority of public decisions involve sizeable components of technical analysis, any change in the relative positions of scientific and political judgment carries with it a displacement in the exercise of power, with possible consequences for participation, deliberation and accountability. Now no less than in 1960s, when Yale University political theorist Robert Dahl used it as the title of his seminal treatment of democracy, the question at the heart of politics remains, "Who governs?" (Dahl 1961). A difference, however, is that technical decision-making is now more visibly and continuously a part of the playing field of politics.

Consequently, there is a need to enlarge the scope of political analysis to take on board, or retheorize, the role of experts in processes of governance. A look at two episodes in some 25 years debate on the quality of regulatory science in the United States underscores the need for conceptual advances.

The recursive politics of regulatory peer review

The quality and reliability of science for public policy have been recurrent themes in the United States for more than a quarter-century (see particularly Jasanoff 1990). Critics of policy-relevant science have sought to ensure its robustness, and a favorite device has been the review of the government's findings and conclusions by other, appropriately trained eyes. This demand supplements the more general requirement of public justification, minimally through notice and comment provisions, that has been a part of the U.S. administrative process since the mid-1940s. On the assumption that policymakers' judgments on science as on other matters will be mission-oriented, and hence potentially biased, critics have demanded that those judgments be submitted to validation by experts, in other words, to peer review. Ongoing controversy over the forms of peer review in U.S. regulatory decisionmaking offers an ideal site for reconsidering the rules of accountability that secure expert legitimacy in that country. Two moments in the peer review debate are of particular interest, the first occurring in the 1980s and the second in 2003 and 2004. Together, they illustrate the power of a framing of policy-relevant science that persistently denies its hybridity and normative content.

An issue that captured the attention of U.S. policymakers perhaps more than any other in the late 1970s was what to do about cancer-causing substances in the environment (for a detailed account of these developments, see Brickman et al. 1985). In 1971, President Richard Nixon declared a "war on cancer," which resonated with public fears of an insidious and irreversible disease that had become, with heart disease, one of the country's two biggest killers. Federal agencies responsible for regulating the environment, pesticides, food and drugs, cosmetics, consumer products, and worker health and safety took up the challenge of working out principles for assessing and controlling the risks of carcinogens. Operating under newly precautionary legislation, these agencies were charged with preventing harms to public health and the environment before they materialized. In the case of carcinogens, this meant identifying the hazardous substances, if possible, before they entered the commercial pipeline or were dispersed into the environment. To carry out that preventive mandate, regulators felt they had to make many conservative assumptions: about the mechanisms of cancer causation (e.g., no safe threshold of exposure); dose-response relationships (e.g., that cancer incidence at high exposure doses should be linearly extrapolated to low doses); and the relationship between humans and test animals (e.g., that humans should be assumed to be similar to the most sensitive test animals). Affected industries argued, for their part, that these assumptions were scientifically untenable and led to irrational, economically burdensome regulation. Agency risk assessments, critics charged, would not hold up to scrutiny if they were peer reviewed by impartial experts with no ties to the agencies' regulatory mission.

It emerged in the ensuing debate that the term "peer review" was highly malleable and functioned effectively as an instrument of boundary maintenance between science and politics, as well as between regulators and their critics (Jasanoff 1987). Virtually all interested parties agreed that the science underlying regulatory decisions ought to be reviewed in some fashion, but there the consensus ended. There were disagreements about who the reviewers should be, what should be reviewed, and how review processes should be structured and organized. In my 1990 study of these developments, I concluded that "peer review," had fallen together with the more general function of expert advice-giving (Jasanoff 1990). Scientific advisory committees had become what I termed a "fifth branch" of government, and they functioned best when they conformed to standards of political legitimacy as well as technical rationality. Advisory processes produced the highest levels of participant satisfaction when they permitted the joint negotiation of technical and normative concerns and when expert advisers remained answerable to the publics affected by their judgments.

The peer review debate of the 1980s ended pragmatically in a victory for agency discretion and decentralized decisionmaking. An influential 1983 report by the National Research Council (NRC), the advisory arm of the National Academies, concluded, against industry advocacy to the contrary, that risk assessment functions should not be located within a single expert body but should rather be carried out separately by each relevant agency, consistent with its particular statutory mandate (National Research Council 1983). Called the Red Book because of its cover color, the report defined risk assessment as a purely technical activity, as distinct from risk management, a process taking account of economic and social factors. Yet background studies commissioned for the Red Book affirmed that risk assessment, too, was a hybrid process, calling for value judgments as well as technical analysis. Those findings buttressed the report's conclusion that risk assessment should remain within the control of authorized regulatory bodies – and, by extension, their legislative missions. Implicitly, the Red Book concluded that process and substance legitimately influence each other in regulatory analysis. While not cognizant of the academic literature in science and technology studies, the NRC report was in this respect compatible with emerging STS insights about the co-production of knowledge and norms (Jasanoff 2004).

In retrospect, we can say that the Red Book's practice was more sophisticated than its rhetoric, but – unreflexively adopted and with no theoretical underpinnings – the practice proved less influential than the rhetoric. Discursively, the report gave strong support to the characterization of risk assessment as a science, a view that powerfully informs regulatory discourse to this day. In terms of practice, the report offered a far more subtle view of the weaving together of analysis and judgment. In effect, the Red Book contained within its covers two contradictory views of risk assessment and regulatory science that would come into clearer focus over subsequent years (see Table 8.1).[6] Politically, however, it was the less nuanced and more easily instrumentalized view that proved more durable.

Table 8.1 Two discourses of risk analysis

Dominant discourse	Insights from regulatory practice
Risk assessment (RA) should be separate from risk management (RM).	Judgment enters into both RA and RM; there can be no clear separation.
RA should not include economic, social, and political concerns.	RA occurs within particular frames which reflect social and political values and may differ across cultures.
RA can be and should be science-based.	RA is limited by uncertainty and ignorance.
There is a clear boundary between science and politics; there exist pre-established criteria by which we can decide whether an analysis is science-based.	The boundary between science and policy is not given in advance; criteria are established by negotiation and convention.

As if to illustrate this point, a second major episode in the politics of U.S. peer review began unfolding in the summer of 2003. On August 29 of that year, the Office of Information and Regulatory Affairs (OIRA) of the Office of Management and Budget (OMB), the economic arm of the executive branch, issued a *Proposed Bulletin on Peer Review and Information Quality.* The *Bulletin*'s stated purpose was to ensure "meaningful peer review" of science pertaining to regulation, as part of an "ongoing effort to improve the quality, objectivity, utility, and integrity of information disseminated by the federal government."[7] Specifically targeted was the category of "significant regulatory information," that is, information that could have "a clear and substantial impact on important public policies or important private sector decisions with a possible impact of more than $100 million in any year." The proposal, it was estimated, would have far-reaching influence across the federal agencies, requiring 200 or more draft technical documents to be subjected annually to OMB-supervised "formal, independent, external" peer review (Anderson 2003).

The *Bulletin*'s principal intellectual justification was that the quality of science crucially depends on peer review. As the text observed,

> A "peer review," as used in this document for scientific and technical information relevant to regulatory policies, is a scientifically rigorous review and critique of a study's methods, results, and findings by others in the field with requisite training and expertise. Independent, objective peer review has long been regarded as a critical element in ensuring the reliability of scientific analyses. For decades, the American academic and scientific communities have withheld acknowledgment of scientific studies that have not been subject to rigorous independent peer review.
>
> (*Bulletin*, Supplementary Information, 68 *Federal Register* 54024)

These statements, and indeed the entire thrust of the *Bulletin*, assumed that science is a unitary form of activity, that peer review likewise is a singular, well-defined process, and that the application of peer review to all forms of science – including regulatory science – can therefore be viewed as unproblematic. Peer review was advanced as a kind of objective audit mechanism for policy-relevant science, to be applied as a backstop to studies conducted by and for regulatory agencies. This characterization downplayed the political implications of removing ultimate control of the review process from the jurisdiction of the regulatory agencies to the OMB, and thereby to a White House with a notably anti-regulatory philosophy.

The *Bulletin* appeared to turn the clock back on years of policy learning. Not only was it oblivious to research findings on the interpretive flexibility of peer review, but it also went against the grain of the 1983 NRC Red Book in calling for a single, uniform process of validation, approved by OMB, for all types of regulatory science. The impulse toward standardization, overriding cross-agency differences in practice, was visible at many points in the proposal text, as exemplified by the following quotations:[8]

> 54024: "Existing agency peer review mechanisms have not always been sufficient to ensure the reliability of regulatory information disseminated or relied upon by federal agencies."

> 54024: "Even when agencies do conduct timely peer reviews, such reviews are sometimes undertaken by people who are not independent of the agencies."

> 54025: "When an agency does initiate a program to select outside peer reviewers for regulatory science, it sometimes selects the same reviewers for all or nearly all of its peer reviews on a particular topic."

> 54025: "it is also essential to grant the peer reviewers access to sufficient information . . ."

> 54025: "the results are not always available for public scrutiny or comment."

> 54025: "experience has shown that they are not always followed by all of the federal agencies, and that actual practice has not always lived up to the ideals underlying the various agencies' manuals."[9]

Not surprisingly, the OMB proposal came under severe criticism from many quarters, including the highest reaches of organized science, where the move to draw regulatory peer review within the supervisory ambit of an already suspect executive branch was immediately perceived as political. In November 2003, the National Academy of Sciences hosted a public workshop at which were aired many research and practice-based objections to the proposal. By mid-December, the end of the official comment period on the proposed *Bulletin*, 187 written responses had been filed, some two-thirds critical of the proposal. At its February 2004 annual meeting, the American Association for the Advancement of Science

(AAAS) adopted a resolution calling on OMB to withdraw the proposal. Reasons offered by AAAS and other opponents included fears of political interference, unnecessary bureaucratic hurdles, asymmetric treatment of experts funded by agencies and corporations (the proposal initially identified only the former as having a potential conflict of interest), and the rigidity of a "one size fits all" approach to review (see, for example, Steinbrook 2004; *Philadelphia Inquirer*, January 25, 2004).

For me personally these developments posed particular intellectual challenges. As an STS scholar whose work had specifically addressed the topic of regulatory peer review, I had a stake in opposing a policy initiative that seemed inconsistent with the basic findings of my and my colleagues' work. I was also aware that my own study of advisory committees could be, and had been, uncritically read as an endorsement of more stringent peer review, with little attention to my observations about the constructedness of policy-relevant knowledge.[10] Breaking a lifetime habit of standing apart from current controversies, I therefore participated in the National Academy workshop and, more exceptionally, submitted written comments to OMB urging that the proposal be retracted. My conclusions that regulatory science is different in context and content from research science, and that "peer review" therefore cannot be uncritically translated from one domain to the other, were referenced in the AAAS resolution and to some extent reported in the media. Their impact on OMB, however, proved slight.

On April 15, 2004, OMB issued a substantially revised proposal, taking note of many of the submitted comments.[11] The new version narrowed the scope of the most stringent peer review requirement to a newly defined category of "influential scientific information" containing, as a subset, "highly influential scientific assessments"; it also granted more flexibility to agencies to design their peer review procedures, and it removed the one-sided restriction on experts whose research was funded by regulatory agencies. At the core, however, the proposal continued to embrace the notion of an autonomous science whose quality and objectivity could be improved in a straightforward way through critical scrutiny by "peers." Instructively, the revised proposal cited my work on advisory committees only to support the propositions that peer review practices are varied and that fair and rigorous review can build consensus around agency actions based on science. That regulatory science is, by its very nature, a site of politics was evidently inconsistent with the deeply entrenched Mertonian discourse of science's integrity, independence, quality and rigor. In this case, as we have seen, the discourse of scientific integrity masked a profoundly political institutional realignment between regulators and the White House. Neither scholarship nor practical wisdom was able to undermine a discourse that offered such substantial instrumental benefits to the ruling interests of the moment.

Cultural practices of expert legitimation

As in the United States, regulators in Britain and Germany have accepted risk assessment as a principled approach to ordering knowledge and weighing policy alternatives, and risk analysis occupies a central place in both countries' practices for coping with the consequences of technological change.[12] Yet in neither European national setting has the methodological robustness of risk assessment received nearly the same attention as in the United States, and nowhere else have political battle lines been drawn around the design of regulatory peer review. Tacitly, at least, decisionmaking in both European countries takes on board the hybrid picture of risk judgments that represented one face of the 1983 NRC Red Book report (see Table 8.1). That hybridity, in turn, demands accountability to wider interests than those of relevant technical communities – forcing consideration of more than simply the body of policy-related knowledge. Accordingly, political representation remains part and parcel of the process of risk analysis in both countries, consciously built into the design of expert committees and consultative processes.

But even though the hybridity of risk judgments is generally conceded, practices for ensuring lack of bias remain partial and untheorized, reflecting different cultural traditions for the construction of public knowledge – traditions that I have elsewhere termed "civic epistemology" (Jasanoff 2005: chapter 10). On the whole, the focus in British regulatory circles is on the body of the expert: accountable judgment is sought through consultation with persons whose capacity to exercise judgment on the public's behalf is regarded as superior, even privileged. Though members of British expert panels can and do represent both technical specialties and social interests, ultimately it is the excellence of each person's individual discernment that the state most crucially relies on. To a remarkable extent the legitimacy of British expertise remains tied to the person of the individual expert, who achieves standing not only through knowledge and competence, but through a demonstrated record of service to society. It is as if the expert's function is as much to discern the public's needs and to define the public good as to provide appropriate technical knowledge and information for resolving the matter at hand.

Needless to say, this faith in individuals' power to see for the people could hardly exist in a more diverse or less empiricist cultural context, where common norms of judging and assessing facts were felt to be lacking. A cost of the British stress on virtuous expert bodies has been to protect the assumption of common vision itself from critical examination. Consequently, a narrow group of experts can with the best will in the world make erroneous judgments on matters that were too complex for their collective reckoning. Britain's infamous "mad cow" disaster of the 1990s illustrated the hazards of blind faith in embodied expertise at the expense of due consideration to what experts know, or can know, and the institutional context in which they exercise their expertise.[13]

In Germany, by contrast, expert committees are usually constituted as microcosms of the potentially interested segment of society; judgments produced in such settings are seen as unbiased not only by virtue of the participants' individual qualifications, but even more so by the incorporation of all relevant viewpoints into a collective output. Reliance on personal credentials is rare in Germany unless it is also backed by powerful institutional supports. To be an acknowledged expert in Germany, one ideally has to stand for a field of experience larger than one's own particular domain of technical mastery. And it is ultimately the institutional context for forming communal expert judgments that matters most to producing social robustness.

The constitution of such bodies reflects something important about what counts as right reason in the German public sphere. The painstakingly representative character of German expert advisory bodies, their membership often specified in detail by legislation, encodes a belief that it is possible to map the terrain of reason completely; an accurately configured map can then be translated into an institutionalized instrument of decisionmaking. An expert within such an institution functions almost as an ambassador for a recognized region or place from among the allowable enclaves of reason. Rationality, the ultimate foundation of political legitimacy in Germany, flows from the collective reasoning produced by authoritatively constituted expert bodies. A paradoxical consequence of this map-making approach to public reasoning is that expert bodies, once constituted, leave no further room for *ad hoc* citizen intervention. They become perfectly enclosed systems, places for a rational micro-politics of pure reason, with no further need for external accountability to a wider, potentially excluded, and potentially irrational, public.

These contrasts help throw the cultural specificity of U.S. legitimation practices, and their solution to the three-body problem, into sharper relief. Professional skills and standing count for more in the United States than the intangible qualities of individual judgment (as in Britain) or institutional representation and balance (as in Germany). In a meritocracy that prides itself on individualism and objective markers of intelligence (Carson 2004), the surest way to become an expert is by climbing the ladder of professional recognition. What an expert stands for or has achieved outside the spheres of method and knowledge is of lesser consequence. Civic virtue is not a prime desideratum in the appointment of experts, although the capacity for team work obviously plays a part in the nomination and selection of experts for important advisory positions.

Of course, U.S. policy is not wholly insensitive to possible imbalances in the constitution of expert groups. The Federal Advisory Committee Act seeks to correct for just this eventuality through its requirement that committees be balanced in terms of the views they represent. Nonetheless, the dominant discourse of policy-relevant science remains unwaveringly committed to Mertonian ideals of purity and detachment, despite all scholarly demonstrations of hybridity and co-production. It is the perceived deviation from the transcendent objectivity of science that most often threatens expert legitimacy in the United States. Allegations that experts have been captured by political interests or by politically motivated research programs erupt in U.S. policy debates with a regularity unheard of in other modern democracies.

None of the three ideal-typical solutions to the problem of expert legitimacy provides for systematic lines of accountability running from experts to wider publics. Intensely political choices of individual experts and groupings remain concealed behind divergent national rhetorics and practices of accountability.

Theory as intervention: regrounding the legitimacy of expertise

Experts have become indispensable to the politics of nations, and indeed to transnational and global politics. Experts manage the ignorance and uncertainty that are endemic conditions of contemporary life and pose major challenges to the managerial pretensions and political legitimacy of democratically accountable governments. Faced with ever-changing arrays of issues and questions – based on shifting facts, untested technologies, incomplete understandings of social behavior, and unforeseen environmental externalities – governments need the backing of experts to assure citizens that they are acting responsibly, in good faith, and with adequate knowledge and foresight. The weight of political legitimation therefore rests increasingly on the shoulders of experts, and yet they occupy at best a shadowy place in the evolving discourse of democratic theory.

I have suggested that expert legitimacy should be reconceptualized as a three-body problem that pays explicit attention to each of the three bodies involved in producing expert judgments: the body of knowledge that experts concededly bring to decisionmaking; the individual bodies of the experts themselves; and the institutionalized bodies through which they offer judgment and policy advice. A brief study of the peer review debate in the United States illustrates the political hazards of too great an emphasis on the first body: the knowledge component of expert judgments. Coupled to an outmoded and uncritically accepted discourse of scientific purity, that emphasis has impeded wide debate by American scholars and publics on the credibility of experts and the institutional foundations of their legitimacy.

A brief contrast with two European political systems shows that the U.S. approach, while possibly unique in its commitment to a transcendental notion of scientific integrity, is not unique in the partiality of its understanding of expert legitimacy. The U.K. emphasis on the embodied expert and the German preoccupation with rational expert collectives each militates against deeper questioning of the constituents of expert authority. More specifically, no national decisionmaking system has as yet taken on board the fundamental STS insight that experts *construct* – they do not simply *find* – the knowledge base on which they rest their hybrid analytic-deliberative judgments. In each democratic society, then, an imperfect framing of the problem of expertise has foreclosed the continuous dialogue between expert and critical lay judgment that is imperative under contemporary conditions of ignorance and uncertainty.

Addressing this deficit in democratic practice requires us to recast the role of experts in terms that better lend themselves to political critique. Key to this move, as I have argued elsewhere, is to import notions of delegation and representation into the analysis of expert decisionmaking (Jasanoff 2003). Under a theory of delegation, experts can be seen as acting not only in furtherance of technical rationality, but also on behalf of their public constituencies, under cognitive and normative assumptions that are continually open to wider review. Equally, citizens need to recognize that governmental experts are there to make judgments on behalf of the common good rather than as spokespersons for the impersonal and unquestionable authority of science. In turn, this means that a full-fledged political accountability – looking not only inward to specialist peers but also outward to engaged publics – must become integral to the practices of expert deliberation.

We come, finally, to a concluding word on the role of scholarship and the relations of theory to practice. The history of expertise as a public problem in the United States and elsewhere suggests that deep reform – aimed not just at current policy practice but at its entrenched ideological foundations – cannot be effectively mounted at the surfaces of already framed debates and controversies. The long U.S. conversation on regulatory peer review illustrates the impediments to making critical voices heard within the press of politics as usual. To challenge, let alone change, deep-seated habits of mind and thought, embedded in resistant institutional practices, requires the would-be critic of expert rule to step out and away from the four corners of ongoing disputes. It calls for the tacit assumptions of the workaday political world to be made explicit, and for new languages to be elaborated to describe previously unseen or taken-for-granted realities. Scholarship provides the platform for such intervention, and the power of the word, backed by historical knowledge and critical analysis, stands ready to be embraced in the project of rejuvenating democracy.

Notes

* In Peter Weingart and Sabine Maasen, eds., *Democratization of Expertise? Exploring Novel Forms of Scientific Advice in Political Decision-Making*, Sociology of the Sciences Yearbook (Dordrecht: Kluwer, 2005), pp. 209–24.

1 For a summary of these charges, see the statement on "Restoring Scientific Integrity in Policymaking" issued by the Union of Concerned Scientists on February 18, 2004, http://www.ucsusa.org/ (visited January 2005). See also US House of Representatives, Committee on Government Reform (Minority Report), *Politics and Science in the Bush Administration*, http://www.house.gov/reform/min/politicsandscience/pdfs/pdf_politics_and_science_rep.pdf (visited April 2004).

2 The Republican strategy included placating the religious right on issues relating to abortion (hence, by extension, stem cell research), as well as industrial special interests opposed to stringent controls on carbon emissions and other forms of environmental regulation.

3 CBS News.com, Text of Bush-Kerry Debate II, St. Louis, Missouri, October 8, 2004, http://www.cbsnews.com/stories/2004/10/08/politics/main648311.shtml (visited November 2004).

4 A notable example of such encouragement in the United States was the 1980 Bayh-Dolc Act, which in effect required publicly funded researchers to seek commercial returns from their work. For critical accounts of the consequences of that legislation, see Press and Washburn (2000); Krimsky (2003).

5 For more on the deep linkages between the construction of scientific and political power, see particularly Jasanoff (2004).

6 Not all of the insights in the right-hand column, to be sure, were apparent to the authors of the Red Book. In particular, issues of framing and cross-cultural variation in risk assessment surfaced in these terms only in subsequent scholarly research, some of which used the Red Book and its assumptions as primary data for analysis. See, for example, Jasanoff (1986) Krimsky and Golding (1992).

7 *Proposed Bulletin on Peer Review and Information Quality* (hereafter cited as *Bulletin*), Summary, 68 *Federal Register* 54023, September 15, 2003.

8 All page citations are to the *Federal Register*, vol. 68, no. 178 (September 15, 2003).
9 I am indebted to John Mathew and John Price for identifying these extracts.
10 It was not the first time my work had been misread in the policy domain as affirming rather than critiquing dominant conceptions of the science-policy relationship. Other similar episodes included a misinterpretation of my work on science advice in a U.S. Supreme Court decision on the admissibility of expert evidence. See Jasanoff (1996).
11 http://www.whitehouse.gov/omb/inforeg/peer_review041404.pdf (visited January (2005).
12 The regulation of biotechnology provides an especially instructive site for observing national practices of regulatory practice and expert legitimation in action. See Jasanoff (2005).
13 In April 2000, the U.K. government estimated that the total cost of the BSE crisis to the public sector would be 3.7 billion pounds by the end of the 2001–2002 fiscal year. *The Inquiry into BSE and variant CJD in the United Kingdom* [hereafter cited as *The Phillips Inquiry*] (2000), Volume 10, Economic Impact and International Trade, http://www.bseinquiry.gov.uk/report/volume10/chapterl.htm#258548 (visited April 2004).

References

Anderson, F.R. (2003), 'Peer review of data', *The National Law Journal*, September 29, 2003.

Beck, U. (1992), *Risk Society: Towards a New Modernity*, London: Sage.

Boffey, P.M. (1975), *The Brain Bank of America: An Inquiry into the Politics of Science*, New York: McGraw-Hill.

Brickman, R., S. Jasanoff, and T. Ilgen (1985), *Controlling Chemicals: The Politics of Regulation in Europe and the U.S.*, Ithaca, NY: Cornell University Press.

Bush, V. (1945), *Science – The Endless Frontier*, Washington, DC: US Government Printing Office.

Carson, J. (2004), 'The merit of science and the science of merit', in S. Jasanoff (ed.), *States of Knowledge: The Co-Production of Science and Social Order*, London: Routledge, pp. 181–205.

Dahl, R.A. (1961), *Who Governs?*, New Haven, CT: Yale University Press.

Dennis, M.A. (1994), ' "Our first line of defense" ': Two university laboratories in the postwar American State', *Isis* **85**(3): 427–55.

Dennis, M.A. (2004), 'Reconstructing sociotechnical order: Vannevar Bush and US Science Policy', in S. Jasanoff (ed.), *States of Knowledge: The Co Production of Science and Social Order*, London: Routledge.

Ezrahi, Y. (1990), *The Descent of Icarus: Science and the Transformation of Contemporary Democracy*, Cambridge, MA: Harvard University Press.

Gibbons, M., C. Limoges, H. Nowotny, S. Schwartzman, P. Scott, and M. Trow (1994), *The New Production of Knowledge*, London: Sage Publications.

Gieryn, T. (1999), *Cultural Boundaries of Science: Credibility on the Line*, Chicago: University of Chicago Press.

Golinski, J. (1992), *Science as Public Culture: Chemistry and Enlightenment in Britain, 1760–1820*, Cambridge, MA: Cambridge University Press.

Greenberg, D.S. (2001), *Science, Money, and Politics: Political Triumph and Ethical Erosion*, Chicago: University of Chicago Press.

Guston, D.H. (2000), *Between Politics and Science: Assuring the Integrity and Productivity of Research*, New York: Cambridge University Press.

Jardine, L. (1999), *Ingenious Pursuits: Building the Scientific Revolution*, London: Little, Brown.

Jasanoff, S. (1986), *Risk Management and Political Culture*, New York: Russell Sage Foundation.

Jasanoff, S. (1987), "Contested boundaries in policy-relevant science," *Social Studies of Science* **17**: 195–230.

Jasanoff, S. (1990), *The Fifth Branch: Science Advisers as Policymakers*, Cambridge, MA: Harvard University Press.

Jasanoff, S. (1990), *The Fifth Branch: Science Advisers as Policymakers*, Cambridge, MA: Harvard University Press.

Jasanoff, S. (1996), "Beyond epistemology: Relativism and engagement in the politics of science," *Social Studies of Science* **26**(2): 393–418.

Jasanoff, S. (2003), "(No) Accounting for expertise?", *Science and Public Policy* **30** (3): 157–62.

Jasanoff, S. (ed.) (2004), *States of Knowledge: The Co-Production of Science and Social Order*, London: Routledge.

Jasanoff, S. (2005), *Designs on Nature: Science and Democracy in Europe and the United States*, Princeton, NJ: Princeton University Press.

Kevles, D. (1987), *The Physicists: The History of a Scientific Community in Modern America*, Cambridge, MA: Harvard University Press.

Kevles, D.J. (1998), *The Baltimore Case: A Trial of Politics, Science, and Character*, New York: W.W. Norton.

Krimsky, S. (2003), *Science in the Private Interest: How the Lure of Profits Has Corrupted the Virtue of Biomedical Research*, Lanham, MD: Rowman-Littlefield, 2003).

Krimsky, S. and D. Golding (eds.) (1992), *Social Theories of Risk*, London: Praeger.

Merton, R.K. (1973), "The normative structure of science," in R.K. Merton (ed.), *The Sociology of Science: Theoretical and Empirical Investigations*, Chicago: University of Chicago Press, pp. 267–78.

Mukerji, C. (1989), *A Fragile Power: Scientists and the State*, Princeton, NJ: Princeton University Press.

National Research Council (1983), *Risk Assessment in the Federal Government: Managing the Process*, Washington, DC: National Academy Press.

Nowotny, H., P. Scott, and M. Gibbons (2001), *Re-Thinking Science: Knowledge and the Public in an Age of Uncertainty*, Cambridge, MA: Polity.

Philadelphia Inquirer (January 25, 2004), Editorial, "The White House vs. Science."

Press, E. and J. Washburn (2000), "The kept university", *Atlantic Monthly*, March 2000: 39–54.

Price, D.K. (1965), *The Scientific Estate*, Cambridge, MA: Harvard University Press.

Shapin, S. and S. Schaffer (1985), *Leviathan and the Air-Pump: Hobbes, Boyle, and the Experimental Life*, Princeton, NJ: Princeton University Press.

Solingen, E. (1993),"Between markets and the state: Scientists in comparative perspective," *Comparative Politics* **26**: 31–51, at p. 43.

Steinbrook, R. (2004), "Peer review and federal regulations", *New England Journal of Medicine* **350**(2): 103–4 (January 8, 2004).

Stokes, D.E. (1997), *Pasteur's Quadrant: Basic Science and Technological Innovation*, Washington, DC: Brookings Institution.

Winickoff, D., S. Jasanoff, L. Busch, R. Grove-White, and B. Wynne (in press), "Adjudicating the GM Food Wars: Science, risk, and democracy in world trade law," *Yale Journal of International Law*.

9 Technologies of humility

Citizen participation in governing science*

The perils of prediction

Long before the terrorist atrocities of 11 September 2001 in New York, Washington, DC, and Pennsylvania, the anthrax attacks through the US mail, and the US-led wars in Afghanistan and Iraq, signs were mounting that America's ability to create and operate vast technological systems had outrun her capacity for prediction and control. In a prescient book, published in 1984, the sociologist Charles Perrow forecast a series of 'normal accidents', which were strung like dark beads through the latter years of the twentieth century and beyond – most notably, the 1984 chemical plant disaster in Bhopal, India; the 1986 loss of the *Challenger* shuttle and, in the same year, the nuclear plant accident in Chernobyl, USSR; the contamination of blood supplies with the AIDS virus; the prolonged crisis over BSE ('mad cow disease'); the loss of the manned US space shuttle *Columbia* in 2003; and the US space programme's embarrassing, although not life-threatening, mishaps with the *Hubble* telescope's blurry lens, and several lost and extremely expensive Mars explorers.[1] To these, we may add the discovery of the ozone hole, climate change, and other environmental disasters as further signs of disrepair. Occurring at different times and in vastly-different political environments, these events nonetheless have served collective notice that human pretensions of control over technological systems need serious re-examination.

While American theorists have often chalked up the failings of technology to avoidable error, especially on the part of large organizations,[2] some European analysts have suggested a more troubling scenario. Passionately set forth by the German sociologist Ulrich Beck, the thesis of 'reflexive modernization' argues that risks are endemic in the way that contemporary societies conduct their technologically-intensive business.[3] Scientific and technical advances bring unquestioned benefits, but they also generate new uncertainties and failures, with the result that doubt continually undermines knowledge, and unforeseen consequences confound faith in progress. Moreover, the risks of modernity often cut across social lines and operate as a great equalizer of classes. Wealth may increase longevity and improve the quality of life, but it offers no assured protection against the ambient harms of technological societies. This observation was tragically borne out when the collapse of the World Trade Center on 11 September 2001 ended the lives of some 3,000 persons, discriminating not at all among corporate executives, stock market analysts, computer programmers, secretaries, fire-fighters, policemen, janitors, restaurant workers, and others. Defeat in war simi-larly endangers the powerful along with the disempowered. In many other contexts, however, vulnerability remains closely tied to socio-economic circum-stances, so that inequalities persist in the ability of social groups and individuals to defend themselves against risk.

'Risk', on this account, is not a matter of simple probabilities, to be rationally calculated by experts and avoided in accordance with the cold arithmetic of cost-benefit analysis.[4] Rather, it is part of the modern human condition, woven into the very fabric of progress. The problem we urgently face is how to live democrati-cally and at peace with the knowledge that our societies are inevitably 'at risk'. Critically important questions of risk management cannot be addressed by tech-nical experts with conventional tools of prediction. Such questions determine not only whether we will get sick or die, and under what conditions, but also who will be affected and how we should live with uncertainty and ignorance. Is it sufficient, for instance, to assess technology's consequences, or must we also seek to eval-uate its aims? How should we act when the values of scientific inquiry appear to conflict with other fundamental social values? Has our ability to innovate in some areas run unacceptably ahead of our powers of control?[5] Will some of our most revolutionary technologies increase inequality, promote violence, threaten cultures, or harm the environment? And are our institutions, whether national or supranational, up to the task of governing our dizzying technological capabilities?

To answer questions such as these, the task of managing technologies has to go far beyond the model of 'speaking truth to power' that once was thought to link knowledge to political action.[6] According to this template, technical input to policy problems has to be developed independently of political influences; the 'truth' so generated acts as a constraint, perhaps the most important one, on subse-quent exercises of political power. The accidents and troubles of the late twentieth century, however, have called into question the validity of this model – either as a descriptively accurate rendition of the ways in which experts relate to policy-makers, or as a normatively acceptable formula for deploying specialized knowl-edge within democratic political systems.[7] There is growing awareness that even technical policy-making needs to get more political – or, more accurately, to be seen more explicitly in terms of its political foundations. Across a widening range of policy choices, technological cultures must learn to supplement the expert's preoccupation with measuring the costs and benefits of innovation with greater attentiveness to the politics of science and technology.

Encouragingly, the need for reform in governing science and technology has been acknowledged by political authority. In the millennial year 2000, for example, the House of Lords Select Committee on Science and Technology in Britain issued a report on science and society that began with the ominous observation that relations between the two had reached a critical phase.[8] The authors foresaw damaging consequences for science and technology if these conditions were allowed to persist. This observation was widely attributed to

Britain's particular experience with BSE, but the crisis of confidence *vis-à-vis* the management of science and technology has spread significantly wider. The European Union's 2001 White Paper on Governance drew on the activities of a working group on 'Democratizing Expertise', whose report promised new guidelines 'on the collection and use of expert advice in the Commission to provide for the accountability, plurality and integrity of the expertise used'.[9] The intense worldwide discussion of the risks, benefits, and social consequences of biotechnology that began in the late 1990s can be seen as sharing many of the same concerns.

These initiatives and debates reflect a new-found interest on the part of scientists, governments, and many others in creating greater *accountability* in the production and use of scientific knowledge. The conduct of research has changed in ways that demand increased recognition. As captured by the 'Mode 2' rubric, the pursuit of science is becoming more dispersed, context-dependent, and problem-oriented. Given these shifts, concerns with the assurance of quality and reliability in scientific production, reflecting the dominance of the 'speaking truth to power' model, are now seen as too narrowly focused. The wider public responsibilities of science, as well as changes in modes of knowledge-making, demand new forms of public justification. Accountability can be defined in different ways, depending on the nature and context of scientific activity – for example, in demands for precaution in environmental assessments, or in calls for bioethical guidelines in relation to new genetic technologies. Whatever its specific articulation, however, accountability in one or another form is increasingly seen as an independent criterion for evaluating scientific research and its technological applications, supplementing more traditional concerns with safety, efficacy, and economic efficiency.

But how can ideas of accountability be mapped onto well-entrenched relations between knowledge and power, or expertise and public policy? The time is ripe for seriously re-evaluating existing models and approaches. How have existing institutions conceptualized the roles of technical experts, decision-makers, and citizens with respect to the uses and applications of knowledge? How should these understandings be modified in response to three decades of research on the social dimensions of science? Can we respond to the demonstrated fallibility and incapacity of decision-making institutions, without abandoning hopes for improved health, safety, welfare, and social justice? Can we imagine new institutions, processes, and methods for restoring to the playing field of governance some of the normative questions that were sidelined in celebrating the benefits of technological progress? And are there structured means for deliberating and reflecting on technical matters, much as the expert analysis of risks has been cultivated for many decades?

There is a growing need, I shall argue, for what we may call the 'technologies of humility'. These are methods, or better yet institutionalized habits of thought, that try to come to grips with the ragged fringes of human understanding – the unknown, the uncertain, the ambiguous, and the uncontrollable. Acknowledging the limits of prediction and control, technologies of humility confront 'head-on' the normative implications of our lack of perfect foresight. They call for different expert capabilities and different forms of engagement between experts, decision-makers, and the public than were considered needful in the governance structures of high modernity. They require not only the formal mechanisms of participation but also an intellectual environment in which citizens are encouraged to bring their knowledge and skills to bear on the resolution of common problems. Following a brief historical account, I will offer a framework for developing this approach.

The post-war social contract

In the US, the need for working relationships between science and the state was famously articulated not by a social theorist or sociologist of knowledge, but by a quintessential technical expert: Vannevar Bush, the distinguished MIT engineer and presidential adviser. Bush foresaw the need for permanent changes following the mobilization of science and technology during the Second World War. In 1945, he produced a report, *Science – The Endless Frontier*,[10] that was later hailed as laying the basis for American policy in science and technology. Science, in Bush's vision, was destined to enjoy government patronage in peacetime as it had during the war. Control over the scientific enterprise, however, would be wrested from the military and lodged with the civilian community. Basic research, uncon-taminated by industrial application or government policy, would thrive in the free air of universities. Scientists would establish the substantive aims as well as the intellectual standards of research. Bush believed that bountiful results flowing from their endeavours would translate in due course into beneficial technologies, contributing to the nation's prosperity and progress. Although his design took years to materialize, and even then was only imperfectly attained, the US National Science Foundation (NSF) emerged as a principal sponsor of basic research.[11] The exchange of government funds and autonomy in return for discoveries, techno-logical innovations, and trained personnel came to be known as America's 'social contract for science'.

The Bush report said little about how basic research would lead to advances in applied science or technology. That silence itself is telling. It was long assumed that the diffusion of fundamental knowledge into application was linear and unproblematic. The physical system that gripped the policy-maker's imagination was the pipeline. With technological innovation commanding huge rewards in the marketplace, market considerations were deemed sufficient to drive science through the pipeline of research and development into commercialization. State efforts to promote science could then be reasonably restricted to support for basic or 'curiosity-driven' research. Simplistic in its understanding of the links between science and technology, this scheme, we may note, provided no conceptual space for the growing volume of scientific activity required to support and legitimate the multiple undertakings of modern states in the late twentieth century. In a host of areas, ranging from the environmental policy to mapping and sequencing the human genome, governmental funds have been spent on research that defies any possible demarcation between basic and applied. Yet, for many years after the war, the basic-applied distinction remained the touchstone for distinguishing work done in universities from that done in industries, agricultural experiment stations, national laboratories, and other sites concerned primarily with the uses of knowledge.

As long as the 'social contract' held sway, no-one questioned whether safeguarding the autonomy of scientists was the best way to secure the quality and productivity of basic research. Peer review was the instrument that scientists used for self-regulation as well as quality control. This ensured that state-sponsored research would be consistent with a discipline's priorities, theories, and methods. Peer review was responsible, with varying success, for ensuring the credibility of reported results, as well as their originality and interest.

So strong was the faith in peer review that policy-makers, especially in the US, often spoke of this as the best means of validating scientific knowledge, even when it was produced and used in other contexts – for example, for the purpose of supporting regulatory policy. In practice, a more complex, tripartite approach to quality control developed in most industrial democracies – peer review by disciplinary colleagues in basic science; the development of good laboratory practices, under applicable research protocols, such as products-testing or clinical trials in applied research; and risk assessment for evaluating the health or environmental consequences of polluting emissions and industrial products. But as the importance of testing, clinical research, and risk assessment grew, so, too, did calls for ensuring their scientific reliability. Once again, peer review – or its functional analogue, independent expert advice – were the mechanisms that governments most frequently used for legitimation.

Signs of wear and tear in the 'social contract' began appearing in the 1980s. A spate of highly-publicized cases of alleged fraud in science challenged the reliability of peer review and, with it, the underlying assumptions concerning the autonomy of science. The idea of science as a unitary practice also began to break down as it became clear that research varies from one context to another, not only across disciplines, but – even more important from a policy standpoint – across institutional settings. It was recognized, in particular, that regulatory science, produced to support governmental efforts to guard against risk, was fundamentally different from research driven by scientists' collective curiosity. At the same time, observers began questioning whether the established categories of basic and applied research held much meaning in a world where the production and uses of science were densely connected to each other, as well as to larger social and political consequences.[12] The resulting effort to reconceptualize the framework of science-society interactions forms an important backdrop to present attempts to evaluate the accountability of scientific research.

Science in society – new assessments

Rethinking the relations of science has generated three major streams of analysis. The first stream takes the 'social contract' for granted, but points to its failure to work as its proponents had foreseen. Many have criticized science, especially university-based science, for deviating from idealized, Mertonian norms of purity and disinterestedness. Despite (or maybe because of) its conceptual simplicity, this critique has seriously threatened the credibility of researchers and their claim to autonomy. Other observers have tried to replace the dichotomous division of *basic* and *applied* science with a more differentiated pattern, calling attention to the particularities of science in different settings and in relation to different objectives. Still others have made ambitious efforts to re-specify how scientific knowledge is actually produced. This last line of analysis seeks not so much to correct or refine Vannevar Bush's vision of science, as to replace it with a more complex account of how knowledge-making fits into the wider functioning of society. Let us look at each of these three critiques.

Deviant science

Scientific fraud and misconduct became an issue on the US policy agenda in the 1980s. Political interest reached a climax with the notorious case of alleged misconduct in an MIT laboratory headed by Nobel laureate biologist David Baltimore. He and his colleagues were exonerated, but only after years of inquiry, which included investigations by Congress and the FBI.[13] This and other episodes left residues in the form of greatly-increased Federal powers for the supervision of research, and a heightened tendency for policy-makers and the public to suspect that all was not in order in the citadels of basic science. Some saw the so-called 'Baltimore affair' as a powerful sign that legislators were no longer content with the old social contract's simple *quid pro quo* of money and autonomy in exchange for technological benefits.[14] Others, like the seasoned science journalist Daniel Greenberg, accused scientists of profiting immoderately from their alliance with the state, while failing to exercise moral authority or meaningful influence on policy.[15] American science has since been asked to justify more explicitly the public money spent on it. A token of the new relationship came with the reform of NSF's peer review criteria in the 1990s. The Foundation now requires reviewers to assess proposals not only on grounds of technical merit, but also with respect to wider social implications – thus according greater prominence to social utility. In effect, the very public fraud investigations of the previous decade opened up taken-for-granted aspects of scientific autonomy, and forced scientists to account for their objectives, as well as to defend their honesty.

To these perturbations may be added a steady stream of challenges to the supposed disinterestedness of academic science. From studies in climate change to biotechnology, critics have accused researchers of having sacrificed objectivity in exchange for grant money or, worse, equity interests in lucrative start-up companies.[16] These allegations have been especially damaging to biotechnology, which benefits significantly from the rapid transfer of skills and knowledge. Since most Western governments are committed to promoting such transfers, biotechnology is caught on the horns of a very particular dilemma: how to justify its promises of innovation and progress credibly when the interests of most scientists are unacceptably aligned with those of industry, government, or – occasionally – 'public interest' advocates.

Predictably, pro-industry bias has attracted the most criticism, but academic investigators have also come under scrutiny for alleged pro-environment and anti-technology biases. In several cases involving biotechnology – in particular, that of the monarch butterfly study conducted by Cornell University scientist John Losey in the US,[17] and Arpad Pusztai's controversial rat-feeding study in the UK[18] – industry critics have questioned the quality of university-based research, and have implied that political orientations may have prompted premature release or the over-interpretation of results. In April 2002, another controversy of this sort erupted over an article in *Nature* by a University of California scientist, Ignacio Chapela, who concluded that DNA from genetically modified corn had contaminated native species in Mexico. Philip Campbell, the journal's respected editor, did not retract the paper, but stated that 'the evidence available is not sufficient to justify the publication of the original paper', and that readers should 'judge the science for themselves'.[19] As in the Losey and Pusztai cases, critics charged that Chapela's science had been marred by non-scientific considerations. Environmentalists, however, have viewed all these episodes as pointing to wholesale deficits in knowledge about the long-term and systemic effects of genetic modification in crop plants.

Context-specific science

The second line of attack on the science-society relationship focuses on the 'basic-applied' distinction. One attempt to break out of the simplistic dualism was proposed by the late Donald Stokes, whose quadrant framework, using Louis Pasteur as the prototype, suggested that 'basic' science can be done within highly 'applied' contexts.[20] Historians and sociologists of science and technology have long observed that foundational work can be done in connection with applied problems, just as applied problem-solving is often required for resolving theoretical issues (for example, in the design of new scientific instruments). To date, formulations based on such findings have been slow to take root in policy cultures. The interest of Stokes' work lay not so much in the novelty of his insights as in his attempt to bring historical facts to bear on the categories of science policy analysis.

Like Vannevar Bush, Stokes was more interested in the promotion of innovation than in its control. How to increase the democratic supervision of science was not his primary concern. Not surprisingly, the accountability of science has emerged as a stronger theme in studies of risk and regulation, the arena in which governments seek actively to manage the potentially harmful aspects of technological progress. Here, too, one finds attempts to characterize science as something more than 'basic' or 'applied'.

From their background in the philosophy of science, Funtowicz and Ravetz proposed to divide the world of policy-relevant science into three nested circles, each with its own system of quality control: (1) 'normal science' (borrowing the well-known term of Thomas Kuhn), for ordinary scientific research; (2) 'consultancy science', for the application of available knowledge to well-characterized problems; and (3) 'post-normal science', for the highly-uncertain, highly-contested knowledge needed for many health, safety, and environmental decisions.[21] These authors noted that, while traditional peer review may be effective within 'normal' and even 'consultancy' science, the quality of 'post-normal' science cannot be assured by standard review processes alone. Instead, they proposed that work of this nature be subjected to *extended peer review*, involving not only scientists but also the stakeholders affected by the use of science. Put differently, they saw accountability, rather than mere quality control, as the desired objective when science becomes 'post-normal'.[22]

Jasanoff's 1990 study of expert advisory committees in the US noted that policy-relevant science (also referred to as 'regulatory science') – such as science done for purposes of risk assessment – is often subjected to what policy-makers call 'peer review'.[23] On inspection, this exercise differs fundamentally from the review of science in conventional research settings. Regulatory science is reviewed by multidisciplinary committees rather than by individually selected specialists. The role of such bodies is not only to validate the methods by which risks are identified and investigated, but also to confirm the reliability of the agency's interpretation of the evidence. Frequently, regulatory science confronts the need to set standards for objects or concepts whose very existence has not previously been an issue for either science or public policy: 'fine particulate matter' in air pollution control; the 'maximum tolerated dose' (MTD) in bioassays; the 'maximally-exposed person' in relation to airborne toxics; or the 'best available technology' in many programmes of environmental regulation. In specifying how such terms should be defined or characterized, advisory committees have to address issues that are technical as well as social, scientific as well as normative, regulatory as well as metaphysical. What *kind* of entity, after all, is a 'fine' particulate or a 'maximally-exposed' person, and by what markers can we recognize them? Studies of regulatory science have shown that the power of advisory bodies definitively to address such issues depends on their probity, representativeness, transparency, and accountability to higher authority – such as courts and the public. In other words, the credibility of regulatory science ultimately rests upon factors that have more to do with accountability in terms of democratic politics, than with the quality of science as assessed by scientific peers.

In modern industrial societies, studies designed to establish the safety or effectiveness of new technologies are frequently delegated to producers. Processes of quality control for product testing within industry include the imposition and enforcement of good laboratory practices, under supervision by regulatory agencies and their scientific advisers. The precise extent of an industry's knowledge-producing burden is often negotiated with the regulatory agencies, and may be affected by economic and political considerations that are not instantly apparent to outsiders (setting MTDs for bioassays is one well-known example). Resource limitations may curb state audits and inspections of industry labs, leading to problems of quality control, while provisions exempting confidential trade information from disclosure may reduce the transparency of product- or process-specific research conducted by industry. Finally, the limits of the regulator's imagination place significant limitations on an industry's duty to generate information. Only in the wake of environmental disasters involving dioxin, methyl isocyanate, and PCBs, and only after the accidental exposure of populations and ecosystems, were gaps discovered in the information available about the chronic and long-term effects of many hazardous chemicals. Before disaster struck, regulators did not appreciate the need for such information. Occurrences like these have led to demands for greater public accountability in the science that is produced to support regulation.

New modes of knowledge production

Going beyond the quality and context-dependency of science, some have suggested that we need to take a fresh look at the structural characteristics of science in order to make it more socially responsive. Michael Gibbons and his co-authors have concluded that the traditional disciplinary science of Bush's 'endless frontier' has been largely supplanted by a new 'Mode 2' of knowledge production.[24] The salient properties of this new Mode, in their view, include the following:

* Knowledge is increasingly produced in contexts of application (i.e., *all* science is to some extent 'applied' science);
* Science is increasingly transdisciplinary – that is, it draws upon and integrates empirical and theoretical elements from a variety of fields;
* Knowledge is generated in a wider variety of sites than ever before, not just in universities and industry, but also in other sorts of research centres, consultancies, and think-tanks; and
* Participants in science have grown more aware of the social implications of their work (i.e., more 'reflexive'), just as publics have become more conscious of the ways in which science and technology affect their interests and values.

The growth of 'Mode 2' science, as Gibbons et al. note, has necessary implications for quality control. Besides old questions about the intellectual merits of their work, scientists are being asked to answer questions about marketability, and the capacity of science to promote social harmony and welfare. Accordingly:

Quality is determined by a wider set of criteria, which reflects the broadening social composition of the review system. This implies that 'good science' is more difficult to determine. Since it is no longer limited to the judgments of disciplinary peers, the fear is that control will be weaker and result in lower quality work. Although the quality control process in Mode 2 is more broadly based, it does not follow . . . that it will necessarily be of lower quality.[25]

One important aspect of this analysis is that, in 'Mode 2' science, quality control has for practical purposes merged with accountability. Gibbons et al. view all of science as increasingly more embedded in, and hence more accountable to, society at large. To keep insisting upon a separate space for basic research, with autonomous measures for quality control, appears, within their framework, to be a relic of an earlier era.

In a more recent work, Helga Nowotny, Peter Scott, and Michael Gibbons have grappled with the implications of these changes for the production of knowledge in public domains.[26] Unlike the 'pipeline model', in which science generated by independent research institutions eventually reaches industry and government, Nowotny et al. propose the concept of 'socially robust knowledge' as the solution to problems of conflict and uncertainty. Contextualization, in their view, is the key to producing science for public ends. Science that draws strength from its socially-detached position is too frail to meet the pressures placed upon it by contemporary societies. Instead, they imagine forms of knowledge that would gain robustness from their very embeddedness in society. The problem, of course, is how to institutionalize polycentric, interactive, and multipartite processes of knowledge-making within institutions that have worked for decades at keeping expert knowledge away from the vagaries of populism and politics. The question confronting the governance of science is how to bring knowledgeable publics into the front-end of scientific and technological production – a place from which they have historically been strictly excluded.

The participatory turn

Changing modes of scientific research and development provide at least a partial explanation for the current interest in improving public access to expert decision-making. In thinking about research today, policy-makers and the public inevitably focus on the accountability of science. As the relations of science have become more pervasive, dynamic, and heterogeneous, concerns about the integrity of peer review have transmuted into demands for greater public involvement in assessing the costs and benefits, as well as the risks and uncertainties, of new technologies. Such demands have arisen with particular urgency in the case of biotechnology, but they are by no means limited to that field.

The pressure for accountability manifests itself in many ways, of which the demand for greater transparency and participation is perhaps most prominent. One notable example came with US Federal legislation in 1998, pursuant to the Freedom of Information Act, requiring public access to all scientific research generated by public funds.[27] The provision was hastily introduced and scarcely debated. Its sponsor, Senator Richard Shelby (R-Alabama), tacked it on as a last-minute amendment to an omnibus appropriations bill. His immediate objective was to force disclosure of data by the Harvard School of Public Health from a controversial study of the health effects of human exposure to fine particulates. This so-called 'Six Cities Study' provided key justification for the US Environmental Protection Agency's stringent ambient standard for airborne particulate matter, issued in 1997. Whatever its political motivations, this sweeping enactment showed that Congress was no longer willing to concede unchecked autonomy to the scientific community in the collection and interpretation of data, especially when the results could influence costly regulatory action. Publicly-funded science, Congress determined, should be available at all times to public review.

Participatory traditions are less thoroughly institutionalized in European policy-making, but recent changes in the rules governing expert advice display a growing commitment to involving the public in technically-grounded decisions. In announcing the creation of a new Directorate General for Consumer Protection, the European Commission observed in 1997 that, 'Consumer confidence in the legislative activities of the EU is conditioned by the *quality and transparency* of the scientific advice and its use on the legislative and control process' (emphasis added).[28] A commitment to greater openness is also evident in several new UK expert bodies, such as the Food Standards Agency, created to restore confidence in the wake of the BSE crisis. Similarly, two major public inquiries – the Phillips Inquiry on BSE and the Smith Inquiry on the Harold Shipman murder investigation – set high standards for public access to information through the Internet. All across Europe, opposition to genetically-modified foods and crops has prompted experiments with diverse forms of public involvement, such as citizen juries, consensus conferences, and referenda.[29]

Although these efforts are admirable, formal participatory opportunities cannot by themselves ensure the representative and democratic governance of science. There are, to start with, practical problems. People may not possess enough special-ized knowledge and material resources to take advantage of formal procedures. Participation may occur too late to identify alternatives to dominant or default options; some processes, such as consensus conferences, may be too *ad hoc* or issue-specific to exercise sustained influence. More problematic is the fact that even timely participation does not necessarily improve decision-making. Empirical research has consistently shown that transparency may exacerbate rather than quell controversy, leading parties to deconstruct each other's positions instead of delib-erating effectively. Indeed, the Shelby Amendment reflects one US politician's conviction that compulsory disclosure of data will enable any interested party to challenge researchers' interpretations of their work. Participation, in this sense, becomes an instrument to challenge scientific points on political grounds. By contrast, public participation that is constrained by established formal discourses, such as risk assessment, may not admit novel viewpoints, radical critiques, or considerations lying outside the taken-for-granted framing of the problem.

While national governments are scrambling to create new participatory forms, there are signs that such changes may reach neither far enough nor deeply enough to satisfy the citizens of a globalizing world. Current reforms leave out public involvement in corporate decision-making at the design and product-development phases. The Monsanto Company's experience with the 'Terminator gene' suggests that political activists may seize control of decisions on their own terms, unless governance structures provide for more deliberative participation. In this case, the mere possibility that a powerful multinational corporation might acquire tech-nology to deprive poor farmers of their rights, galvanized an activist organization – Rural Advancement Foundation International (RAFI) – to launch an effective worldwide campaign against the technology.[30] Through a combination of inspired media tactics (including naming the technology after a popular science-fiction movie) and strategic alliance-building (for example, with the Rockefeller Foundation), RAFI forced Monsanto to back down from this particular product. The episode can be read as a case of popular technology assessment, in a context where official processes failed to deliver the level of accountability desired by the public.

Participation alone, then, does not answer the problem of how to democratize technological societies. Opening the doors to previously closed expert forums is a necessary step – indeed, it should be seen by now as a standard operating procedure. But the formal mechanisms adopted by national governments are not enough to engage the public in the management of global science and technology. What has to change is the *culture* of governance, within nations as well as internationally; and for this we need to address not only the mechanics, but also the substance of participatory politics. The issue, in other words, is no longer *whether* the public should have a say in technical decisions, but *how* to promote more meaningful interaction among policy-makers, scientific experts, corporate producers, and the public.

Technologies of humility

The analytic ingenuity of modern states has been directed toward refining what we may call the 'technologies of hubris'. To reassure the public, and to keep the wheels of science and industry turning, governments have developed a series of predictive methods (e.g., risk assessment, cost-benefit analysis, climate modelling) that are designed, on the whole, to facilitate management and control, even in areas of high uncertainty.[31] These methods achieve their power through claims of objectivity and a disciplined approach to analysis, but they suffer from three significant limitations. First, they show a kind of peripheral blindness toward uncertainty and ambiguity. Predictive methods focus on the known at the expense of the unknown, producing overconfidence in the accuracy and completeness of the pictures they produce. Well-defined, short-term risks command more attention than indeterminate, long-term ones, especially in cultures given to technological optimism. At the same time, technical proficiency conveys the false impression that analysis is not only rigorous, but complete – in short, that it has taken account of all possible risks. Predictive methods tend in this way to downplay what falls outside their field of vision, and to overstate whatever falls within.[32]

Second, the technologies of predictive analysis tend to pre-empt political discussion. Expert analytic frameworks create high entry barriers against legitimate positions that cannot express themselves in terms of the dominant discourse.[33] Claims of objectivity hide the exercise of judgment, so that normative presuppositions are not subjected to general debate. The boundary work that demarcates the space of 'objective' policy analysis is carried out by experts, so that the politics of demarcation remains locked away from public review and criticism.[34]

Third, predictive technologies are limited in their capacity to internalize challenges that arise outside their framing assumptions. For example, techniques for assessing chemical toxicity have become ever more refined, but they continue to rest on the demonstrably faulty assumption that people are exposed to one chemical at a time. Synergistic effects, long-term exposures, and multiple exposures are common in normal life, but have tended to be ignored as too messy for analysis – hence, as irrelevant to decision-making. Even in the aftermath of catastrophic failures, modernity's predictive models are often adjusted to take on board only those lessons that are compatible with their initial assumptions. When a US-designed chemical factory in Bhopal released the deadly gas methyl isocyanate, killing thousands, the international chemical industry made many improvements in its internal accounting and risk-communication practices. But no new methods were developed to assess the risks of technology transfer between radically different cultures of industrial production.

To date, the unknown, unspecified, and indeterminate aspects of scientific and technological development remain largely unaccounted for in policy-making; treated as beyond reckoning, they escape the discipline of analysis. Yet, what is lacking is not just knowledge to fill the gaps, but also processes and methods to elicit what the public wants, and to use what is already known. To bring these dimensions out of the shadows and into the dynamics of democratic debate, they must first be made concrete and tangible. Scattered and private knowledge has to be amalgamated, perhaps even disciplined, into a dependable civic epistemology. The human and social sciences of previous centuries undertook just such a task of translation. They made visible the social problems of modernity – poverty, unemployment, crime, illness, disease, and lately, technological risk – often as a prelude to rendering them more manageable, using what I have termed the 'technologies of hubris'. Today, there is a need for 'technologies of humility' to complement the predictive approaches: to make apparent the possibility of unforeseen consequences; to make explicit the normative that lurks within the technical; and to acknowledge from the start the need for plural viewpoints and collective learning.

How can these aims be achieved? From the abundant literature on technological disasters and failures, as well as from studies of risk analysis and policy-relevant science, we can abstract four focal points around which to develop the new technologies of humility. They are *framing, vulnerability, distribution*, and *learning*. Together, they provide a framework for the questions we should ask of almost every human enterprise that intends to alter society: what is the purpose; who will be hurt; who benefits; and how can we know? On all these points, we have good reason to believe that wider public engagement would improve our capacity for analysis and reflection. Participation that pays attention to these four points promises to lead neither to a hardening of positions, nor to endless deconstruction, but instead to richer deliberation on the substance of decision-making.

Framing

It has become an article of faith in the policy literature that the quality of solutions to perceived social problems depends on the way they are framed.[35] If a problem is framed too narrowly, too broadly, or wrongly, the solution will suffer from the same defects. To take a simple example, a chemical-testing policy focused on single chemicals cannot produce knowledge about the environmental health consequences of multiple exposures. The framing of the regulatory issue is more restrictive than the actual distribution of chemical-induced risks, and hence is incapable of delivering optimal management strategies. Similarly, a belief that violence is genetic may discourage the search for controllable social influences on behaviour. A focus on the biology of reproduction may delay or impede effective social policies for curbing population growth. When facts are uncertain, disagreements about the appropriate frame are virtually unavoidable and often remain intractable for long periods. Yet, few policy cultures have adopted systematic methods for revising the initial framing of issues.[36] Frame analysis thus remains a critically important, though neglected, tool of policy-making that would benefit from greater public input.

Vulnerability

Risk analysis treats the 'at-risk' human being as a passive agent in the path of potentially-disastrous events. In an effort to produce policy-relevant assessments, human populations are often classified into groups (e.g., most susceptible, maximally exposed, genetically predisposed, children or women) that are thought to be differently affected by the hazard in question. Based on physical and biological indicators, however, these classifications tend to overlook the social foundations of vulnerability, and to subordinate individual experiences of risk to aggregate numerical calculations.[37] Recent efforts to analyse vulnerability have begun to recognize the importance of socio-economic factors, but methods of assessment still take populations rather than individuals as the unit of analysis. These approaches not only disregard differences within groups, but reduce individuals to statistical representations. Such characterizations leave out of the calculus of vulnerability such factors as history, place, and social connectedness, all of which may play crucial roles in determining human resilience. Through participation in the analysis of their vulnerability, ordinary citizens may regain their status as active subjects, rather than remain undifferentiated objects in yet another expert discourse.

Distribution

Controversies over such innovations as genetically modified foods and stem cell research have propelled ethics committees to the top of the policy-making ladder. Frequently, however, these bodies are used as 'end-of-pipe' legitimation devices, reassuring the public that normative issues have not been omitted from governmental deliberation. The term 'ethics', moreover, does not cover the whole range of social and economic realignments that accompany major technological changes, nor their distributive consequences, particularly as technology unfolds across global societies and markets. Attempts to engage systematically with distributive issues in policy processes have not been altogether successful. In Europe, consideration of the 'fourth hurdle' – the socio-economic impact of biotechnology – was abandoned after a brief debate. In the US, the congressional Office of Technology Assessment, which arguably had the duty to evaluate socio-economic impacts, was dissolved in 1995.[38] President Clinton's 1994 injunction to Federal agencies to develop strategies for achieving environmental justice has produced few dramatic results.[39] At the same time, episodes like the RAFI-led rebellion against Monsanto demonstrate a deficit in the capacity for ethical and political analysis in large corporations, whose technological products can fundamentally alter people's lives. Sustained interactions between decision-makers, experts, and citizens, starting at the upstream end of research and development, could yield significant dividends in exposing the distributive implications of innovation.

Learning

Theorists of social and institutional learning have tended to assume that what is 'to be learned' is never part of the problem. A correct, or at least a better, response exists, and the issue is whether actors are prepared to internalize it. In the social world, learning is complicated by many factors. The capacity to learn is constrained by limiting features of the frame within which institutions must act. Institutions see only what their discourses and practices permit them to see. Experience, moreover, is polysemic, or subject to many interpretations, no less in policy-making than in literary texts. Even when the fact of failure in a given case is more or less unambiguous, its causes may be open to many different readings. Just as historians disagree over what may have caused the rise or fall of particular political regimes, so policy-makers may find it impossible to attribute their failures to specific causes. The origins of a problem may appear one way to those in power, and in quite another way to the marginal or the excluded. Rather than seeking monocausal explanations, it would be fruitful to design avenues through which societies can collectively reflect on the ambiguity of their experiences, and to assess the strengths and weaknesses of alternative explanations. Learning, in this modest sense, is a suitable objective of civic deliberation.

Conclusion

The enormous growth and success of science and technology during the last century has created contradictions for institutions of governance. As technical activities have become more pervasive and complex, demand has grown for more complete and multivalent evaluations of the costs and benefits of technological progress. It is widely recognized that increased participation and interactive knowledge-making may improve accountability and lead to more credible assessments of science and technology. Such approaches will also be consistent with changes in the modes of knowledge production, which have made science more socially embedded and more closely tied to contexts of application. Yet, modern institutions still operate with conceptual models that seek to separate science from values, and that emphasize prediction and control at the expense of reflection and social learning. Not surprisingly, the real world continually produces reminders of the incompleteness of our predictive capacities through such tragic shocks as Perrow's 'normal accidents'.

A promising development is the renewed attention being paid to participation and transparency. Such participation, I have argued, should be treated as a standard operating procedure of democracy, but its aims must be considered as carefully as its mechanisms. Formally constituted procedures do not necessarily draw in all those whose knowledge and values are essential to making progressive policies. Participation in the absence of normative discussion can lead to intractable conflicts of the kind encountered in the debate on policies for climate change. Nor does the contemporary policy-maker's near-exclusive preoccupation with the management and control of risk, leave much space for tough debates on techno-logical futures, without which we are doomed to repeat past mistakes.

To move public discussion of science and technology in new directions, I have suggested a need for 'technologies of humility', complementing the predictive 'technologies of hubris' on which we have lavished so much of our past attention. These *social* technologies would give combined attention to substance and process, and stress deliberation as well as analysis. Reversing nearly a century of contrary development, these approaches to decision-making would seek to inte-grate the 'can do' orientation of science and engineering with the 'should do' questions of ethical and political analysis. They would engage the human subject as an active, imaginative agent, as well as a source of knowledge, insight, and memory. The specific focal points I have proposed – framing, vulnerability, distri-bution, and learning – are pebbles thrown into a pond, with untested force and unforeseeable ripples. These particular concepts may prove insufficient to drive serious institutional change, but they can at least offer starting points for a deeper public debate on the future of science in society.

Notes

* *Minerva*, Vol. 41 (2003), pp. 223–44.
1 Charles Perrow, *Normal Accidents: Living with High Risk Technologies* (New York: Basic Books, 1984).
2 Ibid. See also Diane Vaughan, *The Challenger Launch Decision: Risky Technology, Culture, and Deviance at NASA* (Chicago: University of Chicago Press, 1996); James F. Short and Lee Clarke (eds.), *Organizations, Uncertainties, and Risk* (Boulder: Westview Press, 1992); and Lee Clarke, *Acceptable Risk? Making Decisions in a Toxic Environment* (Berkeley: University of California Press, 1989).
3 Ulrich Beck, *Risk Society: Towards a New Modernity* (London: Sage, 1992).
4 A pre-eminent example of the calculative approach is given in John D. Graham and Jonathan B. Wiener (eds.), *Risk versus Risk: Tradeoffs in Protecting Health and the Environment* (Cambridge, Mass.: Harvard University Press, 1995).
5 Never far from the minds of philosophers and authors of fiction, these concerns have also been famously articulated in recent times by Bill Joy, co-founder and chief scien-tist of Sun Microsystems. See Joy, 'Why the Future Doesn't Need Us', *Wired*, http://www.wired.com/wired/archive/8.04/joy.html.

6 The *locus classicus* of this view of the right relations between knowledge and power is Don K. Price, *The Scientific Estate* (Cambridge, Mass.: Harvard University Press, 1965).

7 See, in particular, Sheila Jasanoff, *The Fifth Branch: Science Advisers as Policy-makers* (Cambridge, Mass.: Harvard University Press, 1990).

8 United Kingdom, House of Lords Select Committee on Science and Technology, Third Report, *Science and Society*, http://www.parliament.the-stationery-office.co.uk/pa/ld199900/ldselect/ldsctech/38/3801.htm (2000).

9 Commission of the European Communities, *European Governance: A White Paper*, COM (2001), 428, http://europa.eu.int/eur-lex/en/com/cnc/2001/com2001_0428en01. pdf (Brussels, 27 July 2001), 19.

10 Vannevar Bush, *Science – The Endless Frontier* (Washington, DC: US Government Printing Office, 1945).

11 The creation of the National Institutes of Health (NIH) to sponsor biomedical research, divided US science policy in a way not contemplated by Bush's original design. In the recent politics of science, NIH budgets have proved consistently easier to justify than appropriations for other branches of science.

12 For reviews of the extensive relevant literatures, see Sheila Jasanoff, Gerald E. Markle, James C. Petersen, and Trevor Pinch (eds.), *Handbook of Science and Technology Studies* (Thousand Oaks, CA: Sage, 1995).

13 Daniel J. Kevles, *The Baltimore Case: A Trial of Politics, Science, and Character* (New York: Norton, 1998).

14 David H. Guston, *Between Politics and Science: Assuring the Integrity and Productivity of Research* (Cambridge: Cambridge University Press, 2001).

15 Daniel S. Greenberg, *Science, Money, and Politics: Political Triumph and Ethical Erosion* (Chicago: University of Chicago Press, 2001).

16 See, for example, Sonja Boehmer-Christiansen, 'Global Climate Protection Policy: The Limits of Scientific Advice, Parts 1 and 2', *Global Environmental Change*, 4 (2), (1994), 140–159; 4 (3), (1994), 185–200.

17 John E. Losey, L.S. Rayor, and M.E. Carter, 'Transgenic Pollen Harms Monarch Larvae', *Nature*, 399 (1999), 214.

18 Stanley W.B. Ewen and Arpad Pusztai, 'Effect of diets containing genetically modified potatoes expressing *Galanthus nivalis lectin* on rat small intestine', *Lancet*, 354 (1999), 1353–1354.

19 '*Nature* Regrets Publication of Corn Study', *The Washington Times*, http://www.washingtontimes.com/national/20020405-9384015.htm, 5 April 2002.

20 Donald E. Stokes, *Pasteur's Quadrant: Basic Science and Technological Innovation* (Washington, DC: Brookings Institution, 1997).

21 Silvio O. Funtowicz and Jerome R. Ravetz, 'Three Types of Risk Assessment and the Emergence of Post Normal Science', in Sheldon Krimsky and D. Golding (eds.), *Social Theories of Risk* (New York: Praeger, 1992), 251–273.

22 A problem with this analysis lies in the term 'post-normal science'. When scientific conclusions are so closely intertwined with social and normative considerations as in Funtowicz and Ravetz's outermost circle, one may just as well call the 'product' by another name, such as 'socially-relevant knowledge' or 'socio-technical knowledge'.

23 Jasanoff, op. cit. note 7.

24 Michael Gibbons, Camille Limoges, Helga Nowotny, Simon Schwartzman, Peter Scott, and Martin Trow, *The New Production of Knowledge: The Dynamics of Science and Research in Contemporary Societies* (London: Sage, 1994).

25 Ibid., 8.

26 Helga Nowotny, Peter Scott, and Michael Gibbons, *Re-Thinking Science: Knowledge and the Public in an Age of Uncertainty* (Cambridge: Polity, 2001), 166–178.

27 Public Law 105–277 (1998). The Office of Management and Budget in the Clinton administration controversially narrowed the scope of the law to apply not to *all*

publicly-funded research, but only to research actually relied upon in policy-making. The issue is not completely resolved as of this writing.

28 European Commission, *1997 Communication of the European Commission on Consumer Health and Safety*, COM (97), 183 fin. http://europa.eu.int/comm/food/fs/sc/index_en.html.

29 Simon Joss and John Durant (eds.), *Public Participation in Science: The Role of Consensus Conferences in Europe* (London: Science Museum, 1995).

30 In 1998, a small cotton seed company called Delta and Pine Land (D&PL) patented a technique designed to switch off the reproductive mechanism of agricultural plants, thereby rendering their seed sterile. The company hoped that this technology would help protect the intellectual property rights of agricultural biotechnology firms by taking away from farmers the capacity to re-use seed from a given year's genetically modified crops in the next planting season. While the technology was still years away from the market, rumours arose of a deal by Monsanto to acquire D&PL. This was the scenario that prompted RAFI to act. Robert F. Service, 'Seed-Sterilizing "Terminator Technology" Sows Discord', *Science*, 282 (1998), 850–851.

31 See, for example, Theodore M. Porter, *Trust in Numbers: The Pursuit of Objectivity in Science and Public Life* (Princeton: Princeton University Press, 1995).

32 Alan Irwin and Brian Wynne (eds.), *Misunderstanding Science? The Public Reconstruction of Science and Technology* (Cambridge: Cambridge University Press, 1996).

33 Langdon Winner, 'On Not Hitting the Tar Baby', in Langdon Winner (ed.), *The Whale and the Reactor: A Search for Limits in an Age of High Technology* (Chicago: University of Chicago Press, 1986), 138–154.

34 Jasanoff, op. cit. note 7.

35 Donald A. Schon and Martin Rein, *Frame/Reflection: Toward the Resolution of Intractable Policy Controversies* (New York: Basic Books, 1994).

36 Paul C. Stern and Harvey V. Fineberg (eds.), *Understanding Risk: Informing Decisions in a Democratic Society* (Washington, DC: National Academy of Science Press, 1996).

37 For some examples, see Irwin and Wynne, op. cit. note 32.

38 Bruce Bimber, *The Politics of Expertise in Congress: The Rise and Fall of the Office of Technology Assessment* (Albany: State University of New York Press, 1996).

39 'Federal Actions to Address Environmental Justice in Minority Populations and Low-Income Populations', Executive Order 12298, Washington, DC, 11 February 1994.

10 What judges should know about the sociology of science*

In *Daubert v. Merrell Dow Pharmaceuticals*,[1] the Supreme Court firmly rejected the *Frye* test, which had dominated judicial thinking about the admissibility of novel scientific evidence for 70 years. Judges need no longer turn to science to determine whether an expert's opinion has "gained general acceptance in the particular field in which it belongs."[2] Instead, the Court proposed a two-pronged assessment of "whether the reasoning or methodology underlying the testimony is scientifically valid and of whether that reasoning or methodology properly can be applied to the facts in issue."[3]

While *Daubert* seemingly gives judges more discretion than *Frye* did, it also encourages them, as some commentators have already observed, to "think like scientists." Justice Harry Blackmun, writing for the majority, was unwilling to set out a "definitive checklist" for use in reviewing scientific evidence. Yet a determination of "scientific validity" clearly must be central to such inquiry. Where should judges turn for further guidance on how to meet this obligation?

Perspectives from the sociology of science can be applied usefully to the review of scientific evidence in the wake of *Daubert*. It is beyond this article's scope to present the issues in more than outline form, but the approach proposed here promotes deeper reflection about how far the courts can go in determining what constitutes legitimate science.

The practice of science

In recent years, critical studies of science have increasingly focused on the way scientists carry out their work in practice. Investigations into the social structure and operation of science have revealed a picture of scientific knowledge that is distant from the logically coherent but highly abstract accounts constructed by philosophers of science. This new, and in many ways disconcerting, picture of science has particular relevance for the law, because what is at issue in most legal proceedings is precisely the social dimension of science: the matrix of social practices, conventions, institutions, and interests that sustains scientific progress and gives legitimacy to particular scientific "facts."

Below is an abbreviated and highly simplified overview of findings from the sociology of science; these ideas are subsequently brought to bear on some well-known patterns of legal controversy.

Social construction

The most significant insight that has emerged from sociological studies of science in the past 15 years is the view that science is *socially constructed*. According to a persuasive body of work, the "facts" that scientists present to the rest of the world are not direct reflections of nature; rather, these "facts" are produced by human agency through the institutions and processes of science, and hence they invariably contain a social component.[4] Facts, in other words, are more than merely raw observations made by scientists exploring the mysteries of nature. Observations achieve the status of "facts" only if they are produced in accordance with prior agreements about the rightness of particular theories, experimental methods, instrumentation techniques, validation procedures, review processes, and the like. These agreements, in turn, are socially derived through continual negotiation and renegotiation among relevant bodies of scientists.

The process of constructing scientific facts normally takes place within familiar scientific institutions such as the laboratory, the specialist journal, the disciplinary society, or the "invisible college"[5] of experts in a given field. At times, however, non-scientific institutions are drawn into the construction of science, such as when a television program publicizes the risks of a pesticide or a court adjudicates the validity of an epidemiological study that has never been published in the peer-reviewed literature. In these cases, what finally counts as "science" is influenced not only by the consensus views of scientists, but also by society's culturally conditioned views of how things work in nature.[6]

Contingency

From a sociological viewpoint, scientific claims are never absolutely true but are always *contingent* on such factors as the experimental or interpretive conventions that have been agreed to within relevant scientific communities. The contingency of scientific facts refers to their dependence on certain background features necessary for their production. In their normal professional interactions, scientists tend to downplay even those contingencies of which they are aware, and they tend to speak of facts as if they were objectively true. When scientific controversies erupt, however, disputing parties regularly focus on the contingencies in each other's accounts of reality. As noted by sociologists Nigel Gilbert and Michael Mulkay, the objective "empiricist repertoire" of normal scientific discourse is replaced in these instances by a more subjective "contingent repertoire" that stresses the indeterminacy of many alleged facts.[7]

Inscription

The noted French sociologist Bruno Latour has called attention to the fact that science as we know it often takes the form of written texts or *inscriptions*, such as a curve on graph paper, a scattering of dots on photographic film, or an X-ray picture that looks like a supermarket bar code. The inscription (and, more generally, its translation into numbers) is regarded as having a direct relationship to the observed substance of science, although extremely sophisticated instruments and practices may in fact underlie its production. Scientific debate generally takes the inscriptions that are reproduced in published articles as the starting point for discussing natural phenomena. The inscription is a substitute for reality, while "the intervening material activity and all aspects of what is often a prolonged and costly process are bracketed off in discussions about what the figure means."[8]

Deconstruction

For sociologists of science, *deconstruction* means nothing more arcane than the pulling apart of socially constructed facts during a controversy. That facts should lend themselves to deconstruction is a corollary of their original construction. The adversarial structure of litigation is particularly conducive to the deconstruction of scientific facts, since it provides parties both the incentive (winning the lawsuit) and the formal means (cross-examination) for bringing out the contingencies in their opponents' arguments.

Experimenters' regress

Harry Collins, a leading British sociologist of science, has observed that the deconstruction of controversial scientific claims commonly follows a pattern called *experimenters' regress*. Experiments, as Collins notes, are always matters of skillful practice, so that "it can never be clear whether a second experiment has been done sufficiently well to count as a check on the results of a first."[9] When scientists wish to contradict each other's findings (as routinely happens in legal proceedings), the indeterminacy of experimentation provides a natural pathway of attack: Were the instruments properly calibrated? Were background conditions stably maintained? Was the experiment adequately controlled? Were the resulting inscriptions correctly interpreted? Was there a valid statistical analysis of the data? There is virtually no limit to the questions that can be asked about experiments as long as scientists have an interest in challenging one another's observations. A consensus develops around particular scientific theories, methods, and claims only when the incentives for attacking them disappear. Claims that no scientist any longer wishes to challenge or unpack are said to be "black boxed"; such claims constitute the expanding and, for the most part, invulnerable core of scientific knowledge.

Boundary work

The stability of science, according to the sociological view, depends upon negotiated agreements within a research community about a host of issues ranging from the applicable theoretical paradigm to norms of peer review and publication. To maintain the stability of its findings, a community of scientists has to be relatively resistant to criticism from outsiders. Solid state physicists, for example, will only brook criticism from other solid state physicists, just as epidemiologists will reject interventions by experts who have no formal training in epidemiology. Studies in the sociology of science have shown that scientists maintain the purity of their communities through what is termed *boundary work*. People whose criticism the community does not wish to accept are dismissed as members of a different field or, if circumstances demand, as misfits, deviants, charlatans, or outsiders to the enterprise of science.[10] Effective boundary drawing insulates scientific work from unexpected and possibly ill-motivated challenge by inadequately credentialed critics. Boundary work is in this sense an indispensable part of the ordinary practice of science, but the boundaries drawn by scientists can be used to deflect meritorious as well as unjustified criticism.

Applications to the law

The foregoing model of scientific practice provides a useful starting point for explicating scientific controversies, whether they arise at the laboratory bench, in the pages of scientific journals, or in the courts. Recent legal disputes about the reliability of DNA fingerprinting, for example, illustrate both the "constructedness" of scientific claims and some commonly recurring patterns of deconstruction.

DNA fingerprinting was initially greeted by forensic scientists as the ultimate solution for problems of identification. The technique is solidly grounded in biological theory, empirically tested, technologically feasible, and far more discriminating than other widely employed tests of identity. It can be used not only to convict the guilty but to exonerate the falsely accused, to establish paternity, and to reunite families separated by political terror. Between 1986, when DNA identification was first introduced into U.S. criminal trials, and 1990, the congressional Office of Technology Assessment identified 185 cases in which such tests had been admitted into evidence.[11] Given the technique's rapid spread, it is easy to understand why two 1989 decisions to exclude DNA evidence in New York[12] and Maine[13] raised agitated questions about the capacity of courts to deal with complex scientific testimony.

The arguments that led to the exclusion of DNA evidence in these lawsuits, however, seem entirely predictable when observed through the lens of sociology of science. Let us consider first the issue of "bandshifts," which first reached national prominence in a sexual molestation case in Maine. Lifecodes Corporation, the commercial testing laboratory that had prepared the evidence in this case, identified a match between two DNA samples. The bands that constituted the two "fingerprints," however, did not quite line up; the pattern was the same in both prints but was displaced in a way that suggested the DNA fragments in one sample were slightly larger than in the other.[14] On what basis, then, did Lifecodes read the two prints as identical?

The defense attorneys' attempts to investigate this question led to a classic case of deconstruction, in which the validity of a particular scientific interpretation unraveled under critical pressure. The experts from Lifecodes revealed at trial that they had employed a previously unvalidated methodology to reconcile the difference between the two DNA inscriptions. A device known as a monomorphic probe had been used to tag a particular fragment of DNA that is the same in every person. Based on the relative displacement of this tagged fragment, the Lifecodes experts had concluded that all the bands in the seemingly displaced sample should be corrected by a factor of 3.15 percent, a calculation that enabled them to explain away the bandshifting as immaterial—in other words, to declare a match between the two samples.

Subsequent discussion both inside and outside the courtroom led to further deconstruction and experimenters' regress. Once other scientists became aware of the technique used by Lifecodes, they not only found fault with it on methodological grounds, but began proposing alternative techniques they asserted would work better. In a direct attack on the validity of the Lifecodes approach, an expert working for the defense said, "The whole experiment wasn't done with the kind of rigor you would expect."[15]

An exchange of letters in *Science* went even further. One writer criticized Lifecodes for using Southern blotting when "other more powerful techniques" were available, such as the use of "internally tagged" DNA samples and substitution of a sequencing gel for an agarose gel. Another writer suggested that the two samples should be "co-injected" or "co-spotted" in addition to being compared in separate lanes. A third complained that it seemed "overly simplistic to apply a single percentage correction to all the bands in a given lane"; a better approach, he suggested, would be "to spike each DNA sample with a set of marker fragments."[16] Together, these criticisms underscored the fact that Lifecodes' identity determination was contingent on the scientific acceptability of a particular, still contested, interpretive technique: the use of monomorphic probes. Once defense experts and other scientists began systematically attacking this technique, the identity finding that it supported also lost its credibility.

Boundary work has also emerged as a significant factor in determining the validity and courtroom acceptability of DNA tests. Urging caution in the use of the new technique, some have asked whether acceptance by research scientists provides a sufficient guarantee of its acceptability for use in criminal identification.[17] Critics have noted that conditions in forensic laboratories may make the tests less reliable than when they are done in research laboratories. This critique elevates the boundary between research science and forensic science into a legally significant issue. It is worth recalling that a similar boundary proved to be legally persuasive in earlier disputes involving the reliability of blood typing by gel electrophoresis. Courts in Michigan and California divided the "relevant community" of experts into two groups to whom they assigned differing credibility: "scientists" from university research laboratories were deemed more reliable than "technicians" working in forensic laboratories.[18]

Statistical challenges to DNA typing exemplify a different kind of boundary issue that will have increasing relevance following *Daubert*: the difference between a test's general validity and its validity in a particular case. As the OTA study noted,[19] the *validity* of forensic DNA tests does not hinge upon our knowledge about the frequency of various DNA markers in the U.S. population. Yet information from population genetics can be highly relevant to a scientifically reliable application of the tests in specific cases—in particular, to calculating the probability of an accidental match. Hence, a finding that the test is scientifically valid will not alone be sufficient to justify the reliance on DNA typing. The applicability of these tests has to be evaluated case by case, with both forensic DNA experts and population geneticists being given the opportunity to interpret the data from their respective disciplinary perspectives.

In sum, the DNA fingerprinting cases suggest that the courts are a better forum for articulating than for definitively resolving deconstructive questions about scientific evidence. The issues of technique, standardization, and statistical interpretation that first arose in trials involving DNA tests eventually were addressed by expert scientific bodies whose work may help to standardize scientific practices in this area. Thus, in April 1992 a panel of the National Academy of Sciences issued a report recommending that DNA testing laboratories should meet stricter quality control standards to ensure the reliability of their results.[20] Interestingly, Eric Lander, a member of the NAS panel, was one of several experts who had testified on some of these issues several years earlier in *People v. Castro*,[21] the New York case where the reliability of DNA fingerprints first came to public attention.

Judicial assessments

Many of the insights from the sociology of science will seem familiar to judges and lawyers skilled in the interpretation of expert testimony. The community of trial lawyers and judges knows perhaps better than any other professional group just how unruly science often is in practice. Their daily experience confirms that scientists are often sloppy, that they use covert assumptions and untried techniques, and that they sometimes manufacture data points or gloss over results that do not quite make sense in the light of theory, Yet even legal practitioners who are well-versed in the ways of science and scientists can benefit from a systematic account of scientific practice. A more serious engagement with the sociology of science can provide legal analysts with at least three forms of enlightenment.

First, familiarity with sociological accounts of science should help dispel unrealistic and overly romanticized views of the legal process. Is cross-examination really "the greatest legal engine ever invented for the discovery of truth"?[22] The social constructivist perspective suggests the answer may be more complex and ambiguous than lawyers generally admit. Adversary procedures are indeed a wonderful instrument for deconstructing "facts," for exposing the contingencies and hidden assumptions that underlie scientific claims, and thereby preventing uncritical acceptance of alleged truths. The adversary process is much less effective, however, in reconstructing the communally held beliefs that reasonably pass for scientific truth. Cross-examination, in particular, privileges skepticism over consensus. It skews the picture of science that is presented to the legal fact finder and creates an impression of conflict even where little or no disagreement exists in practice.

At the same time, the sociological perspective on science alerts us to be cautious about statements like the following from "junk science" critic Peter Huber:

> Some will always insist that all truth is relative and subjective, that anyone should therefore be allowed to testify to anything, that science must be viewed as a chaotic heap of unconnected and contradictory assertions, and that the best we can do is invite the jury to decide scientific truth by majority vote. But anyone who believes in the possibility of neutral law, as many fortunately still do, must at the same time believe in the existence of objective fact, which ultimately means positive science. The only real alternative is nihilism.[23]

Neither the neutrality of the law nor the positivism of science has stood up well enough to tests of empirical research to justify uncritical belief. Fortunately, however, the alternative is not nihilism, at least as long as we remember that the ultimate goal of the courts is the attainable one of dispensing justice, not the impossible one of finding objective truth.

The second conceptual benefit that the sociology of science can offer to judges and lawyers is to provide a more principled basis for evaluating the validity and applicability of scientific evidence. Seventy years of judicial experience showed how difficult it is to implement the seemingly straightforward dictates of the *Frye* test. For example, courts reached inconsistent results in trying to assign scientific techniques such as polygraph tests or DNA fingerprinting to one or more unambiguous "fields." Work in the sociology of science puts these difficulties into context, revealing them to be special instances of the more general phenomenon of boundary drawing in science. The boundaries around fields, as we now know, are themselves contingent: a scientific "field" is intrinsically a moving target, for its boundaries are defined in relation to particular scientific, historical, cultural, and even political circumstances, all of which may change over time. A technique, moreover, can "belong" to more than one field, and, as in the case of DNA tests and population genetics, courts may discover through experience that a technique that has gained general acceptance in one field may not yet have done so in another—for reasons that are in themselves scientifically valid.

Daubert did well to recognize that "peer review" should not be adopted as a blanket prerequisite for admissibility, replacing *Frye*'s even less workable criterion of "general acceptance." At the same time, the analytic approach outlined above suggests that *Daubert*'s criteria of testability and falsifiability will in their turn prove difficult to implement in courts of law. Whether or not a theory or technique has been adequately tested is as much a social as a scientific question.

If an issue is not contentious within a given community of experts, members will readily agree on whether it has been properly tested. For issues in rapidly moving or frontier areas of science, however, experts will be more inclined to question the adequacy of scientific testing, following the well-trodden paths of experimenters' regress. Trial courts may therefore soon discover that Chief Justice William Rehnquist was not alone in his confusion over how to interpret the *Daubert* majority's criterion of falsifiability.

The skeptical reader may wonder at this point whether the sociology of science will help the courts or whether it will lead them into even deeper trouble. When courts previously faltered in their efforts to apply the *Frye* rule, commentators confidently blamed the vagaries of the legal process for the problem, emphasizing in particular the unrealistic constraints that the adversary process places on inquiries about science. Few thought to question whether concepts like general acceptance in the scientific community—and now *Daubert*'s concepts of testing and falsifiability—made good sense in the light of the true internal workings of science. The prevalent assumption was that scientific truth or consensus were always "out there" for the law to find and that any failure to accomplish this goal was due to imperfections in the law's machinery. Social studies of science pose a fundamental challenge to this relatively comfortable assessment. The difficulty of locating facts, truth, or consensus now seems to be embedded in the way science works. The problem of fact finding originates within science itself, although the law's halting approaches to determining what science has to say on a given issue often add layers of doubt and uncertainty to an undertaking that scientists themselves cannot entirely master.

Courts as participant-observers

This brings us to the third and possibly most significant intellectual contribution that sociology of science can make to the legal process: to provide a more complete accounting of what really takes place when courts engage in scientific fact finding. Clarity on this point will not necessarily bring comfort, especially to those who would like simple rules for solving complex problems. It will, however, help educate the practitioners of both law and science about the limitations of each other's disciplines when it comes to fact finding. An accurate perception of these limits may, in turn, lead to more realistic expectations about what can be achieved in courtroom inquiries into scientific evidence.

Frye, and to a lesser extent *Daubert*, are based on a positivist image of science that does not stand up to sociological, and indeed historical or philosophical, scrutiny. The positivist view presumes that science creates pictures of the real world that the law should merely seek to recover. When courts "find" the facts and opinions of science, or seek to determine the validity of evidence, their role is either to defer to what science already knows or to mimic as far as possible the dynamics of scientific inquiry within the courtroom. A sociologically informed analysis suggests, by contrast, that scientific claims are intrinsically provisional, contingent, and subject to deconstruction under critical scrutiny. Scientific claims, in short, are inherently open-ended, although this property may be clearly apparent only when science is embroiled in controversy. Legal fact finding accordingly reproduces at best a still frame out of the continually unfurling motion picture of science, with all the distortions that such compression entails. Worse yet from the standpoint of scientific positivism, the sociologically open-ended view of science suggests that it is impossible for the legal fact finder to maintain an objective distance from the "facts." In seeking to "find" them, the finder necessarily becomes not just an observer of, but a participant in, the social construction of science.

A recent Fifth Circuit decision, *Christopherson v. Allied Signal Corp.*,[24] vividly illustrates this participant-observer role of the courts in deciding questions about disputed science. Christopherson died of a rare cancer of the liver and colon allegedly caused by exposure to nickel and cadmium fumes generated during battery production at his place of work, Marathon Manufacturing Company. The plaintiff sought to establish this causal link through the evidence of a single expert witness, Dr. Miller, whose testimony was deemed inadmissible by the district court. The case came to the Fifth Circuit on appeal from the district court's grant of summary judgment in favor of Marathon. In an *en banc* hearing, the appellate judges held that Miller's testimony had been properly excluded, in part because of gross deficiencies in the facts and data upon which Miller had based his opinions.

Whether the trial court in *Christopherson* usurped the jury's fact finding role remains an unresolved issue. For our purposes, however, it is instructive to focus on the reasons for the court's ruling that Miller's testimony was fundamentally flawed. Miller had relied on the affidavit of a co-worker, Edgar Manoliu, who had described Christopherson's (and presumably his own) exposure to fumes in the workplace. The court noted that Manoliu's affidavit contained numerous gaps and inaccuracies: it contained no information about the type of fumes breathed by Christopherson or, more generally, produced during Marathon's manufacturing process; it failed to state the chemical composition of the fumes or of the contents of the soak tanks; and it apparently misstated both the number of times Christopherson visited the manufacturing area and the average duration of his stays. Moreover, neither Manoliu's affidavit nor any other source provided Miller with information about "the physical facilities at the Marathon plant, including the size of the plant or the impregnation and soak area, or the ventilation available in these areas or in Christopherson's office."[25]

Our brief foray into the sociology of science tells us that the exercise the court undertook here was a kind of deconstruction very similar to experimenters' regress. Confronted with Dr. Miller's statement about causation, a common type of claim in science, the court delved back into the basis for the statement's production and identified various points at which the chain of inference seemed weak or nonexistent. But the criteria of sufficiency that the court applied to the proposed testimony were of the court's own making, reflecting a quite possibly limited understanding of the nature of causation and proof in cases involving health claims. For example, the court clearly felt that "objective" standards (the chemical composition of fumes, numerical evidence of plant size and exposure) should take precedence over a co-worker's subjective testimony that all was not well in the Marathon workplace.

This is a conclusion that would not necessarily win support from all members of the medical community. In *Christopherson*, then, a scientific claim about causation was deconstructed according to standards articulated by judges, who thus became active participants in determining what evidence was sufficient. The plaintiff's evidence was excluded on the basis of legal or common-sense notions of validity rather than of criteria emanating from the testimony of other experts.

Some practical conclusions

The hardest task for an academic observer of the legal process is to demonstrate that theoretical analysis has useful practical consequences. Will the framework outlined in this article make judicial practice any more reflective or improve the handling of expert evidence by courts? Three general observations on this score are offered, each of which has important consequences for future procedural development.

First, the sociological study of science suggests that science is as much to blame as the law for the seemingly indiscriminate deconstruction of scientific authority in the courts. The contingencies that the law exposes are inherent in the production of science, and, as we saw in the DNA fingerprinting cases, the law may serve a socially valuable function by revealing previously hidden contingencies to both scientists and the public. Yet the procedures for truth seeking in science and the law are profoundly antithetical to one another. Science successfully creates facts because scientists operate in a framework of incremental adjustments and carefully bounded negotiation within communities who share a commitment to closure. Legal fact finding, by contrast, treats all facts as equally contingent in a forum where adversaries have every incentive to overstate the weaknesses in each other's positions. To assess scientific opinion fairly, then, the law may well have to experiment more actively with panels, pretrial hearings, and other non-polarizing approaches to fact finding, including procedures that increase the incentives for negotiation and closure.

Second, it follows from the previous point that legal proceedings should be structured with a clearer sense of the costs and benefits of alternative procedural formats. The panoply of a full-scale pretrial hearing may be appropriate for a mass toxic disaster, where millions of dollars can potentially change hands, or a scientific issue, such as DNA fingerprinting, which is likely to recur many times in the same jurisdiction. At other times, however, the adversary system may be the preferable method for scientific fact finding, both because it is most efficient and because it best safeguards the interests of the parties. The accounts of scientific reality produced by these means may be approximate and incomplete, but the methods of science may do no better in most cases, and they may in any event entail substantially higher costs.

Finally, the analysis proposed here supplies a theoretical basis for the misgivings that the legal community has always entertained about an overly active judicial role in scientific fact finding. When judges exclude expert testimony, appoint their own expert witnesses, or render summary judgments, they inescapably give up the role of dispassionate observer to become participants in a particular construction (or, as in *Christopherson*, deconstruction) of scientific facts. They help shape an image of reality that is colored in part by their own preferences and prejudices about how the world should work. Such power need not always be held in check, but it should be sparingly exercised. Otherwise, one risks substituting the expert authority of the black robe and the bench for that of the white lab coat—an outcome that poorly serves the cause of justice, or of science.

Notes

* *Jurimetrics*, Vol. 32, No. 3 (1992), pp. 345–359.
1 61 U.S. L.W. 4805 (U.S. June 28, 1993).
2 *Frye v. United States*, 293 F. 1013, 1014 (D.C.Cir. 1923).
3 61 U.S. L.W. 4805 (U.S. June 28, 1993).
4 *See, e.g.*, Latour and Woolgar, *Laboratory Life: The Construction of Scientific Facts* (1986).
5 For a definition of this term, see Crane, *Invisible Colleges: Diffusion of Knowledge in Scientific Communities* (1972).
6 The U.S. public, for example, tends to blame diseases such as cancer on chemicals in the environment. For a study of the impacts of culture on risk perception, see Douglas and Wildavsky, *Risk and Culture* (1982).
7 Gilbert and Mulkay, *Opening Pandora's Box: A Sociological Analysis of Scientists' Discourse* (1984).
8 Latour and Woolgar, *supra* n. 4, at 51.
9 Collins, *Changing Order: Replication and Induction in Scientific Practice* 2 (1985).
10 Gieryn, *Boundary-Work and the Demarcation of Science from Non-Science: Strains and Interests in Professional Ideologies of Scientists*, 48 *Am. Soc. Rev.* 781 (1983).
11 Office of Technology Assessment, *Genetic Witness: Forensic Uses of DNA Tests* 14 (1990).
12 *People v. Castro*, 545 N.Y.S.2d 985 (Sup. 1989).
13 *State of Maine v. McLeod* (1989).
14 For details, see Norman, *Maine Case Deals Blow to DNA Fingerprinting*, 246 *Science* 1556 (1989).
15 *Id.* at 1557.
16 *See Letters*, 247 *Science* 1018–1919 (1989).
17 Thompson and Ford, *DNA Typing: Acceptance and Weight of the New Genetic Identification Tests*, 75 *Va. L. Rev.* 45, 56–57 (1989).
18 *People v. Young*, 391 N.W.2d 270, 274–5 (Mich. 1986) (because a theoretical understanding of science is essential, the relevant community of experts is scientists, not technicians); and *People v. Brown*, 40 Cal.3d 512, 533 (1985) (forensic technicians' lack of formal training and background in the applicable scientific disciplines made them unqualified to state the view of the relevant scientific community). For a different approach to the same boundary issue, however, see *People v. Reilly*, 242 Cal. Rptr. 496, 503–4 (Cal. App. 1 Dist 1987).
19 OTA, *Genetic Witness*, *supra* n. 11, at 8.
20 Kolata, *Chief Says Panel Backs Courts' Use of a Genetic Test*, *New York Times* (April 15, 1992), at Al.
21 *Supra* n. 12.
22 *Richardson v. Perales*, 402 U.S. 413, 414 (1971).
23 Huber, *Junk Science in the Courtroom*, *Forbes* (July 8, 1991), at 72.
24 *Christopherson v. Allied-Signal Corporation*, 939 F.2d 1106 (5 Cir. 1991).
25 939 F.2d at. 1113.

11 Expert games in silicone gel breast implant litigation*

Legal historians have noted the relatively late appearance of institutionalized medicolegal knowledge and practices in Anglo-American judicial proceedings.[1] Here at the end of the 20th century, however, the American legal system suffers if anything from a surfeit of expertise. Courts today are awash with scientific evidence, generated largely at the behest of the litigating parties. Forensic science figured crucially in a series of high-profile criminal cases during the 1990s: the identification of telephonic voices (New York State Judge Sol Wachtler's threatening calls to his ex-mistress); handwriting (White House aide Vince Foster's suicide note and the Jon-Benét Ramsey ransom letter); typewriting (Theodore Kaczynski's authorship of the Unabomber manifesto); blood spatters (O.J. Simpson's glove, shoes and car); traces of chemical explosives (the Oklahoma City bombing); intercranial bleeding and 'shaken baby syndrome' (the murder trial of British au pair Louise Woodward). In civil cases, scientific evidence underpins claims of damage from drugs, diet pills, medical devices, electromagnetic fields, environmental pollutants and a host of other hazards, imagined or real. Expert evidence is invoked not only to prove guilt and causation, but also to establish baselines of acceptable behaviour in far-flung domains of professional endeavour, as in cases involving medical malpractice, insider trading, scientific misconduct, nursing, babysitting or child abuse.

As if driven by the law of supply and demand, forensic science, the cluster of scientific specialisms dedicated to the investigation of legally relevant matters of fact, has undergone massive growth and diversification in the past few decades. Indicators of professionalization, such as treatises, journals and associations, have not lagged far behind. A recent 1241-page treatise on scientific evidence testifies to the breadth and depth of this transformation. Its index lists, under a single letter of the alphabet, topics as disparate as 'semen', 'shoewear', 'skeleton', 'skidmarks' and 'smothering'.[2] Similarly hardly an academic discipline has not been called upon at one time or another to satisfy the legal system's insatiable thirst for certified knowledge. Sociologists and philosophers of science, for example, testified against the constitutionality of an Arkansas creationist law,[3] and specialists in ancient philosophy debated the constitutionality of an anti-gay rights referendum in the state of Colorado.[4]

The sudden efflorescence of experts and expertise in legal settings has brought with it a rising concern about the lines of demarcation between genuine and spurious experts, between mere claims of expert knowledge and the real thing. The fairness, not to say the perceived competence, of the legal process depends on its ability to make just such demarcations, but the capacity of courts to do so credibly is increasingly in doubt. For some, the problem reduces to a search for rules or criteria with which courts should be able to distinguish, quite generally, between legitimate science and its meretricious lookalikes.[5] Others have put their faith in process over rules and urged courts to assess the state of knowledge through wider use of specially appointed experts or panels. But such formulaic solutions, as has been argued elsewhere,[6] fail to make allowances for the contingencies that govern the production of scientific evidence. In the great majority of modern legal controversies, relevant expertise is not to be had for the asking, conveniently displayed in well-marked packages in the grand supermarket of science. Like every other aspect of a litigant's story, expert evidence too must be painstakingly pieced together from disparate, contradictory, incomplete and changeable sources.[7] Its function from the start is to support or contest particular accounts of something gone wrong in the world; normative and epistemological commitments are therefore inseparably woven together into expert evidence.

How then should courts tackle the demarcation problem of distinguishing between 'good' and 'bad' expert testimony? If appeal to external scientific authority is excluded in principle, whether in the form of absolute rules or of authoritative processes, clarification has to be sought within the very settings where evidence is made, through a deeper understanding of the mechanisms by which experts gain or lose credibility in the eyes of the law. Expertise is best viewed for our purposes as the end product of a complex game – equipped with its own distinctive moves, countermoves, rhetorics and practices – which can be simultaneously played by multiple players (such as judges, juries, lawyers, scientists, witnesses and professional communities) at varied locations, inside and outside the courtroom. This dynamic model helps us to sort and compare the divergent claims of expertise that come before the courts in complex litigation, such as the silicone gel breast implant (SGBI) lawsuits that have flooded US courtrooms since 1977.[8] Appreciation of the model, finally, provides a basis for refining the judgments that should govern the admissibility of expert evidence in legal proceedings.

How to tell an expert

In everyday life, expertise strikes us as an unproblematic phenomenon with clearly defined boundaries. The word 'expert' has, to begin with, a respectable pedigree in the English language. According to the *Oxford English Dictionary*, Chaucer already spoke of a person 'in science so experte' and of 'Maystres . . . That were of lawe expert and curious'. We have, besides, quite clear intuitions about how to use the term in ordinary speech. A cook, a salesman or a piano tuner, for instance, can be designated 'expert' for simply measuring up to certain conventional performance standards. By contrast, it seems reductionist to pin the label 'expert' on a violinist, mathematician or theatre critic, whose craft transcends any predetermined repertoire of rules. Yet we readily concede that artists, inventors and technicians all possess some form of expertise. Rule 702 of the US Federal Rules of Evidence (Testimony of Experts) begins to tease apart some of these intuitive judgments by acknowledging the varied ways in which expertise can be constituted. Persons may be recognized as experts in the courtroom by virtue of 'knowledge, skill, experience, training, or education'; once they are so certified, they need not, like laypeople, limit their testimony solely to matters known through direct, personal experience. Expertise, as conceived by the law, clearly encompasses the special sort of competence that we term 'science', but it is a significantly broader concept.

While granting that there are varied cognitive and experiential pathways to expertise, Rule 702 does require all would-be experts to show some level of learning or mastery beyond the ordinary. Expertise is not a state to be claimed at will. Yet, in the landscape of contemporary legal disputes, it seems that almost any kind of human experience can be converted, if only temporarily, into a domain of possible expertise. Scientists, used to operating within tightly drawn boundaries of professional authority,[9] find this catholic embrace of expertise unsettling, to say the least. Is the courtroom, then, the proverbial country of the blind where even the one-eyed man is king? The answer, of course, is no. The legal system has as great a stake in distinguishing admissible from inadmissible claims of expertise as science itself. In testing the credibility of experts, the law reaffirms its own credibility. The ways in which it does this, however, are all its own, conditioned by the legal system's peculiar needs, constraints and purposes. Consequently the law's techniques for evaluating scientific evidence do not map neatly onto science's modes of testing knowledge claims. Contrary to conventional wisdom, these discrepancies do not make the law anti- or un-scientific; they merely accentuate the necessary distance between legal and scientific fact finding.

Formal screening of experts has long been a component of legal proceedings. The American federal system determined admissibility for 70 years in accordance with an otherwise obscure 1923 appeals court decision, *Frye* v. *United States*,[10] which decreed that the science underlying expert testimony had to be 'sufficiently established to have gained general acceptance in the particular field in which it belongs'. The *Frye* rule proved difficult to administer consistently, and over time different interpretations of 'general acceptance' took hold in different jurisdictions around the country. Despite this lack of uniformity, the basis for screening experts did not attract much attention outside the legal community until the 1993 Supreme Court decision in *Daubert* v. *Merrell Dow Pharmaceuticals, Inc.*,[11] which many hailed as the case that would liberate federal courts from an onslaught of 'junk science'. *Daubert* overruled *Frye*, holding that it had been superseded by the legislatively enacted Federal Rules of Evidence. Federal courts, the Supreme Court declared, should henceforth subject offers of expert testimony to two basic tests: that of 'fit', or relevance, and that of scientific reliability. To assist the lower courts in applying the latter test, the court proposed four criteria: (a) did the evidence rest on a tested and falsifiable theory or technique; (b) had the underlying science been peer reviewed; (c) what was the technique's error rate, if known; and (d) recapitulating *Frye*, was it generally accepted?

In the glare of publicity surrounding *Daubert* and the efforts to apply it, the moves that legal actors make in constructing experts and expertise have become much more transparent than they were in the shadowy *Frye* regime. Federal judges appear substantially less inclined in the post-*Daubert* era simply to defer to the parties' experts. Rather courts have sought actively to test the relevance and reliability of expert testimony, through proceedings in which expertise is dynamically constructed and deconstructed. Some of the tests applied in screening experts are explicit and rule-like, as *Daubert* contemplated, and have become the subject of vigorous debate and commentary. Others are tacit, invisible, contingent and so unreflectively applied that they elude systematic inquiry. At the same time, the screening process has become palpably more interactive. Judges do not unproblematically apply the legally sanctioned demarcation criteria to a well-defined set of factual possibilities. Instead they (and, where applicable, their appointed experts) respond to specific, situated and strategic moves made by the litigants to establish some expert claims and deconstruct others. By piecing together these cross-cutting manoeuvres, we gain insight not only into what counts as expertise in American law but also into the merits of competing approaches to demarcating expertise.

The game of expertise

The making of expertise within the legal process can usefully be conceptualized as a kind of game in which experts and their claims struggle for credibility in the eyes of the fact finder. As in any game, some of the moves have to be made in accordance with prescribed rules; others are left to the players' wit and imagination. Figure 11.1 lays out the central parameters of the expertise game on an imaginary board divided into four quadrants by a horizontal and a vertical axis. The horizontal axis – labelled *experience* – accommodates moves designed to professionalize the knowledge claimed by expert witnesses. It is not enough for experts simply to embody personal trustworthiness, although this of course is a *sine qua non* of witnessing more generally. In order to claim the special prerogatives that the law accords them, experts have to embody in their own persons the collective judgments of a discipline, occupation or profession. Their success depends on establishing a double claim on the fact finder's trust: not only as individuals, but also as representatives of certified specialist communities. Correspondingly their credibility can be undermined by attacking either their personal or their professional integrity.

The vertical axis – labelled *objectivity* – designates efforts to move expert evidence from the pole of untested or subjective observation (for example, eyewitness testimony) towards that of scientific fact. Expert testimony gains special force when it is seen as conforming to scientific standards. The expert's personal biases and faults then diminish in significance, although (as will be clear in later

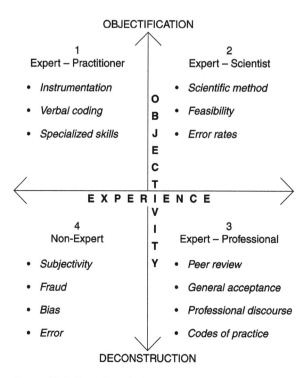

Figure 11.1 Game board of expertise.

examples) the personal dimension never completely disappears. An expert who represents science speaks for a reality presumed to be beyond mere individual experience. The more scientific the claim, the less open it is to personalized attack. Its objectivity is underwritten by science's cultural authority. Following *Daubert*, however, judicial scrutiny can less readily be avoided simply by asserting that testimony is based on reliable science. The labels 'scientist' and 'scientific' have become resources to be strategically deployed, defended and fought for vis-à-vis the judge as well as the opposing party. The vertical axis in Figure 11.1 delineates the moves by which witnesses' claims can either be made to look more like science or else methodologically deconstructed and rendered inadmissible as scientific testimony.

Together, the two axes define the basic strategic spaces in which expertise can be asserted or challenged. Proceeding clockwise from the top left, the first three quadrants all represent spaces in which expertise can be plausibly claimed, but on varying grounds: in quadrant 1, the goal is to enhance the objectivity of lay experience by stressing its skilled, disciplined or knowledgeable character; in quadrant 2, moves are designed to tie expertise explicitly to scientific methods and the objectivity of science; in quadrant 3, expert claims are linked to the judgment and experience of professional communities, but not necessarily to science. In quadrant 4, by contrast, the permitted moves are largely deconstructive: to deprive experts of the resources of specialized 'knowledge, skill, experience, training or education'. The would-be expert is reduced here to the status of a lay witness of no special skill and questionable personal integrity. To succeed in the expertise game, players must press their claims as far as possible in the direction of scientific objectivity and accredited professional experience. In challenging expert claims, the goal is just the opposite: to move claims into quadrant 4, that is, back towards the poles of subjective knowledge and individual experience. Only when pressed into this space can expert claims be said to meet neither the relatively stringent tests of scientific reliability nor the broader measures of professional expertise.

Interpreted within the model of the expertise game, *Daubert* acquires a more complex meaning than it has been accorded by most commentators. It is not, as is sometimes asserted, simply an injunction to judges to 'think like scientists'. Rather, *Daubert* outlines a programmatic view of the possible means by which allegedly expert claims can be moved along one or the other major axis of knowledge certification. The criteria proposed by the Supreme Court are consistent in this respect with the eclectic approach to expertise taken by the Federal Rules of Evidence. *Daubert* implicitly recognizes that expert knowledge, for legal purposes, is not coextensive with scientific knowledge. Of the four *Daubert* criteria, only two (testability and error rates) refer specifically to moves along the *objectivity* axis, by which experts lay claim to scientific reliability; the other two criteria (peer review and general acceptance) refer to moves along the axis of *experience*, from personal to professional, but not necessarily scientific, knowledge.

Daubert did not aim to provide comprehensive rules for establishing expertise and it should not be construed as having done so. The model of the expertise game helps identify some of the gaps in the criteria. 'Falsifiability', for instance, is derived from the philosopher Karl Popper's model of experimental science and has little relevance for other forms of scientific activity. Furthermore none of the criteria explicitly takes account of the role of material resources – such as instruments, reagents, test animals, photographs, software or computerized databases – in producing 'objective' scientific knowledge, even though their pervasiveness in scientific practice is now widely acknowledged.[12] Similarly no mention is made of professional codes or formal research protocols that can be used to underwrite claims of professional knowledge. The criteria, finally, assume a degree of autonomy on the part of judges that does not square with the interactive and locationally dispersed character of the expertise game. The opinion shows neither a reflexive awareness of the judicial role in constructing different meanings of admissibility nor a sensitivity to the ways in which legal discourse might be incorporated into the production of supposedly objective scientific statements. We will return to these points below in connection with the moves made by litigating parties in the SGBI cases.

Playing by the rules

The layout of Figure 11.1 allows cases involving expert claims to be sorted into four 'bins', defined on the one hand by the source of the claimed experiential authority (personal or professional) and on the other by the choice to defend or contest claims of facticity (objectification or deconstruction). In each bin or quadrant, a finer characterization can be produced by describing the specific pathways followed in building up or tearing down the claims of expertise. Was the expert's experience shown to conform to impartial professional standards or was it challenged as idiosyncratic, wrong or biased? Was expert knowledge validated by the test of falsifiability or by that of general acceptance? The metaphor of sorting into bins scarcely does justice to the intricate dynamics of actual cases, which involve simultaneous, competing moves by several actors. In the game of expertise, the contest rarely takes place along preordained positions and stationary battle lines. Winning strategies more often require flexible accommodation to choices made by other players claiming superior scientific or professional authority.

The broad category of toxic tort cases, for instance, can be seen in the light of this analysis as composed of contests between plaintiffs' experts wishing to position themselves in quadrant 2 (upper right), or failing that in quadrant 1, and defendants seeking to press their opponents into quadrant 4 (lower left). An instructive example is *Christopherson* v. *Allied Signal Corp.*,[13] in which a suit was brought on behalf of a deceased worker at a battery manufacturing plant in Waco, Texas. The plaintiffs claimed that Christopherson had contracted a rare and fatal form of small-cell colon cancer as a result of exposure to nickel and cadmium fumes at his workplace. The only expert testimony provided for the plaintiff was based ultimately on an affidavit by a co-worker, whose testimony the court rejected as lacking sufficient markers of reliability: 'We find particularly telling', the court opined, the 'admission in his deposition that he did not know the chemical composition of the fumes nor the mix of chemicals in the impregnation and soak tanks'.[14] Other missing elements included quantitative data on the size of the plant and the soak area, the ventilation system and the dosage and duration of exposure; all these could presumably have been gathered through appropriate instrumentation, but not through unmediated observation. Faced with these gaps, the court concluded that the co-worker's subjective experience of his working conditions could not be packaged as expert testimony.

Skilful deployment of instruments can help clothe individual observations in the guise of credible expertise (quadrant 1), even when no professional warrant is available for particular ways of seeing. Thus, in *People* v. *Marx*,[15] a 1975 California criminal case, a court admitted evidence of bite marks on the victim's body although such testimony was not supported by an 'established science of identifying persons from bite marks'. The court applauded the prosecution experts' 'enthusiastic response to a rare opportunity to develop or extend forensic dentistry into the area of bite mark identification'.[16] Especially persuasive in the court's view was the fact that the experts 'did not rely on untested methods, unproven hypotheses, intuition or revelation. Rather, they applied scientifically and professionally established techniques – X-rays, models, microscopy, photography' to produce data that were independently 'verifiable by the court'.[17] Accordingly the court felt competent to rule that the novel uses of these techniques by prosecution experts raised no serious issues of admissibility.

Not only material instruments, but discursive strategies can be used to rerepresent personal observations as knowledge grounded in professional experience (quadrant 3). In the first Rodney King trial, for example, an 'expert' on police practice persuaded the jury to see a videotape of police violence as experienced policemen allegedly would have seen it. He accomplished this sleight of vision by verbally coding the movements of the victim's body: almost invisible changes in the position of arms, legs and buttocks were classified by these means as 'aggression', calling forth, in turn, such graduated and calculated responses as 'assessment periods', 'escalations of force', 'kicks' and 'blows'.[18] Similar verbal coding has been used with greater and lesser success to convert visual tests of car drivers' sobriety, such as 'horizontal gaze nystagmus', into techniques of expert policing.[19] Appeal to contingently constructed, yet seemingly impersonal, assessment rules can equally be made the basis for rejecting expert claims. An example that gained considerable notoriety in the United States was the idealized code of practice against which the criminalist Denis Fung was measured and found wanting under cross-examination by Barry Scheck in the O.J. Simpson trial. A lesser known but no less revealing example is the list of 'qualifications of expert witnesses in ancient Greek thought' produced by the philosopher Martha Nussbaum in connection with her testimony in the Colorado gay rights trial; by codifying the prerequisites for responsible classical scholarship, she hoped to place some interpreters (and interpretations) of Plato outside the pales of credible expertise.[20]

In quadrant 4 (lower left), we find strategies for moving claims down the objectivity axis, through deconstruction of their scientific merit, or back along the horizontal axis from professional to personal, and hence not qualifying as expertise. Since *Daubert*, for example, sceptical deconstruction of peer review appears to be gaining ground. In a federal district court case, *Valentine* v. *Pioneer Chlor Alkali*,[21] the court rejected an expert's testimony on the neuropathological effects of chlorine inhalation even though he had published an article in a peer-reviewed journal. In explaining its decision, the court produced its own demarcation criterion. Editorial peer review, the judge concluded, was not legally cognizable as 'true' peer review: 'Militating against forensic use of editorial peer review as a proxy for genuine critical examination of purported scientific evidence is the fact that the average referee spends less than two hours assessing an article submitted to a biomedical journal'.[22] When the *Daubert* case itself was reconsidered following the Supreme Court's 1993 decision, the Ninth Circuit Court of Appeals engaged in a similar construction of case-specific demarcation criteria. To strengthen the case for admissibility, it held, scientific evidence should be based where possible on 'pre-litigation research', which is 'less likely to have been biased toward a particular conclusion by the promise of remuneration'. Such a foundation would help to counter charges that the evidence in question 'is not science at all, but litigation'.[23] This ad hoc and unsupported rule was adopted with alacrity by the SGBI defendants, as we shall see below.

Personal integrity is another possible focus of attack in quadrant 4. This is where cross-examination can be deployed to great effect, by revealing personal bias, misconduct, financial interest or inconsistency on the part of individual experts. In the courtroom, the expert's personal credibility is always at stake and the claimed authority of science guarantees no protection against such probing. In *Blum* v. *Merrell Dow Pharmaceuticals, Inc.*,[24] for example, a products liability case involving the drug Bendectin, a Pennsylvania trial judge pointed to defects in the defence experts' professional integrity (evidence of bias in peer review) as well as personal integrity (corporate funding of research) as the basis for down-grading their credibility.

The testimony demonstrated that articles were inserted in 'peer review' journals, without review by independent authorities, but edited by lawyers; that 'peer review' journals published, as valid, the results of 'less than good studies'; that articles were rejected for publication by prestigious journals before being published in the 'peer review' journal, *Teratology*. The testimony exposed scientific literature created for purposes of legal defence. The testimony revealed a sycophantic relationship between 'scientists' and their funding source: the defendant, Merrell Dow.[25]

With this range of illustrations in mind, let us turn now to the construction of expertise by players in the litigation concerning breast implants.

The SGBI litigation: birth of a mass tort

Silicone gel breast implants were first introduced into the American market in the early 1960s as substitutes for earlier, less satisfactory devices, such as wax, fabric, directly injected silicone, synthetic sponges or saline-filled implants. The new product was favoured for its appearance, physical stability and apparent non-reactivity. By the 1970s, SGBIs were in wide use for cosmetic breast augmenta-tion as well as for breast reconstruction following cancer surgery. Some 20 years later, reasonable estimates for the number of women with breast implants ranged between one and two million, with more precise figures probably not ascertain-able.[26] SGBIs were marketed before the enactment of the 1976 Medical Device Amendment to the Federal Food, Drug and Cosmetic Act which required safety and efficacy testing for all implants. Information about the devices' safety was therefore largely the product of anecdotal and ad hoc post-market reporting by users, medical professionals and the media, a problem that was later to plague both plaintiffs and manufacturers. After 1976, SGBIs were subject to review by advisory panels to the Food and Drug Administration (FDA), the regulatory agency whose task it was to decide whether to demand additional testing or to leave the devices on the market. By all indications, FDA exercised its review power lackadaisically and without serious conviction throughout the 1980s.

Starting in the late 1980s, the breast implant story took surprising new turns. There were, to begin with, incontrovertible reports of rupture and leakage from the implants, accompanied by local inflammation, painful scarring, contraction and hardening of the surrounding breast tissue. Even intact implants were prone to 'bleeding', permitting small quantities of silicone to escape and be gradually disseminated through the body. For many women, the localized responses alone were severe enough to necessitate surgical removal of the implants, a procedure that some underwent more than once in the hope of finding a workable solution. More troubling were the increasing reports of so-called 'connective tissue diseases' (CTDs), a collection of auto-immune disorders afflicting the joints, skin and internal organs that included such conditions as lupus, scleroderma and rheumatoid arthritis. Complaints of this gravity could not stay hidden. In December 1990, the CBS television reporter Connie Chung produced a segment on breast implants on her show, *Face to Face with Connie Chung*. She offered 'shocking' revelations of implant-induced disease and charged the FDA with lax regulation and failure to inform women of the risks to their health. Concurrently suits by women with implants began to reach the courts in substantial numbers and with large financial consequences. In December 1991, a federal jury awarded an unprecedented $7.34 million (including $6 million in punitive damages) to a California woman who claimed that she had developed 'mixed connective tissue disease' because of her implants.[27]

Partly in response to these events, regulatory pressure on SGBIs tightened in the early 1990s. Dr David A. Kessler, then FDA Commissioner and an ardent public health activist, requested the agency's General and Plastic Surgery Devices Panel to assess the safety of breast implants. The panel's scientific review, rounded out with three days of contentious, highly charged hearings in November 1991, concluded that not enough information was available to establish the safety of the devices, but that they should remain on the market pending further study. On 6 January 1992, however, Kessler requested a voluntary moratorium on the use of SGBIs to permit the review of additional data obtained from manufacturers in the course of litigation. In its report of April 1996, the FDA advisory panel reaffirmed that the connection between silicone gel and CTDs was not yet scientifically established but recommended restrictions on access to implants while clinical trials were conducted.[28] Acting on these recommendations, the FDA immediately restricted the use of implants to reconstruction after cancer surgery; the agency also proposed strict guidelines for new clinical trials of SGBIs.[29]

The moratorium and its aftermath confirmed many implant recipients' worst suspicions about their health complaints, and the steady trickle of SGBI lawsuits around the country soon turned into a torrent. Manufacturers and plaintiffs alike were caught up in one of the most distinctive, frustrating and messy inventions of the modern American legal system: the mass toxic tort. The total number of SGBI claimants was known to exceed 440 000. Dow Corning Corporation, the market leader in implant sales, recognized that extreme measures were needed to deal with its potential liability. Settlement emerged as the most attractive option for Dow Corning as well as its major competitors. By late 1994, federal procedures for multi-district litigation were used to consolidate some 9600 claims for pretrial proceedings in the Northern District of Alabama. In September of that year, Chief Judge Samuel C. Pointer, Jr shepherded the parties into a $4.25 billion global settlement, with Dow Corning agreeing to pay some $2 billion of that amount.[30] For some months, it seemed that the controversy might actually close, but that impression proved to be illusory.

Several factors contributed to the unravelling of the first SGBI settlement in the following months. To begin with, too many plaintiffs opted not to participate in the global settlement, including most of the Texas claimants, accounting for almost one-quarter of the total number of litigants. Faced with massive uncertainty about the extent of its liability, Dow Corning filed for bankruptcy in May 1995. Science, too, began to emerge as a separate force in the SGBI story, as data became available from the first systematic studies of women with breast implants. On 16 June 1994, the *New England Journal of Medicine* (*NEJM*) published the results of the first clinical trial investigating the correlation between silicone implants and connective tissue diseases.[31] Conducted by the respected Mayo Clinic in Minnesota, this retrospective cohort study compared 749 women who had received SGBIs between 1964 and 1991 with twice that number of women in a control group and found no statistically significant increase in CTDs among the former. The Nurses' Health Study, a Harvard-based survey of some 100 000 present and former nurses, appeared to confirm the Mayo Clinic findings, as did several other studies that followed. As both litigation and scientific research inexorably continued, judges and litigants had to decide how to accommodate the emergent and allegedly independent voice of science into their legal strategies. The model of the expertise game provides a useful framework for analysing the resulting manoeuvres on all sides.

Law meets science: experts in action

Of the many different fora, both state and federal, in which SGBI lawsuits continued to make headway, two attracted special notice for their innovative approach to expert testimony. The first, *Hall* v. *Baxter Healthcare Corp.*,[32] unfolded in a federal district court in Oregon under Judge Robert E. Jones; the other was the federal multi-district litigation, MDL-926, which continued to play out in Judge Pointer's court in Birmingham, Alabama after the breakdown of the original settlement. Central to both proceedings was the attempt to construct an authoritative picture of implant-related disease, a problem that both courts addressed by appointing independent scientific panels to review and sift the available evidence. As of late 1997, the Pointer panel was still conducting its inquiry, whereas Judge Jones had made legal history in *Hall* by ruling inadmissible all of the plaintiff's evidence supporting the claim of silicone-induced CTD. For our purposes, however, it is the contrast between the two court-initiated processes and associated moves by litigants that is of greatest interest. Differences in the strategies adopted by the judges and the parties in the two courts provide compelling insights into the game-like character of legal expertise: even in the post-*Daubert* era, remarkably few moves are fixed in advance, and the scientific stories constructed in the courts bear the unavoidable stamp of judicial predilection.

In search of neutrality

In appointing independent experts to assist them, courts are institutionally concerned, first and foremost, to ensure neutrality with respect to the outcome of the lawsuit. Financial connections with the parties are an immediate disqualifier, as is – ordinarily – evidence of overly close professional or personal relations between experts and parties. Both the *Hall* and the MDL-926 proceedings took pains to screen the court-appointed experts against outright bias, but the methods chosen were far from identical. To identify suitable experts (ultimately, four in number) for the panel in *Hall*, Judge Jones appointed a single special master, Dr Richard T. Jones, who was as it happens the judge's cousin, but also a highly regarded emeritus professor of biological sciences at Oregon Health Sciences University.[33] Judge Pointer's approach was considerably more measured and elaborate. He took over from a group of judges in New York the idea of appointing a *panel* of special masters to designate the MDL-926 expert panel. Six distinguished academic scientists and law professors, each carefully screened for possible hidden financial interests in the case, eventually advised Judge Pointer on the selection of his four expert panellists.

To what extent did these processes actually guard against bias? One notes immediately that *cognitive* bias or interest apparently received less attention from both judges than possible pecuniary interests. The plaintiffs in *Hall*, for example, argued that Judge Jones himself was a source of bias potentially overriding any efforts to secure the neutrality of his expert advisers. The judge's wife had been satisfactorily fitted with implants following cancer surgery in the late 1970s, a fact that Judge Jones acknowledged but did not see as sufficient to warrant recusing himself:

> That doesn't mean that I will admit all evidence as proffered or exclude all evidence as proffered. I will just look at whatever the state of the art is. And that keeps moving all the time, as we all know. But I did want to make that disclosure. And if that creates any problems for anybody, why that's up to you. But I am not going to recuse myself on these cases because of that.[34]

This public confession evidently secured the judge's personal credibility, although his subsequent decision to exclude all of the plaintiffs' evidence was widely seen as unorthodox, unprecedented and a likely overstepping of the admittedly fuzzy line between permissible judicial screening and impermissible judicial fact finding.

A more interesting issue of potential cognitive bias arises in connection with the divergent mapping of the relevant scientific fields by the two expert panels. The *Hall* panel included an epidemiologist, a rheumatologist, an immunologist-toxicologist and eventually a polymer chemist;[35] the MDL-926 panel also covered the areas of epidemiology, rheumatology, immunology and toxicology, but not polymer chemistry.[36] Such differences in scientific coverage are not exactly unprecedented in the annals of evidentiary proceedings. Under the *Frye* rule, courts had frequently disagreed in identifying the 'particular fields' in which novel scientific evidence belonged. Could the reliability of polygraphy, for example, be adequately certified by skilled polygraphers or was additional testimony required from one or more scientific fields, such as neurology, psychiatry and physiology?[37] No clear consensus ever emerged, and excessive scope for judicial boundary drawing came to be recognized as a weakness of *Frye*.

Proceedings designed to establish definitive causal stories under *Daubert* give rise to similar dilemmas. The choice of experts and the fields they represent cannot be dismissed as merely incidental: it goes to the heart of what the fact finder views as contested or as taken for granted. The absence of a chemist on the MDL-926 panel signalled, in effect, that questions about the chemical properties of silicone gel did not merit 'neutral' review. Yet a substantial part of the plaintiffs' argument in *Hall* and other SGBI cases has centred on silicone chemistry, with analogies drawn between silicone gel and silica, a substance known to be associated with auto-immune diseases in exposed workers.[38] Were the two courts, we may ask, seeking to adjudicate the 'same' case through their differently constituted expert panels?

Framing choices: an 'atypical' disease?

That question resonates all the more forcefully when one considers the framing of the plaintiffs' health claims in the two proceedings. Frustrated by epidemiological studies that found no significant increase in CTDs among implant users, plaintiffs' groups began to claim by the early 1990s that science was pursuing the wrong questions and therefore coming up with irrelevant answers. SGBIs, they contended, were not in the main associated with 'classic' CTDs, such as lupus and sclero-derma, but with a more insidious and ill-defined set of 'atypical connective tissue disorders' (ACTDs). Included in this group were ailments that might reflect disorders of the immune system – chronic fatigue, headaches, hair loss, night sweats, swelling, joint pains – but that also occur with some frequency among women in ordinary life. Furthermore the cluster of conditions labelled ACTDs presents serious difficulties for 'objective' medical diagnosis, since the primary evidence of these symptoms' occurrence tends to be the reporting of them by victims. The imprecision of the conditions, together with their high background or 'normal' incidence, make ACTDs a particularly elusive target for epidemiological study.

Not surprisingly, important players in the SGBI cases have sought in various ways to establish – or disestablish – the claims of expert knowledge concerning ACTDs. Marcia Angell, the executive editor of *NEJM* and a vocal advocate of legal adherence to scientific standards, dismissed complaints of 'atypical' disease on the ground that they are impossible to pin down for purposes of scientific study:

> The problem of vague or shifting definitions of disease continues to plague the study of breast implants. When a study fails to find an increased risk of certain diseases or symptoms in women with implants, adherents of the theory that implants cause disease are quick to suggest that the diseases in question are different. It is impossible to study whether something causes illness, however, unless the illness is clearly described. Otherwise, it cannot be consistently diagnosed and its relation to breast implants cannot be

examined. This sort of situation is what Karl Popper, the philosopher of science, had in mind when he said that a scientific hypothesis had to be 'falsifiable' to be meaningful.[39]

In terms of the expertise game, Angell's strategy is to deconstruct ACTD claims as both unscientific (not 'falsifiable') and subjective (not backed up by professionally accredited observation). 'Scientific', in her lexicon, is virtually synonymous with 'epidemiological', a position she articulated even more forcefully in an *amicus* brief, submitted jointly with *NEJM*, to the US Supreme Court in an unrelated case, *General Electric Co.* v. *Joiner*. The brief argued that general causation in toxic tort cases is a 'necessary proxy' for specific causation and can only be established through 'observational epidemiological research'.[40] This move sought to accomplish three important goals at once: to elevate the scientific and professional standing of epidemiology; to render irrelevant the evidence on specific causation, including the less institutionalized, 'new' research on biological markers and bioplausibility favoured by plaintiffs;[41] and to move into quadrant 4 of Figure 11.1 the results of self-reporting studies, such as a study of over 400 000 women health professionals (Women's Health Study) which did find evidence of increased risk of CTDs and which, not surprisingly, has been extensively cited by plaintiffs' experts.[42]

Angell's moves to deconstruct ACTDs and elevate the status 'observational epidemiology' make perfect sense when seen against the backdrop of wider struggles for authority in scientific medicine. The epidemiology that Angell defends, and for which *NEJM* serves as an authoritative mouthpiece, falls distinctly on the 'fastidious' side of the 'pragmatic-fastidious' boundary that the sociologist of science Stephen Epstein identified in his study of the politics of AIDS research.[43] 'Fastidious' science, as Epstein describes it, seeks clean study designs, with low ambiguity, in the hope of producing equally clean results; 'pragmatic' research, by contrast, is more willing to accommodate life's 'messy' realities in study designs, with consequently less clearly interpretable results. As Epstein notes, moreover, these stylistic preferences are not random within medicine but reflect deeper cleavages about the authority and status of 'pure' academic research as opposed to 'messy' clinical practice. The problem for claimants in toxic tort cases is that fastidious approaches are unlikely to detect many of the symptoms they complain of: increased incidence in diseases of ordinary life or diffuse syndromes, often lacking 'objective' markers, and attributable to the synergistic interaction of multiple, poorly understood risk factors. Starkly put, the very atypicality of the SGBI plaintiffs' condition removes it from the investigative purview of 'normal' epidemiological science.

None of the participants in *Hall* explicitly challenged the concept of a single, universally applicable, gold standard for epidemiological research, although such an argument might well have benefited the plaintiffs. Instead the parties confronted the expert panel and the court with diametrically opposed visions of the nature, causes and scientific indicators of ACTDs. The defence argued, on the one hand, that claims concerning ACTDs were (as Angell also insisted) untested and untestable; on the other hand, they cited acknowledged authorities such as FDA's Kessler to support the position that there was no solid scientific evidence tying ACTDs to breast implants. The plaintiffs, by contrast, claimed that epidemiology was too blunt an instrument to establish a definitive relationship between silicone and ACTDs. They therefore presented collateral expertise with respect to biomarkers and other indicators of bioplausibility to shore up their causal argument (see below).

Judge Jones in the end affirmed the defendants' contention that ACTD was 'at best an untested hypothesis', overlooking in the process the more shaded assessment offered by his own epidemiology expert, Dr Merwyn Greenlick.[44] Judge Pointer, cutting a different path, instructed the MDL-926 expert panel to consider the relationship between breast implants and both classic and atypical manifestations of connective tissue disease or immune system disorders; his order listed some 40 separate conditions whose possible link to silicone exposure the panel was asked to review.

Standards of admissibility

Players in the SGBI expertise game have diverged not only with respect to their framing of the central issues in the case but also in their representations of the standards governing admissibility. While ostensibly conforming to *Daubert*'s ruling precepts, plaintiffs and defendants in *Hall* offered the expert panel radically different readings of what the case means and how it bears on particular types of evidence. Generally the defendants sought to hold the plaintiffs' experts to the relatively restrictive moves along the *objectivity* axis, whereas the plaintiffs embraced the more enabling moves along the *experience* axis also sanctioned by *Daubert*.

The contrasts between the two strategies emerged clearly in the summation videotapes prepared by the two sides as part of their closing argument. The defendants' presentation was shot through with references to both *Daubert* opinions, whose criteria were invoked, separately and together, as definitive tests of scientific reliability. Mary Wells, the chemistry expert, opened her argument with a brief 'sag demonstration' to make visible the issue of 'fit'. Allowing the gel to sag out of an upturned jar, Wells contended that none of the plaintiffs' evidence about silica was relevant because it did not concern the kind of substance actually used in implants. She quickly went on to list the *Daubert* criteria, including the 'prelitigation research' criterion announced by the Ninth Circuit in *Daubert II*. The plaintiffs' evidence on silicone chemistry, Wells argued, failed to meet any of the criteria and hence was inadmissible. The fact that witnesses for the plaintiffs, specifically Chris Batich and Leonico Garrido, possessed apparently solid professional credentials was simply irrelevant: "The plaintiffs have not met their burden of proof to establish that the testimony of Dr. Batich or Dr. Garrido is scientific knowledge as required by *Daubert*. The fact that a scientist wants to speak does not mean that the words he speaks are supported by science.'[45] Similarly Jane Thorpe, the epidemiology expert, adopted language from *Daubert II* in asserting,

'Plaintiffs have failed to show in some objectively verifiable way that the experts have chosen a reliable scientific method and followed it faithfully. . . . Atypical disease is a label for non-disease.'[46]

In his closing argument, Michael L. Williams, the chief trial attorney for the plaintiffs, tried for his part to avoid, through careful boundary work, the potentially trumping effect of the negative epidemiological studies relied on by defendants. He began by stressing the absence of research on the condition specifically complained of by the plaintiffs, that is, *atypical* CTDs. A review article by Kessler and other FDA scientists provided grist for his mill, especially the conclusion that 'research is also needed to further address the potential for a long-term association between silicone implants and rare or atypical connective tissue disease syndromes'.[47] Setting aside most of the available epidemiologic findings as irrelevant (because focused only on 'classic' CTDs), statistically weak or flawed, Williams created space for a wider range of expert testimony, including biomarker studies and studies of occupational exposure to silica. The existing epidemiology on ACTDs, his argument ran, provided enough indication of risk to take the plaintiffs' case across the threshold of admissibility, but it was not dispositive on its own. Under these circumstances, any reasonable medical scientist would look to additional sources of information – animal studies, biomarker studies, occupational studies, clinical experience – and this was precisely what he asked the court to do.

Significantly Williams neither mentioned *Daubert* by name nor invoked the criteria. This strategy comported well with the plaintiffs' overarching goal of getting as many as possible experts, and their fields, accepted as both relevant and reliable. Williams wanted the court to take a holistic view of a large body of evidence, none of it compelling on its own, but all of it together conveying a telltale impression of smoke, with smouldering fires behind. Relying implicitly on *Daubert's* injunction that admissibility decisions should be made on the basis of an expert's methodology, not the expert's conclusions, Williams showed from the record that panel members had found the plaintiffs' experts to be reputable scientists using ordinary methods.[48] Another argument used to justify the introduction of non-epidemiological evidence bordered on the equitable notion of estoppel. Williams asserted that pharmaceutical companies had not seen fit before 1991 to conduct clinical trials of silicone implants. They had based their claims about the safety of SGBIs on the very kinds of indirect evidence that they now sought to exclude from the courts. This was not fair. What had historically been the industry standard should now be the standard applied to the plaintiffs' evidence as well.

Williams hereby sought to make the industry's moral integrity and past behaviour part and parcel of the scientific admissibility determination. In less subtle ways, this was the same strategy that SGBI activist groups were following in fora other than the courts. A particularly splashy campaign was waged by the Command Trust Network (CTN), an information clearing house co-founded by former cancer patient Sybil N. Goldrich. CTN placed its advertisements in such highly visible locations as the Op-Ed page of the *New York Times*. All of them carried in bold letters the message, 'Dow Corning Knew', followed by varying graphic charges, such as 'silicone breast implants rupture', 'silicone breast implants leak' and 'silicone compounds kill roaches'. The moral message was not lost on juries. On 18 August 1997, for example, a Louisiana jury found that Dow Corning had failed to test silicone properly for use in the human body and had misled a group of 1800 women about the health risks posed by the substance;[49] however, the dissolution of the Louisiana class action in December 1997 left the ultimate impact of this decision unclear.

Form and function

It should be noted, finally, that the moves in the expertise game are shaped in substantial part by the processes used to elicit expert advice and testimony. A deposition, a pretrial hearing, a panel review or an actual trial each offers distinctive opportunities and constraints for the presentation of evidence. Differences in process between the expert panels in *Hall* and MDL-926, in particular, were significant enough to have a detectable impact on each one's assessment of the available evidence. As noted earlier, the four *Hall* panellists were selected by a single technical assistant to Oregon's Judge Jones. More importantly, they were not court-appointed experts in the sense contemplated by Rule 706 of the Federal Rules of Evidence; instead Judge Jones elected to insulate them from testifying at trial and from possible cross-examination by designating them as technical advisers to the court. Once appointed, the panel operated like a kind of science court, asking questions of the parties' witnesses and watching videotaped summations of the evidence. Only after they had written their reports to the court were the advisers questioned by counsel for the parties. All of the resulting records informed Judge Jones's decision to exclude the plaintiffs' expert evidence.

Larger in scope and possible impact, the MDL-926 process resembled in some respects more a regulatory proceeding than a science court. Judge Pointer, as we have seen, screened the prospective panel members with a sharper sense of public accountability than his counterpart in Oregon. The expert panel was formally appointed pursuant to Rule 706; its members therefore may be called upon to testify at trial, supplementing the testimony of the party experts. There was from the beginning a strong sense that, if the MDL-926 process 'worked', it could serve as a model for other mass tort cases. Consequently a more self-reflective attitude prevailed than in the Oregon court; for instance, Judge Pointer collaborated with research staff at the Federal Judicial Center with an eye to creating an adequate documentary record of the proceedings. The multi-district expert panel met the parties' experts in July 1997 in a three-day hearing in Birmingham, Alabama. Borrowing directly from the regulatory model, the panel also held a shorter hearing with unaffiliated scientists in Washington, DC in November 1997. In keeping with its potential policy-steering role, the panel was asked to comment not only on the possible causal connection between SGBIs and auto-immune disease, but also on whether opinions contrary to its conclusions could be viewed as 'legitimate and responsible disagreement' within the profession.[50]

While it is still too early to evaluate the full impact of these procedural choices, it is safe to conclude that they did influence the parties' strategic options. Judge Pointer evidently took pains to emulate the non-adversarial format of many regulatory hearings.[51] His objective, presumably, was to promote a dispassionate but thorough airing of conflicting viewpoints, with as little lawyerly grandstanding as possible. The summation videos in *Hall*, by contrast, encouraged partisan representations and were designed, particularly on the defendants' side, to take advantage of the visual medium. Williams, presenting the plaintiffs' case, maintained a low-key, almost professorial demeanour, but (as described above) he used the opportunity to impugn the integrity of the industry position. The defence engaged in more obvious stage management, from the choice of tough-talking, severely attired women to make the case for implant manufacturers, to a television clip of Commissioner Kessler denying, in a February 1996 interview on *Frontline*, that there was any evidence supporting the association between silicone and typical or atypical connective tissue diseases. The defendants' epidemiology presentation closed dramatically, with a damaging quotation from one of the plaintiffs' own experts, Dr Goldsmith, whose disembodied words commanded, for several seconds, both the viewer's attention and the video screen: 'At the moment, I must suggest to you that the evidence looks to me as if it's just that, that it's a possibility, and I would have to characterize it as less than 50 per cent. That would be where I am at the moment.'[52]

Conclusion

The SGBI example highlights a very general conclusion about the nature of expertise in the American legal system: what counts as legitimate expertise for purposes of the law is not determined by means of unambiguous rules applied impartially and without variance by solomonic judges. Expertise, rather, is the product of a dynamic process that actively engages a multiplicity of legal actors in constructing, validating and certifying particular knowledge claims as more authoritative than others. On the game board of expertise, players can marshall a complex array of resources – material, discursive, social and moral – in support of their moves to highlight some viewpoints as more knowledgeable than others. Credibility can be gained, most commonly, through moves that seek to professionalize and objectify the assertions of expert witnesses. Correspondingly doubt can be sown and trust undermined through moves that emphasize possible subjectivity and bias in the expert's position. The spaces in which the expertise game is played extend, moreover, well beyond the confines of particular lawsuits, into the more public worlds of television, books, newspapers, public lectures, the Internet, regulatory politics and even unrelated litigation.

Through a comparison of two expert advisory proceedings, in *Hall* v. *Baxter* and the federal multi-district litigation, we have seen further that *Daubert*, far from bringing uniformity to evidence law, has opened up wide new avenues for the exercise of judicial discretion. The gatekeeping power that judges enjoy in the post-*Daubert* era allows them considerable latitude to shape the moves made by other players in the expertise game and to decide, finally, whose moves to countenance as credible or authoritative. Subjective judicial preferences govern in important ways the process of selecting experts, the framing of relevant evidentiary issues, the choice of applicable scientific standards and the procedural framework for soliciting expert evidence. While the parties and their experts also retain independent agency, their moves are controlled to varying degrees by the presiding judge's prior commitments concerning science and expertise. As a result, courts are no more likely to achieve impartiality in interpreting *Daubert* than they were in construing its forerunner, *Frye*. Indeed the SGBI case suggests that, instead of imbuing judges with a deeper appreciation of what makes science 'scientific', *Daubert* has merely provided a powerful new set of rhetorical resources for masking the unexamined assumptions of courts, litigants and even experts.

If expertise is contingently and strategically constructed within the confines of specific legal disputes and, worse yet, if it incorporates the biases and prejudices of presiding judges, where does this leave the legal system's search for reliable expert knowledge? Are all demarcation efforts doomed to failure, with *Daubert* representing only the latest misguided initiative to separate, once for all, scientific fact from fraud and fantasy? The model of the expertise game seems at first to offer only discouraging answers, for it stresses the malleability of expertise, the role of agency and artifice in representing expert knowledge and the inevitable tie-ins between cognitive and normative realities. There is, however, a more optimistic way to read *Daubert* in the light of the proposed model: not as a hopelessly idealized, and unworkable, formula for truth finding, but as an invitation to reflect on and make transparent the foundations of expert credibility. A lawsuit involving scientific evidence becomes, under this reading, an occasion for the 'fact finder' to choose between alternative frameworks of justification. To the extent that a relativizing model for looking at expertise lays bare the moves underlying expert claims and positions, it can only facilitate the task of comparison.

Justice, it is said, should not only be done but be seen to be done in liberal societies. Courts are important fora for the ritual and public affirmation of a polity's commitment to truth and moral order. Increasingly, as well, courts are being enrolled as agents of civic education in societies in which ordinary citizens live most of their lives comfortably detached from the complex machinery of scientific and technological production.[53] *Daubert* bestowed on judges the power to make some of this backstage apparatus more visible in the wake of technological failures, by requiring litigants to display to others the foundations of their supposed expert knowledge. Unavoidably, however, as the SGBI cases illustrate, judges themselves both set the scene and act upon the stages prepared for the litigants' expert contests. For courts to lose sight of their own role in the expertise game – to be seduced into mistaking the play for objective reality – remains the greatest threat to justice.

Notes

* In Michael Freeman and Helen Reece, eds., *Science in Court* (London: Dartmouth, 1998), pp. 83–107.

1 Michael Clark and Catherine Crawford (eds), *Legal Medicine in History* (Cambridge, 1994).

2 Andre A. Moenssens, James E. Starrs, Carol E. Henderson, and Fred E. Inbau, *Scientific Evidence in Civil and Criminal Cases* (4th edn, Westbury, NY, 1995).

3 *McLean* v. *Arkansas Board of Education* 529 F. Supp. 1255 (1982).

4 Martha C. Nussbaum, 'Platonic Love and Colorado Law: The Relevance of Ancient Greek Norms to Modern Sexual Controversies' (1994) 80 *Virginia Law Review* 1515–1651; Robert P. George, ' "Shameless Acts" Revisited' 9 *Academic Questions*, (1995–6), 24–42.

5 See, in particular, Peter Huber, *Galileo's Revenge: Junk Science in the Courtroom* (New York, 1991); Kenneth Foster and Peter Huber, *Judging Science: Scientific Knowledge and the Federal Courts* (Cambridge, Mass., 1997).

6 Sheila Jasanoff, *Science at the Bar: Law, Science and Technology in America* (Cambridge, Mass., 1995).

7 For a compelling account of this process in the context of toxic torts litigation, see Jonathan Harr, *A Civil Action* (New York, 1995).

8 In 1977, a Texas jury awarded $170 000 to a plaintiff claiming injury from breast implants in what may have been the first such successful lawsuit in the country. See Joseph Nocera, 'Fatal Litigation' (1995) *Fortune*, 16 October, 13–15.

9 Thomas F. Gieryn, 'Boundaries of Science', in Sheila Jasanoff, Gerald E. Markle, James C. Petersen and Trevor Pinch (eds), *The Handbook of Science and Technology Studies* (Thousand Oaks, Cal., 1995), pp.393–456.

10 293 F. 1013 (D.C.Cir. 1923).

11 509 U.S. 579 (1993).

12 See, for example, Bruno Latour and Steve Woolgar, *Laboratory Life: The Construction of Scientific Facts* (Princeton, 1986).

13 939 F.2d 1106 (5th Cir. 1991).

14 Ibid., at 1113.

15 54 Cal.App.3d 100 (1975).

16 Ibid., at 107.

17 Ibid., at 111.

18 Charles Goodwin, 'Professional Vision' (1994) 96 *American Anthropology* 606–33.

19 See Jasanoff, *Science at the Bar*, pp.60–61.

20 Nussbaum, 'Platonic Love', 1607–22.

21 921 F.Supp. 666 (D.Nevada 1996).

22 Ibid., at 675.

23 43 F.3d 1311 (9th Cir. 1995), at 1317–18.

24 No. 1982 (Court of Common Pleas of Philadelphia County, Civil Trial Division), 1996.

25 *Blum*, at 70 (Appendix B).

26 Marcia Angell, *Science on Trial: The Clash of Medical Evidence and the Law in the Breast Implant Case* (New York, 1996). See also California Legislature, Senate Committee on Health and Human Services, *Hearing on the Safety of Silicone Breast Implants*, Sacramento, Cal., 5 February 1992.

27 *Hopkins* v. *Dow Corning Corp.* Case C88–4703–TEH (ND Cal. 1992). See also Angell, *Science on Trial*, p.55.

28 Council on Scientific Affairs, American Medical Association, 'Silicone Gel Breast Implants' (1993) 270 *JAMA*, 2602–6.

29 David A. Kessler, 'The Basis of the FDA's Decision on Breast Implants' (1992) 326 *New England Journal of Medicine*, 1713–18.

30   Joseph Sanders and D.H. Kaye, 'Expert Advice on Silicone Implants: *Hall* v. *Baxter Healthcare Corp.*' (1997) 37 *Jurimetrics Journal* 113–28.

31   S. Gabriel et al., 'Risk of Connective Tissue Diseases and Other Disorders after Breast Implantation' (1994) 330 *New England Journal of Medicine*, 1697–1702.

32   947 F.Supp. 1387 (D.Or. 1996).

33   See Sanders and Kaye, 'Expert Advice'.

34   *Andrews, et al.* v. *Bristol-Myers, et al.* U.S. District Court Case No. 94–258–JO, Status Conference Hearing Transcript, 4 April 1996, pp.41–2.

35   Sanders and Kaye, 'Expert Advice', The experts were Dr Merwyn R. Greenlick of Oregon Health Sciences University (epidemiology), Dr Robert F. Willkens of the University of Washington (rheumatology), Dr Ron McClard of Reed College (chemistry) and Dr Mary Stenzel-Poore of Oregon Health Sciences University (immunology).

36   The MDL-926 experts were Betty Diamond, an immunologist, Barbara Hulka, an epidemiologist, Peter Tugwell, a rheumatologist and epidemiologist, and Nancy Kerklivet, a toxicologist: 'Scientific Justice', *The Economist*, 26 July 1997, p.69.

37   For further discussion of this example, see Sheila Jasanoff, 'Judicial Construction of New Scientific Evidence', in Paul T. Durbin (ed), *Critical Perspectives on Nonacademic Science and Engineering* (Bethlehem, P.A. (ed.)), pp.220–24.

38   For a description of the chemical profile of SGBIs, see AMA Council on Scientific Affairs, 'Silicone Gel Breast Implants', p.2603; see also Angell, *Science on Trial*, p.106. On the theories of Nir Kossovsky concerning the molecular properties of silicone, see Gary Taubes, 'Silicone in the System' (December 1995) *Discover*, 65–75.

39   Angell, *Science on Trial*, p.104.

40   Brief of *Amici Curiae*, in the *New England Journal of Medicine*, and Marcia Angell, M.D., in Support of Neither Petitioners Nor Respondents, *General Electric Co.* v. *Joiner* No. 96–188, US Supreme Court, October 1996.

41   See, for example, Taubes, 'Silicone in the System'.

42   Charles H. Hennekens et al., 'Self-reported Breast Implants and Connective Tissue Diseases in Female Health Professionals: A Retrospective Cohort Study' (1996) 275 *JAMA* 616.

43   Stephen Epstein, *Impure Science: AIDS, Activism and the Politics of Knowledge* (Berkeley, 1996), pp.255–6.

44   See Sanders and Kaye, 'Expert Advice', 120.

45   *In re Silicone Gel Breast Implant Litigation*, Defendants Response Videotape, August 1996.

46   Ibid. Compare text of *Daubert II*, 43 F.3d at 1319.

47   Barbara G. Silverman et al., 'Reported Complications of Silicone Gel Breast Implants: An Epidemiologic Review' (1996) 124 *Annals of Internal Medicine* 755.

48   Williams has made this point even more forcefully in unpublished writing since the decision in *Hall*: 'Two facts shock everyone not familiar with the record. First, plaintiffs' experts had world-class qualifications; they included the heads of the Departments of Rheumatology and Immunology at Oregon Health Sciences University and U.C. Davis Medical School, and dozens of other Ph.D.'s and board-certified M.D.'s. ... These highly respected medical school department heads are *not* junk scientists' (personal communication from Michael L. Williams, 13 August 1997).

49   *Spitzfaden* v. *Dow Corning Corp.* 92–2589 (Orleans Parish Civil District Court).

50   Sanders and Kaye, 'Expert Advice', 125.

51   'Scientific Justice', p.69. Public hearings of this type permit a wide range of opinion to be expressed without premature polarization or hardening of views. For further discussion of these points, see Sheila Jasanoff, *The Fifth Branch: Science Advisers as Policymakers* (Cambridge, Mass., 1990).

52   Testimony of Dr David Goldsmith, quoted on Defendants' Video Summation, August 1996.

53   Jasanoff, *Science at the Bar*, pp.215–17.

12 The eye of everyman
Witnessing DNA in the Simpson trial[*]

The trials of OJ Simpson began and ended in a trail of blood. From 24 January to 2 October 1995,[1] the former star athlete and media personality was tried for the double murder of his wife, Nicole Brown Simpson and her friend Ronald Goldman. Just a year after his sensational acquittal, in October 1995, he became the defendant in a civil suit initiated by the victims' relatives. On 4 February 1997, in an equally stunning reversal, he was found liable for having caused the deaths of Goldman and Nicole Simpson. Goldman's family was awarded $8.5 million in compensatory damages; days later, Simpson was assessed an additional $25 million in punitive damages. Blood evidence, presented both verbally and visually, played a crucial rôle in both trials, but it was received with greater scepticism by the jury in the criminal trial. Put differently, the prosecution failed in the criminal proceedings to 'black-box' the DNA evidence in such a way as to eliminate its interpretive flexibility; accordingly, the jury was able to dismiss as insufficient the 'DNA fingerprints' that allegedly linked Simpson to the crime scene. Science's 'immutable mobiles' did not in this case succeed in persuading an audience of non-scientists.[2] In exploring why, I shall argue that, for scientific evidence to carry weight in the courtroom, not only the inscriptions shown to the jury, but the eye that frames them, must be certified as authoritative. The judge's rôle in creating and sustaining such privileged visual positions is the central topic of this paper.

The prosecution's opening argument in the criminal trial explained how the victims' blood was carried from the site of the murders to Simpson's Brentwood estate, first on bloody footprints, then on the door and floor of the white Bronco, then on bloodstained gloves and socks, drop by drop right into the accused's own bedroom. Supported by masses of physical evidence, and given both readable form and personal identity through DNA analysis,[3] the blood seemed almost to acquire a life of its own, with the power to speak for the two victims whose voices had been so cruelly silenced. Yet, shockingly to many observers, the jury acquitted Simpson at the end of a nine-month trial, after less than four hours of deliberation. Ironically, it was not so much the science of DNA typing as Simpson's sartorial vanity that led another jury, little more than a year later, to find him liable for having caused the deaths. The most incriminating piece of evidence in the civil trial consisted of thirty pictures of Simpson shot by a freelance photographer at a 1993 football game. They showed the defendant wearing the rare, size-12 Bruno

Magli shoes that he had once disparaged as 'ugly-ass', and firmly denied owning. Between 1991 and 1993, only 299 pairs of that particular model had been sold in the United States.[4] One pair helped clinch Simpson's guilt more effectively than all the DNA evidence in the earlier trial.

A failure of translation

For many months, from the grisly murders on 12 June 1994 to the 'not guilty' verdict on 2 October 1995, Simpson's fate was thought to hinge on 'DNA finger-printing' (more formally known as 'DNA typing'), a supposedly unerring method of identifying people on the basis of unique patterns in their genetic material.[5] Barely contested when it was first introduced into American courts, DNA evidence became increasingly controversial following *People v. Castro*,[6] a 1989 decision by a New York trial court which ruled that the test's reliability had not as yet been adequately established. That decision sent both scientific and law-enforcement institutions scrambling to close down any further questions about this invaluable forensic technique, and to ensure its unproblematic acceptance by the courts. The Office of Technology Assessment, an advisory body to the US Congress, reviewed the scientific and legal status of DNA typing in 1990.[7] The National Research Council (NRC), the policy arm of the National Academy of Sciences and the nation's most respected source of science advice, studied the technique in 1992; when some of its recommendations were challenged, the NRC convened a second committee to produce a more authoritative follow-up report.[8] The Federal Bureau of Investigation (FBI) launched an immense effort to standardize the procedures for collecting and analyzing DNA samples from crime scenes. Meanwhile, as several papers in this Special Issue show, a rapidly expanding array of private DNA-testing companies hastened to develop reliable systems of peer review and proficiency testing.[9] In 1994, the Federal Judicial Center attempted to systematize the response of judges to this still novel technique: one section of the FJC's refer-ence manual on scientific evidence instructed the judiciary how to ask meaningful questions about DNA typing.[10]

Despite these energetic efforts, closure proved elusive. Both prosecution and defense lawyers in the Simpson case, for example, recognized the still-fluid char-acter of DNA evidence, and rushed to line up allies for their particular interpreta-tions.[11] Charismatic trial lawyers and law professors, well-established DNA-testing firms, staid professionals from state crime laboratories, and even a flamboyant Nobel Laureate scientist,[12] formed a star-studded instructional team for 'the most detailed course in molecular genetics ever taught to the US people'.[13] The prose-cution, along with the majority of white Americans, seemed to accept the DNA evidence as conclusive proof of Simpson's guilt, forgetting in the process that 'blood doesn't talk – people do'.[14] The defense brilliantly aimed its attack on people rather than inanimate inscriptions,[15] charging the criminalists from the troubled Los Angeles Police Department (LAPD) with every kind of deviance, from inconsistency, carelessness and sloppy practice to racially motivated miscon-duct. By the trial's end, the 'mountain of evidence',[16] which prosecutors once had hoped would convict Simpson, had crumbled into an unimpressive, and unpersuasive, molehill.

The causes of this collapse merit careful analysis because its implications reach far beyond the immediate issue of Simpson's guilt or innocence. Was the first Simpson trial, as some have claimed, a truly singular event – unique in its blending of race relations, wealth, sexual jealousy, Hollywood glamour, media attention and the contingencies of local politics[17] – from which no general conclusions can be drawn about legal processes or the public understanding of science? Did the prosecution make a simple but fatal blunder in failing to reckon with the American public's fabled 'scientific illiteracy'? Were the lay jurors simply unable to absorb such complex technical data? Alternatively, if comprehension was not the decisive issue, then why did the jury in the criminal trial give so little credence to the testimony of prosecution experts?[18] Could the DNA-test results have been represented in ways that would have commanded the jury's trust? And do the answers point toward a wider need for law reform, especially in procedures for presenting and evaluating expert testimony?

To begin addressing these questions, we must situate the first Simpson verdict in terms that are more familiar to science studies, and to social analysis more broadly, than to legal inquiry: that is, as a display of radical disbelief in a story that sought centrally to exploit the authority of science.[19] Conventional legal scholarship, with its deep-rooted commitment to the existence of objective facts,[20] offers relatively few resources for understanding what makes, or unmakes, the credibility of scientific evidence in the courtroom. Underlying the law's general rules for evaluating expert evidence is a barely concealed sociology of error – or, perhaps more properly, diverse *sociologies* of error. Evidence ceases to be acceptable in the eyes of the law when it is contaminated by preventable technical or moral failings – for example, a break in the chain of custody, unethical behaviour by a lawyer, dishonesty on the part of an expert witness or reliance on flawed science. The possibility of more radical contingency in the production of evidence lies outside the normal scope of legal analysis and self-awareness.

The dynamics of litigation are partly to blame, since they do much to obscure the complexity of the translations by which samples, artifacts, recordings or pictures become evidence.[21] Offering parties have little interest in presenting their technical evidence in a light that could increase the other side's scepticism. It is safer by far to treat evidence as the product of a few simple, black-boxed operations whose integrity can be defended according to the conventions of the legal game. Thus, for physical evidence, the notion of the 'chain of custody' transports the crime scene to the courtroom through a supposedly unbroken series of physical moves. For scientific evidence, the person of the expert witness contains, and in effect conceals, much of the behind-the-scenes work of translation, from the investigative site through the forensic laboratory into testimony at trial. When these simplifying mechanisms function as intended, the microcosms of crime and court are brought into apparently perfect alignment – as parallel universes whose actions mimic one another exactly, albeit at a temporal remove and in different styles and languages. In this way, admissible evidence transforms the events of the world outside into a courtroom re-enactment through a kind of artifice that claims at the same time the power of accurate representation.

For most legal practitioners, language is still the primary medium of translation between reality and its representation in litigation.[22] The facts of science are transported into the minds of judges and juries through language, strategically deployed – language codified into rules of admissibility, dramatically configured into opening and closing arguments, professionally packaged as expert testimony, and deconstructed through skilful cross-examination. Yet the courtroom is quintessentially also a theatre in which things are not only related but also shown in order to compel belief.[23] Visualization, no less than verbalization, is one of the techniques by which scientific evidence achieves credibility – and so gains, for purposes of legal decisionmaking, the status of fact. Nevertheless, processes for creating, or debunking, visual evidence have received surprisingly little attention in legal analysis, even though verbal testimony is in practice very frequently accompanied by visual supports.

In seeking to manage the interpretive flexibility of facts, the law of evidence has focused first and foremost on various rules and principles, such as the so-called exclusionary rule,[24] or the rules of admissibility,[25] by which judges can screen the parties' proffered accounts to make sure they are not blatantly flawed or untrue. There is a tacit assumption that evidence which is not defective in these ways provides a more or less accurate mirror of reality. In practice, of course, scientific evidence is a far more complex production that necessarily draws on a wide range of social and cultural resources – such as the persuasive power of inscriptions (in our case, 'DNA fingerprints') in western societies, the authority of professional codes and standards, and judges' and juries' commonsense understandings of science. This incorporation of tacit cultural norms into the manufacture of credible evidence deserves more extensive scholarly attention.[26]

In this paper, I address the general problem of the authority of science in the courtroom through an examination of what is involved in making DNA evidence convincing to lay fact-finders. DNA typing is particularly interesting in this regard because, unlike much other forensic evidence, it rests on relatively secure theoretical foundations (contrast, for example, the cases of lie detectors and 'clinical ecology'[27]) and yet it has become highly controversial. The question of vision is crucial to my inquiry. What is it that judges and jurors see when they look at DNA evidence, and what makes their visual experience similar to or different from that of experts? I take it as axiomatic that neither belief nor disbelief in the reliability of DNA evidence should be privileged in probing the reasons for divergent assessments of its credibility.[28] I also follow recent trends in the study of visual representations in assuming no preordained hierarchical relationship between expert and lay perceptions of scientific images and inscriptions: what interests me instead is how each viewpoint may be constitutive of the other.[29] Drawing on transcripts and opinions from US legal cases involving DNA testimony, I suggest that seeing is an essential precondition for believing, but that the right to see is itself in dispute when science comes under legal scrutiny. To establish a privileged point of view with respect to scientific facts, conflicts must be resolved between divergent visual representations of the evidence, between direct and 'virtual' witnessing,[30] and between lay and professional vision.[31] Who resolves such disputes and by what rules, emerge therefore as substantial questions for the legal process.

Bloodstains and signature prints

In a pre-technological era, blood, it was thought, spoke directly to people, telling with unambiguous signs, sometimes even in plain speech, of deeds of infamy. Reminders of that simple belief survive in our cultural heritage, preserved in the resin of literary creativity. Lady Macbeth still walks the stage trying to wash the imagined blood of murdered Duncan from her hands, bloodstains so stubborn that one touch of them will change the colour of the sea, 'making the green one red'. The anxious mother in the Grimms' folktale, *The Goose Girl*, gives to her daughter at parting a white handkerchief into which she has let fall three drops of blood from her own finger. When the poor girl is forced by her wicked maid to dismount from her horse and drink from a stream, the drops of blood call out to her: 'If this your mother knew, her heart would break in two'. In the Rajput legend of Siladitya, the hero's young queen is embroidering a turban of the finest silk for her husband to wear on his return from war. She pricks her finger and a drop of blood falls on the precious work. When she tries to wash it off, the drop spreads through the entire fabric, red stain on green silk, warning her that the husband she loves is dead.

But ours is an age of scientific enchantment. Blood, along with other bodily fluids and tissues, still speaks with authority, but only through the miraculous translations wrought by science and technology. DNA typing is one such miracle, and its unprecedented power to establish the truth is reiterated almost as a refrain whenever people have occasion to talk about its use in law enforcement. Mr Justice Orton, the British trial judge in *Regina v. Pitchfork*, the first murder case to use DNA evidence, introduced the theme of inevitability that soon became part of the technique's mystique: 'The rapes and murders were of a particularly sadistic kind. And if it wasn't for DNA you might still be at large today'.[32] Publicity literature for Cellmark Diagnostics, the private firm that carried out some of the DNA analysis for the LAPD in the Simpson case, boldly announces: 'It is nature's perfect identity test. No other test can give such certainty'. According to an article in *Nature*, DNA typing is 'perhaps the greatest advance in forensic science since the development of ordinary fingerprints in 1892'.[33] New York State's director of criminal justice observes with more becoming, or prudent, circumspection: 'DNA is an extremely powerful tool that enhances the truth-finding function of the criminal justice system'.[34]

So effortless is the translation from guilty blood to signature prints in these popular tellings, that the abbreviation 'DNA' comes to stand, by a potent rhetorical economy, for the entire complex of mediations that lie between: note, for instance, the statements above by Justice Orton and the New York state official, representing DNA as a free agent. Yet the metonymic genius of language that converts 'DNA' into a stark signifier of truth suppresses a world of social activity. Simply collecting samples can pose enormous problems of police work when crimes are committed by strangers. To identify the rapist-murderer Colin Pitch-fork by means of DNA typing, the Leicestershire police had to analyze blood samples from some 2000 young male 'volunteers', aged 17–34, at a cost of about $250 (£160) for each analysis.[35] The sheer scale of the enterprise was staggering by comparison with routine forensic and medical testing. The novelist Joseph Wambaugh gives a memorable if highly coloured account:

> They were drowning in blood. There were vials on every shelf. The freezers were full of it. There was more young British blood flowing in Leicestershire than had been spilled at the Somme.[36]

Especially ironic in the light of Justice Orton's sentencing homily is that none of the heroic effort spent on DNA sampling succeeded directly in fingering the murderer. Pitchfork had persuaded a reluctant friend (he, too, was a 'volunteer', but marching to a renegade drummer) to give blood in his place. Only when the friend confessed the substitution was Pitchfork identified as the principal suspect: DNA evidence then served to confirm the identification.

'You can't see molecules'

Reflecting on the production of evidence in court cases, we recognize that legal practitioners, no less than scientists, are professional fact-makers, who weave objects, images, and rhetoric into narratives designed to compel assent from their intended audiences. Just as experimental scientists use words and inscriptions to project the social space of their laboratories to distant witnesses, so legal advocates seek to transport the crime scene into the courtroom, making it real for viewers removed in time and place from the original events.[37] Legal argumentation, like reports of scientific experiments, appeals to an audience's powers of *seeing* the evidence, as well as reasoning from what is said about it. Visualization in the theatres of both science and law is governed by standardized professional practices, specialist discourses, and particular interpretive conventions. In both kinds of claims-making, facticity (or truth) is established only when the designated audience believes what is signified by the proffered representation.

But while displays of evidence within scientific communities may typically conform to mutually understood rules of representation (both graphic and linguistic),[38] lawyers and their expert witnesses perform before audiences who have not been trained to see reality in similar ways. As a result, the presentation of scientific evidence, and the training of the judge or jury to see it as scientists themselves do, proceed simultaneously in legal settings. Human eyesight, however, is not so easily disciplined to see the 'same thing' in the same way, even when the spectacle is directly accessible to the naked eye.[39] Scientific inscriptions, moreover, pose distinctive problems for non-specialist vision. They are highly mediated artifacts, often seen only with the aid of instruments (telescopes, gravity-wave detectors, electron microscopes, modelling software and, in DNA analysis, electrically charged gels) that confer a monopoly of vision on those who know how to use them.[40] It takes skill and resources to master the relevant instrumentation, and yet more resources to extend the monopoly so gained outward from the locus of scientific activity – the field study, clinical trial or lab group – to wider communities of 'virtual witnesses'. Yet, as Steven Shapin and Simon Schaffer have elegantly argued,[41] precisely such extension beyond an immediate circle of observers is needed to transform scientific claims into matters of fact. And the distant, peripheral witnesses retain, in principle, the right to rebel against the metropoles of science, its 'centres of calculation',[42] by reasserting their own undisciplined and individualized vision.

In legal contests over scientific evidence, the superiority of the expert's trained and mediated vision over the lay fact-finder's unmediated witnessing needs to be formally established; it can never be taken for granted. Sometimes, an image or inscription presented in court is so direct and unambiguous that assent is willingly given to the story it tells, without need of further instruction. In an X-ray photograph, the pair of surgical scissors carelessly left inside the patient's body is visible to all, a perfect translation. There is even a legal doctrine that acknowledges the complete, self-contained nature of such visual demonstrations: *res ipsa loquitur* (the thing speaks for itself).[43] Ordinary fingerprints have come to be accepted in this way, as universally recognized signifiers of truth,[44] although they are the products of specialized, continually changing and potentially contestable instrumentation and technical practices. Even the interpretation of fingerprints, as Simon Cole shows in his paper in this Special Issue,[45] has long been the province of licensed, professional skill.

In sharp contrast with these examples, courtroom exchanges concerning the reliability of DNA typing reveal, especially in early cases, a far from taken-for-granted relationship between expert claims and their reception by lay observers. The questions posed by judges and lawyers exhibit deep scepticism about the experts' capacity to see authoritatively what is denied to other people's senses. The expert witness and the examining lawyer collaborate to instruct, cajole, and rhetorically retrain the fact-finder's eyesight, with greater or lesser success, to 'see' DNA and so, by a metonymic transfer of meaning, to perceive the truth whole.

The theme of DNA's visibility was broached in *Andrews* v. *State of Florida*,[46] the first US criminal trial to rely on identification by DNA typing. A prosecution witness ('*A*' in the following extract) was questioned by the defense lawyer ('*Q*'), who expressed the naïve scepticism of untrained seeing. In this exchange, the lawyer seeks perhaps to impart to the jury some of his own resistance to seeing eye-to-eye with the expert:

A: Generally, you would examine pieces of DNA that would be in the range of one thousand to ten thousand units in chain length. That's a rough approximation. Because you could look at one slightly bigger or slightly smaller.

Q: Not knowing what a unit is, I am still trying to get this down into something a lay person could try to fathom.

A: All right. I tell you what. That one cell in your finger, if you take all the DNA of that one cell out, it would be about nine foot long.

Q: If you could stretch it out?

A: If you could stretch it out, it would be about nine foot long. Does that help you?

Q: It would be pretty thin, though, wouldn't it?

A: Yeah. But if you were – yeah. If you then were to cut it up into little bits, each one would have a specific discrete length you would measure with a real small ruler.

Q: Just the cell that we are talking about, in order to be able to see that, would require magnification under a microscope of what kind of magnification just to see the cell, itself?

A: Depends on how much detail you'd like to see. Couple, hundred fold, you would start to see some pretty good detail.[47]

In another case, *State of New Jersey v. Williams*,[48] it was the presiding judge who crossed sights with the expert witness, asking for a persuasive explanation of what it means, in terms of common, non-expert experiences of seeing, to 'amplify' DNA fragments through polymerase chain reaction (PCR):[49]

The Court: Now when you say – when you reduce it to its pure form, it is about a drop.

The Witness: Well, one has about a drop of fluid. Now –

The Court: Of pure DNA?

The Witness: No, no, no. No, no, no. This is, perhaps, the thing that is confusing the Court. The Court apparently has the idea that you can see molecules.

You can't see molecules. But you can test for their consequence. You simply – one has the idea that you have one of these cocktails. You have one of these cocktails and there is a lid on this thing. A little cap and that's probably about one hundred times larger than what we have. We have this fluid here and we stick it in a thermal cycler and after 30 or 40 cycles the stuff comes fuming out and all of a sudden your laboratory is taken over by these DNA molecules. That's not what we are talking about here, Judge. It is not like – it is not like in one of these things you see in science fiction movies.

The Court: You are telling me whatever it is that is in this tube you could amplify it millions and billions of times. But when I look at what is inside that tube it looks like the same volume.[50]

'You can't see molecules. But you can test for their consequence.' Could one ask for a more concise or compelling statement of the metaphysics of modern science as it pursues things unattempted yet by the unaided eye? Yet in legal settings, as indeed in any wider arena where scientific findings entail normative as well as epistemological consequence, it is essential to enroll the possessors of common vision into seeing the same truths that scientists see with their enhanced capacity for sight.[51] The expert in *Williams* is intensely aware of this obligation as he delves into his repertoire of culturally authorized imaginative resources to pull the judge into his way of seeing things. Shared social myths about the nature of science ('science fiction movies') form part of this repertoire, as do shared under-standings about lawyering: a moment after the foregoing exchange, the expert says to the judge, speaking of the fluid amplified by the PCR process: 'It is a fairly simple cocktail. It is simpler than many drinks I have seen lawyers make for themselves'.[52] The lines of vision intersect again, as the expert appeals to another common cultural resource – the mixing of cocktails – to explain the trans-lation of blood to DNA. It is from such dense cross-hatchings of lay and expert, communal and esoteric, vulgar and initiated – in short, immediate as well as medi-ated – witnessing that credibility is constituted in legal contests over scientific evidence.

Framing vision, constructing expertise

Scientific testimony presents particular challenges for adjudication because courts are reluctant to assert with respect to scientific fact-finding the same unconstrained sovereignty that they assume with respect to all other kinds of facts. The legal community has long taken for granted that the demarcation between reliable and unreliable scientific viewpoints is established in important part outside the purview of the law and can be unproblematically imported into legal proceedings. This assumption underlies the calls by conservative law reformers to eliminate 'junk science' (the unreliable offerings of untrustworthy experts) from the courtroom and to replace it with 'mainstream science'.[53] Rules governing the admissibility of scientific evidence also assume that the demarcation between genuine and spurious expertise is already there for judges to find. Judges are seen as 'gatekeepers', because they have the power to let in the reliable testimony and shut the gate against mere pretence. Thus the 1923 federal appeals court decision in *Frye v. United States* announced the 'general acceptance' test of admissibility.[54] The ruling instructed judges to discover, in effect, which scientific views were gener-ally accepted and which were not; evidence that failed the acceptability test was not admissible.

Of course, the so-called *Frye* rule proved easier to conceptualize than to apply in practice. Courts soon found themselves in disarray, disagreeing on how many experts were needed for *general* acceptance, and whether novel offers of scientific and technical proof, such as radar detection devices to establish speeding viola-tions, voice-prints to prove a speaker's identity, or the statistical analysis of literary style (stylometry) to establish authorship, were generally accepted.[55] Legal commentators attributed the disconcertingly divergent results to judicial 'incon-sistency', and asked for clearer rules to enable judges to discern more reliably just where authentic claims shade off into the grey zone of unacceptability. The 1993 decision in *Daubert v. Merrell Dow Pharmaceuticals, Inc.* was the answer offered by the nation's highest court.[56] *Daubert* replaced *Frye* with the injunction that evidence should be scientifically reliable and relevant in order to be admitted. Reliability, the Court further opined, should be decided according to criteria used by scientists themselves. For starters, the Court offered four non-exclusive criteria: does the evidence rest on a tested and falsifiable theory or technique; has the underlying science been peer-reviewed; what is the technique's error rate; and is it generally accepted?[57]

By looking to externally certified demarcation criteria, the *Frye–Daubert* approach chose to overlook the court's own contingent and case-specific rôle in establishing the preconditions of credibility. Judges, as I have suggested in earlier writing,[58] do not so much *find* as actively participate in *creating* the dividing lines between appropriate and inappropriate offers of expertise. They do so by selectively privileging some expert viewpoints over others, by creating new hierarchies as needed among classes of potentially credible experts (thus, 'scientists' may be more highly ranked than 'technicians', 'treating physicians' than epidemiologists, epidemiologists than toxicologists, and so on). At the limits, they may exclude some experts altogether, or appoint their own experts to provide more neutral scientific accounts than those presented by the parties' experts.

Less blatantly, though no less influentially, judges also import into demarcation decisions their own submerged understandings of the methods of science. Lay perceptions of how science works constitute in this way the template against which courts measure the acceptability of expertise. For illustration, let us turn to a California drunk-driving trial involving a police practice known as 'horizontal gaze nystagmus' – a 'field test' in which inspection of the suspect's eyeball movements (a most literal form of 'eyeballing') provides an index of drunkenness or sobriety. The California judge excluded the evidence, ruling that the administering police officer could not be credited either as a lay witness (his vision was too experienced for that designation) or as an expert (his vision was not properly disciplined by the scientific method).[59] To count as expert, the court indicated, the officer's vision should have been mediated by recognized scientific practices, such as instrumentation or quantification. We return again to the issue of authoritative vision. At the heart of the US legal system's often agonized inquiries into the admissibility of expert knowledge is still the recurring question: 'Whose sight can we trust, if not our own?'.

In a perceptive analysis of the infamous Rodney King case, the anthropologist Charles Goodwin observes that visual evidence acquires special power when it is certified as 'professional vision'. Raw observation, he suggests, is often meaningless unless it can be disciplined into particular 'socially organized ways of seeing and understanding events that are answerable to the distinctive interests of a particular social group'.[60] Goodwin calls attention to three discursive practices – coding, highlighting, and producing and articulating material representations – that lawyers and expert witnesses use to impose meaning on a jumbled mass of visual impressions. In the trial of King's assailants, a murky videotape of the beating was translated into two conflicting narratives, an uncoded lay version and a coded professional version offered by Sergeant Charles Duke, a member of the LAPD but also an expert on police practice. In the victim's (lay) rendition, the tape displayed a single, continuous action, depicting a helpless, unresisting African-American man being viciously beaten by a gang of white attackers. In

Duke's (professional) version, the scene was analytically fragmented into a sequence of disjointed mini-events, in which the jerky movements of the victim's separate body parts offered to trained police officers the rationale for new 'assessment periods', 'escalations of force' and strategically directed 'kicks' and 'blows'.[61] Goodwin concludes, following Foucault,[62] that the power to engage in professional speech, and so to constrain the fact-finder's vision, is unevenly distributed across society. This imbalance makes it extremely difficult for those lacking the resource of professionalism to represent their points of view as rational, credible or true.

Convincing as Goodwin is in deconstructing the expert testimony on Rodney King's beating, he underestimates the contingency of courtroom demarcations between lay and professional vision. Legal inquiry has the power to redefine the very parameters of professionalism from one case to another. Perhaps the most interesting feature of the King trial, in the light of Goodwin's analysis, was the court's willingness to admit Duke as an expert on police brutality, an issue that could as easily have been left as a matter for lay determination. How did Duke, an LAPD officer, lay claim to such expertise? By contrast, in the California decision on 'horizontal gaze nystagmus', expert status was denied to the police officer who claimed to 'see' a driver's alleged inebriation with specially authorized, professional sight; courts in other states have decided the same issue differently. The credibility of professional observation was constituted within the confines of the trial itself, with the judge acting less as gatekeeper than as lexicographer, or definer, of 'expertise'. Episodes from the Simpson case display a similarly active judicial involvement in the very definition of expertise.

A protocol for witnessing

In the Simpson case, conflicts over the credibility of DNA evidence began at the pre-trial stage, in hearings to determine how the blood samples collected at the crime scene would be shared and how integrity would be ensured in their testing. The prosecution considered it sufficient to have a private company, Cellmark Diagnostics of Germantown, Maryland, carry out some of the DNA typing in accordance with the firm's established procedures. The defense resisted this move by questioning whether Cellmark had any privileged claim to credibility. An exchange on 27 July 1994 between Marcia Clark, the lead prosecuting attorney, and Robert Shapiro, a lead defense lawyer, before Judge Lance Ito, centred on the trustworthiness of Cellmark's procedures and, by extension, on the adequacy of 'virtual witnessing'.

Clark sought to black-box Cellmark's expertise, which she argued was appropriately constituted within a closed, professional space defined by the company's testing protocol. The defense experts, she asserted, were welcome to attend and watch the tests being performed, but they could not exercise hands-on control, and would have to remain in this sense outside the periphery of Cellmark's operational rules. Only in this way could Cellmark's professional independence, integrity and ultimate credibility be assured:

Clark: Cellmark is an independent laboratory and they have procedures, protocols, and standards that govern the manner in which they handle their
evidence. They have furnished a copy of these guidelines to counsel and
in that it indicates that outside experts are not permitted to use their
equipment or handle the evidence, and that is for the purpose of maintaining the chain of custody and the integrity of that chain of custody. If
they turn it over, to an outside expert, then they have a break in the chain
with the problems and the complications that may ensue from that.

. . .

But let me clarify what their objection is, now that I think I understand it.
First of all the case samples, these are not blood samples taken from a
hospital in which you are doing a medical diagnosis and you have vials
of blood in large samples. These are crime scene samples. They're small.
The logistical problem of crowding many people around . . . with respect
to having the actual cutting done, the only way that Cellmark can assure
that quality is controlled, or there is quality assurance in the manner in
which the cutting is done is to have their own people do it, and follow
their own guidelines.[63]

Cellmark's credibility derived, in Clark's account, from the very specificity of its
practices. The company's domain was forensic science, a unique kind of activity
whose protocols could not be expected to conform to other forms of scientific
practice, even to customary rules of medical research using similar techniques.
'Crime scene samples', she emphasized, are 'small', unlike the vials of blood
obtained from medical patients. Only a professional body with experience in
handling such samples could be trusted to manipulate ('cut') the DNA in credible
fashion, using its own people and following its own guidelines. Other observers
would simply have to rely on the integrity of Cellmark's rule-governed and expe-
rientially legitimated professional space. As long as the company followed its
own rules, and this *could* be checked by watchful defense experts, its conclusions,
she suggested, should win universal acceptance.

Shapiro's parsing of the determinants of credibility was less deferential and
more democratic. For him, it was not enough to have Simpson's defense experts
simply watch Cellmark's professionals at work, turning samples into evidence
through the company's codified rules of practice. He asked for more active control:

Shapiro: After reviewing the protocol which Ms Clark said we had, which we
did not have until yesterday by fax, it's clear that the procedures
outlined by the laboratory that the prosecution has chosen serve no
purpose whatsoever. For us to have experts there witnessing some parts
of their procedure serves no purpose whatsoever. I talked to Dr Lee
[a respected expert from the Connecticut state crime lab] at length
yesterday on this issue, and he said it just would be an exercise in
futility to merely stand there, under these guidelines, and observe what
they are doing regarding testing procedures, so we would respectfully

again ask the court to revisit the issue of giving us a 50% sample so we can do our own independent testing. Short of that, to give us some access to watch under some defined terms is something that will be of no probative value whatsoever.[64]

One is instantly struck by the predictable, even instinctive use of lawyer's tricks in this richly textured passage: the implicit accusation of bad faith in the late delivery of the fax, and the impugning of Cellmark's independence by calling it 'the laboratory that the prosecution has chosen'. But behind Shapiro's adversarial gibes was a more serious, global objective – the desire to wrest control of scientific fact-making from the prosecution and its designated experts. To do this, he had to deny the power of mere observation to validate the integrity of somebody else's professional practice (simply watching, he said, 'will be of no probative value whatsoever'). Seeing, he implied, must be indissolubly linked to doing, in a seamless, inviolable, self-contained world of technical practice, in order to guarantee the credibility of the inscriptions it produces. So much for Robert Boyle and the force of 'virtual witnessing': here, immanent in prosaic, 20th-century law talk, was Hobbesian scepticism triumphant.[65]

The judgement that Clark and Shapiro called upon Ito to make was not therefore the classic Solomonic one of deciding how to divide drops of blood too small for conventional laboratory diagnosis between two contending parties. More than each side's proprietary rights to the samples was at stake here (although ownership was an issue that Shapiro explicitly raised). In deciding whether to give the prosecution complete control over the samples or to surrender '50%' to the defense, Ito was confronted in effect with opposing philosophies of credibility, founded on different understandings of the connections between doing, seeing and believing. A superficially childish 'custody dispute' over blood samples drew the judge into evaluating the professional lifeworld of DNA typing, as constructed by a private testing company and sanctioned by a police department. By choosing to approve Marcia Clark's theory of witnessing, Ito helped to reinforce the boundary that Cellmark wished to draw between its own world of expert practice and the watching world outside.

Lies and videotape

Rulings that would eventually have an impact on the credibility of DNA evidence did not necessarily concern the manipulation of blood samples to start with. A notable example of such a collateral judgment was Ito's decision to admit a videotape of police activity at the crime scene over the prosecution's strenuous objections. In seeking to exclude the tape, Marcia Clark advanced on behalf of the prosecution an argument similar to Goodwin's claim that 'all vision is perspectival and lodged within endogenous communities of practice'.[66] Three extracts from an admissibility hearing held on 23 February 1995 show Clark trying in vain to establish the need for professional interpretation to make sense of the camera's testimony:

Clark (1):   As the Court can see, at the very point so far when the defense would ask the jury to make an inference, the very point that they're trying to make is obscured. This epitomizes the problem with this whole tape. It looks from this that everyone is standing on top of each other with not two inches between them. We know that is not the case. That obviously can't physically be the case. But it's such a misleading and distorted clip that you can't tell where everyone is standing.

Clark (2):   This is a piece of evidence that is not evidence. This is a distortion, this is a method of confusion, and it does not inform the jury of anything of probative value. In fact, quite contrary. It obscures the fact that it purports to – that the defense says it purports to show.

Clark (3):   Furthermore, and lastly, that they have not produced a cameraman who could tell us where he stood. I'm sure it will be something in the nature of across the street. He will – and someone who will tell us the nature of the lens he used. I'm sure there's some sort of telephoto lens. And I'm sure that if an expert were called . . . they will inform the Court of just how distorting and misleading this really is.[67]

Plain, unmediated eye-witnessing of the videotape, Clark exhorted the court, would not allow the jury to see without distortion what in fact had happened. The tape was the product of a specialized technical practice – photography – with its own internal mysteries of skill and interpretation. It was an encoding of reality rather than a mere reflection of it, and, without an expert decoder such as a cameraman to help them, the jurors would not be able to decode it properly. They would be misled into thinking, for instance, that the LAPD investigators (including, as it happens, the criminalist Denis Fung who was later to be cross-examined by Barry Scheck) were standing on top of each other, when they had actually maintained a proper distance. As in the Rodney King case, the prosecution claimed that the naked eye was not to be trusted with a video. Unless the tape could be seen through the filter of expert interpretation, it was 'a piece of evidence that is not evidence'.

Against this attempt to recast the video as a kind of professionally mediated vision, Johnny Cochran, another of Simpson's lead defense lawyers, offered an appealingly uncomplicated counterargument. The video provided, after all, a form of direct witnessing, as anyone could see. Cochran claimed the perspectival as well as the moral high ground:

> We are the ones introducing the truth here – we're showing a videotape. Now, the fact that somebody can't see somebody's legs, that's preposterous, Your Honor. The part of a videotape, the beauty is you stand there and you look at it, and you can tell where people are standing in the shrubbery. You can see exactly where they are. That's what a videotape is.[68]

Ito was persuaded. Although he claimed to be fascinated by the prosecution's arguments, he ruled in favour of the defense: the videotape, he concluded, was ostensibly 'as accurate a depiction as we will ever get. It is not someone's recollection or interpretation. It's the events as they unfolded'. As if convincing himself of the rightness of this judgment, Ito went on to describe aloud all the comings and goings that he could discern on the tape, without any need for an expert to decode it:

> And *the court is able to discern* from looking at the videotape itself that this videotape was taken at a relevant point when the coroner's investigator, Ms Radcliffe, arrives, she appears to be briefed by Detective Lange. We see Radcliffe and Lange at the top this – *what clearly appears to me* to be the top of the steps. *I then see* them move down to within two steps above the body of Nicole Brown Simpson at the bottom of the stairs. *I observe* them to be looking over the body, and Lange appears to be describing to Radcliffe what is there.[69] [my emphases]

Imperceptibly – signalled only by shifting the locus of visual perception from the third person of 'the court' to the first person of 'I' and 'me' – Ito became Everyman, asserting the supremacy of his own unmediated vision and looking back upon 'the events as they unfolded' through the transparent, and for him truthful, window of the videotape. Yet, not until Ito finished his public-private deliberation was it clear that, for purposes of *this* trial, the videotape would count as a form of direct, not technically or professionally mediated, seeing, so that the jury, like the judge, could view the tape without the aid of intervening experts.

Standardizing vision

DNA evidence was excluded in a number of trials before Simpson's because the inscriptions were produced in accordance with methods that were shown to be *ad hoc*, non-standard and therefore unscientific in the eyes of experts as well as laypersons. What the experts saw and how they claimed to see it were the central issues, and differences among testing laboratories served to undermine particular expert positions. Work in science studies has dwelt in some detail on this aspect of legal controversies, showing how adversarial processes deconstruct credibility by bringing to light myriad tacit and untested assumptions about physical and social reality that enter into the production of science.[70]

In *Maine v. McLeod*, a sexual molestation case, the defense questioned the way in which scientists at Lifecodes, a DNA-testing firm, had identified a match between two samples. The two 'fingerprints' in this case were not identical to the untrained eye: although the pattern looked the same, the bands in one print were displaced relative to the other, suggesting that the DNA fragments in the two samples were of different lengths. The Lifecodes experts had used a mathematical formula to correct for the observed bandshift; this adjustment allowed the lab to find sameness where lay observation might have been inclined to see differences. In this case, the court refused to defer to Lifecodes' visual authority because the adjustment procedure used by the lab had not been reviewed or approved by a wider scientific community.[71]

Standardization offered to testing laboratories and law-enforcement institutions an attractive way out of such quandaries. Standards serve to black-box messy technical practices: behaviour conforming to explicit standards tends to be more resistant to sceptical questioning. Yet, as the Simpson case revealed, standards in the legal context can prove to be a two-edged sword – as much a measure to discredit non-compliant conduct as to protect compliance. Once techniques of visualization are standardized, for example, deviance from the standard can be condemned in normative terms that are equally persuasive to experts and laypeople. For example, Eric Lander, a scientist at MIT's Whitehead Institute who had testified for the defense in *Castro*, and his co-author, FBI expert Bruce Budowle, characterized the early controversies over lab procedures as follows:

> The initial outcry over DNA typing standards concerned laboratory problems: poorly defined rules for declaring a match; experiments without controls; contaminated probes and samples; and sloppy interpretation of autoradiograms. Although there is no evidence that these technical failings resulted in any wrongful convictions, the lack of standards seemed to be a recipe for trouble.[72]

The language that Lander and Budowle used to debunk the efforts of prior workers in the field is striking in its mundaneness.[73] *Anybody* of normal mental capacity can understand concepts like 'poorly defined rules', 'contamination' and 'sloppy interpretation'; even the idea of experimental controls is part of every American schoolchild's basic conceptual repertoire.[74] It takes no special scientific skill or expertise to understand deviance framed in these terms. A jury of high-school students would see the point, let alone a judge. Indeed, as recently as 1996, a Massachusetts judge used very similar discrediting language to exclude evidence produced by the technique of polymerase chain reaction in a Boston laboratory. He found the work 'haphazard' and not done 'by qualified people who follow the requirements that have been standardized'.[75]

Standards, then, can be seen as a translation device that makes expert judgements about technical practices accessible to lay audiences, partly through the medium of mundane normative language. By invoking standards, a sceptical questioner can shift attention from the substantive to the procedural dimensions of scientific practice. As long as no-one questions what is meant by terms like 'haphazard' or 'sloppy', experts and nonexperts can use the same words to assess credibility (even though their underlying opinions about what constitutes acceptable or unacceptable behaviour may not be the same).[76] Judgements concerning the credibility of science appear to be governed by standards of virtue, of ethical and reasonable behaviour, that are not special to science but are widely shared by the culture as a whole. These shared resources of trust and honesty constitute what Steven Shapin terms the 'economy of credibility'.[77]

Barry Scheck, a defense lawyer noted for his successful attacks on DNA-typing evidence, employed such commonsensical norms with devastating effect against the helpless LAPD criminalist, Denis Fung. In a remarkable cross-examination,

Scheck repeatedly confronted Fung with violations of codified methods of DNA sample collection, and with seemingly careless and non-standard handling of samples and other objects throughout the early stages of the investigation.[78] Fung's supposedly aberrant practices (he had not consistently worn gloves, refrigerated samples, recorded entries, requested photographs, worked without spills) were relentlessly juxtaposed against the idealized work rules laid out in a published manual of forensic DNA typing.[79] Fung conceded under pressure that he had delegated some of the work to an even less experienced subordinate and had subsequently tried to cover up this fact. These homely but telling displays of ignorance, incompetence and bad faith not only demolished Fung's credibility (we note that, as a 'mere' technician lacking the social accoutrements of scientific expertise, Fung may have needed an especially dogged mastery of technique to command belief), but also brought to light impediments that no juror could ignore in the rhetorically unobstructed passage from 'DNA' to 'truth'.

But what made it so easy for Scheck to make light of Fung's technical competence? The criminalist's inability to constitute his way of seeing as legitimate professional vision is surely part of the answer. Again and again, as the trial transcript records, Scheck impeached the veracity of Fung's ways of seeing, aided in this endeavour by the videotape that gave the jury its own apparently unmediated access to the LAPD's behaviour at the crime scene. In one tenacious stream of questioning, Scheck planted doubt about Fung's having really seen the bloodstains on the door of Simpson's white Bronco on the day after the murders:

Q: By Mr Scheck: Okay, Mr Fung.
Let me ask you directly, on June 13th in the morning, did Detective Fuhrman point out four red lines, red stains to you on the bottom of the Bronco door?

A: I don't recall him doing so.

Q: When you say you don't recall, are you saying it didn't happen?

A: I'm not saying that. I'm saying I don't recall if he did or if he didn't.

Q: All right. If you had seen four stains on the exterior of the Bronco door on the morning of June 13th, you would have taken a photograph of them; would you not?

A: That would depend, but I don't know. But that would depend on the circumstances.

Q: Let's try these circumstances. You were pointed out a red stain by the door handle?

A: Yes.

Q: You were photographed pointing to that red stain, correct?

A: Yes.

Q: And you're the person that's supposed to direct the photographer during the collection process?

A: Yes.

Q: You're supposed to photograph items of evidence of some importance that are pointed out to you by the detectives?

A: Yes.

Q: In the circumstances of this case, if you had seen four red stains on the exterior of the Bronco door, would you not have directed the photographer to take a picture of it?

A: It would be likely. Yes.[80]

What Scheck achieved in this and many similar exchanges was not merely to make Fung change his mind or publicly admit error. It was rather to negate the prosecution's science-based strategy for making jurors into virtual witnesses; this he accomplished by questioning Fung's visual authority, and thus breaking the chain of visual custody, as it were, at one of its weakest links. With Fung unable to testify that he saw the stains before Fuhrman had a chance to plant them, no amount of subsequent scientific manipulation could empower the blood evidence from the Bronco to bear witness to the crime.

In everyday litigation, as the material constituents of evidence are converted into scientific facts, their humble origins in the work of individual eyes and hands get lost from view, and with this loss comes a forgetfulness about the shared social and scientific foundations of credibility. Lander and Budowle displayed such a conditioned blindness when they acknowledged the troubled prehistory of forensic DNA typing, but dismissed it none the less, on the ground that 'there is no evidence that these technical failings resulted in any wrongful convictions'.[81] Scheck's cross-examination of Fung turned this dismissive assessment on its head by reasserting the primacy of hands-on fieldwork over more theoretically sophisticated expertise; reduced to micro-details, the methods by which the LAPD had attempted to transport the crime scene into the courtroom were shown to be all too fallible. Mundane credibility judgements about Fung's manifold 'technical failings' could then be used with great effect to undermine the prosecution's 'scientific' evidence of Simpson's guilt.

Questions of process

At the beginning of the criminal trial, Judge Ito's calm demeanour and measured responses to the lawyers' and media's frenetic manœuvring won wide commendation. He was praised, in particular, for his allegiance to the emerging 'truth school' among scholars of constitutional and criminal law, a nascent intellectual movement determined to cut across the intense ideological polarization of pro-defense and pro-prosecution positions on the admissibility of evidence.[82] For adherents of this school, 'DNA' promised to be the perfect ally, an able, almost infallible and (important in America's race-conscious justice system) potentially colour-blind assistant in the programme of truth-finding. But a common-law trial is not purely and simply a search for the truth: it is, more accurately, a contest of credibility between two carefully packaged, competing accounts of the 'same' reality. Plausibility is what carries the day: by trial's end, the winning story is the one that strikes the fact-finder as the more believable.

Assessing the credibility of scientific evidence, I have suggested, presents particular difficulties because courtroom science simultaneously appeals to different cultures of belief. Lay intuitions and perceptions of the world, founded upon direct, unmediated witnessing, continually bump up against professionally configured claims of 'virtual' or expert vision. What professionals see with their skilled and instrumentally enhanced capacity for sight, and what they render into words through specialized discourses, overlap imperfectly at best with what lay assessors of the evidence see and hear with their unaided senses: 'you can't see molecules', the experts say, but you should trust us to see them because we can 'test for their consequence'. Trial outcomes in complex cases hinge therefore on the extent to which the judge or jury gives controlling weight to the expert's distanced and instrumentally mediated gaze on reality. In the Simpson criminal trial, expert testimony about DNA evidence had to compete for credibility with other reconstructions of what had or had not taken place at the crime scene (quasi-experiments?), including the famously theatrical demonstration that the defendant's hand did not easily fit into the bloody glove found on his driveway.

Expert witnesses can overcome sceptical challenges like these by seeking to establish a common 'economy of credibility' with lay fact-finders – whether by blinding them with science ('you can't see molecules, but you can test for their consequence') or by making science appear so transparent that no discrepancy remains between lay and expert vision. But the power to persuade does not depend wholly on the talents of particular witnesses or the dynamics of particular cases. Legal rules and practices of general application shape the overall context in which experts testify and may deprive some would-be experts of the opportunity to participate. What conclusions can we draw about the forms that such rules and practices should take, given what we have seen about the construction of privileged visual positions in the courtroom?

Court-appointed experts

In the United States as well as in Britain, clamour is growing to give the judiciary more power to appoint 'neutral', 'independent' or 'impartial' experts to supplement, or possibly supplant, the scientific stories brought to court by litigating parties. In both countries, judges already possess formal legal authority to bring in non-party experts at need – under Rule 706 of the Federal Rules of Evidence in the United States, and in Britain under Rules of the Supreme Court (RSC) Order 40. Until the early 1990s, the American judiciary was notably reluctant to use these powers, for logistical reasons as well as for fear of letting experts usurp the judicial function.[83] Since then, increases in the cost and complexity of litigation have invited a renewed look at this problem. A 1991 report by the American Association for the Advancement of Science (AAAS),[84] and a 1995 report by Britain's Lord Woolf,[85] converged strikingly in their prescriptions for increasing the role of court-appointed experts. In *Daubert*, and more recently in *General Electronic Co. v. Joiner*,[86] the US Supreme Court has also lent powerful support to this move.

Non-party experts possess a number of potential advantages in trumping other claims to privileged witnessing of the facts. Their views come to court bearing an *imprimatur* of impartiality that tends to boost their credibility. As a 'neutral' third eye in the traditional two-party format of litigation, the court-appointed expert might occupy a quasi-judicial position and would form, together with the party experts, a smaller 'facts' triad (a *de facto* Science Court) within the larger 'justice' triad comprised by the judge and the legal advocates. These dynamics could well make lay fact-finders less assertive in turning their own sceptical gaze on the scientific evidence, thereby reducing conflict, but also foreclosing critical inquiry into the mundane, taken-for-granted aspects of scientific practice and the normative presuppositions of experts.

Excluding experts

Rules governing the admissibility of evidence provide another powerful method of enhancing judicial control over the parties' offers of expert testimony. *Daubert* and *Joiner* attest to the federal judiciary's growing frustration with the contributions of partisan experts. These cases assume that legitimate expertise is constituted outside the processes of the law and can be identified by proper application of relevant demarcation criteria. As we have seen, however, expertise in the legal context is – to paraphrase Bruno Latour[87] and Richard Rorty[88] – more the consequence than the cause of demarcation. In designating some witnesses as legitimate experts, and in distinguishing among different forms of witnessing, judges inevitably impose on fact-finding their own understandings about whose vision of the world counts as authoritative (or genuinely 'scientific') and whose does not. In so doing, they limit the range of interpretive flexibility available to lay questioning.

The Simpson case shows that the exclusion of expertise may happen in subtle ways, without formal application of the *Daubert* criteria or other tests of credibility. At two points in the trial – the debates over sharing blood samples and admitting video evidence – Judge Ito was required in effect to choose between competing claims of (visual) authority. By accepting the adequacy of Cellmark's practices and protocols, he took sides in a nearly four-centuries-old argument about the experimental constitution of authoritative knowledge: Hobbesian scepticism was rejected in favour of the view propagated by Boyle's scientific progeny that a test protocol such as Cellmark's can codify a universally valid world of observation and deduction. Similarly, in rejecting Marcia Clark's attack on the authenticity of the defense video, Ito denied that the photographic framing of visual space was an act of technically mediated seeing, requiring decoding by the trained, professional eye of a photographer or film expert. The judge as Everyman asserted his own right to see a universal truth in the moving images of the videotape.

Conclusion: the eye of power

The institutional genius of the courts is their capacity to deliver binding solutions – judgements that people accept as right in both the epistemological and moral senses of rightness. Finality of this kind would be difficult to attain in a lawless democracy of sight, where the fact-finder's right to see was free at all points to challenge the expert's professional vision, and to question its testimony concerning things invisible to the untrained eye. Dispute resolution in a complex society would soon prove unmanageable without some constraints on the deconstruction of expert vision. Not every trial that involves DNA-typing evidence can or should go back to the basics of how scientists see DNA or measure its physical presence 'with a real small ruler'. Like any other working institution, courts have to set some limits on scepticism and distrust. The visual freedom of the lay fact-finder has to be tempered with deference to claims of privileged professional vision, provided of course that expertise is not simply accepted on faith.

Common-law courts have sought to regulate the fact-finder's potentially disruptive power of sight with rules that protect or enhance legitimate claims of expertise. Experts are exempted from the hearsay rule that governs other testimony. More recent strategies for controlling scepticism allow courts to exclude forms of expertise that are seen as unscientific and to appoint, if they wish, their own experts to play a quasi-judicial rôle in fact-finding. These devices strengthen the already considerable authority of judges, enabling them in effect to shape the scientific debate in the courtroom to fit their own intuitive views of how science works and what counts as proper scientific expertise. Moves to enhance the rôle of science in adjudication are thus refracted through a generalist judiciary's understanding of the nature of science.

By following disputes about the credibility of DNA evidence in and out of the first Simpson trial, I have tried to show that drawing demarcation lines between credible and incredible offers of expertise is never simply a matter of rule-following or rule application. Expertise – contrary to what the law may doctrinally presuppose – is constituted or reconstituted to some extent within the framework of each trial. The 'expert' designation reflects not only the judge's appraisal of the qualifications of particular professionals but also underlying conceptions of where professional authority, including the right to see differently, begins and ends. Judge Ito helped to refine the social meaning of expertise just as surely when he ruled on the sharing of blood samples (upholding Cellmark's expertise) or the acceptability of videotaped evidence (denying the need for expert interpretation) as in any more explicit judgments about who could testify as an expert on DNA typing.

The judge's eye, then, is the eye of power. Its authoritative position may need to be accepted in the interests of social repose – but it need not be accepted uncritically. In conflicts over whose perception of the truth or the facts should take precedence, the inevitable plurality of vision that litigation generates must be disciplined in somebody's favour, consistently with wider notions of efficiency, fairness and justice. The innumerable, contingent disputes that any trial opens up between different ways of seeing require someone to turn to as the witness of last resort. This, in western legal systems, is one of the essential functions of judging.

What a democratic society should wish to cultivate, however, is an informed exercise of judicial power, deeply cognizant of its own rôle in constructing expertise rather than unthinkingly ratifying others' ill- or well-founded claims to privileged sight. In an age of heightened sensitivity to difference, and the far from self-evident nature of many truths, we may reasonably ask for judges learned in the subterranean social dynamics of credibility, knowledge and expertise. If the way judges see the world shapes how others in the courtroom must see it, then judicial vision should be trained to acknowledge and criticize its own power to constrain social perceptions of the truth. Justice can no longer afford to be blind.

Notes

* *Social Studies of Science*, Vol. 28, No. 5–6, pp. 713–40 (1998).
1 These are the dates, respectively, of the beginning of the opening arguments in the criminal trial and of the jury verdict exonerating Simpson on all charges.
2 For a discussion of 'immutable mobiles', see Bruno Latour, 'Drawing Things Together', in Michael Lynch and Steve Woolgar (eds), *Representation in Scientific Practice* (Cambridge, MA: The MIT Press, 1990), 19–68.
3 Rachel Nowak, 'Forensic DNA Goes to Court with O.J.', *Science*, Vol. 265 (2 September 1994), 1352–54.
4 Elaine Lafferty with Martha Smilgis, 'The Inside Story of How O.J. Lost', *Time* (17 February 1997), 28–36.
5 The technique is described in Eric S. Lander, 'DNA Fingerprinting: Science, Law, and the Ultimate Identifier', in Daniel J. Kevles and Leroy Hood (eds), *The Code of Codes* (Cambridge, MA: Harvard University Press, 1992), 191–210.
6 *People v. Castro*, 545 N.Y.S. 2d 985 (Sup. 1989). Spurred by criticism from experts on both sides, the court held an extended evidentiary hearing and concluded that DNA typing was a scientifically reliable technique, but that it had not been conducted in accordance with generally accepted procedures in this particular case. As the first decision to exclude DNA typing in a criminal trial, *Castro* underscored the need for properly validated and standardized procedures. See also Lander, op. cit. note 5.
7 Office of Technology Assessment, *Genetic Witness: Forensic Uses of DNA Tests* (Washington, DC: US Government Printing Office, 1990).
8 National Research Council, *DNA Technology in Forensic Science* (Washington, DC: National Academy Press, 1992), and NRC, *The Evaluation of Forensic DNA Evidence* (Washington, DC: National Academy Press, 1996).
9 See, especially, three papers: Michael Lynch, 'The Discursive Production of Uncertainty: The OJ Simpson "Dream Team" and the Sociology of Knowledge Machine', *Social Studies of Science*, Vol. 29, Nos 5–6 (October–December 1998), 829–68; Arthur Daemmrich, 'The Evidence Does Not Speak for Itself: Expert Witnesses and the Organization of DNA-Typing Companies', ibid., 741–72; and Kathleen Jordan and Lynch, 'The Dissemination, Standardization and Routinization of a Molecular Biological Technique', ibid., 773–800.
10 Federal Judicial Center, *Reference Manual on Scientific Evidence* (Washington, DC: Federal Judicial Center, 1994), 272–329.
11 See the paper in this Special Issue by Saul Halfon: 'Collecting, Testing and Convincing: Forensic DNA Experts in the Courts', *Social Studies of Science*, Vol. 28, Nos 5–6 (October–December 1998), 801–28.
12 Kary B. Mullis invented a technique known as 'Polymerase Chain Reaction' (PCR) that permits minute sequences of DNA to be multiplied indefinitely. PCR revolutionized the speed and accuracy of DNA analysis and Mullis, with his bizarre ideas and unbuttoned lifestyle, became a cultural icon. See Emily Yoffe, 'Is Kary Mullis God? (Or just the Big Kahuna?)', *Esquire* (July 1994), 68–74.
13 Eric S. Lander and Bruce Budowle, 'DNA Fingerprint Dispute Laid to Rest', *Nature*, Vol. 371 (27 October 1994), 735–38, at 735.
14 Ellen Willis, 'The Wrath of Clark', *New York Times Book Review* (15 June 1997), 15 (reviewing *Without a Doubt* by Marcia Clark, chief prosecutor in the Simpson criminal trial).

15 Not everyone credits Simpson's so-called 'Dream Team' of defense lawyers with very much ingenuity, preferring to argue that it was the prosecution's incompetence that lost the case almost before it started. On this point, see the account by former Los Angeles Assistant District Attorney, Vincent Bugliosi, *Outrage: The Five Reasons Why O.J. Simpson Got Away with Murder* (New York: W.W. Norton, 1996). As we shall see below, however, the defense lawyers did succeed in bringing the jury into the potentially arcane world of DNA typing by focusing on such mundane activities as sample collection and record-keeping.

16 This phrase was often used by Los Angeles District Attorney Gil Garcetti, under whose direction the prosecution built its case.

17 The Simpson murder case followed closely on the heels of the infamous trials of four white Los Angeles police officers for the brutal beating of Rodney King, an African-American man. The King case was a public relations disaster for the LAPD, especially after the defendant officers were acquitted by a suburban jury in the first trial. According to one line of conventional wisdom, relations between the LAPD and the African-American community were so poisoned by the time of the Simpson trial that even a perfectly conducted prosecution might not have resulted in a conviction. See *New York Times* (4 October 1995), A1.

18 It is hardly surprising that legal commentators have found relatively little to say about the Simpson jury's refusal to credit the DNA testimony. Race in general, and the personal racism of Detective Mark Fuhrman, a key prosecution witness, have been considered sufficient explanations for an outcome that, for the majority of white Americans, plainly beggared belief. But an irony lost sight of in the rush to accept the race-centred account is that the racial explanation itself was not neutrally distributed by race. It was white Americans for the most part who sought to rationalize an otherwise incomprehensible verdict in terms of race: black Americans, including members of the jury, insisted that the evidence had failed to support a guilty verdict. If race was the major factor in the case, then one of its most palpable effects was to make different racial groups perceive the scientific evidence differently. We are directed again to the question of what makes such discrepancies of vision possible.

19 The phenomenon of credibility has long been of interest to social scientists and has recently emerged as an important focus of inquiry in social studies of science. A partial listing of relevant work includes: Mary Douglas, 'The Social Preconditions of Radical Skepticism', in John Law (ed.), *Power, Action and Belief: A New Sociology of Knowledge?*, *Sociological Review Monograph* No. 32 (London: Routledge & Kegan Paul, 1986), 68–87; Augustine Brannigan and Michael Lynch, 'On Bearing False Witness: Credibility as an Interactional Accomplishment', *Journal of Contemporary Ethnography*, Vol. 16 (1987), 115–46; Steven Shapin, *A Social History of Truth* (Chicago, IL: The University of Chicago Press, 1994); Shapin, ' "Cordelia's Love": Credibility and the Social Studies of Science', *Perspectives on Science*, Vol. 3 (1995), 255–75.

20 Case studies and extended discussion on this point may be found in Sheila Jasanoff, *Science at the Bar: Law, Science, and Technology in America* (Cambridge, MA: Harvard University Press, 1995). See also Brian Wynne, 'Establishing the Rules of Laws: Constructing Expert Authority', in Roger Smith and Wynne (eds), *Expert Evidence* (London: Routledge, 1989), 23–55. Instructive, as well, is a recent spate of legal writing attacking critical legal studies and critical race theory in much the way that some scientists have attacked science studies: see, for example, Daniel A. Farber, *Beyond All Reason: The Radical Assault on Truth in American Law* (New York: Oxford University Press, 1997). Notable reviews of this work include: Richard A. Posner, 'The Skin Trade', *New Republic* (13 October 1997), 40–43; Alex Kozinski, 'Bending the Law', *New York Times Book Review* (2 November 1997), 7.

21 I use the term 'translations' here as it is used by sociologists of science to describe the moves by which pieces of the natural world are made tractable and believable in communities of scientific or technological practice. See, in particular, Michel Callon,

'Some Elements of a Sociology of Translation: Domestication of the Scallops and the Fishermen of St Brieuc Bay', in Law (ed.), op. cit. note 19, 196–233.

22 Legal scholars and practitioners disagree about the extent to which legal language should be black-boxed and transported from one case to another as fixed doctrine or dogma. Schools of legal interpretation differ, for instance, in their willingness to refer to a rule's original factual context in deciding whether or not to apply it to a new set of facts: see Robert S. Summers, *Instrumentalism and American Legal Theory* (Ithaca, NY: Cornell University Press, 1982). The difference between the relatively doctrinaire legal realists and the more context-sensitive legal instrumentalists, however, is of degree rather than kind. In either case, language is seen as the primary instrument of persuasion. To acquire rule-like properties, common-law precedents necessarily have to shed their moorings in the messiness of specific facts, just as scientific claims have to cut loose from the contingencies of particular experimental and observational settings. In operating the 'literary technology' of the law, practitioners continually have to judge whether and how far they should deconstruct the applicable legal language.

23 In thinking about belief in the courtroom as a problem of information transfer and mediation (both verbal and visual), I take valuable cues from Bruno Latour: see, especially, Latour, 'On Technical Mediation – Philosophy, Sociology, Genealogy', *Common Knowledge*, Vol. 3, No. 2 (Fall 1994), 29–64; and his comparison of scientific and religious belief in Latour, 'Opening One Eye while Closing the Other . . . A Note on some Religious Paintings', in John Law and Gordon Fyfe (eds), *Picturing Power: Visual Depiction and Social Relations, Sociological Review Monograph* No. 35 (London: Routledge, 1988), 15–38, and 'On the Assumptions of the Virgin Mary – A Meditation on Mediation', paper presented at the conference on 'Histories of Art – Histories of Science' (Boston & Cambridge, MA, November 1995).

24 The 'exclusionary rule' is a principle of modern American constitutional law, with historical roots in the late 19th century, that gives courts authority to exclude testimony obtained through constitutionally impermissible searches, such as those lacking a warrant or probable cause. For a scathing criticism of the modern rule, see Akhil Reed Amar, 'Fourth Amendment First Principles', *Harvard Law Review*, Vol. 107 (1994), 757–819. Amar's evaluation rests on a number of unexamined background assumptions, including the existence of an unproblematic category of 'reliable evidence' which judges should always endeavour not to exclude. Legal commentaries seldom afford much insight into authors' understandings of such concepts as truth and reliability.

25 The leading American case here is the Supreme Court's decision in *Daubert v. Merrell Dow Pharmaceuticals, Inc.*, 509 U.S. 579 (1993).

26 Legal accounts of evidence-making can, of course, be quite illuminating, even when they do not dig deeply into the production of scientific claims, because they shed light on the common cultural resources that support the construction of scientific and social credibility. An excellent example of such work is Joseph Sanders, 'From Science to Evidence: The Testimony on Causation in the Bendectin Cases', *Stanford Law Review*, Vol. 46 (1993), 1–86.

27 Sheila Jasanoff, 'Judicial Construction of New Scientific Evidence', in Paul T. Durbin (ed.), *Critical Perspectives on Nonacademic Science and Engineering* (Bethlehem, PA: Lehigh University Press, 1991), 215–38.

28 Following David Bloor's influential methodological exposition, the key point, of course, is neither to privilege unquestioningly the claims about truth and falsity put forward by particular actors ('impartiality') nor to offer systematically different causal explanations for true and false beliefs ('symmetry'): David Bloor, *Knowledge and Social Imagery* (Chicago, IL: The University of Chicago Press, 2nd edn, 1991), 7.

29 See, for example, Simon Schaffer, 'On Astronomical Drawing', paper presented at the conference on 'Histories of Art – Histories of Science' (Boston & Cambridge, MA, November 1995).

30 For particularly illuminating treatments of the relationship between forms of witnessing and the exercise of power, see Steven Shapin and Simon Schaffer, *Leviathan and the Air-Pump: Hobbes, Boyle, and the Experimental Life* (Princeton, NJ: Princeton University Press, 1985), esp. 55–65; and Yaron Ezrahi, *The Descent of Icarus: Science and the Transformation of Contemporary Democracy* (Cambridge, MA: Harvard University Press, 1990), esp. 67–96.

31 Charles Goodwin, 'Professional Vision', *American Anthropologist*, Vol. 96, No. 3 (September 1994), 606–33.

32 Justice Orton is quoted in a novelistic account of the case by the crime writer Joseph Wambaugh: *The Blooding* (London: Bantam, 1989), 275.

33 Lander & Budowle, op. cit. note 13, 735.

34 Ian Fisher, 'Ruling Allows DNA Testing as Evidence', *New York Times* (30 March 1994), B1.

35 A new technique, 'Rapid Elimination Mass Screening' (REMS), has lowered these costs: Terry Kirby, 'Genetic Testing Breakthrough Allows Mass Screening of Suspects', and 'Faster Genetic Fingerprints Help Police', *The Independent* (London, 26 August 1991), 1, 6. Wambaugh cites a somewhat different figure (£72 for a two-hour blooding): op. cit. note 32, 209.

36 Wambaugh, op. cit. note 32, 214.

37 Among the formal techniques that the law employs for this purpose is the 'chain of custody', establishing the unbroken transfer of physical evidence from the location of the disputed events to the courtroom. A full-blown comparison of the mediations used to produce evidence in science and law could prove instructive.

38 On the importance of language and rhetoric in constructing scientific claims, see Peter R. Dear (ed.), *The Literary Structure of Scientific Argument: Historical Studies* (Philadelphia, PA: University of Pennsylvania Press, 1991).

39 This is the attribute of perception that the Japanese film-maker Kurasawa famously exploited in his classic work, *Rashomon*. On the partial and misleading nature of vision, see also G.K. Chesterton, 'The Man in the Passage', in *Father Brown Stories* (London: Folio Society, 1959), 52–69. Aptly enough for our purposes, the story turns on discrepancies in courtroom testimony by three equally credible witnesses: 'And the figure in the passage, described by three capable and respected men who had all seen it, was a shifting nightmare: one called it a woman, and the other a beast, and the other a devil . . .' (66). As *aficionados* of Father Brown will recall, each man had seen his own reflection in a mirror.

40 The classic account of inscriptions and their role in producing scientific facts is Bruno Latour and Steve Woolgar, *Laboratory Life: The Construction of Scientific Facts* (Princeton, NJ: Princeton University Press, 2nd edn, 1986), esp. 45–53, 89 (n 5), 244–46. Scientists, and for that matter other social actors, make choices in deciding how close to the visual signal they will stay in interpreting it: see Shapin (1995), op. cit. note 19, 264–67, and Trevor J. Pinch, 'Towards an Analysis of Scientific Observation: The Externality and Evidential Significance of Observational Reports in Physics', *Social Studies of Science*, Vol. 15, No. 1 (February 1985), 3–36. On the monopolistic and potentially unlegitimated character of such interpretations, see Shapin, ibid., and Zygmunt Bauman, *Intimations of Postmodernity* (London: Routledge, 1992).

41 Shapin & Schaffer, op. cit. note 30, 55–63. Boyle and his contemporaries drew analogies between experimentation and the legal process. The veracity of both, they noted, could be established by a multiplicity of witnesses, and right actions could be taken on the basis of knowledge so vindicated. Boyle apparently did not have in mind the particular conundrum that would be created by embedding the experimental space – a 'virtual' court of law – within a real legal proceeding, through the vehicle of expert witnessing. This, however, is the quotidian problem of modern law and modern science.

42 Latour, op. cit. note 2.

43 Inscriptions that appear to speak thus plainly to lay spectators may, of course, seem far more problematic to expert interpreters: see Jasanoff, op. cit. note 20, 128–29.

44 Advertising practices offer some evidence to the widespread cultural acceptance of fingerprints as markers of unique identity. Manufacturers of products such as cars and water faucets have employed fingerprints as part of the iconography that distinguishes their products from others. In 1985, the New York State Department of Taxation used the image of a fingerprint to announce an amnesty programme for tax evaders.

45 Simon A. Cole, 'Witnessing Identification: Latent Fingerprinting Evidence and Expert Knowledge', *Social Studies of Science*, Vol. 28, Nos 5–6 (October–December 1998), 687–712.

46 533 So.2d 841 (Fla. App. 5 Dist. 1988), review denied 542 So.2d 1332 (Fla. 1989).

47 *Florida v. Andrews*, transcript of 20 October 1987 (testimony of Dr David E. Housman), 17.

48 599 A.2d 960 (N.J. Super.L. 1991).

49 For an account of the technique's discovery, see Paul Rabinow, *Making PCR* (Chicago, IL: The University of Chicago Press, 1996).

50 *State of New Jersey v. Williams*, transcript of 7 May 1991 (direct examination of Dr Edward T. Blake), 43–44.

51 In modern democratic societies, both the natural and social sciences are therefore simultaneously engaged in creating and satisfying citizens' demands for legitimating demonstrations. See, for example: Ezrahi, op. cit. note 30; Helga Nowotny, 'Knowledge for Certainty: Poverty, Welfare Institutions and the Institutionalization of Social Science', in Peter Wagner, Björn Wittrock and Richard Whitley (eds), *Discourses on Society: The Shaping of the Social Science Disciplines, Sociology of the Sciences Yearbook*, Vol. 15 (Dordrecht: Kluwer, 1990), 23–41; Theodore M. Porter, *Trust in Numbers: The Pursuit of Objectivity in Science and Public Life* (Princeton, NJ: Princeton University Press, 1995).

52 *Williams* transcript, op. cit. note 50, 44.

53 Peter W Huber, *Galileo's Revenge: Junk Science in the Courtroom* (New York: Basic Books, 1991), esp. 192–213; also see Jasanoff, op. cit. note 20, esp. 45–63, 206–10.

54 293 F. 1013 (D.C. Cir. 1923).

55 Jasanoff, op. cit. note 20, 61–62.

56 509 U.S. 579 (1993).

57 For further discussion of the *Daubert* criteria, see Kenneth R. Foster, David E. Bernstein and Peter W. Huber, 'Science and the Toxic Tort', *Science*, Vol. 261 (17 September 1993), 1509, 1614; Foster and Huber, *Judging Science: Scientific Knowledge and the Federal Courts* (Cambridge, MA: The MIT Press, 1997); Bert Black, Francisco Ayala and Carol Saffran Brinks, 'Science and the Law in the Wake of *Daubert*: A New Search for Scientific Knowledge', *University of Texas Law Review*, Vol. 72 (1994), 753–85; John L. Heilbron, 'The Affair of the Countess Gorlitz', *Proceedings of the American Philosophical Society*, Vol. 138 (1994), 284–316; Margaret G. Farrell, '*Daubert v. Merrell Dow Pharmaceuticals, Inc.*: Epistemology and Legal Process', *Cardozo Law Review*, Vol. 15 (1994), 2183–217; Sheila Jasanoff, 'Beyond Epistemology: Relativism and Engagement in the Politics of Science', *Social Studies of Science*, Vol. 26, No. 2 (May 1996), 393–418; Adina Schwartz, 'A Dogma of "Empiricism" Revisited: *Daubert v. Merrell Dow Pharmaceuticals, Inc.* and the Need to Resurrect the Philosophical Insight of *Frye v. United States*', *Harvard Journal of Law and Technology*, Vol. 10 (1997), 149–237; Anthony Z. Roisman, 'The Courts, *Daubert*, and Environmental Torts: Gatekeepers or Auditors?', *Pace Environmental Law Review*, Vol. 14 (1997), 545–76.

58 Sheila Jasanoff, 'What Judges Should Know about the Sociology of Science', *Jurimetrics*, Vol. 32 (1992), 345–59; Jasanoff, op. cit. notes 20 & 27.

59 *People v. Ojeda*, 225 Cal.App.3d 404 (1990); Jasanoff, op. cit. note 20, 59–61.

60 Goodwin, op. cit. note 31, 606.

61 Ibid., 619–22.
62 Michel Foucault, 'The Order of Discourse', in Robert Young (ed.), *Untying the Text: A Post-Structuralist Reader* (Boston, MA: Routledge & Kegan Paul, 1981), 48–78.
63 *The People v. Orenthal James Simpson* (hereafter cited as '*Simpson* trial'), video of pretrial hearing, 27 July 1994 (author's transcription).
64 Ibid.
65 Shapin & Schaffer, op. cit. note 30.
66 Goodwin, op. cit. note 31, 606.
67 *Simpson* trial, videotape and transcript of admissibility hearing, 23 February 1995.
68 Ibid.
69 Ibid.
70 See, generally, Smith & Wynne (eds), op. cit. note 20. On the issue of DNA evidence and its deconstruction, see Jasanoff (1992), op. cit. note 58, and Jasanoff, op. cit. note 20, 55–57.
71 The issue subsequently provoked considerable interest in the letter columns of *Science*: see 'DNA Fingerprinting' (Letters), *Science*, Vol. 247 (2 March 1990), 1018–19.
72 Lander & Budowle, op. cit. note 13, 735.
73 I am here drawing on, but also extending, the valuable work in science studies on scientists' repertoires of challenge and justification: see, in particular, G. Nigel Gilbert and Michael Mulkay, *Opening Pandora's Box: A Sociological Analysis of Scientists' Discourse* (Cambridge: Cambridge University Press, 1984); H.M. Collins, *Changing Order: Replication and Induction in Scientific Practice* (London: Sage Publications, 1985).
74 This is not to say that there is any universal agreement among scientists, or presumably among laypeople, as to what constitutes an adequate control in experimental practice: see Sheila Jasanoff, *The Fifth Branch: Science Advisers as Policymakers* (Cambridge, MA: Harvard University Press, 1990), 75–76.
75 Zachary R. Dowdy, 'A Ruling vs. DNA Evidence', *Boston Globe* (12 March 1996), 1.
76 Consider, for example, the different standards for scientific misconduct that came into play during the investigation of MIT biologist Thereza Imanishi-Kari in the so-called Baltimore case: Daniel Kevles, 'The Assault on David Baltimore', *New Yorker* (27 May 1996), 94–109.
77 Shapin (1995), op. cit. note 19, 268–71. My views here run counter to those of Luhmann and Giddens, as represented by Shapin.
78 Standardized collection methods are equally essential to the project of making credible scientific data, inscriptions, and measurements out of nature's raw materials. For more on this point, especially on the significance of protocols and logbooks, see Bruno Latour, 'The "Pédofil" of Boa Vista', *Common Knowledge*, Vol. 4, No. 1 (Spring 1995), 144–87.
79 The manual in question apparently was an edition of Barry A.J. Fisher, *Techniques of Crime Scene Investigation* (New York: Elsevier, 5th edn, 1992).
80 *Simpson* trial, transcript of 12 April 1995 (testimony of Dennis Fung).
81 Lander & Budowle, op. cit. note 13, 735.
82 Jeffrey Toobin, 'Ito and the Truth School', *New Yorker* (27 March 1995), 42–48. As the trial wore on, straining patience as well as resources, Toobin's flattering picture of Ito yielded to a more ambivalent one that stressed his indecisiveness and lack of energy.
83 Jasanoff, op. cit. note 20, 66–67, 221–22.
84 AAAS-ABA National Conference of Lawyers and Scientists, 'Enhancing the Availability of Reliable and Impartial Scientific and Technical Expertise to the Federal Courts', Report to the Carnegie Commission on Science, Technology and Government (Washington, DC, September 1991).
85 Lord Harry Woolf, *Access to Justice: Final Report* (London: HMSO, 1995).
86 139 L.Ed.2d 508 (1997).

87 Bruno Latour, *Science in Action* (Cambridge, MA: Harvard University Press, 1987), 96–100.

88 See, for instance, Rorty's claim that the 'hardness of fact . . . is simply the hardness of the previous agreements within a community about the consequences of a certain event': Richard Rorty, 'Texts and Lumps', in his *Objectivity, Relativism, and Truth* (Cambridge: Cambridge University Press, 1991), 78–92, at 80.

13 In a constitutional moment

Science and social order at the millennium[*]

New worlds to order

Strolling east along the splendid swath of Constitution Avenue, beyond the recessed lawns of the White House, diagonally across from the back entrance to the National Gallery of Art, the visitor to Washington, D.C. will be drawn to a building whose soaring Corinthian columns signal the presence of something exceptional within. Inside, under the hushed central rotunda of the National Archives of the United States, the now-curious visitor may take her place in the slow-moving line of tourists for a brief glimpse of the three documents that anchor the American state: the Constitution, the Bill of Rights, and the Declaration of Independence. Encased in thick, greenish, helium-filled, bronze and glass frames, elevated on a marble pedestal, the faded parchments are barely readable in the dim, protective light. It is hard to linger long enough to decipher the script; the guards take care to keep the line moving. But the entire setting – the heroic murals,[1] the sober display cases around the circular gallery, the inlaid floor and monumental architecture – encourages a feeling of reverence. This is no ordinary public space; it is the closest thing to a holy of holies in this brashly populist, secular republic.

Yet the ironic observer would note more than a touch of incongruity in the deferential encounter between the spectators and the objects of their veneration. The soft lighting and expensive, high-tech display (the documents descend into an impregnable vault by night) are theater at its postmodern best. The nation whose representatives stream by in all their heterogeneity of sex, race, religion, color, and attire is scarcely recognizable as the one whose blueprints the documents register. Fewer than half the visitors to the National Archives could have voted in the polity contemplated by the founding fathers who look gravely down from their painted murals (Keyssar 2000). Among the visitors are people whose admission to American citizenship would have occasioned a skeptical raising of the eyebrow, if not a shiver of fear, among the sedate gentlemen who wrote those grand, nation-building texts. Their genius, if we choose that term, seems in retrospect to have lodged in what they left unsaid – in a choice of words so flexible that it accommodated an onrush of diversity and change which the authors' imaginations could scarcely have apprehended.

While the written Constitution sits enshrined in glass and stone – and, fittingly, inert gases – it is the practices of government based on the founding texts that have done the most to ensure the republic's survival. For more than two hundred years, the thrust and parry of American political life have been directed toward filling the blanks left open by those historic documents. Judicial decisions played a central role. Early in the nineteenth century, Chief Justice John Marshall's bold decisions in *Marbury v. Madison* and *McCulloch v. Maryland* affirmed the power of judicial review and of Congress to make necessary and proper laws. In the process, Marshall helped establish the proposition that significant political innovation can occur without explicit constitutional reauthorization. Closer to our own day, other landmark rulings of the high court, such as *Brown v. Board of Education of Topeka* on school desegregation and *Roe v. Wade* on abortion rights, have struggled to redefine the rights of persons whose color, gender or, in the case of the unborn, physical invisibility deprived them of status in eighteenth century political life. Still more recently, some credit Chief Justice William Rehnquist with envisioning and carrying through a fundamental reorientation in favor of states' rights on issues such as sovereign immunity and separation of church and state. Between the legal milestones of judicial review and school desegregation, a bloody civil war was fought to cement the origin myth of a nation conceived with such brilliant foresight that its founding principles have survived intact, even though the texture of its public life has changed beyond recognition.

The reality of American politics belies the felt continuity of the founders' vision. Judicial creativity, however, has not been the only instrument of fundamental reform. Over two centuries, American state-society relations have been deeply affected by inventiveness in quite another quarter – science and technology. The principles underpinning the American state were drafted by representatives of a pre-industrial, almost pre-scientific, agrarian society. Since their day, revolutionary changes have occurred in the organization of commerce and industry (Ratner, Soltow and Sylla 1979), spurred by radical shifts in transportation, communication, medicine, finance, and manufacturing. Railroads once thickly webbed the country and then largely disappeared, replaced by highways and, eventually, the aerial routes of civil aviation. Telegraph and electric power lines (Hughes 1983) formed prototypes for today's virtual communication networks. Nuclear power came and went (maybe to return), while the Internet gave newspapers, telephones, and even television a run for their money. Holistic thinking about the environment became fashionable, linked to the growth of ecology, the discovery of chemical hazards, and the birth of commercial biotechnology. Meanwhile, in medicine, human beings were increasingly seen as composites of separately treatable body parts, mental states, genes, tissues, and organs. Technology revolutionized the conduct of war, as the United States, along with a handful of other nations, acquired the capacity to destroy humanity, and earned therewith a vastly stronger hold on the imagination of its citizens.

Since the scientific revolution, the legal and political institutions of the United States, as of other major powers, have changed in keeping with shifting perceptions of the natural world and the capacity to intervene in its processes. So, too, have citizens' self-awareness, expectations of each other, and the norms that reflect these altered perceptions. This coupled development of natural and social orders has, if anything, gained speed and salience as the world narrows. Science and technology, I will argue in this essay, are playing a constitutive role in determining how power will be exercised – and, equally important, constrained – in the emerging global order. In particular, the entanglement of science and technology in three processes of globalization are broad and deep enough, in my view, to merit the label 'constitutional': the redefinition of self, identity, and community; the appearance of the consumer as a political agent, asserting rights claims against commerce and industry; and the certification of 'global' knowledge for use in supranational governance. Through these three prisms, we can see how previously taken-for-granted roles of citizens, corporations, and social movements, as well as their relationships with governmental institutions, are being reconceptualized. Human engagements with science and technology, I suggest, are altering the very foundations of identity, citizenship, and sovereignty, thus silently laying the groundwork for constitutional governance in the 21st century.

Understanding these phenomena is critically important for legal and political theory, but standard analytic tools in these fields need to be supplemented by perspectives from the systematic study of science and technology. In place of the structural formalism and epistemological realism that have marked much orthodox legal and political scholarship, science studies offers a dynamic, constructivist, practice-centered approach that is better suited to analyzing the distributed processes of global constitution-making. Below, I begin by reviewing the contemporary discourses of constitutional change, noting their commonalities and differences. I then reflect on the understandings of law and lawlike processes in the science studies literature, and the treatment of science and technology in legal and constitutional doctrine. With these discussions in place, I turn to the three most prominent nodes at which science and legal order are joined in processes of co-production: identity-making; consumption and citizenship; and global knowledge production. In concluding, I address the implications of these developments for democracy in a post-national future.

How constitutions change

As the United States takes its first uncertain steps across the threshold of a new millennium, one senses that constitutional changes are abroad in the world. Some perceive it in the waning of federal authority and the growing popular alienation from institutions of national governance (Sandel 1996; Nye, Zelikow and King 1997).[2] The extraordinary U.S. presidential election of 2000 confirmed these fears for many: a polled-to-death public split its votes with such stunning accuracy that a statistician from Mars could plausibly have modeled the American electorate as millions of coins tossed in unison (Jasanoff 2001). Europeans deplore the 'democratic deficit' in European Union (EU) institutions (Eder and Kantner 2000) and growing voter apathy in national elections. Others worry that the rise of transnational legal regimes and bureaucracies will sap national autonomy and jeopardize national welfare (Darman 1978; consider also President George W. Bush's retreat from the Kyoto climate change accord so as to protect the American economy[3]). Theorists of sovereignty have focused on the displacement of the state by multinational corporations and global media that have rendered normal modes of participation and politics increasingly irrelevant. Still others see the issue in terms of the formation of new identities and grassroots alliances, creating social movements that do not respect the geopolitical claims of the nation-state. Indeed, as the attacks of September 11, 2001 in the United States so horrifically demonstrated, the devolution of power to non-state actors has shaken fundamental presumptions about what makes a state a state.

Does all this turmoil point only to the decay of existing orders or also to a more optimistic future for constitution-making? It is clear, particularly in the era of globalization, that it is not necessary to hold a formal convention in order to rewrite the fundamental presumptions that bind people to their political authorities. As U.S. experience indicates, radical shifts in social order do not have to originate with, or even be confirmed by, explicit constitutional amendment. Britain's 'unwritten constitution' offers an even clearer example. On the world stage as well, revolutions can and do happen without the benefit of constitutional ratification – as when the Cold War's bipolar order collapsed in 1989. But how do old constitutional dispensations change, and how do new ones emerge? Let us look at three sets of responses, at the levels of national, regional, and global politics. While each offers valuable insights into processes of constitutional change, I suggest that there is need for a fourth model, more suited to times of emergence and more respectful of human involvement with science and technology. This last, I will argue, is a bottom-up approach to constitution-making that has particular significance for global governance in the 21st century.

American history offers an instructive starting point for thinking about constitutional change. In more than two centuries, the U.S. Constitution has undergone only the barest modifications[4]; the text the founders wrote is still the text that schoolchildren study and the Supreme Court pays homage to. Constitutional rights are regarded as among the most cherished elements of national life – to be held, as far as possible, constant, and defended against the corrosive effects of time and social change. Not everyone, however, sees this continuity as real, let alone as reason for bemoaning the end of constitutional creativity. Bruce Ackerman (1983, 1991, 1998), in particular, has influentially argued that the apparent durability of the constitutional order is a major achievement of America's living democracy. At three 'constitutional moments' – the Founding, Reconstruction, and the New Deal – Ackerman believes that revolutionary reform was achieved through inspired but 'unconventional' adaptation of existing institutions and practices. Politicians actuated by transforming ideals successfully claimed to speak on behalf of 'the people' and repositioned the building blocks of government to fit their grandly unorthodox visions.

A different constitutional challenge confronts Europe. Here we have not so much the problem of an ossified, and ossifying, founding text as a search for doctrines to legitimate rule at a higher level than the nation-state. The European constitutional debate is, in this respect, particularly relevant to global constitutionalism. It springs from a similar well-spring of concern: the interests of peace, security, and economic stability seem increasingly to require stronger integration across countries, via new supranational institutions; yet, the cause of democracy seems to be better served through the communal structures long cultivated by nation-states, and hence to favor at best intergovernmental accords (Goldmann 2001, 1–3). This predicament has given rise to more than one school of thought. It has made some European constitutional scholars insist on a minimalist approach, based on carefully prescribed, formal powers delegated to the supranational organs by participating nation-states. This formula would locate the European constitutional framework within the treaties constituting the EU. Reluctance to expand constitutionalism beyond such intergovernmental arrangements stems from a perception, especially among German scholars, that 'Europe' remains for now a notional political space. It lacks a common language or traditions and common media of communication that would enable a fully *European* democracy to form. Pressing for a closer union strikes these observers as unrealistic and threatening to democratic principles (Grimm 1995).

Against the 'constitution deniers,' another school of thought favors a more positive approach to European constitutionalism. The aim of such an exercise, according to Neil Walker (1996), would be to seek out and address in a coherent fashion three sets of questions about the structure of the EU. These concern the logic of the Union (intergovernmental or supranational), the 'democratic deficit,' and the degree of allowable variation among member states. Walker (1996, 288) does not minimize the difficulty of this task: "How, then, is it possible to develop the agenda for the construction of a constitutional identity for a novel political order which draws upon structural principles which are equally capable of resisting reversion to the old sovereign state and progression to a new sovereign super-state?" The answer for him and other modest constitutionalists of the EU lies in developing a mid-range of concepts, such as subsidiarity, that will permit new ways of bridging law and politics. Empirical contexts for this discussion will be found in the intricacies of market integration, currency-making, border security, and comitology rules.

Despite its structural ambiguities and potential, the EU remains at bottom a union built on the sovereign will of nation-states. Globalization connotes something altogether different. It points to the emergence of an ordered political realm that, by definition, supersedes nations. If such a transcendental formation is indeed in the making, can it, too, be said to rest on constitutional foundations? Michael Hardt and Antonio Negri (2000) emphatically answer 'yes' in their ambitious thesis that what we are witnessing at the turn of the millennium is not globalization but the birth of 'Empire.' The order that is coming into being is not, on their account, a Bretton Woods-style piecing together of separate national sovereignties, with power consolidated in international institutions such as the United Nations system. Rather, it more nearly resembles the ancient Roman Empire, a world-formation with its force-fields lying outside the control of even the United States, the only genuine superpower.

The new global Empire, according to Hardt and Negri, has its own constitutional order, but its elements are far different from the institutional building blocks that U.S. or European politicians play with at Ackerman's 'constitutional moments.' Expressing the will of the people has little to do with the constitution of Empire. Hardt and Negri view the imperial constitution as something immanent and unstoppable, almost apocalyptic. It descends from the historian Polybius' theory of Roman government, which saw power as institutionally divided among three centers of action: force with the monarchy; justice and virtue with the aristocracy; and discipline and distribution with the people, or the demos. In modern constitutional systems, these authors argue, this ancient triad was replaced by the functionally tripartite structure of the executive, the judiciary, and the legislature. Now, however, we are caught in another transition – this time toward a 'hybrid constitution' (Hardt and Negri 2000, 316–19), in which the old governmental functions are so networked and distributed as to operate simultaneously everywhere, and therefore nowhere.

The constitutional theater for Hardt and Negri (2000, 319) is an 'imperial non-place.' The transformation they describe occurs almost independent of political will, in defiance of locality, and without discernible ties to social practice or agency. All this is as alien to the temper of Ackerman's analysis as it is to the debates about European constitutionalism. If Hardt and Negri, the theoreticians of Empire, take the high road of constitutional abstraction, the U.S. and European debates can be seen in some ways as taking the low road. Legal traditions, whether in Europe or the United States, view constitutional change in more situated terms, which are in principle more congenial to scholarship in science and technology studies: lodged in particular texts, mobilized by particular actors, and implemented by particular institutions of law and politics.

Yet in one respect all the constitutional discourses we have considered thus far have something in common that differentiates them from most work on the practices of science. Constitutional theorists mostly conceive of change as coming from above, whether through Hardt and Negri's imperial structural realignments, Europe's self-abnegating sovereign states, or Ackerman's inspired judicial and political innovators. But – paralleling Kuhn's (1962) famous argument about scientific revolutions – deep social change can also come about through countless smaller adjustments and accommodations that restructure the basic organization of power. Both kinds of change marked the end of the millennium: the former attracted more notice, but the latter may prove more democratic and durable. Many of these incremental movements were tied in crucial ways to developments in science and technology.

The role of science and technology in the making and unmaking of political order has been largely neglected by political theorists. To be sure, American conventional wisdom attributed the Soviet system's downfall to a form of technology policy: specifically, to President Reagan's determined pursuit of the Strategic Defense Initiative ('Star Wars'), and the resulting costly intensification of the arms race in the 1980s. But this ruinous story of a bankrupt Soviet state further impoverished in search of a bankrupt technology is just another change rung on the all-too-familiar theme of technological determinism: just as 'good' technology drives progress so 'bad' technology, in the Soviet case, brought disaster. Nor have attempts to explain the end of the Cold War in ideological terms proved more satisfying. The fall of the iron curtain was heralded as the 'end of history' (Fukuyama 1992), signifying the demise of the planning state (Scott 1998) and the universal acceptance of the market as the only viable template for economic and social organization. But the stark dichotomy between state and market drawn by many political commentators scarcely does justice to the incredibly complex infrastructures that grew up to undergird both in the modern era. Characteristically, too, deterministic, single-variable explanations of the Soviet system's collapse have offered few insights into the diversity of post-revolutionary orders that sprouted on the dustheaps of an abandoned ideology.

Overall, political accounts of the Cold War's end have displayed little of the subtlety discernible in recent scholarship on technological change (see, for example, Smith and Marx 1994). Yet the tools developed for the study of large technological systems could profitably be adapted to the analysis of such massive social achievements as a state or an ideology, whether they succeed or fail (Latour 1990) Such constructs, no less than fighter planes or power plants, are pieced together from myriad material and social elements that work more or less well together; survival depends on the harmonious functioning of the parts with the whole. Either progressive innovation or radical breakdown could originate, on this account, at multiple points in the system, through agents who question power by political or other means (scientific claims, for instance). Of interest then are the circumstances that permit revolutionary ideas to form and to spread through systems built on other expectations – possibly achieving constitutional status.

What kinds of futures, or communities, are likely to be imagined, and by whom, as we move from a world organized along strict ideological divisions to one where the market now seems rampant? If commitment to nationhood was the glue that held together the dominant cultural identities of the nineteenth and twentieth centuries (Anderson 1991 [1983]), how will the socially and politically significant identities of the coming decades be organized and cemented? How will the new technologies of desire – biological, digital, miniaturized to the nano level – affect identity and agency in the societies of the twenty-first century? With threats of annihilation temporarily in abeyance, and with hunger and poverty receding in many parts of the world, on what basis will people articulate their needs and demands in relation to the formal structures of government? If unwritten and emergent rules of constitutional dimension are beginning to operate in the post-cold-war order, where can we observe these rules being crafted?

Clearly, it is not sufficient to look for answers only in the high politics of globalization, as enacted in international treaties or articulated in the expansion and management of global markets. To comprehend the new constitutional settlements that may be appearing at this historical moment, we must also focus on the ways in which civil societies are responding to novel, technologically mediated possibilities of prediction, manipulation, and interconnectedness. First, however, we must position this analysis with respect to two other relevant bodies of thought:

the discussion of constitutionalism in science and technology studies, and the discussion of technoscientific change in legal scholarship.

Science studies and constitutional law: minding the gap

Given the centrality of scientific knowledge and technological artifacts in contemporary life, it is reasonable to think that the basic ordering commitments of modern societies will be found not only in legal texts, but also, tacitly expressed, in the very organization of life around the products of human ingenuity and knowledge. Constitutional ideas should be embedded in people's collective imaginations and practices, built into their material culture, and worked out in innumerable daily routines that draw upon resources derived from science and technology. Order may emerge not merely, or even mainly, when positive law bestows it or a court affirms it, but also when people assume that they have the capacity and the right to change their behavior in fundamental ways, and act accordingly. Thus, there may be emergent, quasi-constitutional rights that no court has declared nor legislature has decreed, but that are created through altered popular conceptions of what sorts of people we have a right to be, or what we have a right to demand from our ruling institutions. In technologically advanced societies, such changed expectations are commonly associated with transformations in scientific knowledge and advances in technological capability.

To date, however, academic literatures have done relatively little to probe these structuring effects. The theme of scientific and technological progress is not new, of course, any more than its dialectical counterpart, the theme of humanity's problematic adjustment to its own inventions. Both have figured in significant streams of work – analytic, imaginative, minatory, prescriptive – over at least two centuries. On the positive side, are innumerable biographies of inventors and scientists, celebrations of their discoveries, and tales of science's triumph over adversity and disease. On the negative side are many forebodings. Mary Shelley's 1816 'ghost story,' *Frankenstein*, brilliantly captured the terror of runaway scientific ingenuity; today, her concerns persist, under the headings of playing god, flirting with doomsday machines or surrendering to forces outside the creator's control. Philosophers and political theorists have warned of the dangers of hyperrationality and its corrosive effects on deliberation, civic engagement, and individual liberty (Habermas 1975 [1973]; Bauman 1991). The human sciences in particular, as Michel Foucault's oeuvre compellingly documents, can function as disciplinary tools by which governmental power is dispersed throughout society, although these sciences may also open up new possibilities for human creativity (Foucault 1971 [1966], 1979). Still another line of work reflects on the risks and uncertainties of new technologies, and how they permeate the social structures of modernity (Giddens 1991; Beck 1992 [1986]). From outside the western world have come denunciations of science and technology as instruments of dominance, even of violence (Shiva 1993, 1997; Visvanathan 1997). Together, these explorations have done much to destabilize the myth of scientific and technological progress, but in one respect they lack the power of the popular narrative: they reveal deep problems of governance in technological civilization, but they provide few insights into how good orders are achieved. Criticism undoes the complacency of unreflective optimism, but it does not rebuild confidence.

Work in science and technology studies has begun to change this picture by documenting – very generally – how the products of science and technology not only influence but are also shaped by human norms and institutions (Jasanoff et al. 1995). Technological objects, such as ozone holes, genes, smart bombs, computers, climate models, and Dolly, the category-defying sheep cloned from the cells of an adult 'mother,' are all seen by S&TS researchers as repositories of human commitments about what counts as 'good,' whether in reasoning, in making things, or simply in living with one another (Latour and Woolgar 1979; Bijker, Hughes and Pinch 1987; Latour 1988, 1993; MacKenzie 1990; Haraway 1991, 1997). The deployment of technological artifacts engages with and reshapes our perception of social order at many levels: for instance, by redrawing the boundaries between humans and non-humans or nature and culture (Callon 1986, 1987; Latour 1993); by altering fundamental notions of identity (Haraway 1997); and by challenging settled expectations of liberty and autonomy (Jasanoff 1995a).

Among S&TS scholars, Bruno Latour has been perhaps most explicit in calling attention to the constitutional dimension of these human accommodations with the products of science and technology. In his important 1993 monograph, *We Have Never Been Modern*, Latour described the considerable work that human societies do to 'purify' their world of technoscientific hybrids into separate spheres of nature and culture. He termed the resulting settlement 'constitutional' because it deals with one of the most fundamental divisions of social experience: that between 'us' humans and 'other' non-humans, be they animate or inanimate. For Latour the metaphysician, the world of objects is always full of social meaning and normative power. A mundane object such as a speed bump (or a 'sleeping policeman') performs, as its colloquial name implies, functions that are essentially human, albeit rendered without human consciousness. Yet, by locating this construct of earth and asphalt squarely in the domain of inert nature, we, the agents of modernity, set aside any need to reflect on the thing's moral status or the nature of its relationship with us. The world, Latour implies, would be an altogether different place, maybe more terrifying and less ordered, if technological objects were continually reinvested with human characteristics, as nature habitually was in pre-modern societies.

Provocative though these insights are, the regime of sharp demarcations that Latour attributes to modernity markedly contrasts with the fluidity and ambiguity of technoscientific constructs noted by other S&TS scholars (Cambrosio, Keating and Mackenzie 1990; Haraway 1991, 1997; Mol and Law 1994). Like any universalizing theory, Latour's notion of purification fails to account satisfactorily for the divergences one finds among quasi-constitutional understandings in different times, locations, and cultures. Nature is not perceived in the same way by all modern industrial or industrializing societies: different lines are drawn between humans and other species, and different assumptions are made about the degree of interconnectedness between environment and society. Not surprisingly, when it comes to accepting or rejecting particular technological achievements, disparate ideas of what is 'natural' or morally right drive social responses, leading to divergent appraisals of the same processes or artifacts (see, for example, Jasanoff 1995b; Gaskell et al. 1999). In short, the mechanics of demarcation beg for elucidation within specific social, political, and legal contexts. One may ask, in particular, what role prior institutional commitments (including those embedded in formal constitutional law) play in the simplification of hybrid networks into the reductionist framings of *social* and *natural*. Put differently, Latour's constitutional settlement plays itself out in a curiously ahistorical, unsituated, and impersonal space. His constitutionalism is a philosopher's abstraction. To obtain a more textured picture of the ordering power of technoscience, we need to undertake a more grounded inquiry.

Regrettably, legal studies do not instantly provide the hoped for solutions to questions opened by work in science studies. S&TS writings are consistent with the views of a handful of legal scholars working on the intersections of law and technology – for example Lawrence Lessig (1997) on the architecture of information systems, James Boyle (1996) on intellectual property, and Frederick Schauer (1998) on privacy and the Internet – although there has been little systematic conversation between these parallel strands of analysis. For the most part, legal scholarship, limited perhaps by the law's institutional commitments to resolution and finality, has been slow to incorporate the findings of scientific and technological contingency that S&TS research has elaborated over the past thirty years.

There is, accordingly, a noticeable lack of fit between legal discourse and the preoccupations of science studies. Constitutional interpretation makes do with conceptions of liberty, property, human identity and welfare that predate the industrial revolution, let alone today's dazzling developments in genetic, environmental, and information sciences and technologies (Schauer 1998). Rulings that aim specifically to take account of scientific and technological developments – for example, in cases about reproductive privacy, the rights of non-traditional parents, the prolongation of life, the ownership of human tissues, the nature of risk, or the legal status of non-humans (Stone 1974) – show little evidence of engagement with the social and cultural histories of these changes. Indeed, in seeking to defend the fundamental character of constitutional categories, courts and legal commentators often downplay the extent to which our understandings of nature, society and the self have been transformed by two centuries of scientific and technological change.

What makes this lack of reflection on science and technology more puzzling is that legal theory has been hugely influential in bringing to light some of the hidden normative assumptions that underpin supposedly neutral legal rules. Modern versions of Legal Realism, for instance, have refocused the understanding of Realism away from the indeterminacy of rules toward understanding the often-disguised substantive choices embedded in even relatively determinate rules (Fisher, Horwitz and Reed 1993; Fried 1998). Feminist jurisprudence has exposed the gender-based assumptions that undergird much legal doctrine in areas such as property and family law (Bartlett 1990). The Critical Legal Studies movement stressed the ideological contingency of legal propositions that courts often take to be natural and inevitable (Kelman 1987; Kairys 1990). With regard to economic decisions, scholars have questioned the neutrality and inevitability of the 'base-lines' against which constitutional questions are considered. Cass Sunstein (1993) concluded, for example, that the legal distinction between state action and private action presupposes (and hence reinforces) a certain state-created *status quo* that established the boundaries of the *private* to start with.

Despite these turns toward self-reflexivity, legal scholars have not by and large extended their deconstructive and skeptical analysis to the ways in which legal power interacts with the authority of science and technology. An unexamined positivism still marks much writing about scientific evidence, as exemplified by a stream of work criticizing judges, juries, Congress, regulatory agencies, and not least the public for failure to heed the standards of 'good science' (Huber 1991; Breyer 1993; Foster and Huber 1997). Such critiques are often accompanied by triumphalist and historically untenable accounts of technological progress, which represent the law as an awkward impediment to the enlightened march of science. Even at its most sensitive, legal scholarship tends to treat science and law as inde-pendent sources of authority. The two domains are often seen as distinct 'cultures,' with divergent objectives, destined to clash when they occupy themselves with disputes over norms and policy (Schuck 1993; Goldberg 1994). There has been little systematic research on the ways in which modes of authorization in science and the law build upon, mimic or incorporate one another (for some exceptions, all stemming from science studies, see Wynne 1982, 1988, 1989; Smith and Wynne 1989; Jasanoff 1998a,b), even though the historical record suggests that the two cultures have supported each other for centuries in patterns of mutual construction, stabilization, and reinforcement (Shapin and Schaffer 1985; Ezrahi 1990; Shapin 1994; Porter 1995).

More generally, traditional legal inquiry generally takes for granted the boundary between nature and society or knowledge and norms. Laws and rights are held to one side as proper subjects of legal analysis; science and technology on the other side are thought to lie outside the domain of legal expertise. Rights are interpreted as preexisting technology, or at least as lying in an altogether separate normative domain, rather than as being constituted in significant part through technology. Much of the literature on science, technology and the law has thus been framed rather unproblematically in the language of technological deter-minism. Echoing decades-old ideas about culture lagging behind its own inven-tions (Ogburn 1922), law today is frequently seen as lagging behind technology, desperately trying to bridge the gaps created by rapid scientific and technological advances. Thus, genetics and genomics are thought to have leapt ahead, opening new eugenic possibilities, while the law laboriously puzzles out how to protect individual autonomy. Family law is chronically seen as trying to catch up with reproductive technology. According to one account, "genetic testing has made determining paternity simple, even routine . . . But in most states, the law has not caught up with the science" (Lewin 2001). Similarly, the Internet's almost infinite capacity for copying and dissemination is seen as overwhelming the rights of creative authorship. On the whole, technology is conceived of as a threat to rights, which therefore need to be protected through vigilant enforcement of constitutional norms. The analysis of science and technology in the politics of globalization demands more deftly manipulable conceptual categories.

Constructive constitutionalism

I have argued thus far that the constitutional formations of the era of globalization are growing not only from roots in law and politics, but also from human accommodations with science and technology. Neither science studies nor legal theory offer fully satisfying models of sustained inquiry into the ordering effects of technological change. The former has insufficiently engaged with cultural specificity and institutionalized power, while the latter has underemphasized the contingency of knowledge and the law's own role in underwriting science and technology. To find a way forward, we need to step outside the perimeters of current theory and look more closely at the ways in which actors are constructing the present world. Let us return to basic constitutional notions and ask how they are playing out in the global diffusion of science and technology.

In charting this territory, it is best to work with a flexible notion of constitutionalism that is not tied to specific institutional arrangements or codes of law. Constitutions are at bottom balance wheels between power and its abuse. They are devices for ensuring "a form of rule which both empowers a government to carry out the range of functions associated with the modern interventionist state and excludes arbitrary and despotic forms of rule" (Walker 1996, 270). In the postnational era, we may extend this notion of constitutional order by including, in the class of possible rulers, not only governments but other forms of authority that also have power to control people's lives. But the heart of constitutionalism remains the preservation of balance: between enabling and constraining power, and between individual and societal demands. Under each heading, constitutional jurisprudence clarifies and codifies certain communally sanctioned norms regarding what is worth protecting, for and against whom, by what means, to what extent, and through what processes. Laurence Tribe (1978) has referred to these principled substructures as 'models' of constitutionalism. These models, needless to say, respond to developments in science and technology by taking on board changing conceptions of such norms as 'unreasonable search and seizure,' 'privacy' or 'property rights' – all of which are affected by technologically mediated changes in human and social capability.

Yet, this account of constitutionalism leaves untouched certain fundamental ontological problems that are central to the law. What kind of entity, after all, is the state, whose powers constitutions seek to delimit, and what sorts of beings are the individuals whose rights are protected against improper state action? Other puzzles flow from these. Where do judicial beliefs about how to answer these questions stem from? How are the ideas held by courts connected to broader currents of public knowledge and understanding, or to that special branch of knowledge called science? And on what basis should courts decide when some models of constitutional decisionmaking, such as regard for settled expectations or governmental regularity (Tribe's Models III and IV), come into conflict with novel expectations arising from science?

It is here, at the level of constitutionalism's most elementary conceptual units, that we can profitably begin to inquire into the influence of science and technology. To tease out the connections, it is essential to look beyond the formal principles laid down in legal texts and elucidated by courts. We must ask instead how norms of constitutional relevance are tacitly constructed in the daily hum of technological societies: norms that are embodied in technological standards and practices, hardened into material instruments and artifacts, entrenched within professional discourses, and legitimated through public policy. Areas of rapid technoscientific change, as in the fields of genetics, informatics, and environmental science, offer specially promising sites for this kind of interpretive inquiry. Of particular interest are current debates about the self and its entitlements, the rights of the citizen-consumer against centers of private (market) power, and the legitimacy of supranational institutions of knowledge and governance.

Self, identity, community

When the *New York Times* criticizes the law for lagging behind science, what normative position does it seek to convey? We know that paternity can be determined today on the basis of almost foolproof, biological tests that indicate whether a given child is the progeny of the man alleged to be the father.[5] A series of cases involving such tests have come before the U.S. courts, in the form of claims by 'fathers' who discovered their lack of biological kinship to their supposed offspring, sometimes after years of living together in a trusting family relationship. In ruling on these claims, courts have juggled in different ways with the values of genetic and social kinship, support for minor children, respect for reproductive freedom, protection of economic rights, and deterrence of fraud. Not surprisingly, the outcomes look chaotic, more like *ad hoc* accommodations to the facts of the case than like principled rule-following. What principle could possibly explain why a Texas court denies a man visitation rights, but requires him to pay child support for children who are not biologically his (Lewin 2001)? Proponents of the 'law lag' theory would prefer to cut through this tangle and write the scientific 'truth' of paternity unambiguously into the law. Biology should define paternity.

Such an argument not only elevates technological (or technoscientific) determinism to a normative principle (technology *should* drive the law), but it misconceives the subtlety of the connections among science, law, and human agency in constitutional cultures. The novel meanings of selfhood, identity, and community that mark this period of social ferment owe their shape as much to the legal and political contexts in which they originated as they do to breakthroughs in science and technology. These new configurations reflect our ability to see and explain human identity and behavior in altered ways, with the aid of new scientific categories and instruments. But, equally, they are a product of our ability to imagine and enforce preferred identities through culturally sanctioned legal and political means. The Texan 'father' who wished to withdraw support from his no longer biological children – but who might have wished to keep on visiting them – was asserting a sense of kinship that was simultaneously biological and social. His rights were not already present in transcendental form, ready to be 'declared' by a court or conformed to the dictates of science. Rather, like all the newly indeterminate fathers of the genetic testing age, he was a player in a complicated ritual to redefine the meaning of paternity in a time when biological kinship can be dissociated from social kinship at any point in a family's existence. Genetic information, even in this simple context, does not determine identity so much as it enables new identity claims to unfurl.

In other cases, individuals have seized upon genetic information as an instrument of liberation or for building more complex identities and group affiliations. Their behavior confounds the theme of genetic determinism that was current in film and fiction long before the birth of the cloned sheep Dolly at a Scottish research station in February 1997. The older 'technoscientific imaginaries' of genetics were colonized by fears of state control. Aldous Huxley (1946) gave these fears their classic articulation in *Brave New World*, where people were classified and bred for characteristics esteemed by those in power. Throughout the 1980s, academic writing on the coming genetic revolution similarly dwelt on the risks of manipulation and control in connection with techniques of genetic screening, testing, and gene therapy. In the 1990s, however, the reception of genes into culture followed a more complicated script, as people actively asserted claims based on seeing themselves through newly available genetic lenses. Science and law blended into unexpected projects of social action.

Disease groups were perhaps the most prominent, though not the only, early adopters of genetic technology (Callon 1999). The discovery of genes for heritable breast cancer (BRCA1 and 2) led women activists in Britain and the United States to demand greater access to genetic tests and genetic counseling. PXE International, a citizen group committed to finding a cure for the inherited disorder *pseudoxanthoma elasticum (PXE)*, participated in the isolation of the disease-causing gene, set up its own blood and tissue bank, and in an unprecedented move, even filed for a patent on the gene (Smaglik 2000). And in August 2001, stories circulated of a privately held corporation, the San Francisco-based DNA Copyright Institute, that had urged stars and celebrities to copyright their DNA so as to prevent commercial entrepreneurs from producing genetic copies of their valuable 'original' selves. In all these cases, genetic knowledge was appropriated as an added resource for people's self-expression, not as a weapon of control by the state.

To be sure, the possible negative consequences of reading people genetically did not disappear from view, but neither did those potentially affected passively await subjugation. Genetic exploitation emerged as a new front in the longstanding liberation struggles of workers, women, and ethnic and racial minorities against oppression by dominant economic and political interests. Rhetorics of piracy, colonialism and genocide, for example, were invoked and extended in protests by indigenous peoples' organizations against researchers engaged in bioprospecting for rare, medicinally active plants or in devising protocols for sampling human genetic diversity (Reardon 2001). In these cases, social groups claiming fundamental legal rights – representation, equality of treatment, access to various state-sponsored benefits – were created, or reconfigured, through the strategic intertwining of genetics and the law.

Technoscientific activity beyond the life sciences also contributed to movements of self-expression and resistance. One of the darkest manifestations was the apparently self-willed conversion of human beings into missiles and weapons on September 11, 2001, and in the subsequent rash of Palestinian suicide bombings in Israel. These acts, conducted outside the bounds of 'normal' war, turned the narrative of technological progress into a mockery of itself, transforming people into objects, freedom into destruction, and sites of communal life into sites of carnage. That technology can kill was not the novelty here. Rather, it was the rational subject's purposeful embracing of an object-identity, and the resulting human-weapon's denial of compassion, pity or regard for its accidental victims or itself.

Other developments were less uniquely horrible. Information technology substantially lowered the barriers to worldwide communication and thereby facilitated creative processes of identity transformation. Instantaneous electronic communication and the spread of the personal computer made it possible to mobilize communal passions or communal loyalties, cutting across established lines of social identification in unpredictable ways. In cyberspace, states no longer enjoyed a monopoly on the channels of communication. The Internet diluted the power of national governments to command the 'imagined communities' of their citizens (Anderson 1991 [1983]). All manner of organizations could now control a piece of virtual territory, from disease-based groups like PXE International to the Taliban, the Islamic fundamentalists who ruled Afghanistan until after the terrorist attacks of September 11. Using electronic media, non-state actors bypassed the entrenched power of orthodox print and television media to build new group identities and affiliations, supplementing the ties of nationhood.

Some highly stable identities ceded ground, or became blurred, as new opportunities for self-identification were delineated. In the realm of gender, for example, 'transgendered' identities, neither male nor female, were said to have gained ground in the 1990s, partly assisted by the Internet:

> The movement's coalescence, which members say began over the last five years and accelerated in recent months, has gained particular momentum from the Internet, with its ability to connect far-flung people and afford them a sense of safety. On-line groups that began by swapping tips on using makeup and obtaining hormones now also spread word of the latest victims of violence and the next political protest (Goldberg 1996).

The success of various resurgent ethnic fundamentalisms – Jewish, Islamic, Hindu – can similarly be attributed, in part, to the ability of interests back home to tap into the memories, grievances, and (not least) deep pockets of the far-flung representatives of national diasporas (Anderson 1994). New hybrid categories of nationhood (e.g., Non-Resident Indian or NRI) have emerged, extending citizenship outside the borders of the nation-state.[6] Controversies over female Muslim students' right to wear head coverings in French schools or British Muslims' demand for access to state-funded, religious schools illustrate some of the more prosaically constitutional dimensions of these developments.

Corporate rulers, consuming citizens

Redefinitions of individual identity and community form only one strand of quasi-constitutional change in which science and technology are centrally implicated. A second important thread is the assertion of some of the rights of citizenship by consumers against powerful corporations. There is a growing sense that today's formal constitutions do not offer adequate conceptual tools for ordering relations between individuals and private corporations, particularly when corporate operations extend across many national boundaries. Once again, action from below, by potential consumers of technoscience, has underlined the problems and focused attention on the need for solutions.

U.S. constitutional jurisprudence long since recognized that corporate power may not be exercised in ways that thwart legitimate public goals. Even property rights are not held to be sacrosanct if asserting such rights would unacceptably burden the public's lawfully sanctioned liberties. Thus, in his historic 1946 opinion in *Marsh v. Alabama*, holding that a company town could not prohibit the distribution of religious literature on its premises, Justice Hugo Black observed that

> Ownership does not always mean absolute dominion. The more an owner, for his advantage, opens up his property for use by the public in general, the more do his rights become circumscribed by the statutory and constitutional rights of those who use it. Thus, the owners of privately held bridges, ferries, turnpikes and railroads may not operate them as freely as a farmer does his farm. Since these facilities are built and operated primarily to benefit the public, and since their operation is essentially a public function, it is subject to state regulation (citations omitted).[7]

In the great burst of civil rights decisionmaking of the 1950s and 1960s, the Court held that property rights claims could not subvert overriding national goals such as racial desegregation.[8] Cases like these went some distance toward problematizing the boundary between state and corporate action – or between politics and the market. They recognized that claims of private ownership and enterprise are not alone sufficient to justify restrictions on protected public liberties, and that corporate power, when exercised in statelike fashion, needs to be curbed as much as the power of the state.

In formal constitutional jurisprudence, the sense of what constitutes an impermissible constraint on liberty is tied to structuralist notions of power and jurisdiction. The private owner of a company town, or a bridge or railroad operator, or an inn-keeper controls a piece of physical space – like a mini-state – and hence may not deprive persons using those premises or property of fundamental liberties. There is no hint in these cases that technological innovation, historically seen as a motor of progress, can function in ways that equally threaten liberty, without dominion over physical space. Upstream production and marketing decisions by corporations may constrain human behavior down the line as thoroughly as infringements of constitutional rights by the state. By the time products arrive on the market, irreversible ordering commitments have already been built into them that may deprive consumers of important freedoms. Such innovation and design decisions are not open to public questioning or other forms of accountability under existing legal regimes; if anything, they are protected against scrutiny by confidentiality rules and intellectual property rights. The market – which only comes into play when products are already on line – therefore does not function as a good surrogate for democratic control. But cracks have begun to appear in this system as users and consumers assert a more audible voice in the governance of scientific and technological production.

In the aggregate, corporate initiatives in areas like biotechnology, computing, personal communication, surveillance, tourism, and transportation – let alone weapons of mass destruction – hold the potential for a deep restructuring of human behavior. Corporations, too, have in many instances adopted the rhetoric and symbols of statehood, helped along by accidents, deregulation, and management failures that weakened the credibility of states. Thus, DuPont, a U.S.-based multinational chemical company, sought to legitimate itself to wider publics in the late-1990s in terms that straddled the line between product advertising and political campaign pledges. On its website, DuPont embraced the language of sustainability, promising to leave the world no worse off for future generations.[9] A carefully orchestrated barrage of advertisements, built on the slogan 'To Do List for the Planet,' pitched DuPont as a concerned citizen of the world, ready to use its technical know-how (the company's own term was 'knowledge intensity,' as opposed to 'capital intensity') to make life better for untold millions. Like the Hobbesian state committed to defending people against the perils of nature, DuPont promised to protect a global populace against hunger, pollution, and the vagaries of the climate; at the same time, in an appeal to well-heeled consumers, it promised self-cleaning clothes, self-sealing automobile paint, and a material that combines Lycra (a DuPont exclusive) with leather to ensure a poured-on fit. This was no offer to sell a better mousetrap, subject to the laws of supply and demand. DuPont asserted the power and claimed the privileges of an imperial state.

If corporations have taken on the symbolic, rhetorical, and behavioral attributes of states, small wonder that people have found it desirable to assert themselves as citizens against these new centers of power. The idea that major technological shifts should not be undertaken without citizen involvement steadily gained ground in the last decades of the twentieth century. The anti-nuclear protests of the 1970s and 1980s were early indicators of this change in consciousness. The incipient, large-scale commercialization of biotechnology provided further impetus for experimentation with forms of participation and governance. The term 'technology assessment' was taken off the shelf, given a dusting, and harnessed to procedural innovation, particularly in Europe, ironically at the very moment when the United States, a pioneer in this field, dismantled its congressional Office of Technology Assessment (Bimber 1996). Citizen juries, consensus conferences and public referenda were held with varying policy impacts in countries such as Britain, France, Denmark, Japan, and Switzerland (Joss and Durant 1995; Marris and Joly 1999).

By no means all of the deliberative experiments were orchestrated by governments. The politics of biotechnology in the 1990s offers a prime example of newly emancipated consumer behavior. In numerous episodes of resistance against research in plant genetics, activists tore up plots planted with genetically modified (GM) crops. Occurring in both the North (e.g., Britain) and the South (e.g., India), these demonstrations manifested growing reluctance on the part of environmentalists and farmers to accept scientists' assurances that their research was beneficial or even trustworthy. While most biologists continued to insist that agricultural biotechnology posed no threats to human health or the environment, reports of possible risk spread like wildfire through national and international media. In one case, reports by a U.K. scientist that rats experimentally fed GM potatoes showed developmental abnormalities triggered massive consumer rejection of GM products, and changes in British policy toward imports and labeling (Gavaghan 1999; Masood 1999). In another case, a U.S. researcher's finding that pollen from GM corn harmed monarch butterfly larvae received worldwide press, even though both scientists and industry dismissed the study design as too badly flawed for use in risk assessment. Nonetheless, when so-called anti-globalization forces took to the streets in Seattle, Washington and elsewhere around the millennium, monarch butterfly images and costumes provided an instantly understandable, semiotically powerful critique of biotechnology. Demonstrators in effect asserted the right to draw their own scientific inferences, overriding the credibility judgments of expert peer reviewers. Demonstrations, street theater, and consumer boycotts gave evidence that technological innovation was framed as an instrument of governance, requiring ratification by publics as well as experts. By visibly wrapping themselves in the mantle of the monarch butterfly, protesters signaled that industrial research and development could no longer be regarded as off-limits to public review and criticism.

One particular assertion of consumer-citizenship may be read in the future as emblematic of this period of constitutional ferment. This was the case of Monsanto and the so-called 'Terminator gene.' In 1998, a barely known, small cotton seed company called Delta and Pine Land (D&PL) patented a technique to switch off the reproductive mechanism of agricultural plants, thereby rendering the seed sterile (Service 1998). The company hoped that this technology would help protect the intellectual property rights of agricultural biotechnology firms by taking away from farmers the capacity to reuse seed from a previous year's genetically modified crop. Though the technology was still years away from the market, rumors leaked out of a deal by Monsanto to acquire D&PL. Such a partnership could have had enormous implications for both the speed of technology development and its worldwide distribution.

At this point, the technology's corporate sponsors lost control of the situation. The activist organization Rural Advancement Foundation International (RAFI) launched a highly effective international campaign against the technology. RAFI's executive director Pat Roy Mooney is credited with having invented the inspired label 'Terminator technology,' a name that at once translated a complex technoscientific achievement into easily accessible terms and, as in the monarch butterfly case, subverted the distinction between expert and civic technology assessment. Focusing on Monsanto's role, the RAFI campaign gathered support from a network of powerful actors, including the Consultative Group on International Agricultural Research and the Rockefeller Foundation, whose president, Gordon Conway, reportedly talked Monsanto's chief executive officer, Robert Shapiro, into publicly backing down from the company's commitment to 'Terminator technology.' In piecing together transnational politics, civil society activism, popular technology assessment, and enforced accountability from a corporate giant, this episode captured an essential moment in the transition to a global constitutional order.

In sum, these events, which uncomprehending policymakers sometimes dismissed as outbursts of a new Luddism, can be seen as trials in post-national deliberative democracy. They bypassed the electoral process, focused on technology's regulative impacts, and contested the notion that capital-intensive (or, as in the case of DuPont, knowledge-intensive) corporations should have complete leeway to determine the courses of technological innovation.

Empires of knowledge

Historians of imperialism have pointed to the central role played by knowledge creation and appropriation in the formation of the nation-state and, later, in the extension of state power to the governance of vast, dispersed territories in the name of empire. These efforts took the form of classifying people and places, enumerating and keeping watch on them, and making histories or museums of native practices (Anderson 1991; Cohn 1996). From these efforts were born a host of new human and social sciences, such as anthropology, comparative law, geography and cartography (Foucault 1971 [1966]). Analysts of modernity have called attention to the one-sided nature of these activities. The resources and authority needed to produce imperial knowledge rested, for the most part, in the hands of the rulers, and the facts created through their scientific strivings bore, frequently, only a schematic relationship to the lived realities of those being governed (Scott 1998). Postcolonial studies and the emphasis on the subaltern perspective have offered a salutary corrective to colonial sciences, and some recent work has pointed to the complicated, mutually constitutive relationship that sometimes existed between the knowledges of the rulers and the ruled (Storey 1997).

One does not need the special context of colonialism to recognize, as many scholars in science and technology studies have done, that knowledge-making is an instrument of power, and that the scientific workplace functions as a key site for the production of social and political order. Representing the natural world is understood by philosophers and sociologists of science as a way of intervening in it (Hacking 1983; Latour 1983, 1988; also Jasanoff et al. 1995). Visual displays of natural phenomena draw on historically and culturally situated traditions of representation; in a double hermeneutic move, they also sway people's imaginations, and with this their affective selves and capacities for community-building (Fyfe and Law 1988). Methods of measuring and standardizing social or natural phenomena help create the very things they seek to characterize, while concealing the subjective judgments that enter into measurement systems (Foucault 1979; Carson 1993; Porter 1995; Bowker and Star 1999). By consolidating the means of representation in esoteric places, such as laboratories or field stations or archives, the controllers of these 'centers of calculation' form themselves into 'obligatory passage points' in high modernity's exercises of power (Latour 1988, 1990). How do these insights bear on our present era of tacit and unwritten constitutional change?

Globalization offers an obvious entry point. It is talked about in many ways, by journalists, academics, and social activists. For some, the nub of globalization is in the global extension of the free market, with the attendant transmission of capital, ideas, people, and material things around the world, whether it is intellectual property law, Islamic fundamentalism, or Microsoft and Coca Cola (Friedman 1999). For others, more sociologically inclined, it is in the formation of places and subjectivities, cities for instance, that violate or hybridize older social categories and identifications (Sassen 1991). Still others have seen it in the emergence of new kinds of politics, from the rising influence of non-state actors in international negotiations (Haas 1990; Keck and Sikkink 1998) to the production of 'human rights' as a shared, if contested, discourse (Ignatieff 1997). Hardt and Negri (2000), as we have already seen, prefer to replace the concept of globalization with that of Empire. Increasingly, too, television and the Internet have become central players in both the definition and critique of globalization. In these media, action becomes text, readable and indefinitely reproducible; the local becomes global; and the lowly can assume (if only for fifteen minutes of fame) the ancient power of the monarch to command the public gaze. Televised and multiplied, a citizen protest in Seattle or a lethal attack on New York's twin towers acquires, at least for a time, the revolutionary force of a *Communist Manifesto*.

But what of the place of scientific knowledge in all this din of making and unmaking? Does science, despite its contingent, often provisional character have the power to move beliefs, forge alliances, and underwrite norms of global application? Some have argued that this is precisely what has happened in the context of environmental decisionmaking, where knowledge of the biosphere's limited resources and of human interdependence with nature has helped build global coalitions around norms of environmental stewardship (Haas 1990). Similarly, economists would credit the spread of economic knowledge and understanding during the twentieth century with the defeat of socialism at the century's end. The completion of the Human Genome Project at the millennium produced few immediate surprises, but the project's directors used the occasion to preach a new humanism based on the now scientifically grounded observation that, under the skin, human beings are really all the same.

Despite their surface plausibility, claims such as these only open the way to further inquiry for students of science and technology. If scientific knowledge is in fact traveling freely around the globe, what are the social formations and processes that enable its frictionless transfer? If a system of global governance is quietly taking shape, then what knowledge resources has it gathered to itself and where are its centers of calculation? Is there evidence of a new knowledge class that has transcended earlier political divisions and constituted itself as a transnational ruling elite? And if the politics of knowledge historically played itself out in national settings according to well-established rules of testing and credibility, what comparable processes, if any, are arising in arenas of global knowledge-making?

While extended answers to these questions are beyond the scope of this paper, there are many indications that old settlements about where knowledge ends and politics begins are everywhere being reopened and challenged. At the institutional level, we see the rise of a mass of expert bodies of global jurisdiction whose work merges the cognitive and the normative. Constituted under disparate international treaties in areas such as environment, arms control, and international trade, these bodies have the power to certify knowledge and to draw boundaries between acceptable and unacceptable knowledge claims. For the most part, these global experts have operated with traditional notions of what constitutes 'goodness' or reliability in science, accepting published, peer reviewed articles as their gold standard. But the legitimacy of judgments reached on such a basis is often highly contested. Unrest over the technical determinations of bodies like the Intergovernmental Panel on Climate Change or the World Trade Organization attest to the fact that the preconditions for credibility and expertise on a worldwide scale are still very much in flux (Miller and Edwards 2001).

Accompanying the proliferation of new expert institutions is a diversification of what we may call 'global sciences.' These include relatively new additions to the human sciences, such as various forms of risk analysis for estimating global environmental and social hazards; also observable is a cluster of global accounting systems grouped under names like 'sustainability science,' 'vulnerability science,' 'integrated assessment' or 'ecosystem services.' The rise of modeling and simulation, enabled by massive increases in computing power and by sophisticated imaging techniques, has provided a further enormous boost to the ambition of knowing the world in its entirety. A central feature of these 'sciences' is the hybridization they demand of older categories of the natural and the social – violating in this respect the line posited by Latour as modernity's foundational achievement. Self-referential, the new earth sciences constitute the very realities they purport to represent. Their credibility depends not on experimental demonstrations to peer communities, as in the 'pure' fundamental sciences, but on the construction of legitimating practices, such as 'extended peer review,' that require assent from diverse disciplinary and social groups, expert as well as lay.

From a political standpoint, then, the once distinct practices of peer review in science and participation in politics are merging at the global level into novel procedures for ensuring the accountability of scientific and industrial research (Dickson 1984; Gibbons et al. 1994; Nowotny 2001). There are increasing demands for ethics in science, particularly with rapid advances in the human capacity to manipulate the basic biological material of plants and animals. In however inarticulate a way, world polities seem to be rejecting the idea of value-free knowledge and asking for scientific inquiry to make its goals and presumptions more explicit. These and similar developments attest to the erosion of old agreements concerning the objectivity of science and its autonomy from politics. They highlight linkages between knowledge-creation and the institutionalization of power in a globalizing world.

Conclusion: toward post-national democracy

Out of the ashes of the twentieth century the phoenix of a global civil society is struggling to resurrect itself. While constitutional theorists have tied globalization largely to macro-economic and political forces, science and technology must equally be seen as linchpins of the emerging global order. Networks of new knowledge and its material embodiments are helping to frame and stabilize some of the basic elements of a global political system, such as the rights, privileges, and identities of the world's citizens and the powers of major global actors. I have argued that the totality of these changes is constitutional in scope, both enabling and constraining new political formations. Through science and technology, seen as profoundly *social* institutions, many parts of the world today are engaging in what amounts to a tacit constitutional convention. On the table are the nature of the human self, the relations of consumers and corporations, and the certification of knowledge in the conduct of global politics. In all three spheres, the initiative for generating new organizing principles lies not only with corporate and governmental actors, but also in the hands of ordinary citizens and in the proliferating networks of non-governmental associations. In this respect, the emergence of a supranational world order (the 'Empire' of Hardt and Negri) is not inconsistent with continued assertions of human agency.

Realignments of global magnitude will take generations to accomplish, and the contours of the eventual settlements remain but dimly discernible and hard to predict. Let us not forget that it is a contingent as well as an unwritten constitution whose birth we are witnessing. Nevertheless, a few generalizations can be ventured. First, science and technology have not simply deterministically constrained people's freedoms, within limits ordained by preexisting constitutional rights. Rather, science has provided resources that can expand the meanings of identity and community and help redefine the zone of individual autonomy that sits at the heart of all constitutional systems. For good or for ill, science and technology are important aids to human self-expression, not merely iron cages within which a passive humanity languishes imprisoned by forces beyond its control.

Second, without much fanfare or explicit acknowledgment, recognition is growing that technology is an instrument of governance, no less powerful in the hands of private or public actors than laws and regulations are in the hands of government. All kinds of spontaneous experiments are underway to see how far and to what extent consumer-citizens may have a say in the very earliest stages of technological innovation. These range from seemingly irrational, bottom-up acts of resistance, like destroying field trial sites planted with GM crops, to more considered, often top-down exercises in public and political consensus-building on new technologies. Whatever their merits may be, these disparate approaches suggest that the narrative equating technological progress with democracy has come under profound questioning. Technology's claims to benevolent rule must be argued and won today, not simply assumed as they were in older paradigms of development and technology transfer. Publics worldwide want a say in determining what kinds of futures they should live, and as RAFI's successful campaign against the Terminator gene demonstrated, they are sophisticated enough to see that these futures will be substantially shaped by corporate investments in technology.

Third, science's role in underwriting the global constitutional order is associated with new forms and forums of deliberation. These range from more participatory peer reviewing bodies to Internet sites at which the truth of scientific claims is exposed to public scrutiny. Less visibly perhaps, controversies such as those over agricultural biotechnology are challenging scientists' autonomy over the definition of standards of evidence and proof. The fact that findings rejected by mainstream science can exert a powerful pull on global political action should not be interpreted as a sign of public indifference to the truth. Rather, it demonstrates that a new political question has emerged on civic agendas: When is knowledge reliable enough to support collective action? The answer to that question is not seen as lying within the exclusive preserves of scientific authority.

In sum, one of the basic principles of modernity that will surely be reformulated in the course of global consolidation is the sharp disjunction between science and politics, and the separation of processes that secure the authority of scientific claims from those that safeguard the legitimacy of government. Norms of accountability that previously held only between citizens and the state are being extended to experts, with a consequent need for forums in which experts can defend their judgments to wider publics. We observe as well demands for a more 'socially robust' objectivity in science – for facts that can sustain themselves through testing by diverse social groups, rather than solely on the basis of their claimed correspondence to physical reality.

To date, all these changes remain inchoate and uncodified, lodged in diffuse and inarticulate social practices whose collective impact has yet to be felt in the citadels of organized power. To have constitutional force, they should in some sense be explicitly authorized, but by what institutions, organized according to what legitimating principles? The European constitutional debate sets both an encouraging and a cautionary example in this respect: encouraging in pointing to the prospect of an ordered supranational polity; cautionary in delineating the considerable pitfalls that lie in the path of its achievement. Yet, recognizing the very possibility of constitutionalism from below, founded on human creativity and craft, is a prerequisite for its eventual uptake into the practices of politics, law, and governance. It is a first step toward imagining a constitutional order in which the rights of *knowing* citizens – *homo sciens*, beside *homo economicus* – are explicitly acknowledged and given their place in the sun.

All these transformations, finally, demand new kinds of engagement from the social sciences. Disciplinary boundaries based on conceptual categories that are themselves in flux seem ever less appropriate to characterize, let alone analyze, the moving frontiers of global social change. Legal scholarship and political theory in particular will need to accommodate more reflexive avenues of inquiry from newer, transboundary fields such as science studies. The reward, one hopes, will be a richer scholarship of the actual – a re-theorizing of the changes happening in the world about us, and a discovery of new ways to reflect upon, and perhaps intervene in, the courses of scientific and technological change.

Notes

* In Bernward Joerges and Helga Nowotny, eds., *Social Studies of Science and Technology: Looking Back, Ahead*, Yearbook of the Sociology of the Sciences (Dordrecht: Kluwer, 2003), pp. 155–80.

1 The two murals represent Thomas Jefferson presenting the Declaration of Independence to John Hancock, President of the Continental Congress, and James Madison presenting the Constitution to George Washington, President of the Constitutional Convention.

2 The complaint that Americans no longer trust their governing institutions grew in force through the 1990s, along with observations about the public's declining participation in national elections. According to a poll conducted in the summer of 2000, for example, 43% of registered voters said they would watch no part of the Republican convention and 38% said the same for the Democratic convention. The corresponding figures for 1996 were 23% and 21% (Source: Vanishing Voter Project, Joan Shorenstein Center, Kennedy School of Government, Harvard University).

3 'George Bush's Global Warming Speech', *Guardian Unlimited*, February 14, 2002, http://www.guardian.co.uk.

4 There have been only 27 constitutional amendments since the formation of the United States, the most recent in 1992, restricting the power of Congress to raise its members' salaries. Bruce Ackerman (1998, 490–1) has questioned the validity of this enactment, which separated national assent from assent by the states by about two centuries. The failure of the Equal Rights Amendment in the 1970s, despite the growing strength of the women's movement, offers one measure of the resistance to formal constitutional change.

5 While few question the biological validity of paternity testing using DNA markers, the reliability of the results may vary widely depending on the proficiency of the testing institution. On the standardization of genetic testing practices, see Arthur Daemmrich (1998).

6 NRI's enjoy a number of benefits designed to capture some of their foreign earnings for the Indian state. These include a variety of tax and investment advantages and special visa privileges.

7 *Marsh v. Alabama*, 326 U.S. 501 (1946), p. 506.

8 In *Heart of Atlanta Motel, Inc. v. United States*, 379 U.S. 241 (1964), the Supreme Court held that a motel serving interstate travelers could not deny accommodation to

African-Americans on the ground that its services were purely local in character. See, also, *Evans v. Newton*, 382 U.S. 296 (1966) ("Where private individuals or groups exercise powers or carry on functions governmental in nature, they become agencies or instrumentalities of the State and subject to the Fourteenth Amendment," p. 299).

9 The statements have altered in interesting ways over the years. In September 2001, the company posted a statement on sustainable growth that began as follows: "DuPont is on a mission to achieve sustainable growth, which is defined as increasing shareholder and societal value while decreasing the company's environmental footprint" http://www.dupont.com/corp/overview/glance/sus_growth.html. Three years earlier, in 1998, the website offered the following DuPont commitment: "We affirm to all our stakeholders, including our employees, customers, shareholders and the public, that we will conduct our business with respect and care for the environment. We will implement those strategies that build successful businesses and achieve the greatest benefit for all our stakeholders without compromising the ability of future generations to meet their needs" http://www.dupont.com/corp/environment/commitment.html.

References

Ackerman, Bruce A. (1983), *Reconstructing American Law*, Cambridge, MA: Harvard University Press.

Ackerman, Bruce A. (1991), *We The People: Foundations*, Cambridge, MA: Harvard University Press.

Ackerman, Bruce A. (1998), *We The People: Transformations*, Cambridge, MA: Harvard University Press.

Anderson, Benedict (1991 [1983]), *Imagined Communities: Reflections on the Origin and Spread of Nationalism*. Revised and expanded edition, London: Verso.

Anderson, Benedict (1994), 'Exodus', *Critical Inquiry* 20: 314–27.

Bartlett, Katherine T. (1990), 'Feminist legal methods', *Harvard Law Review* 103: 829–88.

Bauman, Zygmunt (1991), *Modernity and Ambivalence*, Cambridge: Polity.

Beck, Ulrich (1992 [1986]), *Risk Society: Towards a New Modernity*, London: Sage Publications.

Bijker, Wiebe, Thomas P. Hughes and Trevor Pinch (1987), *The Social Construction of Technological Systems*, Cambridge, MA: MIT Press.

Bimber, Bruce (1996), *The Politics of Expertise in Congress*, Albany, NY: SUNY Press.

Bowker, Geoffrey C. and Susan Leigh Star (1999), *Sorting Things Out: Classification and Its Consequences*, Cambridge, MA: MIT Press.

Boyle, James (1996), *Shamans, Software and Spleens: Law and the Construction of the Information Society*, Cambridge, MA: Harvard University Press.

Breyer, Stephen (1993), *Breaking the Vicious Circle: Toward Effective Risk Regulation*, Cambridge, MA: Harvard University Press.

Callon, Michel (1986), 'Some elements of a sociology of translation: Domestication of the scallops and the fishermen of St. Brieuc Bay', in J. Law (ed.), *Power, Action, and Belief: A New Sociology of Knowledge?*, London: Routledge & Kegan Paul, pp. 196–233.

Callon, Michel (1987), 'Society in the making: The study of technology as a tool for sociological analysis', in W. Bijker, T. Hughes and T. Pinch (eds.), *The Social Construction of Technological Systems*, Cambridge, MA: MIT Press, pp. 83–103.

Callon, Michel (1999), 'The role of lay people in the production and dissemination of scientific knowledge', *Science, Technology and Society* 4 (1): 81–94.

Cambrosio, Alberto, Peter Keating and Michael Mackenzie (1990), 'Scientific practice in the courtroom: The construction of sociotechnical identities in a biotechnology patent dispute', *Social Problems* 37: 275–93.

Carson, John (1993), 'Army alpha, army brass, and the search for army intelligence', *Isis* 84: 278–309.

Cohn, Bernard S. (1996), *Colonialism and Its forms of Knowledge*, Princeton, NJ: Princeton University Press.

Daemmrich, Arthur (1998), 'The evidence does not speak for itself: Expert witnesses and the organization of DNA-typing companies', *Social Studies of Science* 28: 741–72.

Darman, Richard G. (1978), 'The law of the sea: Rethinking U.S. interests', *Foreign Affairs* 56 (2): 381.

Dickson, David (1984), *The New Politics of Science*, New York: Pantheon Books.

Eder, Klaus and Catherine Kantner (2000), 'Nationale Resonanzstrukturen in Europa: Eine Kritik der Rede vom Öffentlichkeitsdefizit', in M. Bach (ed.), *Die Europäisierung nationaler Gesellschaften*, Wiesbaden: Westdeutscher Verlag, pp. 306–31.

Ezrahi, Yaron (1990), *The Descent of Icarus: Science and the Transformation of Contemporary Democracy*, Cambridge, MA: Harvard University Press.

Fisher, William W. III, Morton J. Horwitz and Thomas A. Reed (eds.) (1993), *American Legal Realism*, New York: Oxford University Press.

Foster, Kenneth R. and Peter W. Huber (1997), *Judging Science: Scientific Knowledge and the Federal Courts*, Cambridge, MA: MIT Press.

Foucault, Michel (1971 [1966]), *The Order of Things: An Archaeology of the Human Sciences*, New York: Pantheon Books.

Foucault, Michel (1979), *Discipline and Punish: The Birth of the Prison*, New York: Random House.

Fried, Barbara (1998), *The Progressive Assault on Laissez Faire: Robert Hale and the First Law and Economics Movement*, Cambridge, MA: Harvard University Press.

Friedman, Thomas L. (1999), *The Lexus and the Olive Tree*, New York: Farrar, Straus & Giroux.

Fukuyama, Francis (1992), *The End of History and the Last Man*, New York: Free Press.

Fyfe, Gordon and John Law (eds.) (1988), *Picturing Power: Visual Depiction and Social Relations*, London: Routledge.

Gaskell, George, Martin W. Bauer, John Durant and N.C. Allum (1999), 'Worlds apart? The reception of genetically modified foods in Europe and the U.S.', *Science* 285: 384–7.

Gavaghan, Helen (1999), 'Britain struggles to turn anti-GM tide', *Science* 284: 1442–4.

Gibbons, Michael, Camille Limoges, Helga Nowotny, Simon Schwartzman, Peter Scott and Martin Trow (1994), *The New Production of Knowledge*, London: Sage Publications.

Giddens, Anthony (1991), *Modernity and Self-Identity: Self and Society in the Late Modern Age*, Cambridge: Polity.

Goldberg, Carey (1996), 'Shunning "he" and "she," they fight for respect', *New York Times*, September 8, Section 1:24.

Goldberg, Steven (1994), *Culture Clash*, New York: New York University Press.

Goldmann, Kjell (2001), *Transforming the European Nation-State*, London: Sage Publications.

Grimm, Dieter (1995), 'Does Europe need a constitution?', *European Law Journal* 1 (3): 282–302.

Guha, Ranajit and Gayatri Spivak (ed.) (1988), *Selected Subaltern Studies*, New York: Oxford University Press.

Haas, Peter M. (1990), *Saving the Mediterranean: The Politics of International Environmental Cooperation*, New York: Columbia University Press.

Habermas, Juergen (1975 [1973]), *Legitimation Crisis*, Boston: Beacon Press.

Hacking, Ian (1983), *Representing and Intervening*, Cambridge, UK: Cambridge University Press.

Haraway, Donna (1991), *Simians, Cyborgs, and Women: The Reinvention of Nature*, New York, NY: Routledge, Chapman, and Hall.

Haraway, Donna (1997), *Modest-Witness@Second-Millennium.FemaleMan-Meets-Onco-mouse: Feminism and Technoscience*, New York: Routledge.

Hardt, Michael and Antonio Negri (2000), *Empire*, Cambridge, MA: Harvard University Press.

Huber, Peter W. (1991), *Galileo's Revenge: Junk Science in the Courtroom*, New York: Basic Books.

Hughes, Thomas P. (1983), *Networks of Power: Electrification in Western Society, 1880–1930*, Baltimore: Johns Hopkins University Press.

Huxley, Aldous (1946), *Brave New World*, London: Harper & Brothers.

Ignatieff, Michael (1997), *The Warrior's Honor*, Toronto: Viking.

Jasanoff, Sheila (1995a), *Science at the Bar: Law, Science, and Technology in America*, Cambridge, MA: Harvard University Press.

Jasanoff, Sheila (1995b), 'Product, process, or programme: Three cultures and the regulation of biotechnology', in M. Bauer (ed.), *Resistance to New Technology*, Cambridge: Cambridge University Press, pp. 311–31.

Jasanoff, Sheila (1998a), 'The eye of everyman: Witnessing DNA in the Simpson trial', *Social Studies of Science* 28 (5–6): 713–40.

Jasanoff, Sheila (1998b), 'Expert games in silicone gel breast implant litigation', in M. Freeman and H. Reece (eds.), *Science in Court*, London: Dartmouth, pp. 83–107.

Jasanoff, Sheila (2001), 'Election 2000: Mechanical error or system failure?', *Social Studies of Science* 31 (3): 461–7.

Jasanoff, Sheila, Gerald Markle, James Petersen and Trevor Pinch (eds.) (1995), *Handbook of Science and Technology Studies*, Thousand Oaks, CA: Sage Publications.

Joss, Simon and John Durant (1995), *Public Participation in Science: The Role of Consensus Conferences in Europe*, London: Science Museum.

Kairys, David (ed.) (1990), *The Politics of Law*, New York: Pantheon.

Keck, Margaret E. and Kathryn Sikkink (1998), *Activists Beyond Borders: Advocacy Network in International Politics*, Ithaca, NY: Cornell University Press.

Kelman, Mark (1987), *A Guide to Critical Legal Studies*, Cambridge, MA: Harvard University Press.

Keyssar, Alexander (2000), *The Right to Vote: The Contested History of Democracy in the United States*, New York: Basic Books.

Kuhn, Thomas S. (1962), *The Structure of Scientific Revolutions*, Chicago: University of Chicago Press.

Latour, Bruno (1983), 'Give me a laboratory and I will raise the world', in K. Knorr-Cetina and M. Mulkay (eds.), *Science Observed*, London: Sage, pp. 141–70.

Latour, Bruno (1987), *Science in Action*, Cambridge, MA: Harvard University Press.

Latour, Bruno (1988), *The Pasteurization of France*, Cambridge, MA: Harvard University Press.

Latour, Bruno (1990), 'Drawing things together', in M. Lynch and S. Woolgar (eds.), *Representation in Scientific Practice*, Cambridge, MA: MIT Press, pp. 19–68.

Latour, Bruno (1993), *We Have Never Been Modern*, Cambridge, MA: Harvard University Press.

Latour, Bruno and Steve Woolgar (1979), *Laboratory Life: The Construction of Scientific Facts*, Princeton, NJ: Princeton University Press.

Lessig, Lawrence (1997), 'Constitution of code: Limitations on choice-based critiques of cyberspace regulation', *CommLaw Conspectus* 5: 181–204.

Lewin, Tamar (2001), 'In genetic testing for paternity, law often lags behind science', *New York Times*, March 11, Section 1, 1.

MacKenzie, Donald (1990), *Inventing Accuracy: A Historical Sociology of Nuclear Missile Guidance*, Cambridge, MA: MIT Press.

Marris, Claire and Pierre-Benoit Joly (1999), 'Between consensus and citizens: public participation in technology assessment in France', *Science Studies* 12 (2): 3–32.

Masood, Ehsan (1999), 'Gag on food scientist is lifted as gene modification row hots up. . . .', *Nature* 397: 547.

Miller, Clark and Paul Edwards (eds.) (2001), *Changing the Atmosphere: Expert Knowledge and Environmental Governance*, Cambridge, MA: MIT Press.

Mol, Annemarie and John Law (1994), 'Regions, networks and fluids: Anaemia and social topology', *Social Studies of Science* 24: 641–71.

Nowotny, Helga (2001), *Re-thinking Science: Knowledge and the Public in an Age of Uncertainty*. Cambridge: Polity.

Nye, Joseph S., Jr., Philip D. Zelikow and David C. King (eds.) (1997), *Why People Don't Trust Government*, Cambridge, MA: Harvard University Press.

Ogburn, William Fielding (1922), *Social Change with Respect to Culture and Original Nature*, New York: B.W. Huebsch.

Porter, Theodore M. (1995), *Trust in Numbers: The Pursuit of Objectivity in Science and Public Life*, Princeton, NJ: Princeton University Press.

Ratner, Sidney, James H. Soltow and Richard Sylla (1979), *The Evolution of the American Economy*, New York: Basic Books.

Reardon, Jennifer (2001), 'The human genome diversity project: A failure to coproduce natural and social order', *Social Studies of Science* 31: 357–88.

Sandel, Michael J. (1996) *Democracy's Discontent: America in Search of a Public Philosophy*, Cambridge, MA: Harvard University Press.

Sassen, Saskia (1991), *The Global City: New York, London, Tokyo*, Princeton, NJ: Princeton University Press.

Schauer, Frederick (1998). 'Internet privacy and the public-private distinction', *Jurimetrics* 38: 555–64.

Schuck, Peter (1993), 'Multi-culturalism redux: Science, law, and politics', *Yale Law and Policy Review* II: 1–46.

Scott, James C. (1998), *Seeing Like a State*, New Haven, CT: Yale University Press.

Service, Robert F. (1998), 'Seed-sterilizing "terminator technology" sows discord', *Science* 282: 850–1.

Shapin, Steven (1994), *A Social History of Truth*, Chicago: University of Chicago Press.

Shapin, Steven and Simon Schaffer (1985), *Leviathan and the Air-Pump: Hobbes, Boyle, and the Experimental Life*, Princeton, NJ: Princeton University Press.

Shiva, Vandana (1993), *Monocultures of the Mind: Perspectives on Biodiversity and Biotechnology*, London: Third World Network.

Shiva, Vandana (1997), *Biopiracy: The Plunder of Nature and Knowledge*, Toronto: Between The Lines.

Smaglik, Paul (2000), 'Tissue donors use their influence in deal over gene patent terms', *Nature* 408: 894–6.

Smith, Merritt Roe and Leo Marx (eds.) (1994), *Does Technology Drive History?*, Cambridge, MA: MIT Press.

Smith, Roger and Brian Wynne (eds.) (1989), *Expert Evidence: Interpreting Science in the Law*, London: Routledge.

Stone, Christopher D. (1974), *Should Trees Have Standing? Toward Legal Rights for Natural Objects*, Los Altos, CA: William Kaufmann.

Storey, William (1997), *Science and Power in Colonial Mauritius*, Rochester, NY: University of Rochester Press.

Sunstein, Cass (1993), *The Partial Constitution*, Cambridge, MA: Harvard University Press.

Tribe, Laurence H. (1978), *American Constitutional Law*, Mineola, NY: Foundation Press.

Visvanathan, Shiv (1997), *Carnival for Science: Essays on Science, Technology and Development*, Delhi: Oxford University Press.

Walker, Neil (1996), 'European constitutionalism and European integration', *Public Law* Summer 1996: 266–90.

Wynne, Brian (1982), *Rationality and Ritual: The Windscale Inquiry and Nuclear Decisions in Britain*, Chalfont St. Giles, UK: British Society for the History of Science.

Wynne, Brian (1988), 'Unruly technology', *Social Studies of Science* 18: 147–167.

Wynne, Brian (1989), 'Frameworks of rationality in risk management: Towards the testing of naive sociology', in J. Brown (ed.), *Environmental Threats: Social Sciences Approaches to Public Risk Perceptions*, London: Belhaven, pp. 33–45.

14 Afterword

This volume was completed during yet another crisis of modernity: the profound disaffection that many citizens of mature democracies seem to feel toward their ruling institutions and modes of governance at the end of what may be called the long twentieth century. Everywhere one turns, there is a sense that traditional forms of representation have failed. Unrest and demonstrations vie with apathy, but both action and inaction signal the same messages: cynicism about the state, an unquenched thirst for change, heightened demands for accountability, and an almost uncontrollable desire for freedom to chart one's own and one's children's destinies. Neoliberalism, the dominant political and policy ideology of the moment, is the construct that seems most successfully to have ridden out this storm of discontent. Neoliberalism offers the dream of a slate wiped clean of state power and the institutions that wield it. For solutions to important public problems, so runs the neoliberal mantra, look to markets, not to states. Yet the Occupy movements of the end of the first decade of the twenty-first century, as well as the distrust and contempt for elites manifested across much of the developing world, suggest that mere displacement of public sector logics by private sector alternatives—most especially by unbridled American-style capitalism—will not prove to be robust solutions for the decades ahead.

Markets have yet to demonstrate that they can deliver equality of opportunity, devise solutions for intransigent ethical conflicts, or develop a workable sense of the common good; and, despite rhetorics to the contrary, modern markets depend on governments to create the stable background conditions they need for their very survival. More fundamentally from the standpoint of democracy, markets create at best thin and superficial solidarities: consumer groupings based on purchasing preferences, united in common commitment mainly when damages threaten, but with little affirmative obligation to build shared values or civic sensibilities. Where then should critical democracy theorists, skeptical toward the discourse of neoliberalism and knee-jerk endorsement of market solutions, begin to look for more generative answers to the problems of governing today's fractious, yet insecure, polities? Can a collection of essays centered on science and public reason contribute in however small a way to alleviating democracy's discontents and to charting more appealing pathways for humanity's future? A few concluding thoughts are in order.

The politics of science and reason

Implicitly and explicitly, this book emphasizes the impossibility of accounting for democratic politics at any scale of governance without taking note of the pervasive influence of science and technology. My vision of what it means for science and technology to be political, however, is quite different from the conventional view that political power impermissibly influences knowledge production and the design of technologies. My argument, in short, parts company from Langdon Winner's famous dictum that "artifacts have politics"—a message that, while right as far as it goes, tends to freeze the meaning of politics and to perpetuate the faulty notion that science and technology could be purified of the biases of power if only we were more attentive. Nor do I espouse the popular thesis, put forward by Bruno Latour and others, that what democracy needs today is a properly representative politics of things—because material objects, whether natural or artificial, belong within the hybrid networks of society, and hence should be invited to participate in its political processes.

I show instead that choices of how to live with scientific and technological innovation are political because they entail normative judgments about the kinds of people we want to be and the kinds of societies we wish to live in. As twin engines of modernity, science and technology have opened up myriad opportunities for people to represent themselves in ways more plastic and varied than the narrow forms of self-representation offered by the referendum or the polling booth. For example, armed with knowledge about their genes, individuals can associate with others sharing similar predispositions to disease, or participate in communities of health and illness by donating information to biological data banks. People can diversify their group affiliations through social utilities, or create elaborate fictional identities through game playing on the Internet. As consumers of environmental knowledge, citizens can take on roles and responsibilities that spill over established political boundaries, as custodians of threatened natural resources, sharers in indigenous knowledge, or members of a united global community concerned about climate change. Artifacts play a concededly important role in these exercises of identity-making and group formation, but more as repositories and enablers of dreams than as moral actors entitled to share deliberative space with human agents. Expanding opportunities for representing human selves and collectives have created new subjectivities and given rise to new demands for access to, as well as control of, knowledge and its technological applications. Politics, as discussed in this volume, arises from attempts to govern these competing visions of what kinds of subjects to be, or not to be, in an era dominated by science and technology.

The process of public reasoning becomes on this account a vehicle for integrating scientific and technological innovation with society's deepest commitments to order: what counts as reliable knowledge; which technologies will benefit society and at what cost; how should uncertainty be evaluated; who should settle controversies; and who should be responsible for unintended harms? Answering such questions involves gathering knowledge, assessing technologies, and evaluating alternative trajectories of modernization. In the intertwining of these strands, we observe not merely the assertion of economic and social power, though these are always present. We see, more foundationally, the co-production of changing natural, social, and moral orders.

Put differently, politics as discussed in this book is not simply a matter of allocating power and resources, including those conferred by science and technology, among existing social groups. Nor is it a matter of recognizing that material objects and sociotechnical systems operate as quasi-agents to shape our spaces of self-articulation and self-governance. Politics crucially involves the crafting of future states of being and forms of life—indeed, imagined communities—which depend in turn on acquiring (and occasionally rejecting) scientific knowledge and the life-changing commodities that science delivers. From intimate and close to home decisions, such as how to bear children or cultivate food, to impersonal, potentially apocalyptic choices, such as whether to invest in nuclear power or synthetic biology, science and technology make available new potentialities and call for new limits. Defining and allocating the prospective goods, while setting bounds on imagined harms, is today the stuff of public reasoning, with associated demands, as the essays show, for new rules of evidence, argument and adjudication. Accordingly, there can be no adequate theorizing of modern politics without asking questions about the politics of public reason.

In offering answers, this book displays the multiplicity of arenas and processes through which the politics of reason plays out, as well as the unstated rules and norms that apply in varied institutional contexts—for example, the "contested boundaries" of regulatory peer review, the "songlines" of risk analysis, and the "game board" of expertise in tort litigation. Normatively, the comparative case studies bring to light tacit values that nation states have embraced in determining what counts as good politics of knowledge. What widely shared notions of evidence and accountability guide public reasoning? Answers given in previous chapters range from the preference for insulating science through naturalizing discourses of quantification in the United States to the emphasis on individual rectitude in Britain, the preference for consensual reasoning in Germany, and the continuing power of personal experience to sway the state's reasons in India. These findings, as I stress throughout my work, are not iron cages that constrain all political actors in a given nation to reason in the same way on every issue. States are too heterogeneous and their institutions too diverse to enforce such rigid uniformity. Courts, regulatory agencies, and international institutions draw on disparate experiences, histories, languages and logics, and all are in principle capable of reflecting on and reforming their practices at need. Yet in stable nation states, there are powerful default tendencies that come into play at critical moments, as when the U.S. Supreme Court in the 1993 case of *Daubert v. Merrell Dow Pharmaceuticals* adopted the unreflexive view of judges as neutral gate-keepers of value-free science. These potent scripts of reasoning tend to be replayed and reinforced unless they bump up against forces knowledgeable enough to recognize them and strong enough to resist.

Reason under law

This volume unabashedly reaffirms the centrality of law and of states in articulating desirable futures for democratic societies, but in so doing it also moves away from structuralist understandings of legality and statehood. That move is necessary in order to do justice to actors, such as the electronic media, that are increasingly challenging state sovereignty, while still acknowledging that states control key resources, preeminently those of lawmaking, that enable citizens to define their identities and represent themselves as autonomous subjects.

For more than two hundred years, the nation state functioned as the governmental form most trusted to meet the needs and interests of the world's growing populations. Governments were expected, indeed counted on, to discern and satisfy public wants; it was what elected representatives were good for. Today, under pressure from globalization and unable to deliver sustained economic growth, states are undergoing significant "status degradation," a term sociologists usually reserve for the downgrading of individual worth. As giant vessels that cannot be turned or stopped at will, today's ships of state look more like rusty relics from a decaying Armada than like majestic standard-bearers for tomorrow's modernity. This outmodedness is most acutely on display when states are called on to regulate technological innovation or assuage public perceptions of risk in areas outside of national security. Already in 1980 I heard a former commissioner of the Food and Drug Administration (FDA), one of the U.S. government's more respected regulatory agencies, characterize his organization as a slow moving target that bleeds profusely when hit; succeeding FDA heads have fixed this image of lumbering vulnerability more firmly in the public mind. Markets by contrast offer appealing models of dispersed imagination and agency, with an agility governments cannot match, and safeguards for rooting out unworkable ideas and institutional corruption before they put down thick and thirsty roots.

As the rights of citizenship increasingly merge with rites of consumerism in wealthy nations, successful corporations are often touted as more muscular, more economically and materially productive than bureaucracies, and better able to deliver the goods that publics want—goods both in the sense of visions of how to live better and in the sense of material commodities that make lives more worth living. Entrepreneurs innovate; bureaucrats only stifle. In the outpouring of tributes after the untimely death of Steve Jobs, co-founder of Apple, in October 2011, a frequently cited saying of his was that people (sometimes used interchangeably with "consumers") "don't know what they want till innovators show it to them".[1] No wonder then that between the iPad and the Social Security card, and even the right to a free public education, it is the iPad that draws forth the more fervent expressions of loyalty and devotion. Besides, to the ideologically minded, 1989 offered a grand global referendum on collectivization by the state as opposed to developing public goods through markets—and markets won that contest hands down.

States are under attack from the left of the political spectrum as well as the right, and deservedly so. Through the sad history of devastating wars, overplanned economies, ruthless dictatorships and violent crackdowns on civilians, modern governments have come to be regarded as oppressive, intrusive, and at their best guilty of a kind of flattening dullness. Their knowledge is far from encompassing; indeed, as all of the essays in this volume demonstrate, state actors see only partially, with vision inevitably shaped and occluded by power and interest. Lulled by their own performances of expertise, moreover, state institutions rarely reflect deeply on their epistemic biases or failings, even in the wake of overwhelming events such as those discussed in the essay on restoring reason. And by controlling the instruments of institutional boundary drawing, states frequently exclude knowledges and perspectives that are not congenial to those at the pinnacles of authority. Why then should we devote much attention to public reasoning? Is it not inevitably a recipe for reasserting a none too thoughtful status quo?

The cases in this book speak against such blanket dismissiveness. Particularly as shown in my essays on the life sciences, there is a productive, even creative, aspect of public reasoning that is too often overlooked by critics. This is the role of reason-giving in helping to shape collective imaginations of the future. Seen from this angle, regulation of science and technology is not simply a matter of setting limits on innovation's risks, but rather a process through which societies decide collectively how to weigh the uncertainties of different ways forward into uncharted territory, and how to allocate the benefits and burdens of alternative courses of action. In designing how to regulate new and emerging technologies, states make room for recurrent moments of ontological politics, that is, the politics of building (and in the best cases continually rebuilding) working relations between things and people: for example, by choosing to treat carcinogens as objects of special regulatory concern; deciding whether or not to import genetically engineered crops; compensating women for untested, ruptured breast implants; or according human dignity to pre-embryos and stem cells. On such occasions, the institutions of public reasoning, both administrative and judicial, serve not only to determine which kinds of materialities should inhabit our worlds, but also how to construct regimes of responsibility around inventions, from engineered embryos to complex financial instruments, that massively reshape the landscapes of liberty.

Understood in this way, the politics of public reason offers an antidote to heedless neoliberalism. In displaying public reasoning as a site of continual epistemic, ontological, and political production, I counter the view that markets alone are sufficient instruments for making collectives capable of informed self-government. Corporations and their assorted progeny, such as wealthy private foundations or the currently much-touted private–public partnerships, possess neither the incentives nor the institutional means to engage publics in informed reflection about the kinds of societies we wish to build through innovation and its tangible, non-human products. Markets, in short, cannot produce knowledgeable and adept democracies. That aim is better served by institutions of public reasoning, created by states under law, that bring into and keep in view what is meaningfully political about science and technology.

Reason as practice and performance

The rise of public reasoning as a policy practice was quite possibly the most important achievement of democracy in the later twentieth century. It happened incrementally, without fanfare, and unheralded by any of the ferment that ordinarily precedes revolutions. Yet laws such as the 1946 U.S. Administrative Procedure Act, mandating governmental officials to give reasons for their actions, responded to some of the most oppressive and widely criticized features of modern government: the growth of faceless bureaucracies, the reduction of human needs and wants to technical calculation, and the subordination of local and experiential knowledge to the tyranny of technical expertise. To the extent that such impersonal bodies as regulatory institutions can be said to think, giving reasons publicly is the device that aligns their thought processes with standards of democratic legitimacy. For example, using the apparatuses of expert advice that I have called the "fifth branch," state agencies can demonstrate that they are not merely enacting their own political preferences. Importantly, in the coupling of democracy with transparency, even reasons grounded in esoteric scientific and technical advice can be subjected to requirements of disclosure and critique.

To date, neither philosophy nor social science has devoted much attention to this practical check on the exercise of executive power or what it means for the ways we should reconceptualize, let alone refashion, our ideas of democracy. This is not for lack of attention to reason as a public activity. From Immanuel Kant to John Rawls, political philosophers have wrestled with the nature of public reason, but largely in order to clarify its optimal logical structure and propositional content and to determine what kinds of arguments can properly be made in the public sphere. The philosophy of public reason seeks to demarcate those domains in which people may freely act upon their personal, non-accountable beliefs (as for example in joining a church, choosing a medical therapy, or deciding to end life support) and those in which, because the consequences plainly affect society at large, only reasons deemed acceptable by the collective may be used to justify one's positions (as for example in ruling on the legality of abortion, opposing a technological facility, or restricting freedoms of speech and association).

The approach to public reason that I offer in this volume is fundamentally different. My objective, consistent with the aims of science and technology studies, has been to investigate how powerful institutions actually reason, not to lay down rules by which people ought to reason in the public square. Indeed, the work gathered in the preceding chapters suggests that efforts of the latter sort are inevitably hemmed in by history and culture. How political communities like their reason served up is both independent of and to an important degree determinative of the kinds of reasons that are given in varied contexts of governance. By displaying public reason as a situated, culturally inflected, political practice, I show that the links between democracy and reason cannot be adequately understood or evaluated from the standpoint of neutral or universal principles. Such principles are not there simply for the asking. Rather, principles seen as neutral are constituted through situated processes of reason-giving and affirmed through repeated use: to borrow Justice Oliver Wendell Holmes's famous observation about the common law, experience, not logic, underpins the practices by which societies go about making what their members deem to be public reason.

Treating reason as a practice has obvious implications for re-envisioning democracy. In seeing how expert discourses are legitimated, for example, one also perceives how hugely relevant but potentially destabilizing points of view are excluded and left outside the ambit of deliberation. Reason, as the essays illustrate, is pieced together through overlapping technical practices, such as quantitative risk assessment, rules for the admissibility of evidence, norms of peer review, and modes of representation on advisory committees. Each practice operates to systematize knowledge and enhance its credibility and value, but each also suffers from biases and blind spots. These are most apparent if we drop the pretense of (and even the aspiration for) reason as a view from nowhere and instead engage in systematic exploration of what actually happens across diverse regimes of reason-making. The comparative method in particular reveals public reason as always an achievement, and what is socially achieved can always be reexamined in hopes of doing better. Most generally, then, reasoning viewed as a social practice lends itself to continual investigation, reflection and reform; reason conceived as a transcendental logic takes refuge in the claimed impartiality of expertise and eludes the possibility of human questioning.

Reasoning about reason

As a contribution to democratic theory, this book straddles the line between critique and affirmation. The individual essays reveal in thick empirical detail, across a wide variety of cases and places, why assertions of truth and rationality in legal and administrative decision making are often less watertight than they purport to be. That recognition, in turn, points to the importance of constantly questioning what it is that power does when it claims to reason. It also underscores why societies need "technologies of humility," those routines of self-reflection that force power to take notice of those who would be hurt if its knowledge is flawed or unduly optimistic.

Together, the essays illustrate the exclusionary effects of dominant structures of public reasoning, especially when dressed up in the authoritative discourses of science and expertise: risk analytic criteria that leave out the distribution and intensity of human suffering; epidemiological studies that ignore the experience of afflicted bodies; rules of admissibility that fail to acknowledge the judge's role in drawing lines between common sense and technical expertise; and expert ethical judgments that foreclose open debate on the moral status of novel, technologically created entities. Uncovering such bounding and blocking practices does not necessarily mean we should abandon them altogether, but knowing how they operate makes it possible to incorporate a deeper awareness of the limits of rationality into public reasoning. This kind of critique by its nature cannot run out of steam. It is the lifeblood of any democracy that takes both the strength of its institutions and their frailties seriously.

Finally, and perhaps paradoxically, the book should be read as a celebration of science and public reason. I see reasoning as one of the essential virtuous practices of modern democracy, provided that it remains conscious of its limits and mindful of its shortcomings. Instead of seeking refuge in allegedly unquestionable scientific facts, a modest public reason would emulate those admirable habits of science that most closely parallel the practices of a robust democracy. This would be a public reason born of civility, willing to engage with unpalatable viewpoints, with honesty to acknowledge its own provisionality and courage to confront radical disbelief. The commitment to such reasoning would be a high achievement indeed. The challenge is not to let imperialist definitions of reason and rationality crowd out the voices of the margins from our painstakingly crafted spaces of reasoning.

Note

1   See for example, James B. Stewart, "How Jobs Put Passion Into Products," *New York Times*, October 7, 2011 ("That doesn't mean we don't listen to customers, but it's hard for them to tell you what they want when they've never seen anything remotely like it.")

Index

Lightning Source UK Ltd.
Milton Keynes UK
UKHW021950150720
366494UK00007B/163